TAKE OUT

QUEER WRITING FROM ASIAN PACIFIC AMERICA

OUT

EDITED BY QUANG BAO AND HANYA YANAGIHARA
WITH TIMOTHY LIU

QUANG'S DEDICATION

For Pau

ACKNOWLEDGMENTS

Thanks to the individuals at The Asian American Writers' Workshop who brought me on as writer, editor and managing director, and for introducing me to a hardworking coeditor and friend. I am grateful to all those who contributed to this project, including Andrea Louie, John Kunichika, Nina Chaudry, Timothy Liu, and especially, Daniel Lee. Thanks also to Annie Lee, Pimpila Thanaporn, Anjuli Dwindhal, Cara Caddoo and Olivia Tam.

Quang Bao is the managing director of The Asian American Writers' Workshop. He divides his time between New York City and Northampton, Massachusetts.

HANYA'S DEDICATION

To Bitter Makoto Dykes

ACKNOWLEDGMENTS

My thanks to the staff, past and present, of The Asian American Writers' Workshop, particularly Peter Ong, Jeannie Wong, Dan Lee, and Andrea Louie. Quang Bao, coeditor and friend, has made working on this book a pleasure. John "Tans" Kunichika has tried to evade me and my various labor-intensive assignments since high school; thanks to him for all his help. Finally, thanks to all the contributors and friends for their enthusiasm and support, in particular Alex Chee, Philip Huang, Timothy Liu, Stephen Morrison, Chris Upton, and Nita Yamashita.

Hanya Yanagihara serves on the board of directors of Kaya Productions and edits The Asian American Writers' Workshop's Asian Pacific American Journal. She lives in New York.

The Workshop would like to thank the Los Angeles City Grant Program, C.J. Huang Foundation and an anonymous foundation for contributing to this anthology.

TAKE OUT: QUEER WRITING FROM ASIAN PACIFIC AMERICA

INTRODUCTION

There is something inherently absurd about anthologies—the good ones feel contrived, the not-so-good ones, embarrassing. What, after all, does "queer writing from Asian Pacific America" mean, anyway? All the writers and artists in this volume identify as gay and Asian, but what other guidelines could we offer them? (Together, we made a half-serious list of things we wouldn't allow in the anthology—for the men: nothing about tricking for money, coming-out stories with only one parent in the room, and characters in mesh tops with peeping nipples. For the women, we declared a moratorium on certain words and phrases: moist, her very inside, silk, sopping, slick, wet, moan.) We knew we wanted to include as many unpublished or little-published writers as possible, and that we wouldn't worry too much about gender equity; far better, we thought, to sacrifice quantity for quality, and in re-reading the contributions from women we've included in these pages, it's a choice we don't regret. But these were only unspoken guidelines, and in the end, we decided to offer no further direction, figuring our submitters would know better than we how to define the subtitle.

One of the joys of a laissez-faire submission policy is the many surprises it offers, both literarily and literally. We never asked anyone to interpret the gay or Asian experience (not knowing what it was ourselves), but, perhaps not so surprisingly, all our writers did just that, although in ways we'd never conceived. Many of the contributions are love stories: E.G. Louie's aching and astonishing story about a boy's first love; Philip Huang's elegant and dark piece about two lovers struggling to fashion a life together under the cloud of AIDS; Larissa Lai's witty and clever inversion of children's fairy tales. And there's some great humor on display here too, from Daniel Lee's sassy collection of poems and Ho Tam's clever portraits of Asian men to Ching Ching Ling's unabashedly materialistic wish list and Natasha Singh's laundry list of dating rules. Even our cover designer and artist, John Kunichika, interpreted this project in ways we could not have forseen.

The best anthology is one that makes you reconsider the genre and audience it claims to represent. We hope you'll agree that this one forces you to reevaluate your conceptions of gay Asian America, however narrow or broad they may be.

Quang Bao
Hanya Yanagihara
New York City, April 2001

TAKE OUT: QUEER WRITING FROM ASIAN PACIFIC AMERICA

TABLE OF CONTENTS

POETRY

PROSE

TAKE OUT: QUEER WRITING FROM ASIAN PACIFIC AMERICA

JONEIL ADRIANO

CONSTELLATIONS

My grandfather passed away on Easter weekend. I found out just as I had finished watching *Postcards from America*, the film loosely based on the autobiographical writings of David Wojnarowicz. One of the scenes near the end of the film depicts David watching his lover dying of AIDS in a hospital room. David thinks about how hearing is the last of the senses to go before death. In those moments when the two of them—David and his lover—were left alone by the nurses, David would whisper into his lover's ear, instructing him that should he see a light, or feel something warm, he should move towards it. If, on the other hand, there was nothing but cold darkness, David told his lover to imagine a state of total calm, like that point in the horizon when sea and sky, time and space meet.

When my dad called to give me the news of Lolo's death, at three in the morning, I didn't pick up the phone on purpose. Instead, I curled up in bed and pulled the covers tight around me. I watched *Postcards* rewinding in my VCR and listened to my dad's voice fill the empty living room through my answering machine. He called again two minutes later, but this time, he didn't leave a message. When my dad called a third time, I finally got the courage to pick up the phone.

"Hello?"

"Pablo."

Dad's voice was still calm and composed. But if you were listening carefully, you would have sensed an unmistakable tone of uneasiness, one that was less pronounced two days earlier, when he called to tell me that Lolo was drifting in and out of consciousness, that Lolo was having difficulty remembering the names of those around him, that Lolo's prognosis was not good.

Dad spoke to me like I was my answering machine, using almost exactly the same words from his message just minutes earlier. There was that same initial hesitation before each sentence, the same monotone recitation, the same unsteady inflections at the same words. I knew him well enough to know that he rehearsed what he had said. We were both compulsive that way. He had probably left the same message to everyone he could think of. He probably even believed, deep down, that if he said those words enough times that they might form a wall, abstracting the horrific events unfolding half a world away until they could no longer make him feel vulnerable.

"Your mom can't stop crying," he told me. He asked me to call her and gave me her number in the Philippines, twice. Then he asked me to repeat the number back to him. When I couldn't get past a busy signal on the other end, he became anxious. He told me to keep trying because he was really worried about her. The truth was: I knew that Mom had all the support she needed from our extended family. My bigger concern was my father, who was all alone in our house in California, hundreds of miles away from his children. Surrounded by darkness and neighbors he hardly knew, he couldn't be near my mother in her time of need, and he was forced to communicate to people in far-flung corners of the globe through wiring and plastic. The world must have felt incredibly immense, and his presence so tragically singular. Dad would never have let on that he also needed someone to help him at that moment.

My younger sister Emmalline was convinced that Lolo must have felt the same way as he lay on that hospital bed: alone. He, too, must have felt so small and incredibly insignificant. After all, he had been devastated when our family left him behind in the Philippines. A few years later, Lola Rosa (his wife) died. During the twilight of his life, Lolo only saw my mother in those hazy days after a stroke. Sometimes he woke up in the hospital convinced he was in someone else's house. He flew into a white rage when the nurses tried to stop him from going home. The hospital always felt hostile and alienating that way: the tubes and machines frightened him. He refused medication and treatment, even when it was to help him cope with the pain. I can only speculate about the extent of abandonment he must have felt in his death bed. I wonder what I would have whispered into his ear if I had been the one at his side shortly before he died.

Emmalline was much closer to Lolo than I was. She was the one upon whom he lavishly flung his affections. Naturally, she took his death hardest. When she was younger, she always said a prayer for him before she went to bed. And then one day she stopped inexplicably. She doesn't even remember the day she stopped; she only remembers a before and an after. When Lolo first became ill, she tortured herself for having stopped praying at all. This last time around, Mom asked her to pray for Lolo, but in my sister's hectic routine of school and work and exams she forgot to do so. Emmalline won't admit it, but the fact that she brought it up with me at all, suggests she must have felt that she had failed Lolo somehow, or worse, that she was responsible for his death.

The night Lolo died, dad also spent a considerable amount of time tracking Emmalline down. When my dad finally found Emmalline at a friend's house, she hurried back to her apartment to be alone. This was two, maybe three in the morning. Less than a mile away from her apartment, a large black object—she thinks a raven, maybe a bat— was flying straight for her windshield. When it was about thirty feet away, the thing suddenly veered to the right and flashed her its chest and belly. By then the object was glowing white. She lost track of it as it disappeared among the trees. Shivering, she felt a very fulfilling sense of internal calm.

————

I'm in a plane, headed for the Philippines. If you have a good sense of geography—and chances are, because you're an American you don't—you would know that we are flying west over the Pacific Ocean. From this high, the sweeping curve of the earth is still only a suggestion. The blue canvas stretched out for what seemed like forever, where it eventually met the sky. If you looked up high enough, you could see star light fighting through the last vestige of day. Emmalline and my dad are directly to my left, sleeping.

All three of us have been on this flight before, but seventeen years earlier, heading in the opposite direction, to California. Back then, I asked my dad if the vast expanse of white clouds below us was snow. Too proud to admit to his son that he didn't have knowledge of the world in its entirety, my dad nodded yes.

In a few hours, the white and blue would turn into lush, green terraced landscape, segmented into small plots for cultivating rice. Mother will be composed. She will be at the airport waiting with Jeffrey. Dad and I will be bearing greetings, letters, cards, messages of hope scripted hastily by relatives scattered throughout America.

————

By the time Lolo died, I would already know Jeffrey for nearly a year, several weeks having passed since our last break-up. In such a short amount of time, Jeffrey and I had built a complex relationship of dependency and repulsion, complicated by my need to prepare for a looming dissertation. He was both my best friend and a lover, but never both at the same time. His expansive empathy was absolutely intimidating.

Mom and Dad, on the other hand, knew very little about Jeffrey, even less of our history together. The picture they have of him is colored by the phone calls I made to them only when the fights Jeffrey and I had were especially exasperating. To their credit, they held back their surprise when I told them Jeffrey wanted to be supportive in my time of need, even if it meant having to take a different flight arriving two hours earlier.

At the airport, waiting for the arrival of the plane with Dad, Emmalline, and me on board, Mom had very little trouble spotting Jeffrey, who at 6'3" and with fiery red hair shaved close to the scalp, towered like a light house above the sea of black-haired Filipinos crowding the doors outside customs.

————

Jeffrey was unchaining his bicycle when I first saw him. I was on my rollerblades, drunk, and waiting for the light on Greenwich Avenue to turn green so I could cross Sixth

Avenue. My head was giddy with excitement. The eye contact was innocent at first, and so were the initial hesitant smiles. At one point, I even thought he might have been laughing at me. But he kept stealing glances and smiling, and he just looked so goofy. None of his clothes matched. He didn't seem to be in any hurry to undo the bike chain, so when the light finally turned green, I took off down Eighth Street thinking that I would never see him.

But Jeffrey was on his bike following me. He was actually following me! It would be one of those fateful moments in his life, I later learned, when he chose to confront, rather than avoid.

The closer Jeffrey got, the more I started to panic. I didn't know what I was going to say, so I started rehearsing pick-up lines and thought about all the possibilities: Is he really following me? Should I be the first to say something? What will I say if he asks me to go over to his apartment?

In the end, our first interaction was nondescript. He turned at a stop light, I decided to follow. He saw me following and turned around to meet me. We exchanged greetings, pleasantries, names, then phone numbers. Just before we parted, he told me that he loved the way I smiled. He called me that night and left a really long, rambling message on my answering machine that I played over and over and over again. For days. The sound of Jeffrey's voice reverberating against the walls was very soothing. When I closed my eyes, I pretended he was sitting on the couch next to me.

On our first date, Jeffrey said he was fifteen years older than I. I found this shocking at first, not because our ages were so disparate, but because he didn't look even close to being 39. I thought he was 32 at most, and on his bike, wearing a white and brown Hawaiian shirt and a fluorescent orange fisherman's hat, he looked even younger. As the night progressed, I found that the age difference gave us a lot to talk about, and share. There was a distance we had to traverse, something for us to do.

We ended the night under the string of lights lining the Williamsburg Bridge. Watched by a partly cloudy sky and serenaded by the East River, our arms and shirts and lips and jeans disappeared into a mass of knots, until a group of teenagers chased us apart by hurling unopened soda cans.

———

This is how I choose to remember Lolo. I was probably six years old at the time. He woke me up at some ungodly hour, dragged me out of bed and dressed me. We walked out the back door. Everyone else was still sleeping, and for the next hour or so, we walked down a gravel path—he barefoot and I in flip-flops. We reached the rice paddies before dawn, making sure to be as noisy as possible in order to scare away the snakes. As we sat on raised earth above the flooded pits, Lolo showed me various constellations in the sky: The Three Kings, the Three Sisters, the Bag of Charms. He didn't know what a "Big Dipper" was. I also remember the stars, bright and vivid as if they had dropped out of a dream.

Then we sat there and watched meteorites streak across the sky. He told me that those flashing lines of light were stars dying and falling to earth. Sometimes, he told me, the stars burned up completely before they reached the ground. At other times, he said, the stars would hit the ground still glowing like massive embers able to destroy entire houses.

"Really?" I asked incredulously.

For the rest of the day, I pondered, in a way only six-year-olds do, what it must have been like to discover an immense five-pointed star—like what they put on top of the tree in Rockefeller Center, only hundreds of times bigger—still luminous and lodged in front of someone's house. I imagined a tall, dignified woman with long grey hair, much like Lola Rosa, scratching her head as lots of young kids milled about excitedly. After the initial shock of finding such a gaudy, over-sized Christmas ornament buried in her front yard, I also imaged that she must have felt incredibly thankful for being miraculously spared. Or maybe she felt distraught enough to curse God for playing such a tacky but vicious joke on her.

———

Jeffrey is looking at pictures from Lolo's funeral service. He is sitting on the swing-bench Lolo built decades ago. It's been three days since Lolo was buried. Inside the house, Mom and Dad are haggling with the neighbors over how to divide up the land. They're being very loud, but they aren't angry with each other yet.

The pictures of the funeral are not very attractive, both because their quality was not remarkable, and because the intrusive camera had captured the mourners in private moments that were embarrassing to look at.

Lolo's face, however, seemed expressionless from every angle. His eyes sunken, skin draped around high cheekbones like old, ratty blankets. Liver spots formed a broken purple line across his forehead. And he was so thin. He had lost so much weight. His shirt collar was way too large, gesturing back to the Lolo that filled out his clothes handsomely. That Lolo is not in any of the photographs Jeffrey now holds in his hands.

Dressed in his sheriff's uniform, that other Lolo once posed proudly next to his bicycle for Lola Rosa's camera. He never talked about those days, but Lola Rosa used to say that Lolo was so striking then. She wasn't exaggerating, because even in his old age, Lolo was still very good looking. He built his own house, spent most of his life tending to his rice paddies, and his body showed it. Age and years of chain-smoking did very little to diminish the awe he commanded from those around him. He was probably the first man I had a crush on.

He must have been good with the ladies. That much I figured out on my own, once I began connecting the dots and realizing that all those other grandmothers were really his mistresses, and the uncles and aunts, bastard children. Lola Rosa, it turned out, never gave birth to my mom or her sister. And it explained why he felt so threatened by my aunt's lesbianism that he cut her off completely for four years, and why I was never fully honest with him.

Looking at his picture, his disarming smile slowly dissolves into a smirk of arrogance belonging to someone who knew the elastic limits of people who were too often forgiving.

And so this man, who lived through American and Japanese colonial regimes, who saw the promises of Quezon left unfulfilled by Marcos, who as a young man shadowed the Bataan Death March, darting between trees to shower American G.I.'s with cigarettes and bags of rice, was still the target of my resentment even in death. The love was still there, of course. It is just much easier for me to resent someone I love, than to love someone I resent.

———

"He looks like he died of AIDS," Jeffrey tells me.

"He had a stroke," I reply. But Lolo did look a lot like someone who might have died of AIDS. In a few years, as more and more people around me began to die, I began to realize that all dead people look remarkably the same regardless of the cause of their demise: they were always thinner, hollow, missing something. I wonder whether I would be haunted by those final images of Lolo when it's Jeffrey's turn to be buried.

"He looks like so many people I know," Jeffrey says as he fans out the pictures in his hand. He stares at me like we're playing poker.

"This place is so different now," I tell Jeffrey. "Everything feels smaller." The wood creaks as we swing back and forth. I point down the road, "That's where a drunk driver ran into a parked jeepney with my sisters inside. And down there used to live an old man with no legs."

The man had little stumps attached to his hips, and he dressed in tattered clothes he never washed. Every morning I used to sit on Lolo's swing bench and watch the man with no legs roll to the market two miles up the road, on something that resembled a skateboard. He would lie down on his stomach and push himself with black, calloused hands. Then, in the evening, I would see him rolling back.

I remember my mom passing along news of the legless man's death like so many rolls over dinner. A drunk bus driver rode his massive vehicle off the side of the road and crushed the legless man as he was making his way back home.

"That was almost fifteen years ago. But I expect him to come back rolling over that rise any second now," I tell Jeffrey.

I couldn't believe such catastrophic changes had been happening in this home, so very far away, itself a place impossible to imagine. Trucks and buses and jeepneys sped carelessly down both directions of the highway in front of us. When I was younger, only a few cars and trucks ever reached this point, mostly filled with people or cargo destined for even farther corners of the country. I remember when there were no hardware stores or shopping malls, only merienda stands for hungry travelers.

Jeffrey couldn't understand. For him, a heightened sense of difference, of alienation, made this place, and his place in it, so very real, so very tangible.

"But to come from your home and feel that it doesn't exist," he told me, "Well, I don't know what that could possibly be like."

"This isn't my home," I correct him, "I'm not even sure it ever was."

Jeffrey places the pictures down on the bench next to him, and puts his arm around my shoulder. My eyes are still trained on the pavement in front of us.

"Every time you move to some faraway place, you leave some fragment of yourself behind to be buried by the people left in your wake," I tell him, "so that by the time you reach your destination, you would already be a different person, a part of you having previously died."

I move my gaze to him now. "Maybe it's not the place. Maybe it's me."

His body shifting in place; the air passing through his nostrils; the shirt fabric sliding across his chest: I listen to the sounds of his thoughts swallowing mine.

―――――

Jeffrey begins leafing through the photographs again. I sit on the swing bench and picture the guava and papaya trees that used to stand where store fronts are now.

I look at the hardware store next to Lolo's house. Years ago there was a small dirt mound where Lola said elves lived; at night, she told us to say "excuse me" every couple of steps just in case we accidentally stepped on one of the elves. If we were rude and unrepentant, Lola would tell us, the stepped-on elf will cause the offending leg to stop growing.

Then I remember Emmalline running into the house, screaming about a faceless white figure watching her from the mound as she sat in the very swing Jeffrey and I now find ourselves.

"The stories," I turn to Jeffrey and say: "I still have the stories."

Jeffrey nods. "I love you, Pablo. If it's any consolation," he says, fleetingly.

"You know, it surprises me how well I'm taking Lolo's death. I mean, I feel that I can be more emotional about it, but at the same time, I just feel spent," I tell him.

"It's called closure," he answers, "and you probably have it."

"But for how long? Closure is never complete."

"It's as good as it's going to get, Pablo. Some people never even find the door they need to close," Jeffrey says.

"Or they walk away without ever closing it," I respond.

He pauses, nods twice, then says in clear, even tones, "Yes, that is exactly what some people choose to do." He understands completely.

———

My mom tells me that on the morning Lolo died, she leaned over his body and whispered into his ear. What she said was this: "We put your spirit in the hands of God and trust that he will take care of you. Don't be afraid." Lolo, no longer able to speak or move, blinked once, then a single tear rolled out of the corner of his eye. I wonder whether the tear was a sign of his mustering the strength to let go, or his recognition of my mother's own strength in being able to let him go.

———

Jeffrey grabbed me by both shoulders. His coarse palms slid up and down my arms, paused slightly to consider the raised skin around my tattoo. Jeffrey's back was against the window, and all I could see was his outline, a black shadow flashing in and out of the shafts of light penetrating the darkness of the room through small holes in the wall.

He told me that he wanted to take me and swallow me whole, except in his broken Tagalog it sounded like he wanted to cover me in rice.

I laughed because I saw the irony in it all.

Slightly perturbed, he switched to Spanish, and when he started to push my shirt up my stomach, he switched again, this time to English. His arms were moving ferociously now, up and down the sides of my torso. They felt white hot against my skin, and left behind traces of his sweat everywhere they went.

Jeffrey took me by the hips and shoved me hard. He pinned the backs of my hands against the wall, and kissed a ring around my forehead. His lips seared holes into my skin. Jeffrey murmured his desires to me, and with each syllable he uttered, I imagined the books back in my New York apartment falling off the shelves one by one.

I didn't resist him. But neither did I reciprocate. Inside, my blood crashed against my forearms with the howls of my mother and grandmother and all the mothers before them. My hands clenched into tight claws and I imagined ripping his back open.

He moved in closer when I didn't push him away—so close that I felt on the brink of falling inside him. His lips kissed my neck the way his entire body kissed mine. I lost track of his hands. They clutched my back as if they belonged there, like they were a part of me. Then fingers reached into my waist band, slid toward the front where they unsnapped and unzipped. The shorts surged down my legs with the last of my reservations. My shirt followed shortly afterwards, and Jeffrey stepped back to remove his own clothes.

I didn't want him to speak so I pressed my fingers against his lips. My parents were napping in the room next to ours, and Jeffrey timed the undulations of his body to Tatay's snoring. Everybody else in the house, and maybe even the whole town, was sleeping through the mid-afternoon heat.

Jeffrey pushed me slowly down to the hard mat I slept on, and with each kiss I felt our skin welding together. His breathing was labored, heavy. His eyes drooped; they pleaded with me to tell him to stop, but I didn't want to. The last vestiges of my consent had unraveled when Foucault and Spivak hit the floor with loud thuds.

My fingers wandered up and down his back. They paused where the vertebra had been thrown out of alignment, and circled it. In the dark, I imagined his freckles like points on a map. I relished the hardness of his bones, the smoothness with which his skin flowed around his back toward his chest. I memorized the spray of pimples on his shoulders, placement of hair in the small of his back. There was no crevice, indentation, roundness or protrusion that remained unknown to me. In the darkness, the clarity with which I saw him was uncanny.

———

When he entered me, I found myself unable to speak. My body began to tremble despite the warmth of the silence around us. I felt him slowly abstracting me. My body became limber. My joints began to pull apart. My skin faded and dissolved into the floor. Beneath him, my body felt unrecognizable, while his remained exactly what it was when we had begun: a shadow of what I have always wanted to be.

NOEL ALUMIT

THE RICE ROOM: SCENES FROM A BAR
A ONE-MAN SHOW

Dance music is heard. Lights come up on a man dancing. Music plays
throughout his monologues.

I. GO-GO GREG

(In a Valley accent) I love my job. Being a go-go boy at The Rice Room is a real big deal.
There's a line of people dying to get in. On a good night, I can clear up to three hundred dollars in tips.

I think of what I do as art. If you treat go-go dancing like art, you get treated
as an artist. An *objet d'art*. That means an object of art in French. I take my work very seriously.

The best part of my job is I get to see everybody. I see who comes in, who is having a good time. I see everybody. I get to meet a lot of them too. I met my boyfriend
here. He gave me a real big tip. Don't get me wrong, I don't go out with every guy who
tips well. This guy is different. Most guys here think I'm just a piece of meat, sweaty skin
with a bulge. That's probably the worst thing about go-going, people think you're easy or
trampy. Most of the go-go boys I know are real decent guys, and not slutty at all. Sure we
dance like sluts, but it's a job, and it stops when we get off the stage.

So my future boyfriend comes to the edge of the stage. He's waving a twenty at me. So
I undulate down, shoving my crotch in his face, expecting him to cram the twenty way
down my Speedos so his fingers brushes against my wanger. Instead, he folds the twenty
sideways and gently inserts it on the side of my bathing suit. He didn't try to grope me
or nothing. I'm thinking, "Whoa, this guy is really special."

He starts having this conversation with me.

"Hey, what's your name?"

"Greg. My name is Greg."

"You dance beautifully. Do you do this for a living?"

"No. Just part time. I'm putting myself through school."

"Yeah? What are you studying?"

"I'm studying to become a rocket scientist."

And he starts to laugh like I said something funny. The truth is I *am* studying to
become a rocket scientist. I did my undergraduate work at Stanford, graduated summa

cum laude in mathematics. Currently, I'm enrolled in the master slash Ph.D. program at Caltech studying chemical engineering and astrophysics.

Being a math major got me started in rocketry. In one of my courses, I was assigned to read *The Rocket Into Interplanetary Space* by Hermann Oberth, which is the first mathematical dissertation on rocket flight that goes farther than the limitations of earth. I mean there have always been rockets around. I mean like for hundreds and hundreds of years. The Chinese used the dynamics of rocket flight in like 1040 AD to fight off enemies and stuff.

A rocket is a like an incredible thrust forward. And rocket science is like the study of thrusting forward. When a spaceship goes into the universe, it requires a severe thrust forward to leave the earth's atmosphere.

Right now I'm doing a paper on different spheres of the earth. Currently, I'm writing about the stratosphere. For those of you who don't know, the stratosphere is that part of the earth's atmosphere which is above the mesosphere and below the troposphere. It's like really complicated stuff. It's OK if you don't understand.

Like I'll talk to my boss Chuck about rockets, the universe and stuff, and Chuck goes off on how the alignment of planets can determine your fate. He goes off on astrology, telling me how he learned it from this guru guy he knew in the sixties and seventies. Chuck is in a time warp, always talking about the good ole days. He's not here tonight. He's visiting a friend.

(*GREG's dance movements transforms into the older CHUCK*)

II. CHUCK

Walter, do you mind if I smoke? Of course you do. I know I shouldn't smoke, you have been telling me that for decades. I'm going to smoke anyway, thank you very much.

I drove by the old neighborhood. I don't know why. I just did. I drove down Hyperion, up Griffith Park Boulevard. Up Hyperion, down Griffith Park Boulevard. Up and down, up and down. Over and over again.

I drove by old hangouts: The Toy Tiger, Pure Trash, and the Riverside Club. They're all gone, you know. The bar scene in San Francisco was pretty hot back then as well...the bars around South Market, Folsom area. What was the name of that one club? The Ramrod. That is what it was called. That bar is gone too. Young people today wouldn't know a good bar if it bit them in the ass. Except for my bar, of course.

The Rice Room is well into its sixth year of existence, thank you very much. You thought I was crazy for opening a club that would cater strictly to gay Asians, in West Hollywood of all places. You should drop by. I know you won't step foot into West Hollywood, but things have changed. They allow Asians into their bars now.

Remember when we would have to show have to show three forms of ID to get in? In the meantime, they would allow a bevy of white boys to saunter in and out without showing proof of any ID. Or they would say we were inappropriately dressed—*us*, not dressed appropriately! Of course they let some blond in with the fashion sense of a peanut. I know the bars in West Hollywood were mean to us back then, but things are different. They are, Walter. You walk down Santa Monica Boulevard today and the joints are filled with Asians. It's different.

I hired a new dancer not too long ago. Filipino kid. From Northridge or Burbank, somewhere in the Valley. It is a well-regarded fact, Walter, that once you come over that hill, your IQ rises ten points. Boy, did his IQ rise. He's the smartest kid you'll ever meet. He's getting his Ph.D. He reminds me of you back in 1972. Strong and smart. We were all strong and smart back then. Back then...remember, Walter? When there was no such thing as Asian. We said what we were: I'm Chinese. I'm Japanese. It was OK to be called Oriental. When a community was only a few city blocks. And we'd watch *The Mary Tyler Moore Show* or *Rowan & Martin's Laugh-In*. We would get up and dance around, like Judy Karne, or better yet, Goldie Hawn.

(*CHUCK morphs into dancing GREG*)

III. GO-GO GREG

There are two people I idolize. The first person is Sir Isaac Newton, OK? Sir Isaac Newton created the basic laws of motion which set forth the analysis of rocket science. Particularly his Third Law of Motion which says: "For every action, there is an equal and opposite reaction." Mathematically speaking, that's big "M," big "V" equals little "m" and little "v." I mean without Sir Isaac Newton I would be studying math instead of rockets. And there are a lot of Asian people who are studying math as it is, right?

The second person I idolize is Goldie Hawn. Goldie Hawn is it, right. You know, from *Private Benjamin* fame. I love her. I love her because I used to watch reruns of *Rowan & Martin's Laugh-In*, right. Well, Goldie Hawn used to go-go dance on that show. It is because of her that go-go dancing is what it is today. I mean before her go-go dancing was like this cheap thing you did in seedy bars. But she glamorized it. She made go-go dancing a respectable form of art. She went on to movies and stuff and won an Academy Award and everything, right. God, I love her. She's so cool.

Of course there's a ton of cool people here. (*Goes into audience*) Part of my job is to mingle with the customer's to give them that full Rice Room experience. *Kamusta. Ni-how. An ya ha seo. Konbanwa.* I've learned to say hi in a hundred different languages. *Bonjour.* My favorite is Guamanian. *Hafadai.* I remember it because it's not a full day. It's half-a-day.

Saying hello in someone else's language makes people feel more at home. They feel relaxed. Feeling relaxed is what it is all about.

(GREG becomes the incredibly manic and fast-talking GEORGE)

IV. GEORGE

I had a very hard day. I wake up this morning with this raging headache. Pounding. Pounding. Pounding. My friend Greg tells me to meditate more often. So I try it. IT DOESN'T WORK! I find myself late to work, because I'm desperately trying to find my glasses. I look everywhere. I pass my hall mirror to discover they were on my face the entire time.

I work for this gay organization. I won't mention the name but they're very big and very influential. I quit my last job in marketing because I wanted to work in a less stressful environment and get away from my straight asshole of a boss. Now I work for a gay organization, the stress is still there, and no matter what anyone says, bosses are still assholes regardless of sexual orientation.

I get to work and phones were going off, the receptionist called in sick, I'm fielding calls left and right. I must have had 32 people on hold at the same time. And while all of this was going on, the only thought that kept going through my head was that at the end of the day, I would go to a bar and relax.

I walk into The Rice Room and I see him. Him. I don't know his name, I don't know what he does for a living, I don't know anything about him. I just know it's him. The man of my dreams. He looks like an Asian James Dean. A rebel. His hair is slicked back with pomade, grooves of hair pulled back, formed no doubt with the teeth of a black comb. Stunning. He's wearing a T-shirt, one size too small, so it's tight, and from my view I could see the muscles of his back tightly, firmly hug his ribcage.

He turns around, and his one-size-too-small T-shirt looks like it's going to rip open from the sturdy pecs of his chest. He lays back on the bar with his elbows resting on the counter, and I could see the outline of little rectangles on his abdomen building and collapsing as he breathes in and out. He's wearing blue jeans, also one size too small. Levi's. Button fly. He's leaning back with one leg out like this, his foot resting on the heal of his black Tony Lama ostrich skin boots, looking like a 1950s matinee idol. I think to myself: it's him. The man of my dreams.

I could see it all in my head. Images popping in my head. Like paparazzi camera bulbs. I would walk up to him and say, "Hi." He would say, "How zit going?" He wouldn't say "How is it going?" or "How are you?" He would say, "How zit going?" And I would look deeply into his eyes and say: "I had a shitty day, but since I've met you my day and any other day from this point forward is a little brighter." And he would laugh, no chuckle, no smile, yeah, smile, and give a reverse nod. He would say, "You're cute, in a Clark Kent sort of way." And I would say, "You're gorgeous, in a way that is indescribable, incomparable, gorgeous in a way that you only possess and no one else." And he would see through my being, see through my soul, see through my glasses, that I'm the only man for him. And tomorrow we'll fly down to Hawaii, where they'll soon sanction gay marriages, start our life together, adopt two children from Korea, save money to send those two children to college, they'll visit us in our home on a hill in Los Feliz, where we would spend the rest of our days until we die only minutes apart, then meet each other as cosmic light on the rings of Saturn where we would spend the rest of eternity traveling from one heavenly star to another...together.

So I'm at the far end of the bar. And I see him. The man of my dreams. I'm working on my third gin and tonic to build the nerve to go over to this guy. Happy hour is in full swing now, and I think to myself: You idiot, go over to him before someone else steals him away; before someone who doesn't even figure into our scheme of flying from star to star for the rest of eternity, comes along, and causes a cosmic imbalance, where I would never meet this gorgeous guy in the first place. Go over. Go over. Go over and meet him.

I take my drink napkin and dry off the sweat on my palms, I put my hands in my pocket to warm the coldness in my fingers. I get up from my bar stool. But just before I go over, I pull out a pen and write with my half-cold, half-warm, half-sweaty, half-dry hand my telephone number on a napkin. I slowly walk over to him and say, "Hi."

"How zit going?" he says, with a smile and a reverse nod.

For a moment, I'm quiet. I don't say anything because he is more beautiful up close than from afar. I take my bar napkin with my scribbled telephone number on it, my name on the napkin is unreadable because the sweat from my palm dampened the paper, blurring the ink.

I say out loud, "Call me." But I pray to myself: God, please let him find me just somewhat attractive. Let him see through my being, see through my soul, see through my glasses and see that I am the man for him. God, please let him see that.

I sit next to him. I order him another drink. "Bartender, another scotch on the rocks." Like they say in the movies. I tell him my name. He tells me his. His name is Richard. Richard. We start to talk. He tells me he's from LA. I tell him I'm from LA. He tells me he loves to read Harold Brodkey. I tell him I love to read Harold Brodkey. He tells me he loves to watch old reruns of *Laverne & Shirley*. I tell him I love to watch old reruns of *Laverne & Shirley*. We talk about how Laverne and Shirley met Fabian on *Laverne & Shirley*. He's laughing and I'm laughing. And I'm thinking this is great. He tells me he only dates white guys—tell him...all of a sudden I'm thinking of the two Korean kids we adopted and how they will never go to college. He tells me he has to go and wanders off to another part of the bar. He neglects to take the napkin with my blurred name and telephone number on it. He walks away. He stops. He turns around. Smiles at me. My heart leaps, thinking that God answered my prayers and this gorgeous guy, Richard, finds me attractive after all. He's willing to leave his boyfriend because he can see my soul. And my soul possesses elements that transcend color lines. Adopted Korean kids, college, here we come.

He looks at me. Richard looks at me, and says, "It was good talking to you. You're kinda cute in a Clark Kent sort of way." He shoots me with his finger. "Catcha later," he says. He leaves. He's gone. I sit at the bar stool, for an hour or two. Go-go boys get on the stage and dance. While I sit here and watch.

V. GO-GO GREG

I have to be upbeat, you know. Everyone is watching you, you know. Who wants to watch a depressed go-go dancer, you know what I mean?

I better take my break now. The club is getting really crowded. You know what that means. That's right. There is a line to the restroom.

(GREG becomes the very still and austere RICHARD)

VI. RICHARD

OPEN THE DOOR!!! I hate having to wait for the restroom. It seems the line to the bathroom is longer than the line to get into this place. All the Scotch I drank is running right through me like water does a faucet.

Listen, you little maggot. My bladder is about to fucking burst. If you don't get out real soon, you're gonna have a pee pond bigger that fucking Lake Superior. You got that asshole? YOU GOT THAT, FUCKING PIECE OF SHIT!

My friends tell me that I need to work on my communication skills. They say: "Richard, you gotta be more sensitive." Fuck sensitive.

I'm mean. I like it that way. I like having people scared of me. They're less likely to fuck with you if they're scared of you. If they're not scared of you—you're nothing. Dispensable.

Imagine: You're walking home. Minding your own business. Walking home from the gym, the Sport Connection, let's say. You're walking down Westbourne on your way to your house off Melrose. A house you got working as a personal trainer, let's say.

You notice a car behind you. It's driving really slow. You don't think much about it. Cars drive slow all the time, right? Plus you're only two blocks, three or four minutes away, from your house and what could happen in two blocks and three or four minutes?

All of the sudden, the slow driving car passes you. You feel a sense of momentary relief. I say momentary because the car stops just ahead of you. Six guys—or was it five— it was six—guys get out and start yelling at you.

"Are you a faggot?"

You try to walk a different direction. Once again: "Are you a faggot?"

You try to walk away, thinking they can't be talking to you, because you try really hard not to look like a faggot, I mean look gay.

As you walk away they follow you. Then you run. And they run. One of them catches up to you, grabs you by the collar, and throws you down. You try to get up. But you feel this whack at the side of your face. Like someone just kicked you. Then you're out of breath because someone just socked you in the gut. Your try to fight back, but you can't. Two guys have your arms. They pulled it so far back that you think you're gonna snap in two. You feel this pain in your chest and stomach, because they're pummeling you. Your try to scream but you can't get enough air into your body to do that because every time one of them punches you the wind is knocked right out of you. Until finally, between blows, you get enough air into your lungs into your gut to scream: "HEEEEEEELP!"

You notice off to your right, a light switches on in a kitchen window. A dim light, but bright enough to notice, bright enough for the guys kicking your ass to leave you alone and speed off. You wait for someone to come out of their house to help you. But you remember people don't do that anymore.

So you make your way home. You want to cry, but a memory from childhood, a saying, a phrase that someone said to you, but you don't remember who, reverberates in you head big boys, men, real men don't cry. So you don't.

You want to call the police, but if you call them, you may have to tell them that you were attacked because you're gay. This was a couple of years ago, you're still in the closet, so you're not ready for that yet. So you don't call anyone.

Instead, you wash yourself up, put alcohol on whatever part of you is busted open, and go to bed. In the morning you tell anyone who asks that you fell or got into a car accident.

For the next two years you try to figure out what happened, why it happened. You keep looking over your shoulder or rearview mirror to see if anyone is following you. You think, if I were straight, this wouldn't have happened. If I were a little scarier to them, if they thought I carried a gun, if they thought I were stronger, if they stopped seeing gay men or Asian men as wimpy or effeminate or weak, maybe they would have let me alone.

OPEN THE GODDAMNED DOOR!!! This guy was nice enough to buy me a drink, a couple drinks, actually.

I'm sitting minding my own business. I'm thinking about how I got to get myself to the gym and work out. I have a forty-four-inch chest. I want to keep it that way. Plus I'm training for a triathalon next month. I injured myself running. So I turn around to stretch my leg like this. Then I see him. Him. My worst nightmare. This Asian guy—coke-bottle glasses, slouched over like he's afraid to be here. He is giving me this look, like he likes me or something.

I see this wimpy, effeminate, weak Asian guy in the periphery of my vision. He comes toward me. He says, "Hi." I say, "How zit going?" He sits right down next to me. He tells me his name is George.

We get into this conversation. We're talking about weird shit, something about *Laverne & Shirley*. I wanna leave, but George keeps talking; I can't get a word in edgewise.

George keeps yapping and yapping. How many *Laverne & Shirley* episodes can a guy talk about? George is really pissing me off. I think to myself: This guy's fucking clueless. He is the kind of guy who makes us look bad. The sight of him makes me sick. I think that it's guys like George that allows people to think that's it's OK to bash the living daylights out of us on our way home. I get so mad, I say the one thing that I know would hurt him: I only date white guys.

I feel victorious. Take that you faggot chink. Score one for the butch guy. And just before you walk away, you see the disappointed look on his face. Your feelings of victory go away. So you turn around and say: "Hey, you're kinda cute in a Clark Kent sort of way." In the back of your mind, you want guys like these to fall off the earth and die. "Catcha later."

OPEN THE GODDAMNED DOOR!!!

(RICHARD morphs into the flamboyant and "queeny" TIEN)

VII. TIEN

God. God. God. God. God. *God.* One of the worst things that could ever happen to anyone happened to me tonight.

The evening started off innocently enough. I get dressed for the evening and decide what I'm going to wear. Blouse: DKNY? Dolce & Gabbana? DKNY? Dolce & Gabbana? I go with Dolce & Gabbana. Trousers: Armani? Versace? Armani? Versace? I go with Versace. Shoes? Cole Haan? Kenneth Cole? Cole Haan? Kenneth Cole? I go with Cole Haan. I grab my makeup purse, jump into the Jaguar, and rush off to the French Market for a bite to eat. I have a mixed green dinner salad with a lemon vinegarette. I jump back into the Jag, rush to the Rice Room. I make my grand entrance. I say hello to 207 people in the first five minutes. They know me here because I was crowned Miss Rice Room 2000. I sit at my table in the back. I pull out my compact. AAAAHHHHH! I see it. There is a piece of green spinach caught between my teeth. I was so embarrassed. I did what any self-respecting queen would do. I ran into the bathroom and I'm never coming out.

(startled) There's some moron banging on the door. Men can be such brutes. Whatever happened to refinement? All of those charming qualities that separated gay men from beasts? Tennessee Williams: gay. Langston Hughes: gay. Oscar Wilde: gay, gay, gay, gay, gay. Men of stature, possessing social graces worthy of royalty. Nowadays, you

can't separate gay men from straight men. Gay men these days want to be butch, masculine. Playing sports for God's sake, trying desperately to appear like other men. What's the use of being gay, coming out of the closet, when all you end up with is being regular?

I mean, refinement and culture have always been associated with the gay man. In some Pacific Islander cultures we are considered blessed, we are the ones who remember the dances and the stories. Parents sent their children to us so that they may be taught those dances and those stories. In the Peking Opera, we were revered as great artisans. We come from a long line of proud and distinctive people. Next year, my homeland, Hong Kong, goes back to China. I've heard about what Communists do to homosexuals, to anyone who deviates from the norm—imprisonment, assault, possible death. Here we are in America, able to be different, to be a group of people distinctly unto ourselves, and what do we do? We strive to be like everyone else, to be accepted like everyone else. Can you think of anything more mundane?

(Leaves the bathroom area and moves to center stage)
(Approaches audience member)

I need to ask you a question. I want you to be brutally honest. Do I look fat? Wait. Don't answer. *(Sucks in gut to appear thinner)* Do I look fat now? That's what I thought that movie *Waiting to Exhale* was all about: a bunch of women sucking in their stomachs so they won't look fat. I was so disappointed. It was about women and the brutish men who ruin their lives. Where are all the gentlemen? My first crush was the gentlest man I had ever met. He was my chauffeur in Hong Kong. His duty was to drive me back and forth to school. We would have made a terrific couple. Him: A rugged, simple human being. Me: Elegant and stunning. There were only a few things standing in our way. He was 32 and I was only seven. He was straight, married, and had a family of his own in some godforsaken village in the Philippines. Still, I'll never forget him. You never forget the one person that made you aware that you are different from the other little boys.

I looked forward to him driving me to school and picking me up. And when other little boys made fun of me for playing with the girls, he would yell at them and scare them off. Lito, that's his name, Lito would say, it's OK if I'm different. Different is good, he would say. "God made us this way for a reason." At the time, I didn't know what God was or religion or anything. I just knew that what he said was comforting. That kind of comfort is necessary. Little boys need some acceptance from other boys, men. Or else you grow up trying to change yourself into something a little more desirable, spend hours on end looking into mirrors trying to remove any residue of imperfection. Thinking that if you were a little more attractive, a little more smart, a little more...that someone would want you, need you, love you.

Lito made me feel that way. He had a child of his own in the Philippines. Working in Hong Kong brought more money to him than working in there. He missed his son, and I wondered if anyone would ever miss me that much. I imagined growing up and marrying Lito. But my family moved to America a year later and I never saw him again.

I can't help but think that someday I'll run into him. Or someone like him. And I'll be ready. I'll be charming, witty and attractive. Perfect hair, skin. He won't have a reason to not like me.

Oh my God. Don't look. I said don't look. But do you see the guy behind me? He is so cute. There's karaoke night every Monday. I come just to hear him sing. He sings my favorite song.

(TIEN sings a song. He sings badly. Suddenly his voice becomes more legitimate, becoming—)

VIII. JOPET

(In a thick Filipino accent)

My dream is to be in *Miss Saigon*. I sang that song for my audition for *Miss Saigon* when they auditioned for the first production in London. In the Philippines, to do *Miss Saigon* means you've made it. It means you are the most talented in the world. At my first audition, in the Philippines, for the very first one in London, they asked my name and to please tell them a little about myself. I said my name is Jopet Walara. I come from a small village. It is so small it does not even have a name. I sang my song, but I was not chosen. I was not good enough back then.

Then I heard they were auditioning for *Miss Saigon* in the States. For Broadway and for national touring. I think Broadway is more better than London. I went to the bureau in Manila to inquire about auditioning for *Miss Saigon* in the States. The man at the bureau said there was big controversy because they were too many foreigners taking up jobs that should go to Americans. Only American citizens can do *Miss Saigon*. So I said I want to become an American citizen. The man at the bureau said that would be impossible. He said there was a long waiting list to enter America, the longest waiting list in the world. A person can wait up to twenty-five years to get here from the Philippines. I said I cannot wait that long. He asked if I had anyone in the States who could sponsor me and bring me over. I told him I come from a small village with no name. A village where no one leaves and no one cares to go. So, no, I don't know anyone in the States who could sponsor me. He said the only way I can come to the US is on a tourist visa, but I can only visit and not stay. I took a great big plane—I'd never been on a plane before—all the way to Los Angeles. When I landed, I did not know where to go. I got on a bus that had a sign that said Hollywood on it. The bus driver asked me where I wanted to go. I said Hollywood. He said I know you want to go to Hollywood, fool, that's what the sign of the bus said, but where in Hollywood do you want to go? I said the only place that I knew—I had heard it the movies all the time—I said take me to Hollywood and Vine. At Hollywood and Vine, I thought I would run into a movie star who could tell me where to audition for *Miss Saigon*. When I got there, the only stars around were the ones on the street. I walked around Hollywood and I saw a sign for a place call the YMCA, which stands for the Young Men's Christian Association. I decided to stay there because I am a young man and a Christian, so why not. I asked a lady at the YMCA how can I see *Miss Saigon* and she told to go to the Ahmanson Theatre. I went to the Ahmanson Theatre and I bought a ticket to go see the show. From the very beginning to the very end, I loved *Miss Saigon* and saw the second act many more times. The last time I saw it, I asked the man behind the glass window how do I audition for *Miss Saigon*. The man behind the window said I had to call the casting people. He gave me a number to call the casting people. A casting lady told me they will be casting for *Miss Saigon* on this day. On that day, I auditioned. I gave them my telephone number at the YMCA. I waited for their call, but they did not call. So I called them. I talk to the casting lady and I said my name is Jopet Walara and I auditioned for *Miss Saigon* and I asked her when do I start rehearsal. She told me there was very stiff competition and not everyone can be chosen. I was not chosen...again. I told the lady I need to be in *Miss Saigon*. To do *Miss Saigon* means you are the most talented in the whole world. I come from a village with no name. I don't want to go back. I don't want to end up like my parents who work their entire lives to have nothing, to be nothing. I don't want to end up like my mother selling measly fruit by the road begging for tourists to buy. I don't want to end up like my father, driving rich kids somewhere as somebody's chauffeur in Hong Kong. I want to be in *Miss Saigon*.

The casting lady said there will be another audition next year. I said I cannot wait that long because I have to go back to the Philippines. The casting lady said auditions do not happen every day, only a few times a year and I would have to wait. I said I cannot wait. I cannot. I cannot. The casting lady hung up on me because she thought I was crazy.

My tourist visa ran out, but I did not go back.

I walk around Hollywood and a nice man stopped me on Santa Monica Boulevard. He offered to buy me food at the Rice Bowl on La Brea. I was so hungry. I ran out of money. I tried to find work, but no one will hire me because I do not have proper papers to be in this country. They said I was illegal. The man who picked me up said he will give me money if I have sex with him. I said OK. The man ask if I were new to Hollywood, because he often picks up guys on Santa Monica Boulevard and he had never seen me before. I said, yes I was new. He said I should do well on Santa Monica Boulevard, because I am a fresh new face in Hollywood.

I walk and walk on Santa Monica Boulevard. I see this sign that says The Rice

Room. I like rice so I go inside. I go to this bar and there are half-naked Asians dancing around on stage for money, like the opening scene from *Miss Saigon*. I like it here. I go to this bar and meet lots of men. I go home with them and they are usually very nice when I ask them for money in the morning. When I audition for *Miss Saigon* they will pick me this time. And they will write a letter to immigration and American Equity and I will get a work visa and I will stay. Someday I will be in *Miss Saigon*.

IX. CHUCK

You know, Walter, I was doing some cleaning. Getting rid of superfluous things in my life. I pulled out my fondue pot. I don't think I'd seen that fondue pot since Farrah Fawcett was on *Charlie's Angels*. That was nineteen seventy—let's see, 2000 subtract 26 years, equals....equals a long time ago. I was never very good at math.

Young men today...I wonder if they would ever know what we did for them, Walter. They think their liberties were all of sudden granted. There were people like you and me in the beginning. We were at the first gay pride festival ever, one dollar organization. I remember all those gay-owned businesses that lined the streets of Silverlake, before AIDS destroyed it all. I remember you telling me in 1974 that we would live forever, that we would be friends forever, Walter. I remember all of these things. I know you remember these things. Me and you would sit around my fondue pot and just remember things. The fun part was me telling how something happened and you remembering it different. Like dancing at some New York disco. How I got so drunk that I slammed into a guy and his blond wig almost came off. In the cab ride home, you told me the guy I slammed into was Andy Warhol. I told you that you were lying because drunk or not, I could spot Andy Warhol a mile away. You said it was and I said it wasn't. I loved telling that story because you would fill in the gaps, like how the kind of drinks I had or the red satin coat I wore. And that story isn't much fun to tell if you aren't there. If you aren't there to fill in the gaps, to make the picture complete, I will be the only one to share my side of the story. And a story with missing parts isn't a story at all. Walter? Walter? I don't know if you can hear me. I don't know if you've heard anything I've said, but I don't want you to go. I know I'm being selfish, but I can't help it. You used to drag me to every bar in town. You introduced me to the pleasures of six-foot drag queens. You were the first person who told me about Donna Summer.

It's time to put away the party shoes, my dear, and rest. I'll be back tomorrow. Your nurse should be here any minute. I'm sorry about the cigarettes. I didn't think second-hand smoke was something you had to worry about. I have to get back to the bar. I have payroll to take care of, liquor to order, got to stay well-stocked or those queens will have my headdress.

X. GEORGE

What I love about this place is it's always well-stocked. It's amazing what a few drinks can do. Screw the world. Bartender, another gin and tonic. Screw the world. Screw Asian men who look like James Dean with white boyfriends. I don't know when it happened. I don't know where I got the idea that a man of my dreams will somehow make me happy. I don't know why I believe it. It's bullshit. It's bullshit. It's bullshit.

I wish I could feel this way when I'm sober. I know I have it in me to be a strong person, truly independent. But I bought into it. The ridiculous notion that I need somebody to be complete. That one plus one equals two, and I was conditioned in the first grade that the higher number means more than the lower number. Well, damn it, why don't I get into an orgy. Maybe then and only then will an orgy of ten people be better than a couple of two people.

Screw the world. Screw the airlines and the hotel industry who offer two for one rates, making a single person feel like he is somehow getting a better bargain in life if he found someone else to be with.

Screw it. Screw it all!! I'll be James Dean, the consummate loner. And I'll be happy. Do you hear me? HAPPY!!! Do you hear me? Happy? Do you hear me? Do you hear me? Do you hear me?

(Music swells. We see GEORGE talking, but the music is drowning him out. GEORGE appears to be screaming. GEORGE drops to his knees.)

Please like me. Please like me. I'll be your friend. You can call me day or night. Please like me. You can have sex with me. Do you want to have sex with me? If you don't want to use a condom that's OK, too. Please like me. Please like me. I know I have it in me to be a strong person. To be truly independent. Maybe someday I'll find a man. *(Enters audience)* I'll enter a crowded place and find some guy, dance real slow, and kiss him smack on the lips. It will happen just like that. I can see it happening in my head. Please like me. Please like me. I'll do anything you want. Anything.

XI. GO-GO GREG

Rocket is an incredible thrust forward. Sometimes a rocket can go so fast that it matches the speed of sound, creating a sonic boom heard for miles around. However, sound can be deceiving. Sound can be so clear and fine that it be heard. But it is still there, penetrating you.

Go-going takes a lot out of you. You try to relax, hanging out at a cafe somewhere, walking down Santa Monica, looking into shops that closed hours ago. I usually meditate or pray. It's a good way for me to calm down. I tell God, "Thanks." Just for whatever. I ask Him to take care of all the people at the bar. Every once in a while, He listens.

(Spot fades on GO-GO GREG. Blackout.)

SELENA ON THE WALL

On his last night, Doug James gave out free drinks to the androgynous club kids with pink hair, the gay guys in cholo drag, the wanna-be actors and dancers who'd heard Queen Latifah went there, the go-go boys, the women who kissed other women, the men who liked to see women kiss, the Asian tourists who read in travel guides that a club in Hollywood attracted an "eclectic" crowd. The club's name was Circus.

Word had gotten round the club that Doug was leaving. He was "going corporate." And all his friends were impressed. Doug told them he bought a suit, trimmed his goatee, and let a man ask him questions at the interview. He didn't tell them he kept the receipt to return the suit in case he didn't get an offer.

"Well, uh, I gotta get trained," Doug said. "Not everyone stays. They fly you to Houston...and, um, if you get cut, they fly you back. Not everybody makes it."

"If you don't make it, will you come back?" someone asked.

He almost said maybe, but he decided to say "No." Leaving had become his main goal; it even eclipsed his obsession with a dead girl. Doug had been there for over five years. Three months ago, he handed a Jack Daniels straight up to a guy named Ric, short for Ricardo, and knew something had to change. "You could fly too," Ric said. And Doug believed him.

―――

He had packed most of his things, and his Silverlake apartment was almost bare. He gave away most of his stuff to his friends. The only things left were his Selena collection, some family photos, and his college degree framed in oak. He would put his Selena collection in storage until it was time to put her back up again. He placed the family photos in a box and would give it to his mother. Most of the pictures he had were of his parents. One picture he would take with him is of his mother, wearing a kimono, and his father, wearing his military uniform. His mother taught him to speak Japanese. This ability helped him in the interview; his employers were opening an office in Tokyo. It was odd hearing Japanese coming from Doug's mouth. He was always asked the question, What are you?, because he had the look of someone in-between. "Hapa," he said. "It's Hawaiian for when you're Asian and mixed with something else."

But mostly, he was mistaken for Latino. Which was fine with him. He loved Latino music; there was a beat and rhyme to it like no other. He memorized songs by the Barrio Boys. When the Barrio Boys sang a song with a Tejano girl named Selena, he wanted more of her. He loved her when she was alive, but he adored her when she died, shot by the president of her fan club.

Doug erected a shrine to Selena, pictures of the dead girl—along with an auto-graphed picture of Jennifer Lopez, the actress who played her in the movie—were taped to his wall. A Selena doll in a pink body suit with flared fabric around the calves and the forearms was by his bed. A biography on Selena sat on a miniature wooden easel in the corner. A poster of *Selena: The Movie* dominated one wall. The dead girl stared at Doug from all angles.

Doug had to work really hard to go to the premiere of *Selena*. He was especially kind to a studio executive who went to the club, asked him if there was any way he could get tickets to the premiere.

"Hi, Bob...um...what's up?" Doug said, sliding him a free gin and tonic.

"My tolerance level." Bob laughed.

Doug was confused. "Huh?" was all he could think of to say.

"Nothing. What's up with you?"

"I was wondering if you knew anybody who could get me to see the movie about *Selena*. The premiere, that is." Doug knew if Bob came through, he'd have to serve him free drinks forever, but it would be worth it. "If it's no trouble." Doug knew that Bob was still trying to pass for 37. "I'd really, um, appreciate it." Doug knew he was giving Bob permission to hit on him, or at least try to, and he knew Bob knew this.

"Consider yourself in." Bob smiled, reaching over to touch Doug's hand.

———

Doug waited for the shuttle bus to take him to the airport to take him to Houston to possibly spend his life in the air. He waited on the curb with his duffel bag that said Nike. He'd always loved Nike. Even when he played baseball, he wore Nike shoes; his team-mates wore Adidas. He was good enough to play college baseball; so good, in fact, the college overlooked Doug's low SAT scores and embarrassing high school grades to award him an athletic scholarship. He wasn't, however, good enough to make pro.

The best part of playing ball was going places, taking an overnight trip to play a game somewhere. They'd go to San Diego or Fresno. Once they even went as far as Reno, Nevada. They took the bus and he was thrilled to see places he'd never gone before. Growing up, he thought he would die in his old neighborhood in Gardena, California.

After he graduated, he needed a job, and asked around at Circus, a club he went to when he didn't have class the next day. He loved the club, the blood-red walls and the lights that looked like moving rainbows. Huge wooden boards carved and painted like clowns welcomed customers at the front door and girls with glow in the dark necklaces walked around with trays of overpriced candy. And the music, the music! Techno, pop, rock, hip-hop, Brazilian rhythms with a disco flair boomed—boomed!—from giant speakers, making Doug think he was dancing inside of a jukebox. Heaven, Doug thought. Heaven.

He started as a bar back, somebody to clean up, fetch booze, and the like, eventually becoming a bartender. He thought he would stay at Circus for only a short time, until something better came along. Usually Something Better meant he had to take some sort of proficiency exam. Even a waiting job at California Pizza Kitchen required a test.

He wasn't good at tests. He got dizzy. In one final exam, he almost passed out on a multiple choice quiz. All of the choices began to look the same, and he haphazardly circled any one of them. He failed. While many of his classmates took three or four classes a semester, he took one and it took all of his concentration to finish.

Something Doug knew—and it hurt him to no end to know this—was that he was not smart. He didn't like to speak, because if he spoke, people would know he wasn't smart. He spoke English well; it was the finesse of the language he didn't get. The way a word could serve as a double entendre, an ironic phrase that made everyone else, except him, smile. There was an "in" joke somewhere and he'd miss it. He was not clever or witty, qualities so many of the other gay men around him treasured. He didn't understand sarcasm. When a mean ole queen said that Doug was the most intelligent person he knew, Doug took it as a genuine compliment and said "Thank you."

He tried to cultivate himself by renting movies, the kind you had to read. After twenty minutes of *Ma Vie en Rose*, he got a headache. The subtitles were going faster than he could read them. He looked through the literature section of a bookstore, but found himself gravitating to the magazines. He tried to hide a part of himself, the part that made him finish a four-year college in eight, the part that made him withdraw deep inside himself when someone was saying something he didn't understand, the part that made him feel that all he could ever be was a bartender and that all his traveling happened in college, with Reno, Nevada its peak.

When the other bartenders talked of things they planned to do with their lives, like the screenplay that was going to put them over the top, or the recurring role on the TV series that was going to put them over the top, Doug cleaned glasses. He didn't know what he was going to do.

What he wanted to do, what made him the happiest, he couldn't get paid for: looking through the Spanish language magazines to find new photos of Selena he could paste to his wall. He couldn't read the magazines, but the pictures were what he wanted. He learned enough about Selena. Anything written about her would be stuff he'd heard before. He knew she was a girl caught in-between. She was a Mexican–American girl from Texas who loved to sing. Despite the fact that she grew up with Spanish in her home, she was always self-conscious about her ability to speak it. Because anyone who came from a Spanish-speaking country knew when a person didn't. Doug knew all about the fear of speaking.

Selena, however, knew what she'd wanted to do with her life, and God love her for trying.

———

Doug had his boarding pass in one hand, and *People* magazine's choice of the world's 50 Most Beautiful People in the other. He watched people coming in and out of Burbank Airport, looking like they had someplace important to be. The act of getting somewhere was an act Doug wanted to learn. He thought of Ric, short for Ricardo.

When the new guy came into the club, Doug spotted him immediately. He had a look about him, something carefree, like he wasn't going to stay too long. Doug liked this guy because he was new, adding a different energy to the club. Doug saw the same old faces, heard the same old music, served the same old drinks. He was tired of the scene. Doug knew once two o'clock rolled around, the music stopped, the neon lights came on, and Circus would be revealed for what it was: a room, just a room. What depressed him was that he knew he would see this room many more times. There was a time when Doug was one of the youngest bartenders there, but now he was one of the oldest. There were some other bartenders who were older, but they liked bartending and planned to do it for the rest of their lives. Those men could do whatever they wanted but they chose to fix drinks. Doug was stuck with it.

Doug watched this new guy dance by himself, slow and out of synch with the music. If it were someone else, he would have looked dumb, ill-equipped to be on a dance floor. This guy, however, looked like he knew what he was doing, and when the stranger looked up and caught Doug staring, Doug cursed himself. The last thing he wanted this slow-and-out-of-synch-music-man to do was think he was interested. It made him vulnerable; he didn't like feeling vulnerable. But the dude smiled—smiled!

Doug was relieved. He was interested, too. It restored the balance of power.

The stranger approached the bar. "Jack Daniel's straight up."

Doug placed the drink on the counter and said, "It's on the house." What Doug was really saying was, You wanna get together later?

"I insist on paying," Ric said, and placed a five dollar bill on the counter. Doug was stunned. Never in his five years of bartending had anyone turned down a free drink. Doug knew Ric was saying, If I take this free drink, I'd have to owe you something— and I don't owe nothing to nobody. "My name is Ricardo, but friends call me Ric." They talked about music, then Ric said, "Wanna do something?" Doug said, "Uh-huh." When Doug's shift was over, they headed into the parking lot.

"So what do you do?" Doug asked.

"I work in the flight industry," Ric said. And for a second, they were quiet. Doug knew not to ask too many questions, because at this hour, in this light—a mixture of moonlight and lamppost—Ric looked perfect: his neatly combed hair, damaged by the heat and smoke of the club, fell into a charming swirl above his forehead and a green tattoo of a Catholic goddess on his left arm seemed to be smiling. Doug didn't want to speak too much, because many a date had been ruined when too much was revealed: a tidbit from childhood or a bad day in manhood made a perfect person less so. Perfect men don't have childhoods: They were born finished products. Perfect men don't have bad days: Their days are endless high school summers.

Ric must have known this too, because he didn't push conversation. Instead he said, "Wanna come to my hotel? They have a cafe in the lobby that's open pretty late." Ric gave Doug directions to get there. Instead of the cafe, they went straight to Ric's room and kissed. Doug tasted the Jack Daniel's that was fully paid for.

When Doug woke, he knew what mornings did to people, the sun took away shadows and added bad breath. He usually left before morning, but this time he wanted to stay. He wanted to know more about the flight industry and asked what Ric did exactly.

"I'm a flight attendant." A conversation ensued about where Ric had been. He mostly did lines to Spanish-speaking countries. He said he got paid more because he spoke more than one language. He was based in Montreal, but when he wasn't flying, he lived in India. Food and rent were cheaper in third world countries.

"How do you become one? A flight attendant, that is?"

"Well," Ric said, "it's more difficult than people think. You gotta know engines and other parts for at least a dozen planes, go through crash simulation, learn how to save a life. It's actually kinda intense. I started with 39 people in my class, and only 23 graduated."

"So they send you to school?" Doug asked. "Yeah, just like school with lots of tests." Tests. Doug cringed. "You thinking of a career change?" "Maybe," Doug said, but he meant a definite Yes.

"Try it. You could fly, too," Ric said.

Doug didn't know if Ric was being serious, because other people encouraged him to do things knowing full well he couldn't. Doug decided to believe *You could fly, too* because Ric didn't know Doug that well, didn't know his limitations, didn't know how dumb he was. For a moment, Doug loved Ric unconditionally, because, for a moment, he felt like he could do what he'd wanted, and possibly be good at it.

Ric got dressed, and looked over at Doug. Doug knew that look; it was time to leave. Doug didn't want to, but he got dressed anyway. He wrote down his number on the hotel stationery and gave it to him. "Will you call me?" Ric said, "I'll do that." And as soon as he said it, Doug knew that he wouldn't. Something else about perfect men: they don't need anybody.

Doug picked up a newspaper on his way home. He combed through the want ads. Nothing. He bought the paper for three days straight. Still nothing. He called four different airlines and got applications to them all. He mailed them in, but no response. In the following months, he called more airlines, and most of them said they weren't looking. He got an interview with a local airline, only flew in California. He'd never been to an interview like this before, and showed up wearing what he'd wear to Circus: jeans and a comfortable shirt. He saw the guys in suits waiting to be interviewed, and knew he fucked up. He turned around and didn't go back.

In his apartment, he wondered if this was a sign. He wasn't a religious person or anything, but felt there were other things out there at work. Maybe whoever was out there was telling him to stay a bartender. It wasn't a bad job, he made decent money. He grew comfortable there. Maybe he belonged in a club. Not too much depth is required. Everything was taken at face value. No one could see how stupid he was. People mistook his fear of interacting with people as aloofness. In a club, being aloof is an accepted, if not admired, quality.

Doug sat on his futon while Selena looked down at him, crumpled want ads on the floor. What a waste, Doug thought. She died young, a waste. Under the soft brown eyes of the Tejano singing star, he thought about his own life. He turned away because the thought of his life made him sad. Everywhere he turned, he saw Selena's image. He felt stupid, stupid for putting pictures of a dead girl on his wall. He wondered if stupid people did this. Maybe he could start a club for stupid people obsessed with dead stars. He could call it The Stupid People Club. He cried, not little tears, not tasteful pin drop tears, but big ones, the size of peas, and he thought how unfair it was that some people got more brains than others. Or led to believe that they have some great talent like playing baseball, but discovering they weren't that talented after all.

Everyone knows when someone is shot down young, laid to rest, buried away, there is something to grieve about, but when you're shot down and still living—now that's a bigger waste. He thought it ironic—he wondered if ironic was the right word—that a girl who had so much to live for died, and a guy with a menial existence stayed living.

He decided to call more airlines, and one told him that they were having an open call, he could come down to the office and interview on the spot, and if they liked him, they'd train him. This time he wore a suit.

———

When the plane landed in Houston, he stuffed the leftover bag of peanuts into his pocket. He waited while everyone got off before he headed into the aisle. He stepped into the airport, and he wondered how the airport in Houston was much bigger than the one in Burbank. He knew that he could be sent back. All he'd have to do was fail one test, and he'd be gone. But Houston—for now, he was in Houston.

LISA ASAGI

PHYSICS

Behind a small eye of a small world, there is a place for things that have disappeared. A buildingless room visited by those who cannot stop searching for the right day, misplaced keys, drops of music, tails of footage. Who look across desks and wait to unpry. In the science of pursuit strangeness happens.

I am walking across a freezing wet lawn. Thousands of miles from home. Greenwich. Tightropes are suspended in a grid above a park. Light bulbs evenly placed are left alive from mistake or tradition. It is so late and I am here as if to move across this one illuminated line would lead instinctively to an ending. As if zero were an ellipse. This is how my mind finds ways to keep moving. It picks up a thread and follows it. As if meaning could become a frame of reference, for me who could never take a decent photograph. In this place celebrated for partitions and beginnings, a small memory of a dream from years ago. It was a dream green with dripping walls of dilapidated factories. I am running through rooms filled with machines, miles of cloth hanging from wires finished drying so long ago they are falling apart. I climb through windows and out into the street. Everywhere, people are waiting in little lots of invisible houses cordoned off by string. Some are eating, others are crying. Street signs, even your building is missing in this dream. I search frantically for your car as light begins to fade, I run until land comes to an end.

Everyday come in with a ring of keys, through a glass door and up the stairwell, into a silence complete as a box fallen in middle of a street. Random and graceful. Slow tossed. In the midst of luminescent night traffic, beautiful streams of red and yellow uncloud an underwater scene of blue. Open the passage between mouth and nose, inhale the velocity of rendered inertia. Invisible movements take place over a tiny clear scarlet sea. The blood of everything nourishes, takes away, will always visit and then go. Leave the body, then the room, returning emotional exhaust over this planet of cities. I am falling again into the night in which you asked me to follow you home. Across the clustering of a city gathered by water. Trees slept and I followed you through hallways that slowly reappeared.

The sound of pennies tossed upon a bed is rain but sun. One morning. How even weather finds meaning in irony and the motion of spirals.

Light pools and seeps beneath waterfalls of curtain. I had been unable to sleep since coming to this place. Your hand a small warm shark dreaming in the reef of my heart. How bodies can whisper. Ribs like gills. Breathing. I could almost hear your voice. Barefoot, slow moving across carpet. How you must have sounded when you were 8.

This is the way the sun cut in while we were still dancing.

In the film of this year, someone is leaning out of a window and wonders how much more the island will change while she is gone. An increase in pressure, electricity of engines, combine to create loss of consciousness in the passenger. It happens whenever departing the island. A density that gathers and drops. An anchor that keeps falling.

Every morning of this week, I have woken later than I should. And each morning I find a stray eyelash on my cheek. When I was very young I would wish for things. A dog, a microscope, my own room. Meteors of concentrated daydream I would consecrate and let fly up into a ceiling so scraped I believed all of them found a way through. When was I old enough to find you, I never wished. I watched. I listened. Searching. Not a boat. A lighthouse. For spaces between. For meanings of glances. Possibilities of life outside of equations.

Science is searching for evidence of existence.

Upon the summit of a remote island, a nine foot mirror has been placed within the mind of a telescope. It is held and adjusted by wires, hydraulics. Operated by distance in order to keep it safe from heat. Emanations of body temperature are waves disturbing the accuracy of reflection. Even the stars in the sky are echoes.

Flying now low over ridges and curves. Muscle and bone under sheets of sand, asleep, it is a quietness almost about to wake and it makes me remember suddenly how far I am from home.

Beneath the desert of southeast New Mexico exists remnants of a reef. Even an ocean can leave an elaborate past. Passages and tunnels. Memories geologists could not help but chart in words like galleries, labyrinths, pearl-filled lakes, unwinds deeply underground. There air is so full of stillness it reaches. Cascades of minerals fall incredible and slow from the stone sky. Walls silently sweat and weep. As if slowness could be unabsorbed.

In a small room, move your hand under my skin. To where you want to be. In the first hour of another life.

DAN BACALZO

I'M SORRY, BUT I DON'T SPEAK THE LANGUAGE

"I like my Asians to look like Asians,"
a lover once told me.

"You have a very feminine face,"
said another.

What is it they expect from me?
What fantasy do I fulfill?
Feminine?
Boyish?
Oriental?

Moving with grace and beauty.

My body
is not the type you normally find in mainstream gay magazine ads.

You know the ones I mean.
Where the men are
muscular, manly—white.

A friend of mine told me
that there was a Japanese guy
at his gym that has a body

"just like a Caucasian."

If I worked really hard,
if I went to the gym every day,
maybe I could have a body like that.

In a crowded hallway I kissed him.
The lights were dim, but I could see him well enough.
And when the eyes failed, the sense of touch allowed me to
navigate every curve and indentation of his chiseled Caucasian body.

I ran my fingers through his short blond hair,
gently caressed his perfect cheekbones,

stroked his muscular chest, his washboard stomach.

Parting my unbuttoned shirt,
his hands wandered over my own slim Asian body.

Did he like what he felt?
Or did I not measure up?
Did he have to lower his standards for me?

My lips traced their way down
from his hardened nipple to
his even harder cock.

I wish my body looked like his.
I couldn't help but think it.
I wish my body looked like his.
Why can't my body look like his?
If my body looked like his,
would that be perfection, then?
If my body looked like his,
would I be more desirable?
If my body looked like his,
would I be happy?

I put my body on display,
dancing on the bar wearing nothing
but a green thong and my Doc Marten boots.

It felt good to have men look at me.
To have my body completely objectified.
But I wonder what they were thinking.
Was my body too thin?
Was my chest too narrow?
Were they looking for perfection?
Did they even know what perfection was?

Did I?

REGIE CABICO

LOVE LETTER FROM ANDREW CUNANAN

Dear Regie,

I am geared to calamity, fragile as baby teeth. Shards every hour of a failure to cope with every day. So much wine, I feel like I'm flying to Europe and I hate airplanes.

★

I've wanted to speak to you ever since I saw you in "How the Sky Fell" at the Poets' Theater. You were so valley. Your performance so wicked, I wanted to kill you. You took an interest in me because I told you I wanted to be an actor. You never cared about my Barney's charge card or the plantations of pineapples my family owns. I got your address from the Asian American Writers' Workshop.

★

I fell in love with you at Mandarin Grill. We sang karaoke, "California Dreaming," remember?

★

On the drive from New Jersey to Miami, bugs shuck their skeletal husks and I imagine both of us near-sighted, swash-bucklers, dangling from a chandelier of hot sex. I have flashed my dimples like an envious boy. Tantrum habits I perfected like a castaway.

★

Let me take a cobalt pencil, make darker your eyelids as I exhale my biography into your left ear. Pull your hair so my fingers breathe through the strands of each tussle, our legs be braided and twined like the shaft of a single goblet. Your shaven blue jaws. Be my rubber ball. My resigned mouse. Let my arms become ropes that I can tie 'round your ribs, kiss every angle of your body. I'm a white fox winding through forested trails of banded muscle and whorls of musk.

★

I have composed impossible lyrics for our pelvis.

Fetal and palming I fuck you.

★

I have told more lies than a psychic hotline. $23 a minute lies. Embellished truths that pay for my hotel, saline solution and gasoline.

★

All I know are the details of condom wrappers and the jolly music of handcuffs.

★

Versace was sucking bacon when he saw me. He tried to smoke his way out of a cordial conversation but I followed him like Magellan. He stretched and his head split, bullets the size of M&Ms tumbled toward him, dried icing thrown at a bride's face. His lids burst. The marble stairs hemorrhaged, sliced open to a purple sky, the salt a mile away. I became witness to his headline. I made that headline. He popped inside his stupid Bermuda shirt.

My auto is slippery with the fluids of men.

I was foot work and firework when I pulled the trigger.

MY PERFECT SILENCE
FOR KAREN CARPENTER

I was born into a Disney menagerie with not a single goal.

It is 1967. Anyone with an amp could have an ambitious hallucination.

When I wake from the cell of my dressing room, I feel the bird's flight in my body. The wing pang, lifting heave, locating itself above my slumped shoulders and part of me shoveling vines with my single voice.

It's just a voice, brunette with bangs, floating, dirigible ready to explode, but can't. So I snatch a pair of drumsticks and love their suspicious feel in my hands. Secretly, I want to smash glass. I hate the color of an obedient deed, so why do I sing its octave?

Notes that open in compassion, ribcage propped apart. My heart lodged too close to my ribs. I'm a tree-limb steady in a highball generation of acid and Joplin slang.

From the surface of a mirror, my body emits hues of yellowish orange. I hear the clucking of distasteful tongues disturb my perfect silence: The motion of twirled knitting sticks and the way yarn licks the air as it snarls toward me. The crocheted mass, an exquisite dangle from my lap. That's the music that's mine. I don't want sex, just synchronicity.

There is a stadium grace when I sing. Sand and the streets breathe the same cacophony of sing-song jangle and station wagons.

I'm able to fill a cavity
with a 4/4 drum riff wedded
with the throat call
of longing.

The camera adds 30 lbs but pounds of what?

30 lbs of silverware
30 lbs of fan mail
30 lbs of stroganoff

My heart beats so fast I enter a slumber. I hear
the winged timpani embedded in my chest.
I enter a sleep.. .. .. A black note floods
the swollen roof of my mouth,
an empty bee-hive home,
a Los Angeles suburb...

If only the skeleton of a girl like the white key of a weathering piano could sing. An ambulance sire...that bird's contralto.

My mother picks me up. Karen I'm sorry...
the clock of attachment stops

TAKE OUT: QUEER WRITING FROM ASIAN PACIFIC AMERICA

GAYE CHAN

QUEER GIRL

INTERLUDE FOR "TABLE MANNERS I & II"

"here, you look for it."

"what is it? tell me what I'm looking for. you are going so fucking fast."

"this whole place is a maze sometimes. everything moving. sometimes you seem like a complete stranger."

"it was her accent that first drew me to her."

"desire has strange origins. did you think it would lead you somewhere?"

"like i was following the trail of western expansion. spreading. smooth. everything, all of this is backwards then forward."

"some would say upward. mobility...eye in the sky. all this stuff in empty parking lots. last night i dreamed everything was humming. i was driving and everything stood there and hummed."

"here, turn right at the next corner."

"every time i breathe i feel you traveling up an artery in my neck. like this car moving through this tunnel. i want to turn off the lights. sometimes i don't want to see where we are going."

QUEER BOY

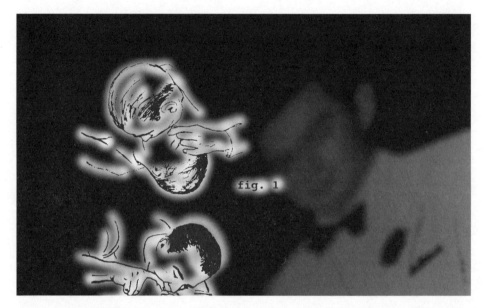

"to you looking is noise, as if blindness could be silence. i wish you could hear the way she says my name."

"everything passing for greek. passing for english and stars. your hair, the color of explorers maps, of horses."

"slow down. we could lose our brakes coming down this fast."

"the sky is so red tonight. i thought it was going to be blue. i thought that moment you stopped moving that i had murdered you. the room stilled and collapsed. all the nerves in my body turned to hair."

"you have no idea do you? how it means. all of this and what it means. you drive and i climb the walls, have no idea what it is. this world is sinking. and still you look at the highway and something else comes for you. like we were cliffs."

"like you were something somebody else could save."

(Lisa Asagi and Gaye Chan)

ALEXANDER CHEE

BURN

In Korea during the summer of the Olympics, the last time Jack Yu saw his grandfather, some of the student activists had set themselves on fire in the streets to protest the continued conflict of the Koreas. Ancestral shrines in the North hadn't been visited since the war began, families remained separated, and the students believed that on the other side of the wall, there were students protesting as well, ready to meet them. Who knows who they thought was in heaven for them. That these burned students would join their ancestors for not having had the chance to visit their shrine once in their lifetimes struck Jack at once as both sad and wonderful. An easy solution, he recalls thinking. Burn yourself instead of the incense.

The students would swarm up from the subways and run through the streets, shouting, and vanish again into the subways. His grandfather would roll up the windows of his black Benz when the tear gas came in on the wind, as they passed through Seoul's crowded tiny streets. Very sneaky, his grandfather would say, sometimes, of the students. And then continue, on another of the endless tourist errands he felt compelled to take Jack on: riding to the top of the Needle Tower. Walking the Secret Gardens. Perusals of national treasures, carefully numbered at the National Museum. A caricature drawn on Picasso Street by an art student. Jack had visited deliberately to avoid the Olympic games, and left before they began. The games would have been unendurable.

Sneaky, Jack remembers thinking: Yes. His grandfather often spoke of how he considered cleverness a uniquely Korean survival trait. This was true, Jack decided then, if you were a surviving Korean. If you were dead, were you not Korean anymore? Were you now just dead, and foolish?

———

Jack thinks about these burning students as he listens to the nine other men in the basement room of the West Village School take turns describing their problems. Group Therapy, Monday nights, early summer, lower Manhattan. Fluorescent light strips color from the cookies and coffee and Jack blinks occasionally from the glare. Welcome to New York, the World's Friendliest City, reads a postcard someone has tacked up on the bulletin board of the room they are in, and Jack reads it again and again from where he is sitting. All of these men are clients of the same therapist and all are gay, all are thirty or so, still attractive, still groomed. All talk through the session about intimacy problems they have with their partners, who are presumably consulting other therapists, attending other group therapies. Jack has yet to share very much. He has spent most of this night trying to figure out why he doesn't talk. Why he feels like he is burning. "I find myself asking why he's thinking about his ex-boyfriends like this," says Paul, a thirty-something Irishman, who shares mostly thoughts about how strange he thinks American gays are, with his boyfriend as the prime example. He pats at his thinning red hair as if to check that it's still there.

Paul's problem tonight is that his lover talks a great deal about the men before Paul, always disparagingly, which has Paul worried about what he feels is his future in this man's esteem. "If he can't remember them nicely, then what was it all worth? I find myself wondering, if he thinks the way I make love is annoying, like it was for him with Derek. Or if he hates the sight of my backside, like he hated John's. I feel caught in questions. Don't much care for it, but I care for him."

"Ask him," Jack says then. Surprised by the sound of his own voice, he continues. "Co-dependency. The way to end it is to ask. I say, be responsible only for what you are told." Paul stares at him. "Otherwise assume that he loves the sight of your backside and the way you make love." And the gathered men laugh. Paul smiles. He's a good sport. He sits down again. He'll not ask anything more about what Jack means. Paul's worries aren't without foundation, Jack is aware: his lover probably can't tell him what's wrong. Jack's a veteran of these sessions. He has come long enough to know how the problems of one relationship can fossilize and turn up later in the next relationship: irrelevant, frozen troubles that remind one of past eras and extinct lives.

Jack stands to share. "I have this problem with pornography." A few heads tonight nod. "I read a lot of it." More heads nod. "And, I find myself turned on especially by pictures of black men having sex with white men. This is disturbing to me." He surprises himself as he says this. He thinks of his lover Ted. Ted had recently decided he wanted to go on a date with someone else, after a year of their being together. Someone he had had sex with before, years ago, who, is black. Ted is white. Everyone besides Jack in this room is white.

"What the heck does it mean to you," Paul asks.

"I guess it's something I can't be," Jack says. "Both of them."

"Is it a power thing, like, you like seeing big black guys rape white guys?" asks another man, Philip.

Jack pauses. His eye fills. He sees heads rolled back, mouths opened wide. Smooth white buttocks parted by gleaming black skin, shined by lube and latex and spit. And the sudden image comes to him of the room of men overwhelmed by sex. "I like," he says, wishing the image away, "that they like it. In the pictures." Some laughter. Coffee tickles a cup and fills it. "And, uh, it's not...rape. Can't rape the willing."

"You're partner is white," says a Fred, likewise a veteran of these sessions.

He is, Jack tells himself. "He is."

"You're a sadist, probably, probably conflicted about it. You want to hurt him, you want him to like it." Fred chuckles when he finishes saying this.

"It's not rape I am looking at," Jack says.

An open relationship, Ted had said to Jack, a few weeks ago. I want to see other people. And Jack had thought about it. I want to see other people too, he thought then. With you. He wanted Ted. He didn't want anyone else. And if Ted wanted other people, Jack wanted that. Wanted to see, Ted against someone else's tongue or dick. The thought that somewhere in the city right now, he might be with the man he'd mentioned makes Jack stick his hands in his pockets to cover an erection.

"The big black dick is supposed to be a myth," someone says from the side.

"So is the little Asian one," Jack offers, holding his to hide it as it expands across the front of his pants.

———

Jack remembers seeing a picture of his father flying through the air, feet first, toward his tae kwon do students. They were each holding a board to either side. His father's feet tore the boards in half. The students grimaced from the force of his impact. Not the same as jumping up and down on the same two feet, this, this was a flying kick. At the time Jack saw the picture, he asked his sister who it was in the picture, he couldn't see his father's face. It's Dad, she says. Can't you tell? Look at those legs. Those are your legs.

Jack has his father's body: short torso, short legs, but tall, somehow. Calves and thighs built to carry much more than the little body atop them. Legs made to stomp enemies, to break doors. My father's body, he tells himself now, after the meeting, as he rubs his stomach, naked in front of the mirror. He has just gotten out of the shower. Jack has been using this body very differently. His father has been dead for several years now and comparisons still make him nervous.

For days now, Jack has had the sensation of burning. Not the pain of burning, but the feeling of burning, the sense that molecules are running and passing, carrying their charges to and fro, matter changing from one form to another, fed by a wind, made from a lightning's tiniest heirs. The air around him shakes in the heat of the invisible form inside him.

"Hi," Ted says, and comes into the room, where he drops on the bed.

"Didn't hear you come in," Jack says. He pulls on a robe.

"Hi."

"How was your night?" He sits down beside Ted. On their white bed, Jack looks down to the shut face of his tired lover.

"Good," Ted says.

"How's your open relationship?"

Ted eyes him briefly and then closes them again. "Good, I think. What's wrong?"

"How is your other boyfriend?"

Ted sighs. "What's wrong? What?"

"Look at you coming home. Like this. What am I supposed to do with you?" Jack gets up and puts on his pajama bottoms, slips his feet into flip-flops. My father's feet, he thinks, looking at them, and flexes the toes. "Why didn't you sleep over there?"

"I wasn't 'there.' That's why. I guess your open relationship isn't going so well."

Jack walks through the apartment, away from the bed, to the dark kitchen which lights when he pulls the fridge open. He pours himself a glass of orange juice. Fine, he thinks. "No," he says. "It's going just fine." He sits in the kitchen to finish his juice, angry until just before he goes to sleep in the living room. "Do you want me to sleep out here?" Jack asks, and even as he says it, he hates having said it. Do you want. Do you want. Like a waiter or a hotel clerk.

In the morning, Ted is gone before he wakes, off to work, like every other day. Jack drinks the last of the coffee and heads off as well.

———

In the closet by the bathroom, Jack keeps his videos. *Movers Gang Bang. Black on White. Zebra Love.* His new favorite shows a man who is allegedly straight, being raped by 10 black men in a row. In the film, he's supposed to be a livery driver who gets caught in an alley in the wrong part of town. Jack has lied to his group, and as he sits watching the video, watching the man get passed from man to man, his skin slick and smoothed by sweat, the cum miraculously vanishing every time it falls on him, he realizes, he will have to tell them. He lied. When he imagines that the vanishing cum has varnished this man's back to a shine, he erupts, and then lies there afterward, the video spilling on, as another man climbs on and into the livery driver.

It's about punishment, he'll say later that week, to the room. I lied. I lied because you were right, and I wanted to be right first.

What's the advantage to being right first, Paul will say. You're just alone with the truth then. You get there first, and then you have to wait for everyone else.

Paul would know, Jack will tell himself afterward. Paul would know.

———

"I don't think it's working," Ted says to him.

"Regarding the group therapy sessions? Or the open relationship," Jack asks. A few nights later, Jack is cooking a piece of steak for them, following a recipe he has just learned. As Ted sits in their kitchen and sips from a glass of wine, Jack rolls the steak in sal-de-mer and herbs. The steak, salt-crusted, as he first sears it on each side and then slips it into the oven, looks to him, for a moment, covered in cum. He runs water over his hands and then tries to answer Ted. He sets his knuckles along the table's edge and looks at him for a long moment. The darkening kitchen of their Soho apartment seems larger somehow. The hum of the air conditioner makes the summer city quiet.

"I think it's helping," he says. "It's hard to see the results. A lot of people get unhappy first, before they get happy. It's like an emotional detox—you have feelings you haven't had all the years since the thing that's bothering you happened. And it's not really for you to evaluate, is it?"

"It was a joke." Ted smiles. Ted wouldn't tell Jack if he had sex with this other man. And he refused in a way that makes Jack think he got this one from his therapist. "I am not going to see him again," Ted added at the time. Jack doesn't feel relieved.

The problem is compounded by the way Jack is attracted to this man, who is also named Ted, but goes by Theodore. They had met separately from Ted and Theodore, Jack and Theodore had. At a party. Theodore is a goofball of a man, lean and energetic, he favors riding his bicycle, keeps his hair shaved close and treats the men he likes like straight men treat women, as pieces of ass. He flirted at the party with Jack, and Jack thinks of it sometimes. Jack thinks of it and remembers being out with Ted on Gay Pride, and running into Theodore on the piers at the end of the parade. Jack was facing Theodore, who, seeing them together, was realizing, Jack could see, what was going on. Ted was facing other friends. Ted was wearing jean shorts cut very high, standing with his legs apart, and Theodore, his eyes on Jack, reached out and sent a long finger inside the shorts, hooking up in between Ted's cheeks, poking firmly between them, and then snaking out again. He smiled at Jack then, raised the finger to his lips, and licked it. Jack was so turned on that when Ted turned to look to see who it was had done this, he let Ted think it was him. Theodore shook hands with Jack then. "Lovely to see you both," he'd said. And raised Jack's hand to his mouth. Jack and Ted had both sunburned that afternoon. "We forget we're not black," Ted had joked, and Jack had thought, Not likely. The burn felt like a blush that wouldn't go away.

They eat the dinner Jack prepared quickly. In bed, Jack fucks Ted, and at one point, Ted on his hands and knees in front of him, head down, his long pale back like a step in front of him, Jack imagines that Ted is Paul. As he does this, he pulls out, and comes across Ted's back. Ted comes into the sheet below him. Jack pushes Ted forward, their heads lie close together, their breath mixing. Jack loves these moments with Ted. Loves the air that has just been inside Ted.

"Yes," Ted says, agreeing with something Jack hasn't said, or said so long ago, it doesn't bear remembering.

———

After the longest of the group sessions yet, Jack goes uptown to a stripper bar called Cleo's in Hell's Kitchen. He checks his hair in the mirrors of the bar and heads downstairs to where the shows take place, a low basement room fitted out with mirrors and parquet and round cocktail tables at the edge of the stage area. He's there because he wants to see a naked black man, live. He isn't there long before Theodore arrives, smiling, and goes right to the table where Jack is sitting alone. "Join you?" he asks.

Jack crosses his legs, erect again. "Sure," he says, and waves his free hand over the chair beside him.

"You're a trip," he says, as he sits down.

Jack smiles at this and the beer he ordered when he arrived finally comes. The waiter stands and looks at them both before asking Theodore what he wants. "He's thinking we don't need to pay for it," Jack says when he leaves.

"I like to pay for it. I like strippers," Theodore says. "It's all good. These boys are beautiful, and they are having a good time." Theodore picks up Jack's beer and takes a long swig. "Why are you here?" He sets down the bottle and waits.

"Same," Jack says. "Sometimes I like to have someone just take their clothes off."

"Go to the gym," Theodore says. His own beer arrives and he pays for it and tips his chair back on its rear legs.

"I do."

And then the dancers are coming on, and the crowd fills quickly. Bad, loud music floats through the room like the cigarette smoke, and the dancers pay a lot of attention to Jack and Theodore's table. They are all under twenty-five, from what Jack can see, and all are Latin. Oiled dark hair, smooth tan bodies, fading tattoos, muscles he can count. One in particular comes over to Theodore, hooks his leg on his shoulder and leaves it there. Theodore pulls money from his pocket and first slides a finger (that finger!) under the G-string's bottom and then pushes back, between his buttocks. The dancer squirms and his eyes pop. Theodore draws his finger back, and smooths the skin there behind the balls. With his other hand he brings the money from his pocket up and snaps the G-string back, so it holds the bill there, behind the dancer's balls. He buries his face in the crotch for a moment and then the boy is sliding back, and the crowd is cheering.

"I love straight Latin boys," Theodore says, and then he brings the finger up again, to run it over his top lip. "Lovely."

We used to have group sex, Jack tells himself afterward on the downtown train, headed home. Now we have group therapy. He climbs the stairs to his apartment. Leaves the smoke-stinking clothes in the hamper. Ted is in bed. I want something of my own, he tells himself, as he climbs in bed beside Ted and the heat of the bed brings a faint glow to his face.

"I want to tell you," Theodore had said, as Jack was leaving. "I am sorry I wasn't more respectful. Of your relationship." This memory keeps Jack company until he falls asleep, much later, wrapped around Ted.

———

"We used to pick up guys together," a newcomer is saying of his lover. His name is Terry. He is replacing Paul, who has graduated, at their therapist's urging. Fred and Jack had decided they were jealous. August comes now, some months after Jack's night at Cleo's. He and Ted are good again, but they still go to their group therapies.

Terry keeps pushing his blond hair out of his face. "It was all right. But soon it became the only way we had sex."

Ted calls his therapy group "ruined beauties." Men who used to get everyone, and now get a few less each year. Terry is the first one who makes Jack think of this saying. The basement room tonight is a cool refuge in a heat wave. All day long, on the streets of New York, Jack has been looking at what seems like, daily, a preposterous number of beauties, still-beautiful: smooth-limbed white boys, muscled and long, their faces tan and smooth like it's their second or third sunburn ever. The hair perfectly cut and mussed, the shorts all the right length. The bargain of a tan, Jack always is reminded, as he looks around the room. More beauty now, less beauty later. Jack works in advertising, he has gone freelance, works only on movie campaigns now. Everyone in advertising tans. Just before he left his firm for freelance, his boss had an eye-tuck. He had probably had his 7,000th sunburn, Jack considers. All these people trying to be a little black. Terry concludes his tale.

"I don't want to leave him. But I don't want what we have. And I don't know how to have what I want."

There's applause at this. Jack claps, uncertain. Not a performance, is it, he asks himself. Shouldn't be. But he still claps.

TAKE OUT: QUEER WRITING FROM ASIAN PACIFIC AMERICA

JUSTIN CHIN

FAITH

Lisa gives me a bracelet,
    a Buddhist trinket she got
when her family went to temple,
a custom to see the beginning
                of each year.

A delicate thing,
    beautiful in its symmetry:
Eighteen beads the unruffled colour
of a chihuahua puppy's tanned fur,
two transparent beads on each side,
    seven more tanned beads each,
and in the center, a large white bead
holding a convex corneal
              slip of plastic,
a white eyeball that reveals,
when you hold it up to light,
the Buddha and his slippers.

If my mother ever saw me wearing this,
she would be gravely upset, grieved;
this small trinket troubling
her firm Christian beliefs,
those she inculcated in her sons.

I do not practice Buddhism.
A charm has only as much power
           as one puts into it.
I wear it because it is such a pretty thing.
And the person who gave it to me
cared enough for my protection:
a reason greater than any faith.

Once, in a Chinese restaurant,
I saw a group of schoolkids kick

the shrine sitting beside the fridge:
the pot of joss sticks, the tea cups
tumbled over, and the oranges scattered
across the floor, the fat laughing Buddha
fell face-down, as if doubled over in hysterics.
The perpetrators of this horror were angered
by the shop proprietor's refusal to serve them.
But did they not realize what they had done?
    Were they not afraid?
Was not the proprietor's faith in his god's
powers to take retribution
        greater than the boys' faith
that the god they had kicked was powerless?

I'm told tales where Buddhist shrines,
Hindu temples, voodoo floats, Christian crosses
    were desecrated
and the persons responsible came
to mysterious and disastrous ends.

Can faith equal faith?

    Is there any equivalence,
or are we weighing elephants against toenails?
What exists in our world, that would allow
us to measure such inequivalence,
        to balance the scales of
culture, faith and fear?

Many months ago, I believed
that my room was haunted. I felt a presence
sitting on my bed, and the cat was sleeping
in her sweet purr on the porch.
        I tried to wake
but felt held down by an invisible force,
my head pressed against the pillow,
my voice taken away from me: I could not
even call out to wake myself up.
    All I could do was pray in my mind,
and pray I did. I suddenly awoke

in a dark still room. This is how I know
I still believed in the god of my youth.

        Can faith equal faith?
Do gods of one faith take care
      of the believers of other faiths?
Who will protect my god
when he falters
        and his faith fails?
Do the gods of one faith take care
        of the gods of other faiths?
Can it change the spleen of our lives?
     Of what we've seen and done,
and what has been done to us?

       Look to Job—
family decimated, crushed
      under eight tons of party lights,
lost, scabbed, ill and tempted;
patient, unquestioning and faithful.

     Idiot simple,
it sometimes seems.

Never mind earthquakes, floods,
storms, collapsed buildings,
serial killers, car accidents,
famine, endless war, another car bombing,
pestilence, flesh-eating bacteria,
untold hatred, the unforgivable,
forgetfulness, revisionism.

Here is my blood-stained faith.
On my wrist, in these boxes of pills,
in this blood test, tubes of scarlet proof,
in this inoculation, dead cells
of ancient diseases flow the fur pelt
of the dog and bit and bit right
through to bone and brain; it is

in this string of obituaries, this book
I am yet to read, this newspaper, these words,
this cure, these half-truths that burst into full
truths, these lies that rot into complacency,
the memory of all the dead and all the living
behind and in front of me, this
is my blood-stained faith.

I BUY SEA MONKEYS

The New Teen Titans save the world

from the world, and stays evil
forces in their dark places;

a page tucked in between their noble
tasks: the promise of bringing life

to life. The drawing shows a family.
1950s compact and nuclear:

Crayola flesh-colored parents and children.
The women have eyelashes, ribboned bows, pearls.

The men have bowties; Dad has a pipe.
Sea monkeys. What miracle of science

could fathom this. Monkeys who live
in the briny depths, who learned to

do acrobatic tricks, and set up house.
How I yearned for a box of miracles.

My own laboratory to bring life
to these amazing pets. My parents

were too sensible for such comic book
chicanery. And the local toy store

would not honor the coupons.
I was too young to understand

the concept of a money order.
I was sea monkeyless

for twenty years. Adulthood
confers certain privileges.

Mr. Frankenstein with charge card.
I finally got my kit.

Crystals dissolved in pure water,
the small plastic tank set

to the right pH to bring life,
eggs poured into the primeval

quench, and in the dissolving
swirl of egg and liquid and fuzz,

little swimming things
swim and paddle against the current.

Not like monkeys in the zoo or even
in the trees. Not flesh coloured.

No snazzy Abercrombie & Fitch tie,
nor Benetton sweaters. How

at the Seattle Aquarium, a small child,
at that wondering age I was

when I wanted those aquatic monkeys,
asks his mother, what are the sea horses

eating? They look like sea monkeys,
she says, and his kiddie eyes that scanned

some other comic book too intently
as I did, start to tear up.

Dream Pet = Fish Food.
Magic sputters into another gutter.

We grow up and figure out the truth,
we realize how hard it is

to maintain and take care
of life, even the ones

that deceive you, especially
the ones we cherish:

I get lazy, preoccupied, go on trips,
holidays, blank days, and return,

the tank is deep-sea green,
saturated, oxygen starved,

little tatters shed and floating
like flakes of a million dead things

in the ocean. In the convex magnifying
bubble of the tank (so you can see the life

you brought), all is exoskeletons,
all is dead, all minute souls given up.

All but one little monkey,
swimming with all his might, all

his filaments paddling in the murky green,
shimmering like the last good cell

in a last good body.
He will live another six weeks,

longer than all his family and species,
then he too will shed his skin one last time,

wonder where everyone has gone
and go there too.

BAO-LONG CHU

DURIAN

Look: it is the width of a man's skull,
Melon green or lemon yellow rind that is hard
As bone and covered with thorns
Arranged in clean rows. Like teeth, but sharp.

Hooked. In Vietnamese, it is sâù riêng
Translated, it means separate sorrows.
It is not a secret we eat this fruit:
The dead flesh fragrance clings

To everything. The truth is the scent
Stays on my skin long after the fruit goes,
Soaks into my fingers, pillows, dreams.
I sleep breathing in the fingered remains

Of this fruit. Difficult to find in Houston,
My mother managed to dig one out
Now and then in a Chinatown store.
After dinner, she would bear the secret

Fruit, centered on a tray like a bridal gift.
I, unable to believe the sharpness of thorns,
Floral fetor, wanted to cover the fruit
With my palms and see how deep

The hooked thorns cut. My mother
Heaved, pulled the heavy fruit close,
My father and I watched the quick
Slip of knife into the ripened slit

Beneath curled stem. Straining, she plunged
The blade down until the hard skin gave up
Its secret: thick yellow segments in twos,
Nestled and closed like fists in anger.

Breaking the solid flesh among ourselves,
We relished the custard-softness, tasing jasmine
And almond oil. My mother would feed
My father. She would linger on his lips.

KEN CHU

QUEER-N-ASIAN

NUMBER ONE GAY SON

MINAL HAJRATWALA

FATHER'S SISTERS

Kamu foi, in your London flat with four flights of stairs
you play the wise crone. Your children
married right, clip words like any Brit;
their wives never wear pants. I know your face
will be mine in forty years:
white hairs sprouting from chin,
strong grey brows, soft torso,
elephant skin. Your first grandchild bears
my name. When you watch boxing on the BBC
you punch the air, swear in tongues:
get em, mara sala, behn chod, bloody fool.

———

On a vibrating sofa at Sears, as my parents shop in housewares
and the Spurs are beating the Oilers on the world's biggest TV,
you Kanchan, divorcee with patchwork face, try to pry
my reason for being a spinster at twenty-three.
Kem? Kem? you ask, why, why, Em ni karvanu,
phrase used to educate a small child,
that is not a thing one does, and I say
No, no, and am finally silent. Your mind
reels on, you recall your grandchild
who loves baseball, sweet girl of the swirling hair
for whom each time we meet I pray, Escape.

———

Youngest with the sharpest wit, do you know they use you
to warn me: This is what you shall become, if
if you don't bite your tongue, if you are stubborn and too smart.
Leela, meaning green. And if you parrot
the family's secrets far and wide, falsify

to brighten your own hue,
then we are blood kin indeed,
bitten nails and yellowed teeth,
shiny hair thick as weeds,
and tales of did-me-wrong,
did-me-wrong.

THE IN AND THE OUT

*"From the seven ways of moaning, it can be understood
whether the light blows to the heart are insufficient."*
—Kama Sutra, 2:7:13

The sound of my own moaning brings me back to myself

& to memories of you

surreal

wet buttons   sore nipple hairs   the great sucking sound

Matta's Vertigo de Eros: Inner black
        geometry of trapezoids   spirals
                    endless pools of deep green oil
                        & in the high left quadrant, an altar
                                the vagina dental   the toothed cunt
                                        fleshy & pink as lungs

A moan is an exhalation
musical as Dizzy Gillespie's breath

Lips open, my note is Aaah

I understand why the surrealists feared the cunt

its sharp hairs   honest eternal wet

I fear my own
hunger:

long-toothed rat in the five-star dumpsters

feeding on remnants of pale women in pale silks

Lips closed, I sing Mmmm

What it comes down to:
My mouth full of you
the sympathetic orgas
a hard slap

What you go down to:
An op art illusion
three lines converge on a point
which can be seen as either peak or hollow

In zazen, Roshi says, Breathe:
Prajna paramita draws in our scattered thoughts

During sex I vocalize my breath

like the Tibetan singing bowl

eternal sound
    the hum in our throat
        a solemn rubbing
            moan bringing me back to my...
                insufficient heart?

Is this the answer to our questions?

the in and the out

shift of lungs, shoulders, blood,
    molecules in the navels of our cells

what they've named
metabolism   respiration   cardiopulmonary exchange

fundamental processes hidden in syllables

buried in the skins of trees

We live among the skinlamps of earth
everything we have is stolen

ore   paper   cotton   ink

Dizzy, breathe me vulnerable trumpets
orchids
the cave in the heart
the vulnerable vulva
the radial ulna
the radical ulcer
the optimum hunger

brown bones of trees ground to this

                              sweet white pulp

                                        under your fingers

PHILIP HUANG

BABY

Such a warm night, not a wisp of fog: the rarest of nights. This is not now, this is 1972. All over the city, windows are being opened (or left opened, the way they've been all day) and sounds drift out: voices, music, water running, the tiny clinking of dishes you might mistake for the twinkling of stars overhead. In the Mission District, above a bookstore, a little apartment begins its vigil over Valencia Street. Now a bit of breeze gets caught in its curtains, hiding and fussing, hiding and fussing, like a toddler in its mother's skirt, so it seems a bashful sort of flirtation from the street, and alternately, the gaze of someone falling toward sleep, a little nap you didn't plan for but don't object to either.

On this pleasant night, in this little apartment on Valencia Street, the shower is running and the story has already begun.

———

When he opened the bathroom door, steam rushed all around him and Baby felt like he was stepping off a spaceship into a dreamy, alien atmosphere: a cloud of moist, feeble thoughts through which the dark voice of a candle throbbed and retreated, throbbed and retreated.

On the bed, he lay down and closed his eyes. "It's my birthday, isn't it?" he asked. "Am I twenty? I'm twenty."

"You are," a voice said. "Are you?"

Above him, Baby heard a match being lit, then the sucking in of breath.

A hand offered him a joint and Baby toked deeply.

"I've got a problem," he said. "I've fallen in love."

"Uh-oh," said the voice wearily.

"I was sixteen," Baby said. "I was in Modesto. I didn't know."

"What's the name of this man? Is it Geronimo? Is it Egg Foo-Young?"

Baby giggled and smoke burst from his nostrils. "Look what you made me do. Stop talking about him," he said, and yawned and stretched. "Just thinking about him makes me horny."

"Oh yeah?"

"Oh yes. Ooh yes, yes, yes."

"What's he do to you so special?" A palm ran down Baby's chest. "Bet I could make you forget him completely." A mouth closed over Baby's mouth and Baby felt the bed sink away beneath him, he was wafting downward into warm swaying water, he was far away.

When he opened his eyes, he looked at Samuel for a long minute, suddenly stoned.

"This is the decade it's all going to happen," he said earnestly.

"What's going to happen?" Samuel asked, also earnestly. "Tell me."

"Oh. Just everything."

"Everything," Samuel repeated, and the two of them stared up at the ceiling happily.

And a thought, like a sheet of scrim, waved over them and unfurled on the edge of language.

———

His mind a train, and in that moment of smoke and tonnage and screaming iron, no matter how brief, he might believe he might be lifted up and away, up and away—

Baby fell on top of Samuel, whose back felt hot and cooked.

Still here. Train come and gone.

A pimple at the base of Samuel's neck looked sleepily at him.

"I'm going in the kitchen," Baby declared absently.

Samuel nodded into the pillow.

What a comforting word. Yes, of course, I'm going in the kitchen. A kitchen, a hearth. A home. The rest could be imagined so long as you had a kitchen.

But there really wasn't a kitchen, as in a separate room. There was a living room, a square of wood floor the size of two parking spaces. In one corner, a fridge and a squat stove, like two giant sucked caramels. Baby padded quickly across the wood floor and pulled a bottle of rum from the fridge.

Back at the home, they had a mess hall. All stainless steel, like those tables where you cut dead people up. Everybody called it "the home," but that was wishful thinking if held ever heard one. He saw what happened to those boys who got picked up by foster families, heard the stories when they ended up back in the home meaner than ever.

He was sixteen when he ran away. It wasn't so hard. None of the doors were locked, no club-footed orderly patrolled the halls. He had simply packed and navigated through the crowd of boys smoking on the steps and then walked to a diner a little ways into town and sat down at the counter next to a trucker who was wiping a plate with a piece of toast. "You must've been hungry," Baby had said. (Was this how men talked to each other?) "Still am," the man had replied.

And just like that, a ride out of town.

And just like that, a ride out of any town.

And invariably, when the day's driving had been done and the truck pulled into some desolate eave, a hand would clap behind Baby's neck.

"Now. How's about some company for the night?" they'd ask, not really asking.

Well, blowjobs could mean company too, Baby supposed. A company that hired anyone who applied. Anyone at all.

One town, then another, some no more than a gas station and few stands of pies or produce. Some no more than a sign on the side of the road: Rushfield, Golden Rod, Bear Creek, Fairfield. After Fairfield, Modesto.

Modesto, the name of a humble magician.

They (Baby and a trucker nicknamed, improbably, Isotope) had arrived in Modesto near midnight, and Baby hopped off and walked across a gravel lot toward the john while the truck was filled up for the last leg of the run toward the Bay. The john was a little concrete hut set before a huge expanse of darkness, and for the single yellow bug-light dangling from its eave, Baby couldn't see where he was headed. He didn't have to piss that badly, but he was aching for a little of the snort the last trucker had given him. As he walked closer, he began to make out the lean knife of a figure just outside the cone of light, so thin it might be a girl, propped against one wall of the john, smoking a cigarette with a careful indifference that Baby immediately recognized. Baby walked slower, trying to see if the figure would look up. It didn't. He passed the figure, and still it didn't look up. Baby rounded the corner and into the door. When he came out, he fished a cigarette from his pocket. "You mind giving me a light?" he asked.

It looked up.

Baby took a breath. He took it right out of his own lung.

Instead of pulling out a match or a lighter, instead of even the cigarette from his mouth and offering it to Baby, the boy leaned forward and brought his face close to Baby's, slowly, until the tips of their cigarettes, extending from their lips, touched.

That was it. They were lit. Every dream, all their years ahead: lit.

A shepherd to follow.

Samuel.

Oh Samuel.

Baby wiped his mouth now and felt his way back to the bed and slipped under the covers. Samuel turned toward him and grunted deeply, a happy sound. Baby's own skin felt clean, but Samuel's was still cooked. Outside, on the street, he heard the heavy doors of a truck unsticking, boots landing on the sidewalk, then the door shutting. Through the window, he could see the panes of the glass on the building across the alley, the drowsy eyelets of their curtains backlit by lamps.

It struck Baby that this was a moment not quite happening, a dream that would haze into white at any moment. This whole life of theirs so far, this sweet night, just a glimmer, without substance, and when he came to he would have to say, "Yeah, man, thanks for the light," and walk off again into the night, across the gravel, back onto Isotope's blue metal truck, and never look back from whatever point he might be now, instead.

The thought fascinated him, and he blinked to see if it were really true. Then Samuel coughed, a sound so real and ordinary that Baby smiled and cupped Samuel's cock until it nodded off and coiled lazily into his hand, and then he felt himself fall asleep with his nose along the lip of Samuel's right ear.

———

Baby was ten again. His Mama was yellow and Sheriff was white.

Black women, some hoisting infants on their hips, floated looks above Baby's head and tisk-tisked.

Look at her, their eyes said to each other. Who she think she is now? Woman like that, who never needed nothing, this yellow whore who never left her plot of land by the railroad where she raised that mongrel of a child ("Look at this child. Damn near a Negro. *Damn* near"), this woman nobody can remember being acknowledged by so much as a nod, who was rumored to have a slanted twat so maybe that's why a nigger would want to touch her (cause an unschooled nigger was nothing if not curious)—who she think she is now? A nobody. Nobody.

Still, nobody deserved what she got.

This slip of a body that two white men had dragged out from beneath her own house and covered with a sheet when they didn't know what else to do with it, that someone (a man, you can bet, yes'm, a man, a jealous man) had hog-tied and slit open and stuffed into the crawlspace, so cut up you couldn't tell that the sheet over it was white originally till someone told you, so cut up even Sheriff held a handkerchief over his nose—covered up, but not before the women could get a good long look at what they had compared themselves to, standing nude before their long mirrors, and what their men would've crawled over broken glass to get a piece of.

———

Not much to look at. Just a small bar with a wood dance floor and light-bulbs the owners smoked out over a candle. A place so half-minded but stubborn, so airy but insistent, it felt like hot shallow breaths on the back of your neck all the time. That's what you walked into, a room poised on the edge of sex, electrified with the possibility of what could happen between men, those deep silent fucks for which time stopped and plunged, and stopped again.

The white boys, all fucked up on something scary, propped against the walls with their johns, would look up once in a while to watch the colored boys make like they were dry-fucking on the dance-floor. And Baby, if he felt like, would throw them a look like a hock of spit—like Yeah? So what?—without losing the roll of Samuel's pelvis against his own.

Samuel was tall but wide, shoulders like volleyballs wrapped in cotton: a flag-ship, a mast cutting high and steady through eddies of men on the dance floor.

Baby possessed a density, a thickness, that spoke of power, like the arc of a bow just drawn back. Half-cocked. Above all that, Baby had the indifference of a man who was used to being looked at. Men looked at him and their mouths went sour from suck-ing on their own tongues, their noses ached with sniffing.

If anyone knew the choreography of Baby's body, it was Samuel.

For it was Samuel's body that traced out the complex logarithms for Baby to follow.

For when they danced, they talked with their hipbones in a language only peo-ple born with the dance could understand.

Hold still. Now grind.

I'm slowing down, where are you?

Give me more.

Careful what you wish for.

Give it. Give it.

People in the room still?

For when Baby danced with Samuel, the walls of the room, the floor beneath, all fell away, ribbons from a box that held only him and his.

———

Sheriff bent down and looked Baby in the eye.

"You know what this is?" Sheriff touched the metal star on his chest. "You know what this means, boy? Means I got a right to ask questions and people got an obligation to answer me. Baby, look at your Mama there. look at her and think real hard about what I'm going to ask you because I'm only going to ask once. Baby: Where's your Daddy at?" Baby didn't answer. He wasn't ever supposed to talk to a white man, even when asked a question he knew the answer to.

His Daddy was a soldier. His Daddy had said to his Mama, "Soon-Hee, this is a table. This is a kettle. And that there's a baby." His Mama had said, "Table. Kettle. Baby."

All his life, Baby never knew another name. His Daddy had said that morning, "Baby, you go outside and play. Look what a fine day it is. T's a fine day, ain't it? Go outside and play. I need to have a word with your mother." Then he had winked and patted Baby's tummy and guided him out the door.

So what does a white man, a sheriff at that, know about what a black man is capable of? Baby looked at the railroad tracks running all the way down to the sky until something on the edge of his vision rustled.

The mass under the sheet had managed to sit up, bolt-straight, and lift an arm. She was pointing at the railroad. Her jaws moved up and down. She looked at her son and pointed at the railroad more intently.

Baby tried to help. Yes, Mama. That's right. The train. That's where he went. The train.

Her eyes darted between Baby and the horizon. Still she pointed, like a young child trying to show a parent where the monster was hiding. The air was hazy with flies, the trees clogged with anything else born out of the Mississippi mud that's small enough to fly. Baby tried to please his mother by looking where she pointed, to show he understood. After a while, he realized it wasn't the railroad at all he was looking at, but the long ragged range of Samuel's spine.

————

For it was Samuel who knew of the tea saucer on Baby's back that was filled with cream. That was soft, runny cream left out in sunlight, the one sure mark that he was something other than black.

No one knew where to place a man like Baby, with his dusty high yellow skin and his hair real straight in some parts and real kinky in others, with his one eye hooded and the other a clean blade of almond. It wrapped him, the approximating stare of strangers on the street disguised as a passing glance. Wrapped him and cleared a foot-long radius on the sidewalk.

Samuel was a quarter Indian himself, but you couldn't tell by looking. Bones cut so sharp and skin so dark, his head seemed in silhouette even in full light, all apples and angles. Kissing the skin of a man like Samuel, that's the glimpse of evil. Skin so oiled and dark you run the danger of seeing your own face in it, seeing your ugly please me please me face that no one ought to see lest you turn to salt.

Samuel said his mother's people a few generations back hunted buffalo, though Baby knew that buffalo haven't been free on the continent to hunt for well over a century. They made stuff up as they went along if someone wanted a story. If Samuel's people hunted buffalo, then Baby's people built the Great Wall of China. ("Maybe that's how they built that damn wall, with buffalos," Baby mused.)

Samuel always laughed that if they had a kid together, they'd end up with one hell of a wrong-looking child.

Well, children weren't something too much on Baby's mind. What's he want with a child anyway? But you talk long enough about something that you don't have, never going to have, and it starts to mesh right into the grain of your life so that you forget what fiction is. If Baby drank a beer at breakfast, Samuel would frown and say, "Aw, now, Papa, what kind of example is that for our son?" If Samuel left some toenails on the pillow, Baby would chide, "I can't be cleaning after you once that child comes!"

Sometimes when he was alone, Baby would sense something vague just to the left and back of him, some sense of a round-headed child, a little girl maybe, sitting there waiting to get her hair braided. And he'd touch his throat and laugh at himself for thinking such a ridiculous thing and ache a little bit.

―――――

Baby said: I'm sorry. I didn't know what he was doing to you in there. I thought he was making love to you in there.

She was standing now, on the steps of the porch. She was barely grown, Baby thought, barely a woman. She dipped her head and fanned the back of her neck with her hand. Open gashes draped her torso. Bones gleamed from beneath the wounds like the eyes of animals hiding in her body. Her breast peeled to either side of the longest gash and the thick hairs of her genitals were clotted with blood.

Baby fetched a glass from the house and filled it with water from the pump, but she didn't want any. She seemed preoccupied. Again and again, she rubbed at her wrist, her palm. Killing time. Waiting.

And he might have mistaken it for a twitch, but there was no mistaking. She winked.

―――――

Samuel whined at breakfast about the milk being too cold.

"Too cold? You getting fussy, or you just getting fussy on me?"

"I ain't kidding, Baby. Something about my head, I don't know what, but that cold is hurting my head, like right here, right at the back of my neck." He rolled his head to demonstrate.

"Oh," Baby said dismissively. "I get that, too, when I eat ice cream too fast. Just take small sips then."

Samuel didn't snap back but sat holding the back of his neck. With his other hand, he raised the glass to his lips and took small sips like Baby said.

Samuel had to be down on the corner by eight each morning to catch the bus, take a transfer, then a train, and be at the warehouse by nine, an easier schedule than when he was just a packer and had to be there at six. Now he took care of orders and worked a clean nine to six shift. Baby himself flitted through jobs, gas stations and restaurants, mostly in the gray cold months of the year, but when the weather brightened, as much as it does in the city, he said his farewells to employment. It wasn't that they had money, had the luxury of unemployment. They were making it month to month as it was, but certainly more than he was used to. Samuel didn't mind that Baby didn't work; he was union now, and making good-enough union wages to keep them both afloat.

Most mornings Baby woke with Samuel and put a couple eggs on the stove and some toast in the oven while Samuel showered and shaved. Baby would stand with a glass of coffee halfway to his lip while he tried to remember some dream he had the night before, the apartment filling with the comforting sound of water running and food cooking while they both adjusted themselves to the mundane demands of the day and the populated world. After Samuel left for work, Baby would sip coffee in the window and watch the street begin to wake:cars with music drifting out as they passed, children walking in clusters to the bus stop, the grocer across the street setting out displays of oranges on the sidewalk. Then maybe a nap till noon or a bit after. And then he'd decide where he wanted to go that day: maybe to the park, but maybe just see what the old bookstores and record shops might have that he hadn't seen before. He'd set out of the house with a sense of adventure, though his adventures usually never extended past the ten-block area of his neighborhood. It was also the sense of renewal, a sense of freedom to invent his daily persona: He could be the bemused stroller, taking delight at every windowfront, sitting anonymously good-natured in a taqueria; or he could be something darker, at the station, posing the practiced casual pose from his old loitering days, cataloging the real hustlers who worked the station's men's room, washing their hands for long minutes, checking the shine of their hair in the mirror along with prospective johns. Occasionally one of them would try to catch Baby's eye, but immediately they'd know him for what he was, and there's nothing worse, nothing, than one whore propositioning another.

This undocking, this drifting through the day: It was a present he gave himself. A person could let himself wander anywhere he pleased, so long as he had a harbor to return to each night.

———

That evening Baby met Samuel at the train, like he always did Fridays, but Samuel wasn't there. After half an hour, Baby walked home alone, muttering to himself. Ever heard of a phone? Ever heard of calling someone to say you going to be late?

"Brother!"

Baby hadn't seen the man or the commotion behind him. Two blocks up a crowd had taken over the street, dancing in the dimming light. Too festive to be another war protest.

The man who called out to him looked overjoyed. His blond hair was wrapped to approximate a head of dreadlocks. The man threw up his hands to imitate a goal post, so excitedly that he nearly fell over. "It's over, Bro. It's over!" he cried.

That was the thing. No men left in this town except fags, college students and hippies.

Baby tried to walk past but the man kept at his side.

"I mean, shit! Haven't you heard yet? Saigon?"

Baby stopped. "What about Saigon?"

"Saigon fell! It's over! The war, man. You know, the war's over!"

When Baby didn't react, the man paused and took a good look. Sometimes the angle of lighting brought out the narrowness and upwardness of Baby's eyes, accentuated the wide cheeks that sloped into the corners of his mouth. And a yellow streetlight could bring out certain tinctures of his skin—

"Hey," the man said. "You guys won. Congratulations." He joined his fists together at his chest and made a little bow at Baby and then skipped off toward the crowd.

Crazy-ass cracker.

What the hell was there to celebrate? He didn't follow the war too closely but Baby knew it was lots of brothers out there in the jungle, and brothers who got their legs blown off, and brothers who just plain died. And on the flip-side, Vietnam. Held seen enough villages on fire, seen enough dirty crying children to last him another lifetime. The whole thing was a mess. So again, what the hell was there to celebrate?

And this was a thought that came uniquely to Baby: how you gonna talk about who won and who lost to a man that came from two peoples who, in another generation, in another war, had been bent on putting bullets through each other's heads?

He turned the corner and took the long route home to avoid the crowd, shaking his head. The wind was lifting leaves off the ground. He wanted Samuel.

———

"Might as well live close to your work," the old Samuel had shrugged the night they had arrived in San Francisco.

They were standing in the lobby of an old hotel like those you see in old movies with comic, fumbling bellhops. Curls of wood climbed the tall, tall ceiling, dull brass panels gazed serenely from the elevators, and the parched paper on the walls swirled with so many flowers that Baby's nose twitched with the acrid scent of open roses. Thin pale women in beaded dresses might spill laughing from the elevators at any moment. But everything looked heavy, as if logged with water. Nevertheless Baby had smoothed the legs of his jeans and patted down his hair as they approached the counter.

"We need a room," Samuel had told the clerk.

"Two hours or four?"

"We need a week."

"Room open on the sixth floor. Shower and toilet located at the end of the hall. Cash only and don't leave nothing on the sheets," the clerk recited to the women in his magazine.

When they were walking to the elevator, Baby whispered, "Where are we?" He didn't want to disturb the old men sleeping on the velvet armchairs by the fireplace, although there wasn't a fire.

"This is the Tenderloin," Samuel explained, as if that said it all. The elevator gave a sigh when they told it to move. Samuel asked, "Those truckers, they ever give you money? D'you ever ask?"

"Sure. Sometimes."

"Good enough," Samuel said.

Nights were for work, but days were for themselves: for bare-chested naps in Dolores Park, chess games at the Wharf, scenes from a movie, a montage of summer days. They didn't have to work every night. Sometimes they had a stretch of three or four days to themselves. If they worked, they worked simultaneously. That way, neither of the them would ever have to sleep alone.

One week passed. Then another. Pretty soon, a whole month. The weather started turning chilly earlier and earlier in the day, Baby remembered. Then one morning, when he staggered home from a job, placing one foot in front of another up all those steps that seemed both shallow and deep (was he going up, down? Was this the right building?), down the dark hall whose doors oozed at him like the bellies of large animals, when he finally steadied the nauseating swilling of time long enough to work the complex machinery of the doorknob (a key! a lock!), Samuel was not there. Baby stood in the little room for a long, long time (Samuel might've just stepped out for a few hours, but no, no: Look how bare the room looks, the light gray instead of bright), and then the floor rose and rose until it pressed against his face and the last thing he remembered thinking, so lucidly and calmly he could hear it even now:

Well, that's the trouble with being a sheep: You might love the shepherd, but you can't tell him what to do or where to lead you.

But he had been wrong, wrong. For a hand had reached into his deep white sleep and pulled him up by the collar.

And then that hand slapping his cheeks.

And then Baby's own voice screaming, accusing.

And then Samuel's voice: "No, no. I didn't. I'm right here."

And Baby bobbed to the surface.

Samuel had turned out Baby's elbow and found the tiny clot nestled inside there like a beetle. But there had been no questions, no more words. There would be time for all of that later.

Time for all of that later.

Were they ever that young? That memory wavered uncertainly in his account of their life so far. It felt tied off from the years that followed, like a knot in a clown's balloon. For the Samuel who had strode confidently to the hotel counter, who slipped like a bug through a hungry city and its lymph nodes of truckstops and men's rooms, the Samuel who could be drenched with the breaths of breathless men, that Samuel seemed to Baby now, and had Baby known enough to admit it, so youthful and affecting in his confidence that life's rules could be mastered. But more than that, and this saddened him: also irretrievable, like a toy lost in the water, like, yes, a childhood game that they've had to give up for this life without magic.

Baby sighed now as he climbed the last flight of stairs.

That was why he clung to Samuel so. They were utterly alone in the world, in the sense that no one else knew the grimy, exciting fairy tale, the furious youth, that they had stepped out of once, once upon a time.

———

When Samuel walked in through the door, he looked so limp and chewed up that Baby couldn't find the heart to be angry.

"I'm sorry," Samuel said, sagging against the door. "I just plain fell asleep. Can't explain it. Rode all the way out across the Bay before I woke up." He sniffled and rubbed his nose. "You mad?"

Baby looked him up and down.

Samuel asked for a kiss. His voice wobbled.

"Hells no," Baby said. "And don't you look to get me sick too."

But he lighted a kiss on Samuel's forehead and put him to bed.

In the kitchen, Baby hummed along with the rice as he chopped up a leek to go in with the mushrooms. Sure is a nice feeling to have your man in bed. Sure is peaceful to have your man be asleep and not be fussing over how much butter you cook your own damn mushrooms in.

Another voice said, Amen, and Baby nodded.

When he tried to wake Samuel for dinner, he got waved away. "let me get some sleep," Samuel said heavily. "I'll be fine by tomorrow, I promise."

Baby felt Samuel's forehead. Hot. Definitely hot.

"Sure," he said, "Sick gets what sick wants."

It was early enough to be restless, and Baby had counted on going to the club with Samuel, but now it looks like he's staying home. It's different when a sick man's in your bed. Can't be hopping all over town when a sick man's in your bed.

Summer nights meant music and long shiny trucks and tough young men in tight jeans under the window. This time of year, the night air was cool and pleasant, like the cool of a chilled beer can just under your nose. Young men called to each other, to passing cars. Young men who escaped the draft for lack of papers or eyebrows, the same young men who looked tough and available on the benches of Dolores Park. Baby tipped the bottle to his mouth and listened to their friendly greetings.

Hey. Where you been, where you going?

No place, man, no place.

After the dishes, Baby went through the pantry: beernuts, canned olives, bean spread, bags of salty stuff. That Samuel, he liked to eat some crap. He'd eat frosting out a can all three meals if you let him. Behind a gallon jug of salsa, Baby found a tiny box wrapped in red. Sneaky, Baby thought. He had half a mind to open it, but his birthday wasn't more than a week away. If he can wait twenty-four years for this birthday, he can wait a few more days. He put the box back and tried to watch TV, but it was all the same, on every channel: news of Saigon, women running, dragging babies, running toward the Embassy, mashed against an iron gate like pressed flowers. Baby yawned and finished his beer and turned off all the lights, washed up, and slid into bed naked.

Samuel felt like a loaf of dough left to rise under a heavy towel. Instinctively, his head turned away and revealed his neck. Baby placed his face into the crook made there, but he couldn't sleep.

———

Distinctly he recalled the cushion of his mother's body underneath him, her tiny steps blurring after a while into flight, that teenage body blowing down the streets, the world blowing by, the two of them born along the ground.

What's that word? Buoyant. Buoyancy.

Did she run like that, with a baby strapped to her back like a bundle of kindling, a baby that she could hold up to the powers-that-be at the embassy and push on a plane to anywhere, anywhere at all, because, after all, that baby was one of their own, even if she weren't—

No. She didn't have to. Because his Daddy married her. He married her when he didn't have to, when he could've left her to rot and starve in the fields his men had left smoking with bodies.

It had been a clean, safe passage.

"This is a table. This is a chair. And that there's a baby."

"This is a railroad, Baby. You know what a railroad really is?" his Daddy would ask, then laugh his deep laugh. They would squat at the edge of the tracks, Baby between his Daddy's knees, their fingers on the steel rails, waiting. Then the tremor, a tiny bird heart beating, and Baby would look into his Daddy's face. "Now? Is that it? Now?" But his Daddy's face would be calm, his eyes closed. The tremor grew more and more, a bird heart, then the heart of some larger animal, a dog's, then a horse's, the feather and fur and hide growing thin until it seemed the heart was beating bare in their palms, until their fingers, still on the rail, began to shake, the dense wall of sound washing closer and closer. "Now?" Baby would ask, getting scared, his legs growing soft. A boy had been killed on the tracks the summer before, his shoe caught between the wood ties. "Now?" The conductor started to blow his horn, once, then twice, then just let it wail, but his Daddy would only shush him and press his fingers to the steel.

"Trust me, child. Not yet, not yet—"

Then at the last possible minute, Baby felt his body lifted upwards and backwards, into the air, as if blown by the wind from the passing train, blood rushing through the cords of his little neck, his heart lurching and pumping clots of thoughts and his Daddy screaming "Hallelujah!", but then, just then, his feet would land on the coarse gravel again and his Daddy's arms would unwind from his torso, and it would grow peaceful and still and green again.

"Wasn't that something?" his Daddy would say. "Something, wasn't that? Remember that feeling, Baby. Anytime you think you know what fear is, anytime you forget what the joy of living is, remember that feeling. And you remember that I pulled you back. Me, your Daddy. Never trust anyone else to do the same for you."

Eventually the silence took over Baby's mind. Such quiet and darkness, he couldn't tell how much time had passed since he first lay down. He imagined the ceiling was the surface of a sea and they were deep below, where all there is to do is concentrate on the act of breathing. Gently he slipped off Samuel's underwear and tucked his hand where Samuel's thighs branched.

———

But Samuel wasn't better by morning, nor the day after that. The whole weekend he stayed in bed and let Baby play mother. Baby cooked up some tea he bought at the herbal pharmacy down the street. He helped Samuel into the bathtub and sponged him. Who's my baby? Who's Baby's baby? On Thursday, Samuel felt good enough to get up and move around. Just as well, cause it was Baby's birthday.

Samuel leaned against the side of the fridge with a glass of wine—no, with his third glass of wine—and watched while Baby chopped and boiled and washed. A small ham was sitting royally in the oven, a pot of rice simmering with its clean easy smell.

"Did I ever tell you," Samuel began. "Did I ever tell you how beautiful you are?"

A radio was playing the next floor down, sad and faraway. Why was it that faraway music always sounded so sad? The lightbulb, yellow and failing, flickered absently.

Baby put down his knife. "You drunk, that's what you are. Leave me alone and let me finish cooking."

Samuel circled Baby's waist and kissed his ears. "You want to do something crazy?"

Baby's dick stiffened against the sink. His mouth turn up with thoughts of something illegal and wet. He turned around in Samuel's arms and pressed himself into Samuel's crotch.

"Well, do you?" Samuel asked.

Baby could feel Samuel begin to rise under his pajamas. "Maybe. Maybe not."

Samuel moved down onto one knee.

Baby let out a peal of laughter. "Shit," he said. He began to unzip his unfurling crotch, but Samuel's face, just below, was full of piety instead of flirtation, earnestly instead of foreplay.

"Baby, quit. I'm being serious here," Samuel said, but didn't continue. He stole a look at the ceiling, which, Baby supposed, was the closest Samuel ever came to being religious.

"Let me tell you a story," Samuel said. "OK, a story. There was this man once," he said. "This boy, actually, this kid who thought—Wait, that's dumb. OK, wait. Geese. No, wait," he said, and then stopped. "Wait."

Baby waited. Samuel got this way sometimes when he drank.

"OK," Samuel continued. "Remember when we just arrived here, living in that hotel? You remember?"

Baby nodded suspiciously.

"There was one night when I'd headed out the door thinking I was just going to find a john, make some quick cash, whatever. But then a bus came, and I thought, sure! And then another bus came and I thought, why not! I don't know. I just kept going and going, one transfer after another, not really sure what I was doing, but all the time doing it just the same. I thought, Baby don't need me. He'll be fine. And what I need him for? Baby, you know how geese, when they're born, their minds get stuck on the first thing they see, be it their mother or an alarm clock, and they follow it forever? Baby, I saw that was starting to happen with you, you were starting to get stuck on me, and Lord knows, if you follow me I'll lead you someplace awful."

Baby's vision milked over. "Why are you telling me this?"

"I'm telling you this because I came back. Because I knew I had to. And wasn't I right? Wasn't I? When I opened the door, I thought you were dead, Baby, dead! But then you started screaming, you remember? Screaming, You fucker! You fucking left me! Didn't you! Didn't you!" Samuel tried to laugh at this, but he only managed to clear his throat. "And I thought, Yes, yes I did. And then, No, no. I couldn't have, could I? Could I have?" Baby leaned back, hoping the counter was still there. His knees were turning to dough and liquid pushed up his throat, but Samuel caught him square in the eye and held him. "Listen, Baby. I been thinking. I been thinking a lot, specially these few days when you been taking care of me. Listen to me, Baby. I'm telling you this. I'm telling you this is how it is." He looked down a second and when he looked back up, he was sober. "This is it, right here. You and me. Two people get so used to making a life together they don't want nothing else. Maybe there ain't nothing else out there. Maybe all there is is in this room, right here, right now."

Baby could have said lots of things. He could have argued or said something smart. But he just stood there like someone dumb, holding out his hand like a begging cup as Samuel slid the ring onto his finger.

———

"You follow me. You follow me forever," Samuel said.
Baby said yes, yes.
"Won't be no place awful, I can promise you that."
Baby thought, yes, good, promise.
You a married lady now.
Amen.

———

Tell me, Baby. Tell me why. Why's a man got to kill a woman like that?

Sheriff's voice trailed off. He looked sadly down at his palms, and Baby knew suddenly what he hadn't wanted to know, what he had known all along, about that white man and his white heart beating beneath his metal star.

Then Baby was off.

Not so much running but slipping along the smooth rails. He could hear the train though it was miles off now, the shudder of the wood ties beneath like the timbre of a low growl that tired more and more. When the house, too, disappeared, he stopped and untied the bundle from his back, and carefully, carefully he peeled back the first layer of pale cotton. But there was only another layer, and another, until all there was was a tangle of cloth in his hands. Where were the bright eyes, the tiny fists? Where was Samuel? A dream. Samuel was next to him, a thick lump under the sheet. Baby placed a palm on the sheet to calm himself but there it was, there it bloomed, under his hand, spreading in a circle, spreading wider and wider. His palm came away wet and red.

No no no no no—

Another dream.

———

The air outside was wet and cold and thin, almost not enough air to breathe. Baby sat in the windowbox looking at Widow Matthews caning down the street with her eyes set dead ahead of her, determined to fight the wind and gravity itself. If the weather was warmer, Baby would've dangled out the window and called out to her, but now she seemed just another old woman trying to get herself home before dark. Her steps were labored, just left of sync.

Heavy.

Yes ma'am. That's the feeling.

New decade was coming tonight but Baby felt just tired. More like something was ending.

Samuel settled between Baby's legs with a blanket around himself, his face turning orange with the sunset. Baby fed him a bit of wine from his own glass. After a while, they fell asleep. After a little while longer, they were on the bed making love.

Samuel felt a little skinnier, it was true.

Maybe a lot skinnier. Flesh ain't what it used to be. Samuel's skin, that fearful oiled skin, now took on a dullness and a thinness, like cigarette paper near the cherry, like Widow Matthew's cloudy eye. Holding Samuel, Baby imagined they were two elderly folks resting up for the remainder of their days. Then he thought, Why, we ain't even thirty yet!

Baby tried to remember what they used to feel like to each other naked, but he couldn't. Body grows with you. It was gradual, like an iceberg. You keep your eye on it and it don't seem to move at all, but if you look away and look back—

Baby entered Samuel gently, gently.

Who's moving? Who's still? like gin sinking through water, sugar rising through cake. Can't tell what's one and what's the other.

They fell asleep again and again, weaved under and over white dreams. In the distance, firework and guns popped faintly.

He was dreaming of Samuel's face, seen that first time, the smile spreading like breath across the glass of those cheeks, bathed in yellow like a wash of sepia-tone, the sad and sweet quality of a time and place you could ache for but never see again. Another lifetime. That was what struck him. What had struck him, what he had already felt, all those years ago, on the edge of Modesto, a sense of nostalgia so sudden and fleeting that he had no choice but to chase it.

And the man next to him now was surely the same man, but not quite. Not quite the same.

"Bad dream?" Samuel asked.

"Yes. A bad dream."

"Do they find him this time? Whoever killed your Mama?"

"No. They never do."

"Oh," Samuel said. "Poor Baby," he cooed. And then, "Tell me again. What's she look like?"

"Oh, real cute."

"Is she smart?"

"Oh, real smart. Reads anything you give her."

"That's good. That's beautiful."

They laced hands over Samuel's heart.

In this way, a third person entered their lives.

In this way, Baby and Samuel became parents.

———

When Samuel died, tall blond grass grew up around the bed.

Baby's mother came and stroked his hand.

Poor Baby—

Is a train coming, Mama?

Poor little Baby.

She took out a bit of rope and made a loop around his wrists. He put his chest to the ground and she made a loop around his ankles.

He's gone, Mama. So you were wrong. He didn't kill me. Maybe I killed him.

After a few minutes, when he didn't hear anything else, Baby knew his Mama had left him for good.

People in the room still?

It's over, Bro. It's over.

What's over?

You know. The story. This is how it ends.

Slivers of sunlight, like knives seen edge on, cut through the slats of wood above, crawling closer as the sun winded across what had to have been a spectacular sky.

Beneath him, the softest earth, though nothing grew.

See? Didn't I promise you? That if you followed me, it won't be no place awful, Baby.

That's the price, ain't it? You love someone and it don't ever end. Not even when he does.

Baby knew too what he should have said to Sheriff.

You ask me where my Daddy went? You'll never know where. No one will. He jumped on a train that come passing by after he killed Mama and he somewhere far. He was scared. He seen his own face in Mama's skin, seen such evil, the only thing he could do was cut it up.

But who killed who, I ask you.

I begged my Daddy to take me with him but he wouldn't. He said the strangest thing. I still remember it. He said, There's a story here you don't want to know and I don't want to tell. He said, You know what a railroad is? A railroad is a piece of the ladder God climbed to heaven after Creation and then kicked to the ground after. Touching the tracks is like touching a piece of sacrament, a piece of His hem. And being on a train is just man's way of trying to get to heaven without really earning it. That trails going to run and run, but it won't never pull in anyplace.

Now what kind of life is that?

What kind of life you suppose that is for my Baby? For my sweet, sweet Baby—

———

Such a warm night, not a wisp of fog.

A sleight of hand, a magic trick. If you blink, if you cough, you've missed it.

In their little apartment on Valencia Street, Baby and Samuel are laying on the bed, talking softly.

"This is the decade it's all going to happen," Baby says. What does he mean? He doesn't know what he means.

"What's going to happen?" Samuel asks. "Tell me."

"Oh," Baby says, after a moment. "Just everything."

"Everything," Samuel repeats.

And the two of them look up happily at the ceiling where they don't see what's already beginning to happen, to unfurl, a thought like a sheet of scrim, how it waves and opens and opens and opens. A banner. A painting. They can't see it.

In the painting he will to go to the bed. He will kneel there and not move, an entire day, an entire night, whispering into the cooling clay of Samuel's cheek.

But Samuel can't hear. He is far away. When one is so close to the end, what he hears is the darker song.

Can you hear me? I love you. I love you. I—

Do. I do.

THE INTERVIEW

Once the knock came, you wait for it every morning. Silence can mean anything. Your father's instructions are clear: Stay in bed. Whatever happens, if you hear a knock, pull the covers over your head, pretend to be asleep, but stay where you are.

That's what you'd done wrong the first time. You answered the door. You were stupid.

You were lucky. The man had asked to come into the house, but hadn't insisted on looking in the bedrooms.

When it was certain the man had driven away and would not come back, your father told you to go get your mother from the closet. At the kitchen table the three of you tried to eat breakfast, but you just picked up your fork and then put it down again. Your father looked your way every few minutes. "Next time, why don't you just invite them in and tell them everything," he suggested.

"Or maybe," he said, "maybe you want them to take us all away."

You tried not to cry. You didn't want all of you taken away. No, you didn't. Really. But you almost ruined everything. Yes, you did.

Then your older brother sat down at the table and asked for a glass of juice. Held slept through the morning's events. When he heard what happened, he looked at you. "Dumbfuck," he said. "No brains." Your mother stroked your hair.

"Is this my little retard?" she asked. "Is it?"

―――――

Your son is stupid. But he's young, barely a teenager. He trusts people. He's not a survivor. He's not like your other son, the older one, the one who understands about deceit, who already has the slick, indifferent look of his father. In public you praise the older son for his smartness, for his quickness.

You're a survivor. You lived in Arizona for three years.

Secretly you love your younger son more. This is the child you slept with on the floor of a motel room for three years. This is the child who is still closer to the dream of children you had when you were a bride. You ache for him. You ache with the knowledge that soon your husband will take him away from you too. It's already beginning to happen. Already his soft, broad face is burning away. Already he is beginning to turn deaf to you. You know too that once a child is damaged, you've lost him forever.

―――――

Your son is stupid. He is weak. He has the softness of his mother, the womanly tendency to accept defeat.

Sometimes you think of your wife in the first years of your marriage. You think of yourself, tall and successful, a man for whom no luxury was undeserved, not even the doctor's prize daughter. You think of your friends, all men of wealth, with their thick, loud wives, and you remember, with pride, the way your friends looked at your slender bride. Sometimes you think of the plush apartment in Taiwan, the highrise, the view all the way to the sea, the furniture in pale teaks, the coppered walls and the low hum of the air conditioner on certain summer days when the smog rolls and tumbles beneath your veranda. The bedroom wrapped by a long vanity like a fur stole.

Sometimes you can still see your wife sitting at her ivory vanity, choosing powders and perfumes, making up her face.

Sometimes you dream of your wife, someone still slender and smooth-skinned, trailing through that apartment with your tiny son in her arms, and your own voice saying, "Bring him to me."

You can still feel her weight resting on the arm of your chair during mahjongg games, her long legs crossed under your palm. Sometimes you remember how easily she once fit into your hands, her waist the perfect neck of a vase. You must remember that, or else how will you go on?

These days you live in a small rented house in the ugly gray heart of Los Angeles. A small blue house constructed entirely of spotted linoleum, the seams of the drywalls held wearily together through the plague of earthquakes as if by will alone, haunted incessantly by a dampness that taints the first breath of the morning with a metallic aftertaste. In the shower you stand perfectly still, for fear of touching the caked tiles.

But it's your house. You signed the lease. You sign the checks every month. It's yours.

Three years ago you sent your wife and kids to live with your brother in Arizona in that motel of his so you could marry Terry Bedford for her papers and then divorce her. Now you sell cars and your wife works at a video store with a porn section. She doesn't speak too much English. She doesn't have a work permit. She doesn't complain. She doesn't tell you how hard it is for her at the video store.

Sometimes you get home before your wife does, though it's late enough. Sometimes your younger son is awake and alone in the house, watching Johnny Carson. Your other son is off somewhere. You sell cars. Your boss is a Vietnamese son of a bitch who tries to cut into your commission. You've had a long day. Everyone tries to screw with you, wants a better deal. Your suit looks good, but it's dirty. You want to shower and eat. You tell your son to heat up some food but he pretends to not hear you the first time, so you say it again.

You're still angry at him. You're angry at him for not having more brain than it requires to wake you when someone knocks at the door at 9 A.M. on a Saturday. You think of him inviting the man into your house to catch you in a lie. When he finally woke you, you were startled. You cupped a hand over your wife's mouth and woke her and hid her in the closet and then caught your breath before greeting the man sitting—yes, sitting, like a guest—in your living room.

You don't know how old your son is. You know school can't be going too well for him because you never see him with friends and he never mentions other kids. He's already starting to get that tall gangly quality of the men in your family, and your skin tingles at the memory of puberty. He's the kind of kid you, and probably your older son, would've bullied in school. At the dinner table, you read the paper and he keeps his eyes on the TV. Over the top of the paper, you look at your son's dull profile. He'll never be good-looking. He'll go through the world with his face like an open invitation. He's a commoner. A sheep.

You feel suddenly you should say something to him, anything, the way your father might have done when you were a boy, but your wife comes through the door just then, and, predictably, she goes to the child.

————

You're a survivor. You wake with your husband's hand over your mouth and you hide in closets. You're a mother now. You do what you need to do.

Your father was dying when you were pregnant with your second child. Life is so full of simple ironies. You had hoped he would live to see the child, and he did. He was a kind doctor. Strangers came out for his funeral. You were the oldest daughter, the most beautiful one out of all the sisters. At his funeral you cried. The sting of birth had left you weak. Your mother held the new baby like flowers someone handed her for a picture. You cried and cried. Because the last kind man on earth had died.

You're a survivor. Your mother is a survivor. She survived the Japanese. One by one, she survived the marriages of her daughters.

Sometimes teenagers come into the store and try to rent adult videos. You tell them no, get out of here, and they say rude things to you and laugh and run off. Sometimes no one is in the store at all. The owners are friends of your husband. They pay you in cash. Sometimes when you are alone in the store, you think of what you could do if you had enough cash. Nothing specific, really, but when you see your son's face at home, you feel ashamed.

———

You're a survivor. You slept in your own bed for three years because you understood that your mother wanted to sleep on the floor. Deep down, all women want to sleep on the floor. Of course, you're speaking metaphorically. You don't do that very often. Your mind is precise. You're going to be a doctor when you grow up. You're going to cut people open in precise lines.

Your little brother doesn't think it's fun, but you do. He doesn't like challenges, puzzles. You, on the other hand, look forward to long night sittings with your father plotting out the narrative, anticipating questions, patching holes in the story. The burden falls mostly on your father. All you have to do is not contradict anything he says. If he tells them you walk to school, you don't tell them you take the bus. You certainly don't tell them your mother drives you to school. Your father says if you believe in what you're saying, you're not really lying.

———

No, sir, I haven't seen my mother since we left Taiwan. My parents are divorced. My father remarried in the States. Her name is Terry Bedford. I met her once. She's nice.

Yes, sir, I lived with my uncle for three years in Ar-li-zo-na. He owns a motel. My brother and I shared a bed. Our father lived in L.A. He visited us four times a year.

I make my own lunch, and my brother's, too. Our father brings food home after work. I don't do the laundry but I sort the clothes and fold them after. We shop for groceries on Saturdays. I look after my brother when my father's at work. We play Atari. I don't know where my mother is. It never occurred to me to wonder how she's doing.

I want to stay in America, sir.

I want to be an American doctor when I grow up.

———

It's not fun. It's scary. You sit and go over the details again and again but you can't remember everything.

You don't want to make your mother disappear.

After you answered the door that morning, your mother had to disappear for a little while, just in case. She packed two bags.

Your father has invited Terry Bedford over for dinner. You and your brother clean the house upside down, make sure there's no trace of your mother anywhere. Your father makes steaks for four. Terry Bedford is blonde. She's very happy to meet you, heard all about you, and hugs you. She was married to your father for two years, divorced now for just over four months. Your father is sometimes gone all night, and you understand that he is with her, to keep her happy and unsuspecting, even if they are divorced.

She hugs you and her bosom is large. She brought a pie. Her hair is blonde but dry. She has pimples around her mouth. When she smiles, you notice her overbite.

You've never been this close to a white person before, except for the teachers at school. You've never seen your father speak English before. He speaks very well. Suddenly he is a different man. He tousles your hair and looks adoringly at you and your brother. Your brother smiles too. Everyone is smiling. Terry Bedford asks you about school, but your father told you before she arrived to keep your mouth shut. You pretend you don't understand what she's asking and smile.

Near the end of the evening, you and your brother stand next to Terry Bedford in the kitchen. She kneels and puts her arms around the both of you. Your father takes a picture. You all take turns taking pictures with her. In the kitchen. In the backyard. Living room. Porch.

This is why your father invited her over. He needs to document that Terry Bedford is on good terms with you. That she has been over in the house so there's no need for surprise visits. That this is not a fraudulent relationship.

After she leaves, you clear the table. Your brother slips out the back door. Your father watches TV. You can smell his cigarette.

You miss your mother. You wonder if this means she can come home soon.

———

You're a survivor.

Your father was a drunk. Your mother was useless. She was insane from as early as you can recall. She sent your older brother away to live with the sheriff as a houseboy to earn money. You had a younger sister who was also useless. She frightened easily. Your older brother, possibly your only ally in the world, resented you, though it wasn't your fault. The sheriff had turned out to be a cruel man. Your brother suffered while you pocketed money from the family liquor store. You had girlfriends. You married into a doctor's family.

You're a survivor. When you were eighteen you were drafted into the Navy. Once you were off the coast of Japan when your ship sank. It was January. Half the crew died, but not you. In the black frozen sea you watched another ship come to rescue you. In that long cold hour you watched the others sink, you made promises to yourself you no longer remember. The rantings of a teenager. When you married you decided no son of yours should ever have to be sheep. Your sons will be kings among men.

One day you heard that your brother had moved to America and bought a small motel. So why not you?

When you came to America to look for a woman to marry, you sent your wife and kids to live with your brother.

You imagine that your brother made love to your wife. Of course he did. It doesn't bother you.

Terry Bedford used to walk through the apartment with a cigarette in one hand, and an ashtray in the other, ashing as she walked. For some reason you found this terribly exciting. Terry-bly. Ha!

———

No, wait. Something is wrong.

That morning, when the man knocked and you opened the door. That morning, after the man left, when your father sat down and smoked a whole cigarette before telling you to get your mother from the closet—

Think about it. He smoked a whole cigarette first. She was hiding in there and he smoked a whole cigarette first.

That's not what's wrong.

The air ducts connect the living room directly into that closet. Your mother would've heard, quite clearly, from the closet, even with the intervening door shut, the whole conversation, the man saying goodbye, your father closing the door, the man's car starting and then the thump as it dropped over the curb and then the minutes of silence, of your father's breath drawing deeply from the smoke. She would've known the man had left. She would have known it was safe to come out.

Why would it be necessary for you to go tell your mother the man had left?

Why would she have stayed in there all that time?

———

You imagine your husband making love to Terry Bedford. You know she has large bosoms. You wonder how she feels like. In one picture she's kneeling in your kitchen with her arms around your children. You imagine kissing her bosoms, the sweaty flesh between her breasts. Unexpectedly you think of your husband's brother. You think of his loneliness. You think of going back to your mother.

It's early morning. It's still dark outside. The boys are dressed. You scramble a plate of eggs. You smooth your younger son's hair as he eats. Your husband is on the phone with his lawyer. You've taken the day off though you're not going anywhere. Your husband comes to the table. He says maybe they'll question the boys, maybe not. Probably they'll question the older one but not the younger one. He tells you to expect a call.

After they leave, you take a cigarette from your husband's jacket and light it. He won't miss it. The windows brighten more and more and then it's mid-morning.

———

You wait in a line. The room is full of people in lines. It's a large room, one wall of windows overlooking the gray grids of the city. It's loud. People have brought their small children. Spanish and Cantonese and English and one or two children are crying and fussing and crying. You can't think. It's hot. You're thinking too much.

Your younger son is asleep in a chair across the room. Next to him, your other son is reading a magazine. You're easily wearing the most expensive suit in the room. Your lawyer will meet you in an hour. He's a short Cantonese man who knew your wife's family back in Taiwan. When he arrives, you're still in line.

You smile at the black woman at the window, who gives you a number. You find a seat next to your sons. Your lawyer sits next to you. He says he doesn't think they'll interview the boys, at least not separately.

———

You're not really sleeping. You're listening to the voices all around you. If you knew Spanish, you'd know what the family next to you is quietly fighting about.

In your head you see an empty house. You see the Arizona desert, as you saw it the first time from the plane. You see your brother leading you through the crowds of the airport. You are by yourselves. You've left your mother back in Taiwan. You see your brother making your lunch every morning, walking you to school. You see a family of men.

If you believe what you're saying, you're not really lying.

———

A voice calls out your number, then repeats it. You nod at your lawyer. You nod at your sons. A man with a folder takes all of you into a hallway. You smile, shake his hand, introduce your sons and your lawyer. You keep smiling. You try to look the part of a hearty immigrant with a dream sparkling in your eyes. The man doesn't care. He points to a row of chairs outside of a door and tells your sons and your lawyer to wait there. You follow him into a small office.

———

I met Terry Bedford at the car lot where I work. I sold her a used Toyota, a blue '85 model in very good condition. She invited me over for dinner because she wanted to help me with my English. She knew how to cook Chinese food. On our honeymoon I took her to Las Vegas. She wanted to meet the children but I thought they might not like her. They were very close to their mother. Their mother abandoned them. In Taiwan. She met another man and didn't want to have anything to do with them. That was 1983. She didn't even care that I was going to take them to another country. I sent them to live with my brother in Arizona because it would've been very difficult for us otherwise. I didn't move them to L.A. after I married because I wanted to start fresh with my new wife, and two children by another woman would've made it very complicated. Terry Bedford is a good woman. She wanted children of her own and I didn't want to have any more. It's very sad. Our divorce was finalized this summer. She came by a few weeks ago for dinner. She liked the boys very much. I have pictures if you want to see.

I wish things had worked out with Terry Bedford. You understand how that is.

———

While your father is in the room, you sit and flip through a magazine about tennis. You think about your backhand and the rotation of your shoulders through a ball. Perfect. Your brother sits next to you with his knees against his chest. Every few minutes he looks at you but you don't feel like being bothered. You're cool. You're an adult. You're ready. Your father comes out of the room. The man shakes your father's hand and they stand in the doorway, whispering. Is it your turn now? Is it your brother's turn? You look at your brother. He looks shit-faced and you hold him together with your eyes. You hope the man will point at you first.

———

Your father comes out the room. You can feel it, spreading from the inside of your nose and then up to your eyes. For a moment everything goes out of your head, everything your father had made you memorize. You look at your brother but he won't look back. You're going to vomit. You're going to slip. You're going to ruin everything.

———

You fell asleep after the cigarette. You didn't have any dreams. When you wake you don't move. It's past noon. You don't turn on the TV. You don't go to the bathroom. You lie on the side of your face and look at your hand. It's very hot. Your cheek sweats. You think of the car in the driveway. You wonder how much gas is left in the tank, how much cash you have in your purse. It wouldn't be a long drive. If you left now, you could be there by nightfall. You would stand at the front desk and ring the bell and he would come out, expecting another tourist or another businessman coming in for a convention at the bigger hotels, but then he would see you. His face would light up.

You hear a ring. It rings again and again and stops for a few minutes, then rings again. It's not in your head. You look at the phone and then back at your hand.

You're back at that long ivory vanity, your face centered near the bottom of a tall mirror. Late morning, all the late mornings of that first year compressed into one. Start from there. You can see your husband moving toward you in the mirror. You feel his one hand lifting your hair, and then his other hand slipping under the neck of your robe and circling your breast.

Slow it down now. Pay attention.

As his hand parts the robe, keep your eyes steadily on your face. Look carefully. But you don't see it. There's nothing. There's nothing other than some embarrassment, some gratefulness. Not even the emptiness of children waiting to be born. It's that moment you keep going back to, combing, trying to remember how your face looked, the private moments of a woman at her mirror, the face only you yourself have seen— But it's no use. You couldn't have been warned.

The phone rings and rings, but you don't move. You keep looking at your hand until it blurs.

It doesn't matter who's on other end, what news, what fate. It's not the signal. The signal lies somewhere much deeper. It's been calling all this time, tingling, rattling just under your skin. Hold still. Hold absolutely still.

If you move now, if you move just one finger, you'll never stop. You'll never stop.

T.C. HUO

A DEEP BLUSH

I found these pages in the closet of the apartment I had just moved into, in north Berkeley. I had spent half of the summer apartment hunting.

These pages, most likely by a Cal student tormented by his own untested homosexuality, had remained in the closet since 1975. And all this time various tenants, apartment managers or the cleaning crew, either left it there, treating it as something out of sight and out of mind, or had failed to discover it, this unstapled lyric of desire which had turned into a relic. About time for this humble, yellowed, dusty lyric/relic, to come to light. I fetched it from the closet.

But first, as a believer in facts and a skeptic of imagination, as a future practitioner of journalism in the coming century, in other words, as a graduate student in journalism, I must follow my sense of ethic by not adding what the pages themselves lacked; namely, physical descriptions of the speaker himself. I must leave the pleasure of imagination to you.

Take a moment, then, to embellish an Asian American male. Summon his height, weight, torso, physiognomy. Form your picture of Jerry Who, the owner of these lines of tormented passion, and fixate that picture as you follow the destiny of his budding love life. Also imagine—or recall, if you will—the era of sweeping bell-bottoms, spellbinding marijuana, Bee Gees and ABBA, the end of Vietnam War.

Fix the male image in your head, and let's begin.

———

JERRY 1975

I wanted to talk to him and ask him out for dinner tonight. I should be friendly, very friendly. Even before I walked in, my heart had gone erratic, my throat dry. I should have planned what to say and how to say it. Once I caught his eyes across the room. I wished I had the guts to walk up and talk to him, asking him questions the way he asked me questions that Friday afternoon. Now it was my turn to make the move.

My supervisor was doing some paper work at the table next to him. I walked up and began to talk to my supervisor, and as I was talking, I sensed his eyes—I sensed that he had risen his head, aware of my presence in his proximity, but I kept my head down, avoiding his eyes. I kept talking to my supervisor. Only after I returned to my seat did I steal a glance. This time he neither turned around nor raised his head. He would have to be a fool if he didn't know I was staring.

Usually I would leave work as soon as I could. Today I stayed around waiting for a chance to speak to him, ask him out for coffee. A student, a uniformed, four-eyed fifteen year old, sitting on the desk, was talking to him, and he stood by her listening and looking receptive. 4:30. Time to go. She was still talking. I couldn't hear them. The learning center became empty. He seemed to be unaware of my presence (I am a shade, ten feet away from him, imperceptible behind the door): I kept casting glances at him and he all that time had his eyes fixed on that student, listening to her. I fiddled my fingers on the table. Finally conscious that I had no business staying around, I walked away.

My lab partner Karen Kwan and I entered a coffee shop on Telegraph Avenue. As soon as we sat down with a cup of espresso, Karen brushed her long hair with a sweep of her hand and began, "So tell me about your crush." She leaned forward.

I almost blurted out with "his" but caught myself in time and I swallowed the masculine pronoun back down my throat (the "he" got stuck in my throat, "he" caressed my throat). "Her ignoring me doesn't bother me as much now," I said. "At first it was bad. Right after the coffee date she became a stranger."

"And you to her," Karen said.

"Not looking at me, not a glance as if she never knew me."

"Her back against you?"

"One day, there, way ahead of me at the intersection, crossing the street, she turned her head, saw me—just a look—then turned away, kept on walking west."

"She didn't even wave?"

"Not waving a hand. No. And here, forty feet south from the intersection where she was crossing, as I walked I watched her walk away. Forty feet of impossibility, no hope."

"The end." Karen sighed.

"I stop expecting any friendly gestures or signs of interest. I've decided to ignore her—but last Friday—"

———

Last Friday I wore my favorite short-sleeve shirt, pink and soft against my skin. Fridays were game days, and the children gladly gave up their textbooks and pushed away educational games like chess and took to horsing around instead. We Calstudent tutors became mere babysitters. Some of us, Bill being the prime example, took on the role of big brothers and big sisters.

At first I heard Bill's voice and somehow I knew he would come over and talk to me—a matter of approach. First, he joked with the kids at the other end of the table, sitting there like their big brother. At this end of the table, hearing his voice, I looked up. The deeply tanned half-Chinese, half-Hispanic disengaged himself from the kids grouping around him; he stood up and crossed over the bench (watch those brawny thighs, the pair of long legs astride) and sauntered over with a leisurely pace (the male stature) and asked how I was doing: How's school, he asked. Good, I said, not knowing what else to say, not having anything to say to him, and not saying anything else. Just a curt "good." The Cambodian girl—from the first wave of Southeast Asian refugees arriving in California—across from me stopped drawing, raised her head and said, "Your friend's here," idly shaking her pencil. I said he was her teacher and she had better behave and show respect by calling him Mister. He stood there for a few minutes, across from me behind the newcomer girl. I shouldn't have spoken to her in such a severe tone. Not knowing what to say, I looked up again—with a smile?—met his eyes, and for a moment I thought the look meant what I thought it meant. That did it. While he stood there I was surprised at myself that I had nothing to say. Nothing to say to him. He stood for a few minutes and then walked away.

———

"Take care of your feelings first," Karen said.

We had left the coffee shop and now were headed toward the campus.

"Doesn't the eye exchange make you feel the person is interested in you—that look filled with," I let out a deep sigh, "amor?"

"I remember, once, at a bus stop there were this man and a woman. Chic is the word for them, the man in the large bell-bottoms, platforms. He asked me when the bus was coming. I said, in five or ten minutes. When he asked, he smiled gently and looked at me straight in the eyes, very gently."

That would befuddle my head: when someone smiled at you and looked at you, the eyes gentle, like that, it's easy to get confused—that amorous gaze.

"He was with a woman although they didn't act like a couple: her mouth puckered, her look sour, the two were silent. The man asked again, was it sixty-five cents. Seventy-five, I said. Again the friendly smile."

Pedestrians wove past us on the busy sidewalk.

"Suppose I go around smiling the way he did, smiling at strangers, to classmates, professors, to co-workers, just to befuddle their heads."

"You might want to try it out. Smile. A woman appreciates that."

I would fall for his eyes, his gentle gaze, tempted to respond. How misleading. "No doubt he was her boyfriend," I said. Can't trust those eyes.

———

I had on a white shirt with tiny black and blue stripes. I changed into my favorite pair of sweeping bell-bottoms with a silver-buckle leather belt. I left the very last button of my shirt unbuttoned, and, rather than tucking it in, tied the two sides into a bold knot, so my belly button would show. I slipped on the pair of platforms. The sweeping bell-bottoms, the large collar white shirt, my black hair—I looked good. I went to work, humming ABBA's "Dancing Queen." Sweet 17, although I was no longer 17. The sky blue, the lawn green.

The tune of the "Dancing Queen" followed me on the sidewalk I passed a car parked by the curb. With my sunglasses arched on my forehead I checked myself in the car window. It reflected how well matched the jean bell-bottoms and the shirt were, how well they fit together. You can dance, you can dance.

I entered the learning center. As usual, the kids played games this Friday afternoon. They chased each other around the tables, shrieked freely, and burst into sweat. The meeker ones would draw.

Beset by the children, I tried to study chemistry. But my concentration had been pulled loose in shreds because Bill sat three tables away engaged in some activities with a surrounding circle of children, and because by him stood a well-dressed young woman who looked like his natural right hand, a fresh blossom to foil the green leaf that was Bill. He apparently didn't see me. Made no difference whether or not I was around, whether I flowered wide open because of the presence of this green leaf, my man. He must have taken a look at me while I tried to read.

Why suffer? Why not leave? The clock on the wall read 3:40. I had been in the learning center for less than thirty minutes. I turned around at Bill's direction: the circle of children had disbanded and the gallant was now talking to the four-eyed receptionist. In my seat, I knocked my left high heel on the floor. Toc toc toc. Still talking to the receptionist. My left foot turned and knocked again. Toc, toc, toc.

He didn't see me as I put on my sunglasses, didn't turn to look as I got to my feet, the knot in front of my belly button trembling in plain view, didn't even hear the tic toc tic toc as I stomped out. He didn't see how well matched the bell-bottoms and the shirt were, how clean. Didn't see the butterfly knot I'd tied.

"Are you playing games?" my roommate Eric Stone asked as he took a beer from the refrigerator. "I wonder if she has been doing the same thing you do, avoiding you because, let's face it, she's attracted to you." He opened the beer can.

"Avoiding me because she's attracted to me?" He and she could be so tongue-twisting, so hard to say it right.

"Exactly. Women like to play hard to get. The cat-and-mouse game." Eric walked into the living room.

"It seems unlikely," I frowned, pondering on the sofa, "since I had come over to her first and bluntly paid her a compliment that Friday afternoon." If only Eric knew it was the other way around. You're good-looking, Bill said. He who I thought had never noticed me now sat less than two feet away and gazed into my eyes. A man had paid me a compliment. My first.

"To say what you said that day doesn't take much courage, let me tell you. I do it all the time."

I knew straight men and boys did it all the time—to make their move—because the impulse to pay the opposite sex a compliment came so naturally to them. Their heterosexual instinct. A matter of course. I had seen boys—still in middle school, still wet behind the ears—wait for their girls with a bouquet of shy roses or carnations in their hands. It had never occurred to me, even now, in college and on any special occasion, to do such a thing to a boy I liked, to Bill—just as it was not the practice, I supposed, for the girl to win a boy with a gesture of gallantry. Yes, straight males did it all the time, young or old. In every sense of the word: They did it.

"Is this the same Chinese gal?" Eric asked.

"She acted like nothing happened, not letting on that she was flattered."

"Women are shy. Pal, deep down she is flattered. Trust me. Next time, buy her some flowers. That will fix it." Eric gulped down the beer.

It might have been bold of me to call Bill, but I needed to act; otherwise nothing would result from the first encounter. The compliment he gave me would be the beginning and the end. I called him up. Did I talk to you, Bill asked, his voice opaque, indecipherable, aloof. Yes (I could scream into the phone), you came and talked to me, remember? Remember?

"I gaped at the phone with astonishment. I wished I had not called her to ask her out for coffee. So today after I signed out I walked straight to the door and didn't turn around even though she was leaving also."

"Good for you, Jerry." Eric slapped my back with his bear hand. "Act like you didn't see her. Just keep the game going, attracted to each other yet acting nonchalant. That will conquer her. Trust me, pal."

———

"The end. This time it doesn't even hurt," I told Karen on the phone.

"Feeling indifferent, numb?" Karen probed.

"A few weeks ago, her indifference hurt badly."

"Now you begin to do likewise, acting indifferent."

"Now, looking at her: Sure, she looks good, but I don't feel connected to her anymore." Referring to Bill as a "she" got increasingly easier.

"Susie said liking a woman and finding her attractive are two different things."

"You told your sister?" I sat up in bed.

I must have raised my voice because it took Karen a second or two to speak. "I didn't tell her much. She said you are trying to force a physical relation." An increasingly remote prospect now. I listened on, "Women don't go for that. She doesn't even know your name. And because of your attraction to her, getting to know her is hard to do: The attraction stands in the way."

"Your sister should be a psych major," I snorted.

"Now, don't be sarcastic. She simply offered her perspective as a woman."

"Now is the end. Last Wednesday, on my way to sign out, I heard a guy, two other tutors, and she talking about a party. Earlier I saw the guy giving her a piece of paper, which must be, what else, the invitation."

"So they talked about a party."

I signed my name, took a look: Apparently Bill and the girl were absorbed in whatever they were talking about. Heedless of me. Heedless of my platforms. I hesitated: whether to walk around them and leave, not saying hi, or chirp in, throw in a line or two—hey, what party are you talking about. Act casual.

"I walked around them, looking straight ahead, since in any case she wouldn't return the look."

"Even so, you still want to leave a good impression," Karen said.

"Every Monday, Wednesday, and Friday, an expectation is there, something to look forward to."

"Susie wants to know if you're still meticulous about what you wear to work," Karen added.

What did she think? I rolled my eyes toward the ceiling. "Today she didn't look at me although she was close by, so close, as if I were a stranger—"

———

"No no, not that, invisible is more likely," Eric Stone said, standing in the living room, again with a beer can in his hand. "When her sight excludes you, that's the end," Eric said.

"The end? Today, she stood behind me, signing out, leaving at the same time too. She could have left earlier; instead she chose the moment I signed out to sign out." Kneeling on the floor, I leaned over the small table and swept the spellbinding scent toward me, beginning to breathe in slowly.

"Or maybe she didn't plan it: It was time to leave, and she came to sign the time sheet and it did not matter who stood before her or behind her, you just happened to be in front of her," Eric said.

I sucked in some more of the mind-opening smoke. "I wished she had planned it, though. She could have waited until I left. Instead she had to pass me."

On the street I was talking to a fellow tutor. The red light stopped us so that Bill had time enough to catch up. Green light. He passed me, right by the side, looking straight ahead, going his own way.

"Hi, I wanted to say." My voice trailed as the smoky scent took me to the beginning of floating oblivion.

"Did she do it on purpose?"

"She could have avoided me by going a different way, or, better yet, walked slowly so that she wouldn't catch up with me—so, so she could have done it on purpose, just to let me see her, just to treat me like a stranger."

"She enjoys treating you like a stranger, it seems, like she had never seen you, like she's blind to you," Eric said.

The orange glow of the twilight slipped through the slanted white jalousy into the room. This Twilight Visitor, who brought a moment of glory into the room by adorning the walls with the orange imprints of his presence, would leave soon. Even as they appeared on walls and corners, the imprints began to fade. I inhaled the curlicue of oblivion. More than half of the simple, orange patterns on the walls had disappeared. I watched the retreating steps of the Twilight Visitor as I murmured, "She likes to do that, she does." The living room darkened. The Twilight Visitor had left.

———

So, this was the room where the two roommates carried on their conversation, the straight one drinking beer and the gay one smoking pot for the first time perhaps. I glanced around the sparsely furnished living room. By the window I had set the computer I bought in 1994, already inadequate for my use. In 1975, a white jalousy had hung down the window.

I touched the wall. How many times had it been repainted, since 1975, after these two roommates had moved on, or moved out? How many layers of paint? And the floor, they must have stood here, on this very spot. I squatted on my haunches and ran my hand over the floor. Coolness passed through my hand.

Early September, and the days were getting shorter. On this late Sunday afternoon, I watched the revenant shafts of light play in the living room.

———

"What she does is immature," Susie said. "I expect an adult to be cool."

All three of us sat around a table, in the same coffee shop where Karen and I had our first talk. This time Karen showed up with her younger sister, Susie.

"So why force the issue? Why do you let her hurt you? Call it an end." Susie took a bite of the bagel.

How could I? I watched Bill as he passed me. As he walked away, I watched him and thought: He looks good. I said, "I don't understand why she treats me that way."

Karen said, "She can hurt you because you're still hung up on her looks, since she, as an adult, is not that mature—according to Susie." Karen glanced sideways at Susie with a slightly teasing smile.

Susie returned the bagel to the saucer. "Not the way she behaves," Susie puckered her mouth. Her pageboy short hair at this moment gave her a stubborn, willful look.

As if to test her sister's depth of knowledge of the human heart, Karen turned to Susie. "Is she a flake, like what you said she was?"

"A flake. I'm positive."

"Still, you like her looks," Karen eyed me.

His back, broad and powerful. "Her back, broad and powerful—she's a swimmer," I added, and quickly brought the cup of cappuccino to my lips. I took a purposeful sip, my eyes on the mouth of the cup.

"That's the problem with you men. The first thing about a woman you see is her body." Susie threw me a glance full of disapproval. "You should give her time. Go slowly. Get to know her personality first."

"I do know a bit about her personality," I half protested. "The day she saw me she didn't have the friendliness to wave her hand but turned her head away and walked on instead."

"See, in this case, when you find out things about her, you're hurt. If she likes you why does she act that way? And give you the contrary message? This is a lesson for you," Susie said.

"Susie, you're too hard on him," Karen eyed her sister.

"Just trying to help."

I stared deep into the mouth of the cup. "I used to—and still do—act indifferent to the wo(man) I am attracted to. I even avoid her because I inevitably become tense if I get too close: I might lose self-control."

"If her body is not the first thing you see, you won't be anywhere near losing your self-control. Believe me." Susie finished her bagel.

———

"So now you avoid her, you walk away, you pretend not to see her, you stay away from her. You never come close enough to make a conversation possible. You're a great help to yourself, Jerry." From behind the couch, Eric slapped his beer hand on my shoulders as I curled in the couch.

Yet has Bill ever made the effort? It was he who started acting distant by turning away from me. I'd thought of having a talk with him. I would ask him What is the matter? That day, crossing the street, you didn't even say hi. Why? What does he think is the matter with me, the way I continually stare at him—that I want to know. I'll tell him I am attracted to him.

"I've thought about having a talk with her," I said. A pause, then I looked to Eric Stone. "What if she's lesbian?"

"That solves the problem!" Eric threw up his hands. "Then she can tell you what she really thinks of you: Quit the come-on, I'm a dyke."

"Why can't I tell if someone is interested in me or not?" I dug my hands into my hair, elbows on my knees. "What does it mean when she looks at me? She still does."

"That tells you two things. Either she's a dyke, or a flirt."

Few men, I felt like telling Eric, would walk up to a man and say this: You're good-looking. Had Bill not meant it?

"It's a blatant come-on signal," Eric said. "She has the hots for you."

"If so, why did she become distant?" I want to tell Bill: It's embarrassing, staring at you like that, so impolite. . . .

"She's coy. She wants you to look at her, so look at her. It's not offputting, not at all," Eric said.

Bill could be wondering—hence his looking at me?—why I look at him when I should pay attention to my tutees. Certainly it's rude to stare at a stranger. So doesn't he know that I am attracted to him? The fact that I couldn't help looking at him? That if he's a leaf, I will be the flower, and if he's a branch, I will be the leaf, and if I am a tree, he will be the root. "I shouldn't have forgotten myself though, that day we had coffee," I told Eric.

"By smiling too much you forgot yourself? Come on." Eric put on an incredulous expression.

"I was too visibly pleased."

"That repulsed her, all right," Eric grunted.

Was Bill disillusioned? But he really looked at me that day, straight into my eyes as I looked at him, the man with a broad and powerful back. A swimmer's back. He really looked at me. Stared, gazed, if you will.

"Suppose you have a talk with her over a cup of coffee," Eric kept on. "What's the worst thing that can happen? You find out she's a dyke? Congratulations, pal. You're free. And remember to thank her when she tells you she thinks you're a weirdo—that's why she looks at you, because of your weird behavior. She wonders why you stare at her. Now it's the time to act gentlemanly. You kiss her goodbye, like a gentleman. No, no, correction. You shake her hands, man-to-man. You tell her that's the last she'll see of you. And run for your life."

———

Yesterday Bill talked to a tutor, a young Asian man. I wondered if Bill, in a low seductive voice, said to him what he'd said to me: You are handsome.

But when Bill talked to a woman I thought he was straight. Bill would look at a woman the way he looked (used to look?) at me. Enraptured? She lost herself in his gaze and his whole heart poured out for her.

———

"The idea that she likes you seems far-fetched now. If she likes you she wouldn't ignore you. She wouldn't." Susie addressed me in the same coffee shop. She bit into a bagel. The three of us sat by the window facing the sidewalk on an early Saturday afternoon.

"Because you were distant and ambiguous," Karen explained to me.

"That's not it," Susie corrected her sister. "She needed time and he"—eyeing me—"was too desperate."

"She could be uncertain about herself, uncomfortable about expressing her sexuality," Karen said, the psych major.

"That could be it," I said. Bill was probably uncomfortable with his sexuality. The machos had a harder time.

Susie's eyes grew big. "So she fought with herself, she became distant, she pulled away? That's too bad though, too bad for both of you."

"I wish I can cool off so I can help her, ask her what is bothering her, listen to her, be her friend," I said.

"That's more important than just wanting her," Karen leaned forward to pat my hand.

At this point a familiar voice said, "May I join you?" Eric from outside stood by the open window. "Hi, Karen." Karen and Eric had met a few times in my apartment. I introduced Susie to Eric. Eric smiled as he leaned to me across the window and whispered in my ear, "So this is the dyke." I sat straight up and cleared my throat. "Susie is Karen's sister."

Eric pulled a long smile. "Susie, nice to meet you."

"Come join us," Karen grinned and pulled a chair from a table.

And Eric stepped into the coffee shop.

———

I made an appointment with a psychiatrist in school. But unlike Karen and Eric, the psychiatrist was a stranger. How could I tell a stranger—especially a straight man—the most intimate, terrifying details of my life when I couldn't bring myself to tell my friends? Referring to Bill as a "she" always pained me. It weighed on my tongue. This fakeness. Changing the sex of my lover made me anguished, it dragged me through a slow death. I asked to see a female psychiatrist.

In the office, on the therapeutic couch, I realized how infinitely easy and comfortable it was to use the feminine pronoun, to come across as straight. I stammered, "On the other hand, if—" and I almost blurted out with "she" but caught myself in time, "he's out, if he's comfortable with his own sexuality, he'll want to explore." And thus my lover, whose masculine pronoun bore such heavy physical weight, was released from the trap of my throat.

In her chair, the psychiatrist looked stony, seemingly without any intention to lead me on and open me up.

I braced myself. "And he'll discover soon that he's in demand—that's what happens to someone good-looking: People will soon pay attention and compliments to him, ask him out. They are for him to choose: the cute and boyish, the athletic and butch, the dressy and sharp, one date after another." The unresponsiveness of the psychiatrist made me sense the banality of what I said, my senseless, crazed, imbecilic rambling. I might as well be talking to a block of wood.

The next few sessions fared as badly. The psychiatrist still looked wooden and remained professionally indifferent. I could barely squeeze two words out of her. Perhaps the challenge was how much I could tell and how far I would go in the telling. My face growing powdery red, I pushed myself further, "If he's dealing with the issue, then I'll be caught up in it, I'll be hurt, as I am now. He pulls away because the attraction is too dangerous, too maddening. He could be wondering why I keep staring at him all the time. If he's disgusted with me, he didn't have to look at me at all." As I said this, I decided to quit future sessions.

———

"I don't see how you can be so nonchalant," Karen said, again in the coffee shop.

"Outwardly perhaps," I said.

"Susie said you play hard to get."

"Moi?" Campiness could be so provocative. And deliberately, I crossed my legs.

"But you've done your part: You've asked her out."

Bill's turn was long overdue. I didn't respond to the heterosexual Karen.

She pressed on, "Did she look at the time sheet that day after you left? As she signed the time sheet, did she look up your name?"

He? She? I didn't feel like talking.

"Well, did she?"

"That afternoon she stood behind me, not saying a word," I said.

"Susie said the girl thinks you are a freak."

"Karen, do me a favor. Stop talking to your sister about me, OK?"

"I didn't. Eric told her."

"What?"

"They have been going out. On dates."

So, granted by the heaven, approved by the earth, the straights did it again.

———

I ordered a lunch plate. The waiter brought the soup. As I tasted the soup, I felt a shade sliding past. Come join me, I greet this invisible figure, smiling and eyeing him and smiling. This non-person sits down. Keep me company, I say, eyeing him and he eyeing me eyeing him.

I finished the soup. After lunch I would go buy a new brush.

A young Asian man passed the restaurant window. He wore a red blazer. Sweeping jean bell-bottoms. Right height. Even with the pair of platforms. Tic toc tic toc on the sidewalk. Nice soft black hair. He was the kind you would call cute; boyish, that is. He looked good. Bill would have come up and said that to him. Paid him a compliment, looked him in the eyes. *You are good-looking.*

———

Friday again. Past 3:30, the clock on the dashboard indicated. Even if I went in to work I would have little to do other than sit around until I couldn't stand it any longer, and bored, I would leave early. 3:44. Even if I went to work I wouldn't stay long. Plus, I didn't want to be seen—I didn't want him to see my sour face. I was prepared to be seen though: I wore a blue-striped shirt, and a new pair of jean bell-bottoms.

Four o'clock. Thus debating and reaching a futile conclusion—while waiting in the car—I decided to go to the only place that would contain me, my apartment. I started the car.

The cars inched forward. Through the car window I saw someone jogging on the sidewalk, in shorts and a sweat shirt. I honk, smile: Come in. I would open the door for Bill. Rivulets of sweat around his forehead—his heavy breathing. Rivulets of sweat crawl down his body: sweaty arms, sweaty back. Trembling slightly, my hands on his shoulders, standing on tiptoe, I reach up, run my tongue around his temple, along the curve of his ear: salty. Feeling his insubstantial breathing on my neck. His hair brushing against my earlobe.

Once in the apartment, I turned on the record player. *Young man.* Fetched the pair of tight jean shorts. *I say young man.* Put the shorts on. Put on a black shirt. I smiled in the mirror and began to pose. *YMCA. YMCA.* After making a few movements with my hands while rhythmically twisting my waist, I changed into other shirts: a white one, a light green, another two black shirts, the white cowboy jacket. I danced in front of the mirror and smiled and knew I looked good.

Now dancing to the tune of "Disco Duck," I began to feel better.

Disco.

Disco, the duck quacked along.

Disco.

Disco, the duck quacked again.

And the singer and the duck sang together, *Disco, Disco Duck.*

All day today I felt low, disliked myself. Now I felt ready for summer, I wanted to do something wild, like wearing the pair of wanton jean shorts. I wondered what Bill would be doing tonight. My hair made me look good, although I didn't have the kind of brush I wanted. I took off my clothes. I had forgotten to smile. Yes, a smile could truly change my mood. I should smile more often.

TAKE OUT: QUEER WRITING FROM ASIAN PACIFIC AMERICA

PAOLO JAVIER

HEARING FORMS

I like Hakeem. Or anyone
willing to dance at
the drop of a hat. To
saddle up left of center in
a room and wave the
white flag in wake of
East Indian moyennes.
Be game for hip-hop, too
out of the blue toss
rhymes my way by
A Tribe Called Quest.
He's rejoicing when
laughing, roaring frankly
like the oven he feeds
at Earl's on Fir.
His shyness Kevin warned of—
so much for that.

Just now—this minute—
he's come by the bookbin.
Glides inside as if right through
the door I'd fastened.
Slowly sheds jacket off, bag
swaggers to center
clearing away cabinet, chair, desk.
He cut a move—
diminished the room?—no,
à la Carroll's Alice, Hakeem
hit the ceiling. I ought to
give capoeira a try, meet
his friend, he said, a half-Fijian.
Once more, have here—
shift's final hour—
company: His.

Anything goes with Hakeem.
Later we might stop for pizza,
peek into the Bhangra jam
at SOB. If a bust, those snug
orange couches roost
in the lounge. Wednesdays,
Victoria's a DJ in The Pit.
Or the arcade jukebox—
we'll purvey it, rap back
rap lyrics, contend
the form: Us both, almost
sure to call it Poesie.

UNTITLED

Can I be more
curled up than
this? that

can't be—
on your lap as
a baby my
head is a ripening

fruit.
Quiet now—
a morning

seen in your
own still
life.

OCTOBER SNAP

I.

Yellow leaves fall on the sidewalk, so the storeclerk sweeps.
Yellow leaves tumble past my weeds. My landlord emerges yellow

in a gold Camry. Down a camera creek of Mercurys a sleek
Continental glides. Content in a rental, with a panda on his back a

man passes. He makes a pass, pauses, the sun in his mouth. He has
hurt teeth. Off-yellow, fall. Trees leave. The storeclerk weeps.

II.

The Writing on the Wall

'There are no words.'

That's my camisole I wear for sleeping.

Would you like to see your present now, or

later? I don't want to be another story, you

know? You mean you won't wanna hang out before

you go? You're a real prince!

III.

'I miss you, but I
am trying
not to.' Not our miscue

or toes that winter,
our slippers
in the shower.

TAKE OUT: QUEER WRITING FROM ASIAN PACIFIC AMERICA

RICHARD KIAMCO

POWERSHOWGIRL: UNACCESSORIZED

[RICH *as narrator*]
Originally, I'm from the Midwest, born in the cornfields of Illinois.

But I was abducted by Asians. More specifically, overachieving Filipinos. I grew up in the rice paddy doctor dynasty. In the '60s, the United States strip-mined Philippine universities of their academic gold. My parents were the cream of the crop of their schools. The U.S. Government flew them over in exchange for their talents. My parents were 'intellectual mail-order brides.' My father graduated king of engineers, was *Wall Street Journal*'s engineer of the year for Rockwell International. My mother, a doctor by age 21, was an international award-winning medical phenomenon. And there I was, in kindergarten, with the weight of their histories on my shoulders...(*sighs*).

I grew up thinking *Gray's Anatomy* was a coloring book. My kitchen counter: (*panning*) toaster, rice cooker, blood pressure machine. For Thanksgiving dessert, while the neighbors had pumpkin pie, we had flu vaccines.

Birthdays, American girls had the add-a-pearl necklace. Each birthday they get another pearl to add. We had the add-a-product doctor's bag.

First year—bandages. Second year—stethoscope. I was the only third grader with malpractice insurance. Embrace the agenda.

―――――

At third grade, my father said to me,
DAD (*with Pinoy accent*):
It is not enough to get perfect grades. In order to be an attractib candidate por medical school, you must be "well-rounded," diversified in your skills.
[RICH *as narrator*]
He sent me to a special summer camp.
"Carpenters Camp…"
Bob Villa for toddlers.
Our final project was to build a dwelling that we would sleep in. While the other boys were building caves and the castles,
I was busy building a kitchen with a breakfast nook.

S'mores, boys? Mmmmm, yummy.
By sixth grade, my father said,

DAD *(with Pinoy accent)*:
It is not enough to have skills from de classroom. You must go out and apply it in de field.
[RICH as narrator]
So, for my sixth-grade summer, my parents bought a fire-damaged house on the other side of town—burned on the inside but still standing. We rebuilt it. I spent my entire sixth-grade summer rebuilding this house. Well, actually, part of vacation was spent looking at colleges and studying for the SAT…. I'm eleven years old and I'm studying trigonometry!

––––––––

Here I am, in the one-acre lot of the charcoal bungalow with grass as tall as I am, a weed eater and a surgical mask from my doctor's bag.
Buzzz buzzz buzzz *(cutting weeds)* and there's this boy, Mike, from school, riding by on his bike…he invites me over to his house to play. *(put down the weed eater, tear surgical mask off and throw back at charcoal bungalow, run around the corner to his house)* And Mike is playing basketball, watching TV and eating junk food.
MIKE:
You wanna twinkie?
RICH:
Um. *(pause)* No, thank you. Mom says that Americans have poor diets.
MIKE:
Oh. OK…*(eats twinkie)*
RICH:
I have to go now.

I come back and I tell my mom.
RICH:
Mommy! I met this boy, Mike, from school, and he was playing basketball and…
MOM *(with Pinoy accent)*:
Do you know why, Reechard? Because Americans are lazy! They have poor diets, they watch telebision, and they have low aptitude in the math and the sciences.
That is foolishness. Be carepul of that! SSSSSST—oy!

RICH:
I never understood what that "SSSSSST—oy!" thing meant. I mean what am I?
SSSSSST—oy *(panting)*
I'll be a good boy, ARF!
I'll get good grades, ARF!

I'll go to med school, ARF!

I'll squash my soul, destroy my self-esteem only to regain it after thousands of dollars of therapy as an adult...ARF! Embrace the agenda!

[*RICH as narrator*]

We did have some vacations where we actually went somewhere interesting—other than Northwestern University or Yale. The Wisconsin Dells, about 2 hours north of Chicago—canyons, rivers, ducks...but it wasn't enough for my dad to just get there on time. It had to be an "educational experience." We had to get on the expressway...

DAD *(with Pinoy accent)*:

"Find a semi-truck, place the car in de slipstream behind the semitruck, the sweetest spot ob lowest air resistance..."

RICH:

And I'm in the back seat with notebook and pencil calculating the 'mechanical adbantage.' Dad checks my work. (*yells out the car window*) "SAVE ME! I'm 11 years old!! (*looks at view*) I wanna watch ducks!"

Meanwhile, I was struggling with my own sexual tension. Back at age four, in the basement, the Sears repairman was fixing the freezer.

————

RICH:

HI! I'm four, but I'm an overachiever in all fields!

I run upstairs to get root beer (*turns*) because root beer is for special occasions only.

I have my own personal stash hidden in the library behind the books. (*Comes down the stairs*)

"These are my white seersucker pajamas with pink-n-blue building blocks with bears with balloons...elastic waist with snap crotch. Thirsty??"

(*Hands bottle over*)

You're welcome.

(*Twisting elastic waistband in finger*)

My Bugs Bunny alarm clock is broken, can you fix it?

It's in my bedroom...

[*RICH as narrator*]

It didn't work out, though.

He couldn't handle me being on top.

I grew up to be the kid you all hated in high school. The super-mega-maxi-overachiever.

I aced every class. I was on every third page of the yearbook. Student Council President, editor in chief of the newspaper, editor in chief of the yearbook, peer counselor, spelling bee champ, dance troupe captain—surprise—(*pose*) flag corps captain (*twirling*) sticks with scarves! Don't mess with me FFFFFFT, rifles! (*Release imaginary rifle into the air, spin, and catch*) Butch and femme, yeah! (*pause*)

OK, I admit it. I was on the math team. Champion Mathelete...got first place in region- als geometry, competing in the oral and written categories for 'convexity theorems.'

I beat every valedictorian in my state. Eat me. (*Blowing nails, rubbing on chest*) No pocket shield—RAW!

I was a nerd, I was a brain, *but* I dressed cool. I designed all my outfits.

Passed home-ec class with flaming colors.

And I dressed all the homecoming queens,

(*Aside to the audience*) The girls, bitch. It was Illinois, not NYC...

I was in that rebel without a cause, trendy without taste, Duran Duran period.

(*Easing into poses*) Slouchy suede boots , leather jeans, with double-wrap belt with ammu- nition and a gun holster, (*drawing gun pose*) Fffffpt! Pow!

Ffffftmppow! Powerblouse with a cowl neck, four-inch shoulder pads on my shoulders and arms, 'cause why stop there? Blue hair, crimped and spiked, with scars shaved into my head randomly, not symmetrically—"I didn't want to look mainstream" Eyebrow & eyeliner makeup—kabuki wannabe—

But NO EARRING...

I didn't want people to think I was femme. (*Sigh, pose*)

All decked out for school in the morning, and Dad would just gawk—

DAD:

What are you doing? W–What is dis?

RICH:

Dad, it's trendy! Very eighties, androgyny? It's big in Europe!

DAD:

What part?

[*RICH as narrator*]

I come out to them and they're totally shocked. Hello? Did you miss the last decade? Did you miss the whole (*Click, click, pose pose, gun holster bullets pow! shoulder pad pose blue hair crimped pose Boink hair kabuki eye pose...A Chorus Line dance combination- singing*) "One! singular sensation..."

(*Freeze in classic top hat jazz hip pose...*)

(*Shrug*) They did.

So, I talk to them.

_____

RICH:

Do you love me? I've always been a good boy. And I don't want to start lying to you. (*Pause, deep breath*) I'm a homosexual.

Mom bursts into tears, dad blacks out

I kicked the slant out of both of their eyes (*Kick*) BONK!

Dad comes out of his coma,

DAD (*Crying*):

We love you. We'll always love you, no matter what. (*Hugs RICH*)

We'll cure you. I have a baseball bat and glove in de garage. I'll go get them.

MOM:

Reechard, this is your favorite rice candy buud, buud EAT THIS,

and this is the bible, READ THIS! I will pray for you.

_____

[*RICH as narrator*]

Mom lit enough candles to start global warming.

So I agreed to go to family therapy. Their agenda was to fix me, my agenda was to get a blow job.

DAD:

Reechard, dis Saturday morning, we will do welding in de basement.

No more carpentry! Too much decorating with carpentry...PSSST—oy!

[*RICH as narrator*]

I'm down in the basement and I've got the shield, the torch and the toolbelt.

(*Realization, singing*) Y-M-C-Gay! What did dad know?

DAD:

We want you to STOP theatre. STOP dancing and singing...No more *Chorus Line*! STOP sewing. And STOP doing (*pause*) dat thing, you do…!

RICH:

What thing?

DAD:

You know! Dat thing you do…(*Cryptic*) with your eyes...

RICH:

(*Pause, thinks*) Oh you mean—(*Eye thing, sighs*)

DAD:

We want you to join de football team and de wrestling team.

RICH:

Uh, Dad, that's not a cure, that's foreplay.

(*To audience*) Imagine me on the football field? Or on a wrestling mat?

REFEREE:

(*Whistle*) TWEET TWEET!! Illegal hold!

RICH:

But I'm still scoring! Mmmmmm, touchdown, endzone. Jazz hip, twenty-yard line.

[*RICH as narrator*]

I came flying out of the closet. (*Fosse moves*) 6,7, 8..

Not only am I gay, I'm *not* going to Med school.

(*Kung Fu kick, sensei accent*) Ooooh you dishonor your family! Prepare to die! (*Kung Fu knife arm moves*) Ohhh...Suddenly, my parents became Japanese. (*Shrug*)

DAD:

You can be gay but you must become a doctor, so dat people will not know dat you are...dat way. Some people are known as 'Jimmy de Greek,' I will not have my son be know as 'Rich de Gay.'

[*RICH as narrator*]

[*One week later*]

[*TV announcer voice*] welcome to TEENAGE, "Chicago's number one television talk-show...tonight's special guest, RICH KIAMCO, GAY TEEN."

(*RICH waves, mouthing "Hi Mom...Hi Dad." Pause, eye thing, sighs.*)

R. SKY KOGACHI
WRIST

A loose wrist is a weak wrist and my wrist is the weakest joint in my body. During certain occasions my wrist has predictably gone flimsy. At a bar or a club, I may suddenly lose all motor control of my wrists, leaving my hands to flail about with every gesture of my arms. The time I spend on the sales floor in a clothing store is proportional to lost wrist control. And especially when socializing with others suffering from the same, it becomes a contagious disease.

We frequently gather as a makeshift support group at a local café to reassure ourselves that our problem is common, shared and bearable. It is a dangerous group to sit with. Rather than helping each other learn to control our wrists, we encourage each other to let wrists be as loose as possible. After the night really gets going, the flying wrists become so outrageous, we are slapping each other—sometimes playfully, sometimes painfully. But being slapped by someone with the same problem is infinitely better than being slapped by anyone else.

I have struggled at times to keep control over my wrists. I concentrate so much on this effort that they simply become painful to move. This does just the opposite, effectively locking my hands in place, parallel with my forearm. My movements look robotic as I struggle with everyday tasks such as speaking with hand gestures, typing or grasping things such as dreams. Daily life becomes a painful struggle.

It is difficult to strike a balance between these two states.

At times when it is neither painful nor flimsy, it functions normally without any reminder or forewarning to the problem. They are wrists like any other. They look like any other, although much thinner than normal, if there is such a thing as a normal-sized wrist. So thin are they that the slightest cut may mean cutting off my hands entirely.

To cut these wrists is to cut off the problem. The loss of control, the pain. When I was younger, I wanted that so much. How much better I thought my life would be without these wrists. But these wrists are mine and I now hold them up to the world. Limp or locked, they provide me with nothing more than opportunities to be who I am.

TAKE OUT: QUEER WRITING FROM ASIAN PACIFIC AMERICA

LARISSA LAI

THE SALT FISH GIRL
(AN EXCERPT FROM *SALT FISH*, A NOVEL-IN-PROGRESS)

When I was fifteen and still many years from marriage, I fell in love with a girl from the coast. She was the daughter of a dry goods merchant who specialized primarily in salt fish. It was, in fact, her father's trade that brought her to my attention. She stank of that putrid, but nonetheless enticing, smell that all good South Chinese children are weaned on, its flavour being the first to replace that of mother's milk. They feed it to us in a milk-coloured rice gruel, lumpier than the real thing and spiked up good with salt for strength.

You might say saltiness is the source of our tension. Stinky saltiness, nothing like mother's milk. The scent calls all kinds of complicated tensions having to do with love and resentment, the passive-aggressive push-pull emotions of a loving mother who nonetheless eventually wants her breasts to herself, not to be forever on tap to the mewl-ing, sucking creatures that come so strangely from her body and take over her life. Especially knowing from keen observation of her mother before her, that we eventually grow too monstrously huge for the memory of our births, and that we will eventually leave. Why give away too much of yourself, especially intimate bodily fluids, when you know you'll eventually be abandoned, with or without gratitude depending on luck. Give 'em salt fish congee early and you'll forget about 'em sooner and vice versa.

That's the problem with girls. They leave. You can't rely on them. Of course, in these modern times of difficulty and poverty, you can't rely on boys either. Who knows if or when their overseas uncles will call for them, change their names, call them "son" instead of "nephew," and leave you in the dirt. The red earth, I mean, that's the classical term, isn't it, so bloody and morbid, those old sages. So my mother started me on salt fish congee early. Who could blame her? She was never the type meant for motherhood. If it weren't expected of her, if she had had other options, she'd have been an empress or a poet or a martyr. Something grand, and perhaps a bit tragic. She loved those old sages, with their subtle cleverness and sad girl stories. But leave those to me. I didn't ask for them mind you, I'm as much a puppet of fate as anyone else.

———

I noticed the salt fish girl on market day. My mother had bribed me with a promise of sweet sesame pudding to do the shopping. Trying to make up for lost time, I guess. But why bother offering me sweet now, when it's salt I'm hooked on. She thought she could

117

change me, but it was a bit late for that. Besides, while the sticky pot may be a great place for drowning spirits, its dark thickness doesn't entice. Perhaps later, when I've learned to love my dark self, thick and heavy, but sweet as sugar in spite of everything. Until then, it's stinky salt fish I'm after.

I went to the market more because I wanted to get out of the house than because sesame pudding does anything for me. Little did I know that my mother's intentions behind the black sesame pudding had nothing to do with making up for any neurotic, return-to-infancy, childhood-deprivation fantasies on my part. That she had something infinitely more immediate and material in mind.

I'm not saying that my take on the matter was entirely fabricated, mind you. My mother was thinking about abandonment. She wanted me out of the house that day so she could invite nosy Old Lady Liu the go-between over to talk behind my back about matters matrimonial. I know some girls are betrothed at ages much more tender than mine, but still! I was only fifteen. Wouldn't there be plenty of time for that later?! Talk about morbid, self-fulfilling fantasies! Oh sure, I know it's tradition. I know my mother isn't personally to blame, that she was just doing what all good mothers are supposed to do if they want their daughters to live respectable lives. Note I didn't say happy. We all know that joy and sorrow are entirely matters of fate and have nothing whatsoever to do with planning.

So she had only my welfare in mind, but did she have to start so early? It was a cruel trick of patriarchy to make her the agent of our separation which she so dreaded. Dreaded and longed for, just to have it over with. It was a complicated black sesame pudding she stirred up that afternoon.

As for me, I went to the market with my baby brother strapped to my back and a belly clamouring for something savory.

As we approached the market, a young woman turned the corner down a dark alley, one strong brown arm bracing a basket of salted dainties atop her lovely head. The scent of the fish, or perhaps her scent, or more likely still, some heady combination of the two, wafted under my nose and caused a warmth to spread in the pit of my belly. I followed her right to the entrance of the market, ignoring the rice-wrap and sweet potato seller whose wares I otherwise would have paused to ponder over.

I followed her right to the salt fish stall that she ran with her father. She set the basket down among numerous others filled with tiny blue-veined fish so small it would take twenty to make a modest mouthful, and others filled with long dry flats of deep ocean fish the length of my forearm and half again. I bought enough to flavour a good-sized vat of congee and then breathed deeply to still my mind for the rest of the shopping.

After that I was hooked. The recollection of her bright eyes and lean muscular arms reeled me in as surely as any live fish seduced by worms, or perhaps more accurately by shreds the flesh of their own kind. I made it my job to do the family's marketing in spite of the fact that it fell on top of all my regular chores, of which there were many—fetching water, feeding the chickens, sweeping the courtyard, taking care of my baby brother and chopping all the meat and vegetables for every meal. I was frugal, had an eye for fresh goods, and was a good bargainer, so my mother was happy to send me. Besides, my Saturday morning absences were a perfect time for the go-between to visit.

So while my mother secretly sweetened-up that meddling old nanny-goat, I managed to see the salt fish girl once a week, except when she went back to the Coast with her father for more supplies. At first she took little notice of me—just another skinny village girl with bad skin and bony fingers. She sold me my fish without a word beyond the few necessary numbers and then turned to the impatient aunties eager to get home for their morning congee.

Whether it was because I was such a staunch regular, or whether it was because of the way I gazed at her above the smelly baskets over which black flies hovered and dirty hands exchanged coins, I don't know, but she began to recognize me and put aside choice bits of merchandise in anticipation of my arrival. As she passed me the pungent preserves and took my coins, she stole a quick glance or two and flashed a shy smile through which her crooked teeth peeked endearingly.

A number of months passed in this manner before I worked up the gall to invite her to come with me when market day was over. Of course I would catch a scolding for shirking my days duties when I got home, but the adventure would be well worth the bother. In the late afternoon, we walked down to the river together, lay down in the tall grass and played tickling games until the stars sprinkled down from the night sky and covered us like bright, hungry kisses.

Then we separated. I walked home reeking of salt fish, took my anxious mother's scolding with a brave and defiant face, went to bed and tumbled into a deep and contented slumber.

The following week, I announced my decision to become a spinster. Tradition allows this, if the family is agreeable and there is no protest from the local magistrate. My mother was furious. The go-between had found a suitable husband for me in the neighbouring village. He was the youngest son of a silk farmer, which was a common but respectable trade in these parts. He was blind in one eye, and ugly as sin. He was the only one of his brothers who had been sent to school and rumour had it that his father wanted to find him a position with the government. My mother had been making arrangements for us to meet that week.

"Forget it," I said. "I've got arrangements of my own."

"I never raised you to be so cheeky, I'm sure," she said.

"True. But aren't you glad I'll be here with you when you grow old, rather than scrubbing undies for my mother-in-law?"

I showed her all the money I had saved spinning silk for other village families, and announced that I would pay for my spinsterhood ceremony myself. I refused to eat until she acquiesced to my will.

It was harder for the salt fish girl. No spinsterhood tradition was observed on the coast and her father was dead set against her picking up the nasty customs of the locals. He forbade her to see me.

I hadn't expected this little difficulty. I had assumed she would follow my example. I hadn't asked myself what I would do if she wasn't able to. Did I still want to enter the sisterhood on my own? It is hard to retract such a grave decision as I had made without losing clout to make further autonomous decisions regarding one's life. Worse still, some of my sisters were upset with me for choosing spinsterhood for less than spiritual reasons. I sat tight and continued to see it through even as I plotted how to rescue the salt fish girl.

———

Her father could not stop me from coming to the market. I continued to buy fish from her until one afternoon, in a fury, he closed his stand early and marched her to the mud hut on the edge of the market district which was their home when they were doing trade in town.

Desperation made me bold. I went to his stall the following market day, hoping to see her. I didn't, but the pungent odour of salt fish inspired a plan. Pumped full of fool's courage, I went up to him.

"Where is your daughter?"

"Thank you for your concern, but if you don't mind my saying, it's none of your business."

"That may or may not be the case," I said, more boldly still, "but won't you tell me anyway?"

"She's sick at home, no thanks to you."

"Then tell her I wish from the depths of my heart that she would get well soon and come to see me," I responded politely.

If there had been fewer people standing around watching, he would have reached out and slugged me. I could read the restraint in his eyes. As it was, he refused to sell me any salt fish, but pointed me in the direction of the butcher instead and said perhaps the man with the bloody apron could do something for me.

I thought to stay and argue, but decided I'd better back off for the time being.

The next market day, I passed by his house just as he was leaving. I heard his daughter pleading with him to be allowed out, to be taken along to the market. He refused sternly and locked her in the back room where she wailed loudly long after he was beyond earshot.

An hour later, I approached him at his stall.

"Where is your daughter on this auspicious market day?"

"She's at home with a fever, no thanks to you."

"Tell her I am praying to the Goddess of Mercy for her health and hope that she will come and see me soon."

He grunted.

I tried to buy some fish, but he said I didn't deserve it and would find what I deserved at the execution grounds on the other side of town. I would have spat at him, but there were too many people watching.

The following market day, when I approached him, he lunged at me in sheer fury, grabbed me around the neck and squeezed as hard as he could. I choked desperately. It took five big men, including the bloody-aproned butcher, to pull him off me. The first thing I could smell when I could breathe again was salt fish. The stink of it made me want to live more than ever.

I walked around the marketplace at a furious pace, contemplating. The sky grew dark and the vendors one by one began to close their stalls. My stomach started to grumble. I hadn't eaten since early that morning. I circled the market place looking for a cooked food vendor, but they had all packed up and gone home. The poultry man was busy with his fowl. He had three unsold chickens which he was trying to pack into the same basket, but they squawked and pecked at each other, as though each was to blame for her sister's unhappy fate. Suddenly the basket burst and the chickens ran about clucking madly. One ran farther afield than the rest. On an impulse I took off after it. The poultry vendor, in a hurry to get home, yelled after me, "If you can catch it, it's yours." The chicken led me right to the salt fish girl's back window, where I pounced on it and clutched it, squawking, in my arms.

She leaned out the window dangling a heavy fish hook. Expertly, she hooked me by the scruff of my collar and pulled me, chicken and all, into the house. "You could try to be a little more subtle," she said.

The chicken kept squawking. She drew a fish gutting knife from her skirt and solemnly slit its throat. Blood spurted up in a long arc, and drenched me in a dark shower.

In the downpour I hatched a plan. "Pack a bag," I said. "We're going to escape."

She gave me a mop and some clean clothes. I sopped the blood up quickly, put on the clean clothes and helped her out the window. With the chicken in one hand and the bloody clothes in the other, I jumped out after her.

We dug a shallow hole in the backyard, buried the bloody clothes and then ran to the river. There, we stole a skiff and floated downstream.

————

In the morning, finding his daughter missing, the old merchant ran to the police and accused me of kidnapping. The police searched my parents' house and found nothing. They said I had not come home since setting out for market the previous day. Eventually, questioning led the police to the bloody-aproned butcher and the other four men who had dragged the salt fish merchant off me the day before.

"Perhaps," said the butcher, "he's accusing the girl to conceal something terrible he's done to her. Surely it's at least worth searching his house."

The police made a careful search of the merchant's house and found nothing but baskets and baskets of sweet and pungent salt fish. The merchant shot a scornful look to the butcher, who stood in the doorway. The police were just about to call off the search for the day, when the youngest of them noticed some newly turned soil behind the house. As I had hoped, the bloody clothes were unearthed and identified by both my parents and the butcher as mine. The poor old salt fish merchant stood accused of murder.

Many miles downstream, munching on boiled chicken, I chuckled at the thought.

The salt fish girl asked me why I was laughing and so I told her. But instead of laughing with me, she pulled a long face.

"What's wrong?" I asked.

"I don't want my father to die," she whispered, and began to cry.

It's a bit late for that, I thought. You should have said so a long time ago. But I said nothing and put my arms around her. I could feel her heart pounding inside her ribcage. She sobbed and howled so desperately that I said, "We could go back. We'd still be in time to save him."

But she shook her head through her tears. "What's done is done," she said. "What happens is what's meant to be."

I held her and said nothing. She continued to weep and eventually sobbed herself to sleep.

And that, I suppose, was the beginning of our quarrels.

FISH BONES
(AN EXCERPT FROM *SALT FISH*, A NOVEL-IN-PROGRESS)

After my supposed murder by the salt fish merchant, my mother grew morose and melancholy. I was her favourite daughter. She had never much cared for my brother, in spite of the fact that he was her only son. For, you see, he was not a child of her womb, but of a concubine whom my father took ten years after I was born, just as my mother's eyes were beginning to show their first dark shadows, her hair, its first pale strands.

It was a good time for silk, and my father's business, like that of many of his neighbours, was booming. At ten years of age, I already played a big part in the family business. My small, nimble hands were of the type deemed perfect for the work of unravelling cocoons. We were not so well off that we could easily afford a concubine, but my father was something of a braggart, always wanting more than his neighbours, always wanting to prove himself superior. He also often made a fool of himself. In drinking games, he would often drink to excess trying to prove how well he could hold his liquor. In gambling games, he took risks beyond the call of common sense, because he never wanted to seem to be losing. Had he been any other man, he would have landed us in the poor house before we even had a chance, but my father was blessed with incredible reserves of luck, and as a result, never came to any serious harm, regardless of the extent of his foolhardiness.

But this is a fairy tale, and of course, he was a kind man, my father, and generous. I only want you to understand what his flaws were so that you will understand later why things turned out as they did.

So at the end of particularly good season, having sold reels and reels of well-spun silk to the foreigners at a good price, he had enough money in his pockets to buy a concubine. A wiser man would have put the money away for harder times to come, but my father was not a wise man.

He took the money and asked my mother to buy him a concubine. He looked her right in the eye. Perhaps he noticed the wrinkles beginning to form around it, perhaps he noticed the dark melancholy shadow beneath, perhaps he did not. He asked her and she did not flinch or weep or accuse. She took the money and went to the city. She came back with a beautiful young girl, fourteen years old, fair as the full moon and so slender her body seemed to sway in the wind like the bamboo that made a green, living fence around the perimeter of the village.

She also came back with a story about how people in the city were coming down with a terrible coughing disease where pieces of lung were known to have sometimes come up in the phlegm. "Bad city air," said my mother, "nothing to worry about."

The girl's name was Heavenly Peace, but she was so lovely we just called her Heavenly for short. My mother was always gracious and kind to her. If she felt the weight of her own years or the slightest twinge of jealousy, she never said so, but treated Heavenly with the kind of benevolent indifference that tradition required of a well-mannered First Wife.

When Heavenly became pregnant, my mother graciously congratulated her. If she felt a little tightening around her heart, she mentioned it to no one, although she did switch to a more expensive face powder that came all the way from the barbaric lands of the foreign devils who had set up shop in the city. Her mother, retired from her professional life as a village midwife and living with her son, sent it to her at her request. And if, in the meantime, Heavenly started to look a little more pale than normal, if her constitution seemed a little weaker than it had been when she arrived, my mother was not going to be so ungracious as to mention it.

My father, being a foolish man, spent more time than ever with Heavenly. Perhaps he did pay my mother less attention than he had before. I still believe he loved her deeply, but she would not have been amiss to doubt it.

Heavenly went into the labour in the middle of a typhoon. The bamboo growing around the perimeter of the village swayed wildly in the wind, whistling the whole time. The chickens clucked and fussed in the henhouse. Our roof shook. Heavenly and my mother began setting out buckets in the front yard to catch the rain and that was when the cramps started. There would be no fetching the village mid-wife that night. Fortunately, my mother had assisted her mother enough as a child that she knew what to do. She chased everyone but me out of Heavenly's room and sent my sister to boil water. Heavenly shrieked and screamed and coughed. She was not yet fifteen years old and her thin body was less suited to this purpose than it might have been later. I, personally, was terrified. I had never seen so much blood in my life. My mother remained calm and cool throughout the whole thing. She instructed Heavenly to breathe deeply and eased a screaming red thing from between Heavenly's legs. The moment my brother had fully emerged, Heavenly closed her eyes and fell back. My mother's nose twitched as though with a suppressed sneeze. "It's a girl!" she shouted, uncertainly at first, and then again, clearly, "It's a girl!"

What brought my mother to utter such a lie, I can only imagine. My mother was not an unkind or vindictive person. It must have been an impulse, perhaps one that she regretted later, who is to say if she won't?

When Heavenly woke and asked to hold the baby, my mother passed him over. But the moment Heavenly received him in her arms, she began to cough. At first, my mother thought it was nothing, but then Heavenly coughed louder and more deeply. She coughed and then she couldn't stop coughing. Up from the very bottom of her lungs she horked the thickest, greenest, foulest-smelling phlegm. My mother snatched the baby back. "You're tubercular," she said. "Safer to bring baby up on formula."

Heavenly died the following spring, two weeks after her fifteenth birthday.

———

My father figured out my mother's charade soon enough. He did nothing to put an end to it, but rather humoured her, and the child too, who saw nothing amiss. But I knew that he was a brother and not a sister. I had seen the little knob he had where I had none, and I knew what that meant, at least in the reductive way that children understand what gender is. I knew also that I was not to speak about it, and so I didn't.

That's why I say my father must have really loved my mother. Her charade clearly went against his personal interests. All men in those days wanted at least one son, and it didn't matter who gave it to him. If he wanted her son and was willing to wait, and willing to take the chance that there would be none, he must have really loved her.

They got along much better after Heavenly died. My father gambled and drank less, according to my mother's wishes. Our silk business prospered, and my brother, in his frilly dresses, grew into a sweet little girl.

After a time, my father came down with the terrible lung disease that was decimating children and old people and the occasional able-bodied man or woman with a ferocity that defied reason. When the day of my supposed murder by the salt fish merchant arrived, it was more than his weakened system could take.

———

My brother was still a young child the year of my self-orchestrated murder. He had a slight build and wonderfully fair, pale skin like his mother. I remember people pinching his cheeks and commenting on it when we went to the market together. It always made me furious, being of the dark-skinned persuasion myself. If they didn't think he was a girl, I might not have felt the nip of competition keenly as I did, but my knowing he was a fake made their compliments all the more maddening.

After I was gone, my brother took over many of my chores. Not the marketing—he was still too young for that. But he began to feed the chickens and chop vegetables and carry water.

One day shortly after his thirteenth birthday, he went to the river for water. He dipped his buckets in, one after the other. As he was hooking them to his pole, he saw a flash of red out of the corner of his eye. When he looked more closely he saw a little fish with red fins and golden eyes not more than two inches long staring up at him from the bottom of one of the buckets. He took it home and dropped it into the fish pond by the entrance to his alleyway, and took the water into the house where our middle sister stood beside the stove chopping vegetables. She gave him a bowl of rice and told him to eat quickly and then go cut firewood. He ate half the bowl and stuffed the rest into his pockets. On his way to the woodpile, he stopped by the pond and sprinkled the rice on the spot where he had left the fish.

And so the days passed. My brother shared all of his meagre meals with the pretty fish and worked harder and grew thinner and paler than ever. In contrast, the fish got bigger and bigger. Its fins grew longer and redder. Its eyes grew more golden and bright. When my brother was sad, he would go the the side of the pond and call to the fish, and the fish would come to the bank and gaze at him from just beneath the water with its brilliant golden eyes.

If my mother watched him sometimes, she never let on. My brother looked so much like the dead concubine it was hard for my mother to truly love him as her own. Perhaps she felt odd about continuing to dress him in girls' clothes, especially now that her husband was dead and there was no chance of another male heir. But she continued the charade, perhaps out of spite, perhaps out of habit. Besides, she and my brother were hardly close enough to talk freely about such intimate matters. And he looked so much like the concubine. But sometimes when she looked at my brother from a certain angle or in a certain mood, it seemed as though my father were peering out at her from behind the veil of Heavenly's face. Then my mother would grow melancholy and reproachful, or else she would fly into a fury of frustration at having lost her husband so early, because of another woman who didn't even want him for herself, but rather as carrion for death.

It was a strange relationship that developed between them. When he looked to her for love and affection, as a needy child will, she could not bear the sight of him. But when he was not conscious of her gaze, her eyes followed him like a greedy dog, jealously watching the concubine and waiting for my father's ghost to show itself in the child's mouth or eyebrows.

This was how she first noticed the fish. My brother often dawdled at the pond after finishing his day's chores, and there he would lose himself in the fish's golden eyes as he poured out his loneliness and confusion. It was those moments when our father's genes seemed to manifest most fully. Through my brother's eyes the old man seemed to gaze out with a sad kind of longing that my mother found particularly heart-wrenching. When she realized the object of that gaze was not her but some weird little fish, it was all she could do not to weep with jealousy and longing. She shook with emotion in her little hiding place in the mulberry hedge from which she had taken to spying on my brother. All those years of carefully practiced grace had finally gotten the better of her, and now jealousy and discontent leaked from her soul like a slow poison. To make matters worse, she had an ulcer.

One day when my brother was out cutting firewood, my mother went to the spot beside the pond where he usually waited for the fish. She sprinkled a little rice into the water. The fish didn't come. She tried this on a number of occasions without any luck.

Determined to outdo the little fish, my mother went to the market. She bought yards and yards of Indian cotton, the kind of stuff of which the British were so fond. Out came the scissors, the brightly coloured threads, and needles sharp enough to poke your eye out. My mother cut and sewed, snipped and tucked, darted and hemmed until she held in her hands a perfect little Victorian maiden's dress with all her anxiety and strange wishes sewn neatly and mercilessly into the seams.

Well! My brother was so shocked he nearly fell down when she gave it to him. "If you're going to be a girl, you may as well be well-dressed," said my mother. My brother, who had secret penchant for things Western, shimmied out of his pants and his high-collared blouse and put the thing on. He sashayed to the well for water.

As soon as he was gone, my mother snatched up his old clothes and donned them herself. She went to the pond and called to the fish as she had seen my brother do. The fish came to the surface. It was more than three feet long and its bright scales shimmered under the water. It looked up at her with intelligent eyes. My mother drew a needle sharp lance from behind her back and speared the fish through the belly with a single thrust. She tossed it up onto the bank where it fell with a splat! The fish was dead.

She trussed it up and nonchalantly threw it over her shoulder. She took it to my sister and asked her to steam it. Such a heavenly aroma wafted out of the kitchen half an hour later. My sister was an excellent cook.

On his way back from the well, my brother stopped by the pond to show his dress to the little fish. He stood beside the pond and called to her. He called and called until his voice grew hoarse and a little deeper than usual. He called and he waited until my sister came looking for him. "Time to eat," she said. "Fish."

A look of horror flooded over my brother's face.

My sister had set the table neatly, with lots of little vegetable dishes surrounding the big central platter. In the platter lay the fish, in a puddle of soy sauce and steaming juices, its eyes cooked white and its little body sprinkled decoratively with shredded ginger, green onions and dried banana flowers. My brother burst into girlish tears.

"What's wrong?" said my mother. "You sick?"

"Where did you get the fish?" said my brother.

"Found it in the pond. Wasn't doing us any good in there so I caught it and took it home. You like fish don't you?"

My brother began to wail again and would not stop until long after my mother and sister had devoured the fish, claimed it dense and succulent, cleaned up, and gone to bed. When the moon rose full and white, he tumbled into a troubled sleep and began to dream.

In the dream, he saw the fish again, wavering under water. "Take my bones and polish them," said the fish, "Hide them. Whenever you want something, all you need to do is ask."

My brother was not particularly superstitious by nature. He woke to the crow of the noisy rooster more angry than sad. In the night, his feelings toward my mother had turned from apologetic inadequacy to the fury of injustice. "No more Mr. Meek and Mild," he swore, "from now on I must defend myself." He polished the bones and hid them behind a loose brick in the wall. He turned his mind inward and began to plot his revenge.

Once, while he was out feeding the chickens, on the other side of the wall in which he bones were hidden, he found himself craving sweets. My brother had a sweet tooth, but his craving was seldom satisfied. My mother was frugal, and almost never brought such things into the house. And when she did, they were unlikely to be intended for my brother. After feeding the chickens, he went to the river for water. When he returned, out of breath, with buckets sloshing, he found a pot of black sesame pudding bubbling on the stove. He was sure it was the magic fishbones that had fulfilled his wish. He slopped some into a bowl, slurped it back joyously and washed the bowl clean just before his mother returned with a package of real French coffee and and box of date and nut candy. "Out of my way, mui mui," said my mother. "Go help your sister sell eggs."

The chickens had been laying furiously for the last week or so, as though their little avian gonads were spiralling out of control. Omelets, custard and egg drop soup: They couldn't eat them fast enough, and so our sister had taken to selling them on the corner. My brother went out obediently as though to join her, but as soon as our mother had closed the door, he slipped around the side of the house and set up a few old crates by the kitchen window. From there, he clearly observed the arrival of the old go-between and the whispered deal-making between the two women. As soon as he got the gist of the conversation, my brother climbed off the boxes and ran to his sister, who still had fourteen eggs rolling shamelessly about on her red cloth. "Ma's going to marry you to an ugly old man," he told her. "The go-between's in the house right now. All that's left is for him to take a look at you in the new blue suit you're making, and if he likes what he sees, then off you go."

Mid-Autumn Festival arrived. People made or bought paper lanterns for their children, dressed in their finest clothes and went down to the river to look at the moon and one another's little packages of candlelight, softened and tinted by the many-coloured stuff of the lanterns. My sister and mother were planning to go down to the river. My mother told my brother to mind the house. "You're so morose," said my mother, "you won't have a good time anyway. Why not stay at home and make sure we don't get robbed?"

My brother protested, but his scene was hijacked by my sister, who claimed she couldn't find the blue suit she had just finished making for the occasion. My mother flew into a panicked fury, and finally had to lend an old suit of her own to my sister, one that was just a little too worn, and on which the stitching and embroidery were less fine than the delicate lines and figures that had poured from my sister's hands. They left the house late. My mother's eyes were creased with worry and fury, her movements agitated. My sister followed meekly behind her, ashamed of her error and worried about the viewing which was to come. Let's be gracious and just say that they left, feathers flying, looking less than their best.

As soon as they were gone, my brother retired to his room. He pulled the loose brick from the wall. The fish bones tumbled out, and after them, a little heap of blue fabric. This was a long time ago. Who knows how my sister's blue suit got there? Perhaps, terrified of her impending fate, she had hidden the suit behind the brick with the intention of disappointing the ugly old man. Perhaps my brother, fed up with his daily persecution, had stolen the suit in revenge for all the slights he had borne at my mother's hands. Perhaps the fish bones had something to do with it. What does it matter?

Point is, my brother had the suit. He was a sucker for good fabric. The oily softness of the silk and the fineness of our sister's stitching sent him into raptures. He slipped out of his work clothes and into the liquid smoothness of the suit. He braided and pinned his hair. If, on account of his advanced adolescence, his skin was less clear than it had been in earlier years, what of it? He scooped up the fish bones and returned them to their place in the crevice brushing his fingers against something soft as he did so. He reached into the hole and drew out a pair of the daintiest embroidered shoes. These he placed on his wondrously tiny feet, and, stopping to buy a lantern from a paper artisan selling them on the corner, made his way down to the river.

Well! My mother and sister noticed him right away, dressed as he was in my sister's beautiful suit. But try as they might to approach and scold him, they seemed unable to push through the crowds without losing sight of him. He recognized the young man his mother had selected for my sister—not an ugly old codger at all, but the handsome son of a well-to-do merchant family; a step up in the world, some might say. My brother smiled at the man demurely and then cast his eyes quickly downward. The man looked pleased. He tried to approach more closely, but my brother eluded him as deftly as he had my mother and sister.

He couldn't avoid both parties the whole night. There arrived an unfortunate moment just around midnight when he found himself standing between them on the path. Tall river weeds blocked his way to the water and to the village on the other side of the path. Both parties approached him, each with its own, eager reasons. My brother panicked. He leapt into the river weeds in the direction, fortunately, of the village, accidentally tripping over a rock and losing a dainty shoe on his way up. He didn't stop to retrieve it. He dashed through the reeds and bushes and hurled along the embankments between the rice paddies, using mulberry bushes for cover as much as he could. He scrambled into the house, squirmed out of my sister's suit, stuffed it back into the chink in the wall and replaced the brick. He put on the tattered suit he had been wearing earlier that day, went down to the kitchen, settled into a chair beside the stove and pretended to sleep.

When my mother and sister came home, there he was fast asleep beside the stove, looking as though he had never left. They searched the house for the suit and found nothing. No sign of a single, dainty slipper either. Puzzled and irritated, they went to bed.

The following morning, my brother's tired eyes and rough, pimply skin made them doubt further that they had actually seen him the night before. While they could have as easily fed each other's certainty about what they had seen, this time they only reinforced each other's doubt.

"I don't think it was him we saw," said one.

"I thought I did," said the other, "but now I'm not so sure."

———

Later in the afternoon there was a knock on the door. Two of the merchant's servants appeared, looking sheepishly apologetic. "Sorry to bother you, auntie," they said. "Yours is the only house in the village we haven't searched. The merchant's son has fallen in love with owner of this slipper." One of them drew the impossibly tiny shoe from his pocket.

"Hmmph!" said my mother. "Thinks he can get out of his contract with me so easily, does he?! I didn't bring this girl up to be humiliated so! What do you think she is, a lump of cow dung to be discarded at will?!" She pushed my sister forward.

"If the shoe fits..." one of the merchant's servants said, and then instantly regretted the double entendre. The other held out the shoe.

My sister strained and pushed, squeezed and shoved, but to no avail. There was no way her big flat peasant foot was going to fit into that shoe!

"We know you have another daughter," said one of the servants. "Your neighbour told us."

"There's no way the shoe will fit her clumsy foot," said my mother.

But of course she was wrong. Remember, my brother was the child of a very shapely concubine. Not only did the shoe fit his foot, but he drew another out of his pocket to match it. The servants swept him up and lowered him gently into a red sedan chair. They put a veil over his pimply face, then hoisted the chair into the air and carted him away.

What was my brother intending? Did he actually plan to marry the merchant's son? Just how liberated you think China was in those days? I hate to say it, but my brother was a man's man after all, or should I be more clear? A manly man, a he-man, a het-man. This might be a fairy tale, but my brother was no fairy. The minute he was presented to the merchant's son, he dropped his silken pants and shook a prodigious prong in his admirer's face. Then he turned, shed the rest of his clothes, wiggled his bare, pimply butt at his would-be in-laws, and took off in the direction of his mother's house. On her doorstep he announced the arrival of his esteemed surname's next patriarch. Buck naked and too obviously a man, he stepped over the threshold and refused to don women's clothes ever again.

You'd think someone who had lived the greater part of their life as a woman would have more sympathy toward the gentler sex. Not a chance! "Nothing gentle about them," said my brother. From then on he laid down the law and ruled the house with an iron fist.

DANIEL LEE

LIMERICK TO A BITCHY DRAG QUEEN

Said, "Hey Miss Thang, you're a troll!
So go home and smoke out your bowl."
I'd tell you, "You suck!"
But that's how you fuck
When it's time to douche out your hole.

REQUEST

Fuck me
I'm bored.

WHEN LETTING GO/FUCKING

This time I'm not holding back
Not holding back the
five spice
sweet rice
priceless
heaven-dressed
devil-fuck of mine.
Not holding back Astarte,
Jezebel, Delilah, Salome
Not holding back
the thigh bitin'
prose writin'
sin sellin'
holy dwellin'
supernatural sex
prophecy in me.

Not holding back
white fetishizer!

Not holding back
Asian colonizer!

You can't
Suzy my Wong
Flower my
Drum Song
can't
half-eat my peach
nor dodge my reach
for your
deviation
elation
climax saturation
This I'll do for you

out of mercy
out of convenience
out of the good graces
of my pelvis

This lovin'
This lovin' is criminal
in all 50 states 'cause
my fuck sweats queer
front in rear
lasting
lasting like a lesbian
like a lesbian comin'…
just comin' & comin'…
comin'…
comin' & comin'…
comin' & comin'
comin' & comin'
comin' 'cause
my rhythm drills out and in
just comin'…
comin' & comin'
comin' again,
again & again & again
again like an itch—relentless bitch
again cause
I can fuck like the IRS
indict like Lewinsky's dress

I'll make your nose bleed
I'll free your scream seed
This ain't no cheap thrill
So here's your Playbill

And once you've tasted this
Blowpop dream lick,
can you handle a
nicotine-fuck fit?

You'll keep comin' back
to swim
in the pool of my
homo sex drool

You'll keep comin' back
to tongue tango
between the halves
of my ass–mango

You'll keep comin' back
to trip
from the spit of my
acid dipped lips

You'll keep comin' back
to tap
into the rollin' joys
of my lap

You'll keep comin' back,
comin' back,
when I let go
and fuck you,
fuck you like
I really mean it.

DONALD LEE

EXTRA BUTTER

I didn't ask for the anal probe. I don't recall the request. Shit happens, I know. But it has a particular way of happening to me. Each Friday minute after 6 P.M. I spend at work should be compensated only with eyelashes torn off from the person who is keeping me from re-entering the outside world. Eyelash per minute. That's fair. This time that person is LaTavia, the fuckin' rude rep from Mercury Express.

"Look ma'am. It's not that I won't help you. There's nothing I can do. Your package will be delivered by the next available courier. Please hold."

"Hello…"

Dead silence.

A different rep came on, "Mercury, Wanda speaking."

"Yeah, LaTavia was helping me."

"Hold on."

"Mercury, this is LaTavia."

"LaTavia, it's Bebe again from Imperious Bitch."

"Who you calling a bitch? Bitch!"

(Click.)

Shit. Perhaps I can squeeze in a drive-by shooting at Mercury before my hair appointment.

6:30 P.M. Never really used digital clocks until I started working here. Time was hardly the issue before. I used to come and go as I please. Now I'm a prisoner of time. Like I'm a slave to everything. Turkey pastrami with melted Jack cheese, Barney's, and, of course, my hair dresser. It's hard enough to score an appointment with Stfan on such short notice. Besides, it's Friday. Doesn't the weekend mean anything to my boss? Plus, I don't recall reading any fine line restrictions in the six-page memo on summer hours.

When I started temping for Imperious Bitch (you know their tag line: "IB classy. IB sassy. Hip label for junior execs with a downtown flair"), all I wanted was a paycheck and free samples. Now that I'm a regular clockwatcher, I could care less about that over-priced, off-the-shoulder-feathered-cape-wrap dress I've been messengering to the warehouse all day. But I still look good in one anyway. It's not so bad, really. Within three months at Imperious Bitch, I was able to save enough money for a tiny studio on my own. I could even afford to keep my baby. Cat, that is.

Ivanjou, a slightly overweight, or in my eyes, *opulent* Russian Blue, is not waifish, to say the least. Boy, can she eat that Fancy Feast. Not only does she match my recent passion for anything Russian, she is cool and luxurious, personified in a cute package. A reflection of me. How grand! She's truly the only thing that keeps me sane in this mad, mad world. My furry pillar of calmness. I absolutely adore her. I even bought her a leather collar, studded with cubic zirconia from QVC's Diamonique Hour for Pets. It's darling, I tell you. I know all my neighbors think Ivanjou is a bit obnoxious. But how can anyone not love the way baby flaunts her royal feline status by parading about with her shimmering choker? After all, it's only befitting for a feline of a blue-blood lineage to wear a jeweled collar. Presentation is everything. Nothing is sacred when it comes to Ivanjou. In fact, I named her after two child models: Ivanka Trump and Bijou Phillips, both of equal familial fame of a tragicomic history. I also considered naming baby after my two idols, Martha Graham and Bianca Jagger. But "Marthca" just doesn't exude that *je ne sais quoi* I was aiming for. I settled on Ivanjou after consulting with the *Cosmo* horoscopes. *Cosmo's* advice for Aquarius: Get out of the zombie parade. Be frivolous. Find a new idol. Admiring others will lead to self-renewal. Just don't over do it. No one likes an annoying groupie. Fashion suicide of the month: sandals.

6:50 P.M. Damn. I'm all outta cigarettes and the courier service hasn't called yet. That'll cost me another ten for Stfan's tip for being late. Maybe I should just cancel my date with Mark. For all I know, he could be a major jerk. Besides, my hair's a mess. I feel like crap. And I still haven't finished work.

Funny thing. Just as I pick up the phone to call Mercury Express, a call comes through.

"Um…hello?" Don't recognize the voice.

"Hello. Is this Mercury? I was about to call you guys."

"Nonono. It's me, Mark."

"Oh…Mark."

"Yes. Hi. Bebé? Is it?"

"No. It's actually Be-be, as in the alphabet, 2 Bs."

"Bebe. I'm sorry…I…I was just confirming our plans for tonight."

For a second, I wished I had never responded to that chance meeting ad in *Single Metropolitan*:

Thursday night around 7:30 in Penn Station. You are the beautiful brunette in a pink T-shirt with an IB logo and bright yellow jeans. I'm the guy in the blue denim jacket you smiled at as you went down the escalator. We locked a gaze across the 2 train platform. You Downtown. Me Uptown. Been missing your smile ever since. Let's ride together sometime. Please call Mark at Box #3666.

What can I lose? More time? I might as well take a chance. It's not like I'm going out with LaTavia.

"Sure. Extra Butter around 8ish, right?"

"Yeah. Sounds great. So will you be wearing that pink shirt again?"

Like that's my only outfit! God, I hope he doesn't wear the same denim jacket. I cringe at the thought.

"I'll be wearing that same denim jacket."

Damn. It's too late to back out now. I'm going out with a guy who does not wash. Gross beyond gross!

"How quaint." I fake-smiled over the phone. It was the best response I could conjure under such circumstances.

"Um, so…yeah, well…you can't miss me. I'm pretty easy to spot. We'll find each other inside. I'm sure." Vagueness was my only defense at this point.

"Alrighty then. So, I guess I'll see you at 8. Extra Butter. Can't wait."

"Yeah, see you there."

Perfect. Anal probe just getting deeper by the minute.

Hanging up, I thought, Why is he so exact? Nobody's ever punctual, especially for a pseudo blind date. And the way he assumes I'll be wearing the same clothes is so typically male. Is that what I want—"a typical male"? On the other hand, I do like saying the name "Mark." Mark. Mark. Mark. How bad can a "Mark" be?

Soon after, Ms. Satan, herself, LaTavia called to confirm the delivery. Finally. Sure enough, the phone started ringing all over again, but fuck it. I got hair business to take care of. So I hopped a cab downtown to Stfan's salon.

For three weeks I'd been burning in hair hell. Thank heavens Stfan, my savior stylist, squeezed me in last minute. If you haven't already heard, according to last month's *Fashionista*, Stfan's salon was rated with four knockout blow dryers. It was reportedly, "a ringing endorsement for gauche she-males with classic weave problems." Whatever that meant. I've been with Stfan ever since I moved to New York two years ago. Strange. I did, however, notice the shift in Stfan's staff and clientele toward the upwardly mobile/sexually ambiguous. Along with this new crop of clients, Stfan's fee jumped as well. But that didn't cut my trust in Stfan's magic scissors. I remembered how Stfan salvaged my passé Pat Benatar 'do to a slinky shag, which helped me land my job at IB. Sure, the prices may be outrageous, but a Stfan signature cut is worth every Imperious Bitch's dime. My philosophy on money: Why suffer a financial diet when there are better diets around? I mean, last month was not in my budget, but it has passed like the wind. Who has the time to bother with money matters? Certainly not me.

As soon as I stepped into the salon, Stfan's staff of East Villagey types surveyed me as if I was Kathy Lee at a sweatshop. Stfan was not in sight. So I took a sigh of relief. At least he's not pissed off waiting for me. He's probably rescuing some other hair emergency in the back. Reorienting myself from the industrial techno beats and the ever-so bitchy crew, I decided against making the first move. I'm the customer, I said to myself. So instead, I side-glanced my way past the glammed-up cast with facial piercing and plunked down on a pillowed junk sofa awaiting service. A setting like this requires a proper disposition. A few minutes later, a Japanese girl dressed like a cartoon character comes my way.

"You need help or somethin'?"

"Yes, I have a 7 o'clock with Stfan," I said, maintaining my composure.

"Stfan cancelled all his appointments tonight. His boyfriend needed a Tae Bo partner," this Japanese girl panned as if I should've known this.

"What? I just talked with Stfan earlier! He said he'd accommodate me," I nearly hollered.

"Well, he's gone, girlfriend. No need to get loud! Jeez. If you like, Gish'll do the job," the Japanese girl, maybe boy, queened out at moi.

Already unsure of tonight's events, I quickly balanced my options. I could either risk it with this Gish and possibly walk out with a decent 'do or suffer my style with humidified hair. This was a major SOS. For all I know, Gish could really butcher my hair. The last harrowing hair experience I had was back in college. The cut was so horrific that I had to miss a whole semester of courses, causing me to make up the credits in continuing ed, a.k.a. Drop-Out Central. No. This won't do. It's best to brave a stylistic defect for one night than a whole month. Anyway, Mark is a guy who wears the same jacket. He probably won't even notice my hair. Reassuring myself, I left the salon and head to meet Mark.

On my way, I remembered I forgot to tell Tina, who was cat-sitting for me, where I put the cream for Ivanjou's collar rash. So I call home. No answer. Tina must have turned the phone off. She's an odd one.

Tina, my ex-roommate, is a credit card hippie I met in college. Although she comes from a well-to-do family, Tina prefers the granola lifestyle. I inherited, or rather dispossessed, Ivanjou from Tina, who's better off pet-less. That girl seems to acquire allergies like one collects stamps. According to Tina, she can't read certain books because of their paper stock. Shakespeare, sorry. Fitzgerald, forget about it. Never mind Nietzsche. To this day, Tina is the only self-certified bibliophobe that I know of. Tina also maintains a regular peanut/pill diet. They are the few products she has no allergic reactions to. Not yet, that is. Overall, she was a decent roommate. Chatty, but nice. Chemically inclined, but nice. And at times overly flatulent, but nice. We separated on good terms with Ivanjou as our bonding factor.

Tina thought it would be fun to have a plaything to coo over in the apartment. I couldn't understand why Tina would risk her health for a cat but agreed it would be a nice accessory for the apartment.

At first, all was well. Then the onslaught of sneeze attacks followed by skin rashes invaded Tina's fragile frame. Even though Tina insisted that her all-knowing herbalist, who's Chinese, prescribed her something that would alleviate the symptoms of animal allergies, I remained skeptical.

Tina religiously took the medicine, composed of ancient lotus roots mixed with saliva from pregnant sparrows. Amazingly, she survived the sparrow saliva as well as having Ivanjou for a couple of more weeks until I moved. After that, baby was solely my responsibility, which I gladly took on. Too bad there isn't a hypoallergenic breed for kinds like Tina. However, she still occasionally cat-sits for me.

7:50 P.M. Almost there. I rushed, clutching my cell. Extra Butter, Extra Butter, Extra Butter., I chant in my head. I recall the gallery invite Mark had sent me. A retrospective of neo-avant-garde artists' works restructuring the socio-political paradigm of American culture. "Negotiating Hatred: A Paradisaic Paradox in Contemporary America," on view now through November 26 at Extra Butter. Interesting. But is it appropriate for a first date? Mark's assemblages are exhibited there. How presumptuously pretentious for him to invite a girl he hardly knows to his opening. At least he's a successful albeit strange artist. "Negotiating Hatred?" "Assemblages?" I hope he's not one of those "adventurous" artists who sticks a bunch of prosthetic appendages or missing doll parts in his work. If so, he's definitely trying too hard.

To my surprise, I was greeted at the gallery by a distraught Tina. Apparently, Tina had been waiting for me all night at the gallery.

"What's wrong?" I asked, more intrigued than worried.

"It's Ivanjou. I think she's dead," Tina said. "I tried calling you but I couldn't reach you anywhere. So I came here instead."

"Dead? What do you mean? Where is she?"

Tina slowly reached in her backpack and gently retrieved a half-dead Ivanjou. My poor baby.

"She was doing fine when I went to the bathroom. She'd been furiously scratching at her collar. But she seemed fine. When I came out, she was gasping on the floor. I thought she was coughing up a fur ball so I didn't take much notice. But then, she didn't stop. I tried raising her arms but it didn't help. So I rushed here to find you. I didn't know what else to do."

"You moron! Have you considered calling the vet? Oh, my poor Ivanjou." I tearfully cradled Ivanjou in my arms. "C'mon precious. Bebe's here." Ivanjou remained nonresponsive, a furry dead weight.

A crowd began to gather around us.

"Bebe, is that you? I thought it was you," I heard Mark say, emerging from the curious crowd. "You said you were easy to spot, and you were right. Nice outfit you got on."

"Can't I have a moment here with my preciously departed without you mocking me?!"

"Oh, it's all the rage. Homeless Eskimo, the new line from IB. My friend got one in sable brown," said a woman in the crowd.

"Just leave me alone!"

"Calm down, Bebe. What's the matter? Cat got your tongue?" he joked, not knowing the crisis brewing with my baby.

"You fuckhead!"

"Yeah, go back to negotiating hatred, you nosy bunch. Can't you see her cat is knocking on heaven's door? My friend needs time alone," Tina said trying to defend me.

"You too, Tina," I said as I pushed my way past the crowd to the open streets.

"Wait, I didn't mean it that way. I like your dress, cape, whatever. You look great. Wait. Come back! I love Imperious Bitches! Bebe!" called Mark, who's never quite on the mark.

Alone and still crying, I laid Ivanjou down on a nearby park bench. Not knowing what to do, I took out my brush and began combing my tangled hair. After fixing myself, I decide to brush Ivanjou as well. Presentation is everything. I start to brush Ivanjou slowly and softly, feeling the motion of each stroke. Then my strokes gradually increased like I was possessed. For no reason at all, I vent and brush Ivanjou viciously like a mad woman. Fuck this shit. Sometimes, you need to deep six today for tomorrow. Extra Butter. Extra Fucker! Mother Butter Fucker! I was so focused on consoling myself that I didn't even notice Ivanjou meowing away, confused by the combing commotion.

Meow.

"Ivanjou! You're alive!" I yelled joyfully. The cat looked at me and meowed knowingly. "You got me so scared, precious. Ivanjou! Ivanjou! I want you, Ivanjou!

"I'm hungry. Want some Fancy Feast? Let's chow, huh? We'll go home and have a fancy feast together! Just you and me," I said, lifting Ivanjou in the air. I wrapped baby in my arms and begin walking back to my tiny studio, all the while leaving behind a shimmering cubic zirconia covered in fur on the park bench.

You know, I didn't ask for the anal probe. I didn't wake up today wanting the anal probe. I didn't ask for the anal probe! I didn't ask for the anal probe! I didn't ask for the anal probe! But shit happens anyway.

RUSSELL LEONG

PHOENIX EYES

At the same Buddhist temple downtown where my friend P. and I used to go whenever he visited L.A., I prepared to don the grey robes of a layman. There was no chance of my becoming a monk, but I wanted to hear the five precepts for myself.

A dozen people would take the vows today. The monk would state the same precepts to each of us. Some simply nodded their heads in affirmation; others answered with a soft "aye." I was the last to step before the altar. Now the monk was repeating to me: "Do not kill sentient beings. Do not steal. Do not lie. Do not drink alcohol. Do not have improper sexual relations." At the fifth precept, I balked. The monk looked me directly in the face. I cast my eyes downwards. My days of pleasure and sensation it seemed, would cease. I was past 40. Yet sweat was flowing down my back. I squinted in the haze of the burning punk sticks and yellow candles.

———

Twenty years ago, I graduated from Washington State College with a double major in theater arts and business communications. Ba and Ma had high hopes of me, of a wife and children soon, and a stucco duplex where they could live with us in their old age. When I told them I would never marry, they threatened to disown me. From then on, I did not show my face at family banquets, at baby parties, or even at funerals. It was as if I, the offending branch, had been pruned from the family tree. I was hurt, then angry. But I also felt free to pursue my life as I saw fit. As always, older sister supported me after I explained to her why I wanted to live in Asia.

"If I'm going to make it as a theater designer in America," I said, "my training in Asia ought to open a few doors. Look at black artists in Paris. They make it there first, before they come back here." I promised to keep in touch. I promised to send money for the folks if I had any to spare.

But beside my artistic ambitions, and unbeknownst to my family, I was leaving the U.S. because I had fallen for an airline steward based in Taipei. We had met the summer before on a Tokyo-Taipei flight—I had been spending July studying Mandarin. He would be my first Chinese lover; at the time in the States, Asian men going together was considered "incestuous." Even if we were attracted to men of our own race, we didn't move on it, fearing we'd be ridiculed.

Every other month, I drove my beat-up blue Mazda from Pullman to Seattle, where I would spend a weekend with the steward. When I finally graduated I worked the summer to save for a ticket and then in the autumn moved to Taipei to join him. His tenth-floor condominium was on Chunghua Road, near the hotel district. The teakwood furnishings were a far cry from the wooden crates that had surrounded me growing up in back of a grocery store by the tracks in Seattle's International District.

Besides sex, he wanted me to serve him—draw the bath water, polish his shoes, massage his brow with green eucalyptus oil, teach his friends dirty jokes in English. Even with my help, he took half an hour to tie a silk ascot around his neck; I took one minute to throw on a T-shirt and Levis. He drank at odd hours and chewed candied ginger and Wrigley's gum to cover his breath. Where was love, I asked myself. It was hell. After six months, it all ended one night after I was eyeballing the singer at the Hilton Skylounge. The steward and I got into a brawl in the parking lot. He kicked me out the next day.

That year—1972—Nixon, Kissinger, and Winston Lord broke twenty years of Cold War policy toward China. I was stranded on a hot, dusty street in Taipei, with a hundred dollars U.S. in my pocket, a duffel full of clothes, and an art-and-business degree to my name. I sat at a fruit stand, drinking a concoction of condensed sweet milk, crushed ice, and mango, trying to decide what to do with my life. Taiwan was a small island near the equator shored up by coral reefs, U.S. dollars, and cheap labor. In all fairness, the Portuguese were right when they named it Formosa, beautiful island. Between the hills and the sea, though, shanties hugged the dirt, poor relations to the mountains of condos and mansions above them. Certainly I did not want to be overwhelmed by lack of money, by lack of love, or by too many English students, which is what usually happened to foreigners forced to earn their keep.

I found a cheap room in a pre-war Japanese-style boarding house. A notice posted on the inside of my door read, in Chinese, "Do not use over 30 watts, no loud music, clean the toilet after you're done." The absentee landlord, a widow, would rifle through our rooms while we were at work, unscrewing bulbs with too high a wattage and unplugging radios and television sets. But the boarders, mainly office workers, tolerated the "widow's house," because of its convenience to bus lines and the low rent. Jerry-built townhouses edged up to either side of the wooden structure. It had been beautiful in its day, but now it was only a matter of time before this colonial relic would be demolished.

———

Before I ran completely out of money and out of luck, I ran into P. at the National Palace Museum. I was taking notes and sketching Tang dynasty terra cotta burial figurines. I noticed how the wide sleeves and low bodices—fashions influenced by the foreign traders who plied the Silk Route—accentuated the body. These styles seemed to reveal, rather than hide, the body's robustness. Absorbed in my observations, I was startled when a man standing next to me suddenly began speaking in perfect, high-pitched English: "You're an ABC on a summer visit?"

"Me? Yeah, like you said, I'm an American-born. Here to learn what I can. How did you know I spoke English?"

He looked me up and down, smiling and pointing to a stocky, half-naked clay figure tethering a yellow-glazed horse.

"Persian or Turkish, not Chinese, " I said.

"Imported labor," he said. "Exotic, like you. You'd have been a good model for a stable boy."

I blushed, realizing that no local boy would have dared enter the museum dressed as barely as I was—in cutoffs, tank top, and plastic sandals. I retorted: "And you are a Tang prince waiting to mount the horse?"

———

It was P. who brought me out—to the hung kung hsien, the international call line. The circuit was made up of high-priced young men and women who made themselves available in Taipei, Hong Hong, Manila, Bangkok. As the tiger economies began to flourish in the seventies, so did the demands of Western businessmen for after-work entertainment. Most of our clients were German or American, with a few English, Dutch, or Spanish—and even a few Asian businessmen thrown in. On our part, we could be of any nationality, Taiwanese, Thai, Chinese, Vietnamese, and of any gender: man, woman, or pre- or post-op transsexual.

We hung out in the same cafes and shopped at the same boutiques. After our clients spent over $100 on food or clothing, we'd get a 5% kickback—and a New Year bonus in an embossed red envelope. As I saw it, food is food to the belly, and cloth is cloth to the back. Most of us ordered vegetarian dishes for ourselves, but for clients, we selected the richer braised meats and fancier seafoods that they preferred.

The boutiques were staffed by the same slender, clear-skinned young men or women. The clothes, as everyone knew, might have been labeled "Bluette Mode-Paris," but they were knit in a local factory that made "imports." No matter, the salesperson would try the clothes on for the buyer in the private dressing room. My well-built buddy, Wan, would wear nothing under his trousers. A certain Ivy League professor known for his translations of Sung poetry, loved, whenever he was in Taipei, to stop at the boutique, and have Wan undress and dress for him.

———

As P. taught me, the main thing was not what you did in bed, or even how good you looked; the key to referrals and comebacks was skill and charm in "talking, walking, welcoming, and leaving." You had to make your client feel intimately involved, you had to make him long for your presence after he'd left. After all, P. said, if they could afford you, they could afford someone even younger or better-looking. But not necessarily smarter or more personable. A street hustler or bar girl didn't need education or social graces, but an escort or companion did.

That meant you had to know at least two languages and the common cordialities in Japanese, Chinese, and English. Read the newspaper everyday. Know your food. Hold your liquor. Don't order the most expensive entree or wine, but something appropriate to the season, to the country you were in. "Take a lesson from me," P. said facetiously. "In Kyoto, don't order Szechuan pork. Admire the view from between the shoji, and accidentally brush your hand on your client's thigh without looking directly at him." Bringing his hand to my face, P. suddenly traced my lips with his fingers. "Save this part for me."

Last, but not least: Keep it simple, but as good as you could afford. No white shoes or polyester shirts. Not too much jewelry or luggage. When business was slow, P. said I might consort with horny American sinologists from prestigious Ivy league schools who'd come to Taipei to hone their classical Chinese. They were suitable for conversation and culture, as they loved to pontificate about their studies, but not for their allure or their dollars. They were the orientalist tightwads of the Orient, he joked; they didn't know much about fashion, food, or how to spend money. But, as P. said, you could always learn a bit more about Sung-tzu from them. "That might come in handy with your next client; watching the moon from the hotel balcony, you could recite a stanza or two."

P. didn't need the money like we did, but he did what we did anyway, for pocket change and for fun, he said. Sometimes, after double-dating with clients, or having drunk too much of our favorite cognac, P. and I would fall asleep on the same bed, feeling safer in each others' arms.

One morning, after waking up together, he had a sudden desire, he said, to visit the lotuses that would now be at the peak of their bloom. I asked him why today, because I knew that he had a valued client flying in.

"Then I'll just cancel him. He can wait until tomorrow." He dressed, tossed me a Diet Coke and a banana, left a message for his client, and rang for a taxi. We were on our way to the Lin Family Gardens, just south of the city, a classic 18th-century Fukienese family compound. We passed through endless corridors, dank rooms, and carved door lintels to the lotus pond in the back. There seemed to be no tourists anywhere. From the depths of mud and dark water, hundreds of white lotuses had pushed themselves up to reach the sun. Upon seeing these, he began to tremble. I put my arm around his shoulder. His grandmother, who had raised him, had always looked forward to the beginning of summer and the blooming of lotuses in the small rock pool in back of their family house. As the third wife of her husband, and being from a country background, she had the lowest status in the large household. Her room was the smallest, her clothes the most meager because she could not produce a male heir. Yet she had raised P. as her own son, picking his hair for lice, bandaging his scrapes when he would fall. Each year, during the two or three weeks that lotuses were in full bloom, she would, just before dusk, pour clean water onto the bulb of each pale flower. At dawn, she would, with a tiny spoon, collect what water remained on the flowers into a jar. This precious liquid, mixed with morning dew, would make the purest water for tea, enough to brew a single cup, which she would sip with him.

––––––

The red taxi whisked me to the peaks of Yangminshan estates, to where the sour smog of the city basin gave way to the scent of pine and jasmine. The doorman smiled and opened the black-lacquered double doors, flanked by two sago palms.

Making my way to the outdoor bar, I spied Tan Thien, the thin, effeminate scion of the Tan Tan ice cream family, which had branches all over the island and was establishing plants in Singapore. Then there was Jerry, a muscular Taiwanese, kept by a restaurant owner in Osaka. And Marie, a French-Algerian student who had found it more exciting not to study Chinese—we'd had a brief affair. One night when we were making love I went on and on about the Jun vases I had seen that afternoon at the Palace Museum. She told me that I opened my mouth at all the wrong times, instead of putting my lips where they belonged—quietly between her legs. She swore at me in French, and I at her in Cantonese, and we parted. After me, she drifted to pretty-boy types who usually borrowed money from her and never paid her back. About then, I think, she started going out with older businessmen, again through P.'s referrals.

I kissed her lightly on the shoulder. "Marie, ni chen mei li. You look wonderful." And she did, in her simple black cotton dress and pearl earrings, her upswept chestnut hair.

"So do you, Terence. But you're as dark as a peasant. Your phoenix eyes give you away, though."

"Eh?"

"Longing and lust. That's what I see in them."

I kissed her again, and moved on.

I moved among Otto's usual crowd of slender Asians in their twenties, and important antiques—a gilt Burmese Buddha, oxblood porcelain vases filled with orchids, and

Ming country furniture.

Otto was a Swiss cookware manufacturer, and a regular at the Hilton Skylounge. Because of his bent for Asians, he kept villas in Jakarta, Chiang Mai, and Taipei, along with his family home in Geneva. He preferred, he said, the sensual aspect of darker Malays, but tempered with common sense, "at least one quarter of Chinese blood."

I pressed the gold pinky ring chiseled with my Chinese surname tightly against my palm. We were all accessories. Whether we were from the country or the city, whether pure-blooded Chinese or mixed with Japanese genes during the colonial occupation. Or Malay. It didn't matter. We were beads on a string. A rosary of flesh. We gave up our youth to those who desired youth. There was some room for variation, for beauty was in the eye of the beholder. I myself was called "feng yen" or "phoenix eyes" because of the way the outer folds of my eyes appeared to curve like the tail of the proverbial phoenix. Such eyes were considered seductive in a woman, but a deviation in a man. Thus, the male phoenix sings by itself, as it dances alone.

It was at one of Otto's get-togethers that I ran into Li-ming again. He was a well-known modern dancer who once asked me to design a stage set for him that would give him the illusion of height and weight—he was well under five-four. I ended up creating a series of painted silk banners that moved up and down on invisible nylon strings. During the last act, the banners slowly lowered behind him, effectively shutting out the rest of the troupe, so Li-ming appeared much taller. The editor of *London Dance Magazine*, who was making his annual Asian junket, saw the performance at the Sun Yat-Sen Memorial Hall and the editor was impressed not only with the dancers and the stage set, but with the designer, me. We had ended up at a Taiwanese restaurant eating garlicky sauteed squid, boiled peanuts, and noodles, downing it all with beer and getting thoroughly drunk. I was in no mood to talk design with the balding British editor because I had been smitten with the dark long-haired waiter. I gave the editor my card and insisted my friends take him with them.

After slipping the manager a few bills, I asked my waiter to spend the night with me. Even though I'd moved out of the "widow's house" to my own fifth-floor studio, I'd never bring people home. P. was the only one who would visit and sometimes stay the night. So I drank coffee until the last customers and the manager left around three in the morning, and the steel door clanked down over the entrance. I helped sweep the floor and refill the condiment jars—pepper sauce, soy, and oil. In the airless basement dining area, the waiter set the air conditioner higher and put on a tape of Dionne Warwick. We pulled out the table from between two red vinyl banquettes, then pushed the upholstered seats together. We lay on the slick vinyl, sweating and breathing hard, undoing each other's shirts. In the darkness, I fumbled for the glass jar on the table that now blocked the aisle. Pouring the liquid onto the palm of my hand, I sniffed it: sesame oil. I began to massage his shoulders and the small of his back, steadily working the oil and sweat between his legs.

The barking of dogs on the streets awakened us. Bleary-eyed, he stumbled to the kitchen and fried an egg over leftover rice. We ate and drank last night's cold tea in silence. His damp hair fell in a mop over his forehead. I brushed it away from his eyes. We smelled of sesame, stale cologne, and sweat. He smiled and shrugged his bare shoulders. Could I introduce him to customers, he asked me, as he had to pay for his brother's tuition in a private English-language school. He wanted to know if I had any American "friends" studying in the colleges who needed companionship. I pulled out a $50 bill from my pocket. "My pleasure."

"No," he said. "Brother, you are Chinese. We look the same. Swear the same. Fuck the same. I chu'uang tu'ng meng—-though we sleep in different beds, we have the same dreams!" I hugged him, and promised to bring American friends to his café in the future

———

That's where my dual career began: in Taipei, then onto Hong Kong and Osaka. Twice a year, P. and I flew to Hong Kong to set up private parties and modeling shows for jaded wives of rich businessmen. A family limo would meet us at Kai Tak airport. When their husbands were on trips to the U.S. or Japan to meet their mistresses, we would set up parties for these tai-tais, who paid well for good-looking men. Struggling (but handsome) students, and out-of-season soccer players were my specialty. Women, we found, went for the strong thighs and tanned calves of the players, which performed more diligently than the listless limbs of their pale husbands.

One thing led to another. Shopping for fabrics one day in the Landmark Mall with a Mrs. Chi, we were introduced to her Tuesday-night mah-jong partner, a gallery dealer from Shanghai. His gallery, Contempo, showed modernist Chinese artists from the twenties and thirties, now very collectible. He would take the time to educate younger collectors, including me, about painting styles that derived from Qi Baishi's minimalist renderings of fruits, flowers, and vegetables.

The following day he drove the four of us to the Chinese University of Hong Kong to see paintings by the eight eccentric Qing masters of the Yangzhou region. They were, he explained, the 18th-century precursors to the art of the New China. Yangzhou was near the tributaries of the Yangzi River and the East China sea, a cosmopolitan metropolis based on the salt and fish industries. I was impressed by his erudition. At the same time that he could appreciate esoteric old masters, however, his sensual tastes ran to young, unschooled hairdressers and bartenders with thick hair and bright eyes. Through him, my appreciation of Chinese modernist painting—and of men—improved.

Men were no problem, but I couldn't spend money on this caliber of paintings. Twice a year, I sent some money home to Ba and Ma, care of my sister. Besides, my own studio in Taipei was as spare as a stage, with books, a bed and desk, and track lighting. I needed spaces to exercise, to create, and to escape. Out of odd pieces of stone and lava rock I had assembled a rock garden on the balcony and potted some bamboo to hide the high-rise apartment across the way.

I was three years on the Taipei-Hong Kong-Osaka circuit before I got to do anything bigger in London, Canada, or New York. P. and I used to match our clientele in the same Asian cities so that we could rendezvous later and compare notes. In the meantime, I was the only Chinese American male on the hung kung hsien. Despite my eyes, I never considered myself exotic or different. But I used my English and art background to advantage with my clients: mainly men, but an occasional female. I always sent flowers to the women after I left them, usually a spray of pink orchids, and a subtle-patterned tie to the men. In Bangkok, on a trip with a Chiu Chow businessman, I had picked up three dozen silk ties at discount. My callbacks and referrals were no worse, and probably as good, as men who were much better-looking. I had strong features, and never hid the irregularity of my slightly rough skin with makeup, like the others who tried to smooth their imperfections. I smiled or complimented a person, however, only when I really meant it. I guess even my jaded clients could appreciate that.

———

Evenings, I would drink with middle-aged Chinese or Japanese businessmen: average length of marriage, eight years; one wife, maybe a mistress, two children. The Japanese were fastidious about their skin and bodily cleanliness, bathing before and after sex, so I preferred them. Then again, Chinese from Hong Kong or Singapore enjoyed talking, and eating, before and after the act.

After dinner I would go to the Club Fuling, a bar for Japanese and foreign businessmen near the Majestic Hotel, in the Shilin district. Unlike other clubs, the Fuling had no neon sign, just an engraved bronze plate with the club's address. Membership was by referral. New members—and that included locals and foreigners—could only join through an introduction. No street trade. Even we—companions, escorts, or entertainers—had to pay a nominal fee.

Entering the inner courtyard, I would pass through a Japanese garden with its plantings of red-leafed nandina—heavenly bamboo, and wisteria. Two entrances led to different parts of the club. The left door, sheathed in verdigris copper, led to a western-style bar with leather and chrome chairs and glass tables. The right entrance, sheathed in rosewood, led to Japanese tatami rooms, and was considerably more expensive due to the imported foods served. I usually worked the western-style side. No food, just local salted peanuts and dried cuttlefish.

The club's waiters were at least five-feet-eight inches tall. Some were of aboriginal origin from the Hualin mountain area; others were ethnic Chinese from Seoul or mestizos from Manila. The club catered to Japanese and Asian men over 40 years of age. Being a shorter generation due to the war, the patrons were fascinated with younger and taller Asian men. The waiters turned heads and opened wallets. They were dressed elegantly, in white linen shirts, black slacks, and black patent-leather shoes. They slicked their short hair back behind the ears. They would never go home with clients, otherwise they would be fired. Each had been selected and trained by the Fuling's rich owner, a local trader who had made his first fortune exporting refrigerators to Southeast Asia.

———

Daytimes, I would read, go to museums to research, or go shopping. I recall that one day, as soon as I entered the neighborhood around Lung Shan Market Street, my shoes started kicking up dust. Lung Shan was in the older, western side of the city near the river, for locals, not fixed up for tourists. The air was raucous with the voices of straw-hatted peddlers selling everything from watches to perfumes to human-shaped ginseng roots laid out on blankets on the street.

The leveling of some pre-World War II housing blocks had turned the sky yellowish-gray with dust. Shoeshine boys prodded me until I gave in. One examined the leather of my shoes and said the hide must be expensive. "We do not have this here." I turned to him and nodded my head, mumbling that a friend had sent them from Hong Kong. I tipped him a dollar for polishing them.

In the middle of the sidewalk, people with shopping bags were pressing around something or someone that I could not yet see. I walked toward the crowd. Edging my way to the side I saw a man sitting on the ground, with a short haircut. His eyes did not look up. He was a young man no older than I, pale skinned, with the leanness of a soldier. His straight shoulders ended abruptly at the armpit. It was warm, and he wore no shirt. His gray pants were rolled up to his knees.

He was painting. I looked at the crayfish emerging as his toes deftly controlled the bamboo brush. A bowl of water, a wooden box full of various tipped brushes and tin pots of paint were at his knee. Passersby tossed coins into a tin cup.

I squatted down so as to be the same height. A voice in the crowd shouted "How much?"

He said: "75 dollars."

"Too much," the voice said.

He calmly answered: "I don't lower my price, but neither do I raise my price for anyone." With his feet he pushed two pebbles to each corner of the painting to hold it down. Squatting, he repositioned himself to prepare another sheet of white. This time he bent over, inserting the brush into his mouth, between his teeth. As he bent down, I could see the inverted triangle of his shoulders and back tapering to his bare waist. Someone kicked the stone on the corner of the unsold crayfish painting. He lifted his eyes for a second and looked at me without expression. I lowered my gaze. The green carapace of a grasshopper emerged. Coins continued to drop into the can. The crowd thinned out, and then thickened again with the newly curious. His tongue flickered pink for a second, to moisten his lips. He had gleaming white teeth, except that one was badly chipped. His forehead and chest were lightly glazed with sweat and a line formed on his brow as he continued to paint in the humid afternoon.

Had he been maimed? Or had he been born without arms? His pupils were the gray of an agate. As I examined the crayfish painting, I wondered if he washed his face in a plastic basin at home. Or if his sister or wife or mother did that for him. How did he bathe or cook or make love? Despite his lack of arms, he seemed to have a part that I lacked.

The pock-pock pock of a monsoon shower took us by surprise. Quickly, he used his feet to roll up his paintings, before the rain could spoil them. From the crowd, a younger man, perhaps a friend, helped him scoop up the rest of his materials. He rose from his haunches. He was taller than I expected. The shower was now a torrent, and the painter and his friend turned into a muddy alley off the main street. Without thinking, I hurried after them, sloshing my way through uneven, potholed streets. The rain pummelled down; I sought shelter under a doorway. When the rain stopped, as quickly as it had begun, they were nowhere to be seen. Soaked, lost, and breathless, I flagged a cab to take me home.

———

That evening, I went back to the Club Fuling where the head waiter introduced me to a number of visiting Japanese businessmen. We had a few drinks, before I settled on Tanabe-san. He had a wife and children, he said. Every year he would go back to Osaka to impregnate her, to "keep her busy." I laughed, only because I had heard the same line several times before. He said that I reminded him of a well-known Kyogen actor—with the same square face, ruddy complexion, and red lips. We spoke in halting English, with a bit of Chinese and Japanese slang thrown in. I would write down the characters in kanji for him on a paper napkin. As I did so, he gripped my wrist in his hand.

His blunt fingers were strong. He asked if I had ever been bound. I said no, that I didn't do that. He laughed. He put my hand over his wrist and told me to squeeze as hard as I could. I did. He said, "Too weak. You've never lifted a shovel or a hoe! We must use other things." I asked "what things," and he pressed his glass of bourbon to my lips. He had his ways. I looked toward the bar. The bartender squinted at me, out of the corner of one eye. It was the "O.K.—he's clean and solvent" signal.

We taxied back to his hotel. He turned on the bath water. I turned on the television, ordered two Remys from room service, and stripped down to my jockeys. I had emptied both glasses before he emerged from the dressing room in a blue-and-white cotton robe. Flustered, I began to run my hands over the covering that concealed his body.

With a click, he opened his leather valise. It was full of thick white cotton cords, organized by length. He had me tie his wrists and arms back, pinioned to the sides of his body. Between the bands of white, his blue-and red-tattoos glowed: dragons and serpents attempting to escape from their prison of bound flesh. I placed my lips on the head of the red serpent that encircled his chest. Then I drew back until I could bend my knees and place the soles of my feet on his belly.

I worked my toes downwards, foraging in a triangle of dark hair until I managed to insert his cock between my feet. With my soles, I kneaded until it became engorged, the bluish veins pulsing beneath the skin. I did not touch him with my arms or hands. Flexing my calves and thighs, I pressed my feet together until finally he could not contain himself. At that moment, in my mind, I could see the painter whom I had lost in the rain.

At 15, I remembered reading Thomas Mann's *Death in Venice*. I saw that perfect beauty could kill, as the pursuit of it had killed Aschenbach and quite a few of my friends. Death, like beauty, could arise slowly, through frustration, liquor, or disease, or strike quickly, through anger, accidents, or suicide. I decided I could live better with imperfection, as long as I could live with myself.

––––––

In time, as my theater and design work materialized and I began to earn more from those efforts than I did from "other" work, I told myself that I would leave Asia for good. I was happy that I had been able to put a hefty down payment on a stucco duplex for my parents, who were, at last, able to tolerate me, in their way. From L.A., where I had settled, I flew to Seattle for my father's 70th birthday banquet. I had not been publicly seen at a family banquet for 20 years, though I had seen Ba, Ma, and Sis briefly, on and off.

That afternoon, Ba put on his Brooks Brothers navy suit, bought in San Francisco; Ma donned her best jade rings and pendant. Sister was in charge: she had arranged the menu and tables at the Hong Kong Low; bought the 24-karat "long life" gold peaches from the jewelers, made sure that a play area for infants and children adjoined the main room. During the dinner, members of the Hop Sing Association praised Ba's contributions to building a high school in the Pearl River district that he was from in Guangdong; the International Settlement Civic Association of Seattle gave him a plaque; and sister, on behalf of the two of us, talked about his virtues as a father to his daughter, the pediatrician, and to his son, the designer. I had no words to say, but led the toasts after the speeches.

Accompanying my parents from table to table, I felt the heat and sweat seep from my body. I could see questions in people's smiling faces: Where are his wife and children? Why isn't he married yet? Does he make money? What exactly does he do for a living? I was imagining things, I told myself—these kith and kin of Cantonese farmers and small businessmen didn't really care that much about me to begin with. If I had stayed in Seattle and lived their lives, I would be asking the same questions. I was glad when we reached the last table to toast. We lifted our shots of brandy, like I did at my own farewell meal at the Club Fuling, before I left. There, the members of my adopted family—P., Marie, Wan, Tan Thien, Otto, Li-ming, and the others whom my blood family would never meet—used me as an excuse to toast each other, the future, and the next man they would meet. I suddenly felt orphaned with my memories. At the same time I felt moved to see Ba and Ma in public, flushed and beaming, until the last guest had shaken their hands.

Sis and I drove them back to their apartment where I picked up my bags.

"Bye-bye, Ba, Ma, " I said. "Have a good trip. Sis and I have already reserved the hotel in Vancouver and boat tour."

Without ceremony, Ba suddenly thrust a large package wrapped in recycled green Christmas paper and twine, into my arms. Ma told me to open it. It was a red Pendleton blanket, a Pacific Northwest specialty. He grunted. "For you—king-size—big enough for two, eh?" Ma said: "See the label here—all virgin wool. Not a cheap one. We get it close-out." I could only nod my head. My eyes were wet. I had not realized how much I had missed them all. Sis touched the material but didn't say anything. It was late, so I bowed to the three of them. And I left for my hotel.

———

P. moved also moved to the West Coast—San Francisco, after I had moved to Los Angeles. Wherever he moved, his family would buy him apartment houses to manage.

The last time I saw P., five months ago, I noted that his features had aged well. In his late forties, he could still pass for 35. He attributed his glossy black hair, pale smooth skin, and flexibility to his Southern Yunnan ancestry. I always thought that it was due to his vegetarian diet and yoga. He had no outward symptoms of the disease. At the time, he was drinking bitter melon fugua juice daily, a native drink favored by Beijing researchers studying immune-building drugs at John Hopkins Medical School.

A card I had got from him, postmarked San Francisco, read, in Chinese: "Dear Terence/When my feet leave this earth the calendar will turn a new leaf, with a new birthday on a new month/Light incense for me, wherever you are./ P."

I had called immediately but his line was already disconnected.

Three days later, I read about his death in the Chinese paper, but the family and the police did not disclose details. The family whisked the body back to Taipei. No funeral services were held in the states. His family had apparently not been willing to admit at all that the myth of Asian invulnerability is simply a myth. But they were not alone in their desire not to see or hear about AIDS. In Asian families, even in the nineties, you just disappear. Your family, if you have one, rents a small room for you. They feed you lunch and dinner. They leave the white Chinese deli boxes pushed up—discreetly or not—against the door. Asian families do not want to have anything to do with what the American welfare system can offer the afflicted: Supplemental Security Income, food stamps, Medicare, hospice care, etc. They simply could not call AIDS by its proper name: any other name would do—cancer, tuberculosis, leukemia. Better handle it yourself, keep it within the family. Out of earshot.

———

Perhaps our lives were marked, as our bodies are destined to be beautiful or maimed, before we are born. But neither prayer nor desire worked to bring anyone whom I loved back. Only now I can say his name, because now it doesn't matter. Peter Hsieh, the beloved grandson of the general, Hsieh Hung, who so valiantly fought the enemy during the Sino-Japanese Resistance of the thirties. Now there's nothing more to fight against, or resist.

Even though I'd myself tested negative for the virus, I'm afraid of simple moves: Today I won't open the door and walk across the street, not even for a six-pack of beer or aspirin. I don't trust cars, pedestrians, clerks, janitors, nurses, bank tellers, not even children anymore. Nothing to do with the L.A. riots, car jackings, or fear of being robbed in this city. It's something else entirely.

I thought that I was prepared to accept the news of his death. But I wasn't. Rereading his card, I began to tremble from the fear and beauty of his words, "A new birthday in a new month." Being nominally Buddhist, he believed in rebirth, and in good or bad karma begetting similar karma.

———

Enveloped by spiraling smoke, the monk had been waiting for me to answer. His clean-shaven pate and face were beaded with sweat, but his black eyes were steady and cool. I had repeated "yes" three times to each of the precepts, including not lying, not stealing, not drinking, and not killing. And, finally "yes" to the last, not having improper sexual relations. If taking these vows would change things, or if it was too late to change my life now, I did not know. Dok. Dok. Dok. Dok. Dok. As he began to strike his mallet on the wooden fish-drum, others in the room picked up the chanting, Nam mo ah ye da fo ....

I could sense his presence nearby. He was not the one whom my eyes had sought and loved, or the one who had already lived and died. He was another—the one still waiting to be born.

JONATHAN H.X. LEE

ON A BROKEN THREAD

On the bus of mother:

Walking along the railroad tracks,
Carrying clean underwear,
To change if necessary,
Mud curling, living around my toenails
 become toejam,
Hot-mucky me.

I won't miss her—my mother,
Spreading food on the table,
I don't remember climbing down the tree
 running to the house;
Open window—odor of her food calling.

Can't wait to cook a few kernels of corn,
I could see them shining golden,
In the cold-nightlight

There was a worried look in my
 mother's face;
(What is it?)
She came to the front window,
And called for me,
Looking up and down the twilight railroad,
Up and down the acacia tree,
(I did not answer)—she returned to the
 kitchen.

I woke up when the man next to me,
He shook me vigorously:
"You were crying in your sleep"
("It was just a dream," I said apologetically)

Walking to the door of the bus
Entering a waiting room,

Suddenly it came to me:

It was not a dream,
It had actually happened,
It had come back to me—in a dream
I had forgotten it.

How could I forget such a significant event,
In my childhood—how could I have
    forgotten;
The tragedy that was to condition—so much

Of my life—living on the streets.

CHEN LIN

TO GROW A ONE-HUNDRED-POUND CABBAGE

As if it were an extension of himself, twice
the man describes this thing as huge—this boulder-size
vegetable with leaves big enough to cradle and float
a fleet of babies down a stream. Huge.
Of course

no secrets would he reveal—wouldn't want to
spoil the competition. Just a quick highlight on the ideal
conditions: three straight months of Arctic sun mixed
with perpetually wet Alaskan soil. Does he fertilize?
Yes. Mulch?

On the day of the fair, the contenders are gathered,
a pageant of giants and the oddly formed. Breathless,
he hauls his prize on the scale. Before gravity has a chance
to settle the score, the gears are already turning: up
next year's

planting schedule, spike torches in the plot
to warm the frigid sun-smeared nights. Only espionage will
uncover his scheme to conquer the cabbage's frontier, these years
spent peeling away at the tightly wrapped head to get to
the heart.

PAPER
FOR JAMES

I can't believe we've come full circle. One
year completed. Now begins the count. A
reed of a number, one. Still, it's the start.
Perhaps that's why it's observed with paper
and grows in worth from there each year. Silver,
gold and diamond, the stuff that builds empires
and knocks them down. In truth, though, what endures
is a record more clear than any mere
artifact, the wisps of memory held
in things. Although this, too, is an object,
and fragile enough to fade in the sun,
it comes from a long geniality,
a history of materials bound
to capture the seasons of lovers' hearts.

CHING CHING LING

LUNCH DATE/WISH LIST
A FOUND POEM

Ching Ching,
I've made reservations for 1 so
We won't have
To wait. Is this
Fine?
Yours, H

H—
1:00 is *comme il faut*.
As we steadily emerge from
the clamorous hoi
polloi, the stinking agora of the masses,
and into the radiant Apollonian
light, our destined perch on Olympus,
the less time we spend waiting in
line, the better. Make the reservation at 1
so that we can swoop in past
the lemmings and be served
with priority.

Sometimes I make myself sick
with these jokes.
NOT because they are
sickening in and of themselves,
but more because
I suspect I would do
exactly as I suggest given the chance.
BUT NO, in fact, I think I would
REALLY be a model of elevated
grace and charity. In fact, I
do believe I
might even be a Philosopher Queen,
and a Saintly temporal Princess.

For the time being, though,
I'll settle for lots of money so
that I can buy one of
those new Apple laptops that can play DVD.
I saw one last night and it
blew my mind.
The picture and the sound were not to be believed.
Would you be a doll and
buy me one for Christmas.
    (It's only 4 grand, darling.
    Petty cash, really.)

Just for fun,
here are some other things on my Christmas list:

Furniture from B&B Italia
wraparound modernist sofa
in chocolate brown
        (gorgeous)
        down filled head board
        Mahogany platform bed frame

Tiffany money clip engraved "C I R"
        (the C should be inverted as in the
        English E II R= Ching Ching Regina, Primus)

Bang & Olafson stereo
        (with top-of-the-line speakers, naturally)

flat-screen HDTV and DVD player
        (with sub-woofer to
        enhance the sound)

lifetime supplies of A&W cream soda
and Samantha Smoothies
        in all flavors

lifetime supply of Dewars Scotch
        (I know, it's not the best, but it's all
        I know)
        And Maker's Mark bourbon.

Complete set of Vuitton luggage
        in green Epi leather

Large size De Kooning canvas
        (from his earlier years, the cheerful stuff
        I have a large white wall just crying out
        for something dramatic)

In a pinch,
I'll settle for some oversized
Asiatic thing as long as
it's full of frolicking monkeys

To die for
Venetian candle holders:
           frighteningly anthropomorphized apes
           in pewter, wearing menacing gold masks
           and sporting golden harnesses with
           angel wings on the back.
           They hold the candle in an outstretched hand
           and a rapier in the other
                     Absolutely amazing.
           Available at Gumps in San Francisco
           for $500 piece.
           Yet again,
           chump change
                   (I'd of course expect both.)

Wusthof knives
for the professional chef
        (I'll settle for Henckels or Sabatier)

All-clad, pans and kettles

Sub-zero
under the counter,
refrigerator

built-in
Viking oven
        (range too, but separate)

Henry Miller "Aeron" chair

vermillion lacquered boxes
               (from Ching? Ling? Ming? Dynasty.
               Whatever.)

cowhide armchairs
   by LeCorbusier

shatoosh throw in camel
               (for snuggling up while watching a DVD)
actually, anything in endangered animal hide.

Mongolian lamb throw,
backed with shatoosh
               (as a bedspread)

zebra skin, backed with shatoosh
               (alternate bedspread)

rhino horn mounted on
gleaming tropical hardwood—
in a pinch I'll settle
for antelope horns as long as they have
a nice tortoise-y pattern

leopard skin to drape over my sofa

red venetian glass goblets

Jeep Grand Wagoneer, circa 1975

Jussara Lee suits
         and shirts
         and socks

a pet, housetrained
cappuccin monkey
               (desexed, so as not to become
               troublesome come puberty)

2 black pedigree pug puppies
               (Chang and Eng)

small, rather elegant pistol
>> (to dissuade would-be burglars,
>> errant roommates and
>> busybody neighbors

a maid

>> (credentialed)

Ever,

Ching Ching

R. ZAMORA LINMARK

A LETTER TO CLAIRE DANES FROM A FAN IN MANILA

"The place just fucking smelled of cockroaches. There's no sewage system in Manila, and people have nothing there. People, with, like, no arms, no legs, no eyes, no teeth. We shot in a real psychiatric hospital…" — Claire Danes to *Premiere* magazine

Dear Claire —

It is ghastly indeed: this city
crowded with cockroaches and people
who walk without legs, drive long
chrome-plated coffins without arms,
and stare imperiously at you
without eyes. Not to mention
squatters sleeping on stilts,
island panhandlers, again without arms
and legs, highway beggars,
again without eyes and hair,
and sidewalk dwellers whose walls
are painted with huge signs
reminding people not to dump trash,
piss, shit. By the way,
how was San Francisco? Are you now
back in the East, Boston or Manhattan,
that is? I am forever still in Manila,
writing you with much concern
because the City Mayor has called
an emergency meeting to ban
the showing of all your movies,
including *Les Miserables*. The papers
and glossy fashion magazines are
naming you "Unknown," "Uncouth,"
"Uncultured," "Unconscious." Word
has it that Brooke Shields is here too,
gambling at Heritage Casino on Roxas
with fishermen and politicians.
Is it true? Is she with Andre?

Are they still together? But
what you said about this city
of roaches and missing extremities
are bold impressions I cannot hold
against you, for first-time travelers
from First World countries all undergo
cultural seizures here; tics
of the mind responsible for setting
off a series of generalizations
and assumptions about bugs,
blindness and amputation. Not
excluded from this list are Filipinos
in America, like cousin Jennifer
from Daly City, Tito Bert in Wichita,
and Tita Joan in Pasadena. Claire,
I would like to invite you back
to Manila. Make another movie.
A romance, and not one filmed in a psycho
ward. Do it with Matt, Damon or
McConaughey or Broderick, but
preferably Dillon. Or why not
Matt Mendoza, Manila's own
achy-breaky heartthrob? And bring
with you, once more, your dollars,
your talent, and this time,
crutches and roach spray.

SAVED BY BERTOLUCCI

Vince, this is Mom. I just ran into Mrs. Edralin at Safeway Beretania and she told me that
her next door neighbor told her that you were in a beauty pageant. Is this true? Ay, dios
mio, what will I tell your Dad when he finds out? Call me. *beep* Hi, Vince. This is Art.
Arturo Dwayne Johnson, the new Mr. AmPIL All-Around winner. Sorry you didn't get
the grand prize, but better first runner-up than no runner-up, right? Anyway, just calling
to wish you a good time in the third world. Bring lots of condoms and Evian, heard the
water there gives you the runs. I'll be in Queens by the time you get back, so see you

next year *beep* Vince, it's Dave. Call me when you get a chance. My number is nine four five, eight four nine six *beep* Ay naku, Vince, Mrs. Sakamoto from next door just called to tell me you placed first runner-up daw in the beauty pageant. Totoo ba? You better call and tell me the truth so I know what lies to tell your father. I'm sure he'll find out sooner than later *beep* What? Screening calls, Mr. API? This Edgar, call me back. I stay home. Hurry up. I don't got the whole night *beep* Congratulations, Vince. This is Dad. I just got a call from your mother and she told me you placed second in a scholarship contest. Don't feel bad, hijo, I know how much of an overachiever you are but second place is not that bad. The main thing is you did your best *beep* Vince, I know you're at home so just pick up the phone. Pick up the phone, Vince, because I know you're right there standing in front of your answering machine and staring at my voice, so just pick up the phone because I got something juicy for tell—

(*Vince answers the phone. Edgar, who normally expresses himself in the Hawaiian-Pidgin English vernacular, is speaking in a very exaggerated tourist-from-the-mainland English. An English that is part Valley Girl talk and part-farmspeak. Vince tolerates it at first but gradually becomes irate.*)

—This better be good, Edgar.

—Where were you all day?

—I mean, like, have you been out all day, or are you, like, simply ignoring the importance of being me?

—I've been home all day, trying to pack.

—So, like, how's it going, Mr. API?

—You tell me, you're the one who called. And quit using that Haolified voice on me, Edgar. It doesn't suit you.

—Pardon me?

—Quit talking like a Haole!

—You mean, stop speeching like you?

—No, I mean like them local Japanese teachers we had in grade school. The ones who thought they were far superior than everybody else because they thought they sounded just like their Haole husbands when the fact of the matter was their Pidgin English accent did not only get thicker but they also made the English language sound as if it was in dire need of a good Preparation-H shove.

—But don't you think the English language needs some loosening up? I think so. That's why I prefer to talk to you in Pidgin cuz Pidgin ain't stiff.

—And I am?

—Hate to say it, but yes, Vince. (*Edgar resorts to Pidgin English.*) You can be real stiff, li'dat, and when you stiff as one corpse, you act and sound just like them Haoles and Katonks from the mainland. No breaths and no colors, li'dat. In fact, in all the years you knew me, not once did you open your mouth and mind to Pidgin English. And till this day, I still cannot figure out why. Maybe you just simply too tone-deaf or too tongue-tied.

—No, Edgar, it was because I was taught not to speak it, remember?

—No tell me you really buy all that crap about you ending up with one bleak future if you speak Pidgin English, Vince. Maybe you just —

—Just what?

—Maybe you just lacking in Local pride.

—Fuck you. I'm proud to be Local.

—Vince, remember how that bitch Mrs. Takemoto used us for talking Pidgin? How she always used to threaten us and tell us that if we keep speaking in Pidgin, nobody was going take us seriously? Well, it wasn't hard to figure out that she wasn't only putting down Pidgin, but she was also trying to make us believe that the only way to get ahead or be important in this world is to talk and think like Haoles. Sometimes, I feel like going back to Kalihi-Uka elementary and slapping her in the face with my 4.0 GPA report cards and my Honolulu City College diploma. But, you know what? I cannot cuz my own parents used to tell me the same ole shit.

—But you're versatile, Edgar, remember?

—I know, which brings me to the fact that the difference between me and you is that I can speak standard English and at the same time keep my Pidgin and Local mentality too, whereas you cannot.

—Bitch.

—Takes one to call one.

—I'm hanging up.

—Chill, Vince, I was just practicing English.

—Practicing what?

—Practicing English. That's what Dr. Dumpit calls it.

—Shit, Edgar, of all the nights in the year, you decide to practice English a couple hours before my trip to Manila.

—Jeez, I was only practicing English cuz I was just informed couple hours ago that I got the job at Northwest Airlines.

—Congratulations.

—Can you sound a little bit more bubbly than that, please, like in your Mr. AmPIL intro?

—Ha, ha. You're so funny, Edgar, I forgot to laugh.

—Better be nice to me from now on, brah, cuz once I pass probation I can bring anybody I like anywhere in the world with my fuck-buddy passes.

—You ain't fucking me, that's for sure.

—Northwest called me this morning to tell me I got the job cuz I passed my Tagalog as my second language proficiency exam. I going fly to Minneapolis next month for training. Oh, I cannot wait, Vince. Imagine me up there: a Local Queen ramping down the aisles of heaven, pushing my golden cart and asking the men, in my Haole-like voice: Will that be chicken, fish, or me, Sir?

—Where is Northwest going to base you?

—I find out two weeks before graduation. I wrote down San Francisco as my first choice, Hawai'i as second, but with my strings of bad luck with park queens lately, I probably going end up in Wisconsin.

—Is this the juicy self-important news you called me for?

—Of course not. God, Vince, you think so lowly of me. I know I self-important and I know that I own the rest of the globe that don't belong to Rand McDonald's.

—You mean, McNally.

—McDonald's, McNally; po-tay-toe, puta-to; same smell. Eh, no forget that I may act as if the world revolves around me but I also make it circle other people too.

—Yeah, only when you're sleeping.

—Bitch.

—Like you, thank you.

—So how does it feel to be the new Mr. API?

—Actually, I'm trying to erase it from my memory.

—Well, you can just forget trying to forget it cuz you have over five hundred people to remind you that you never dreamt the whole thing up, and that you really are the new Mr AmPIL API.

—Fuck you.

—No, thank you. I don't know why you're getting all upset for, Vince. It wasn't that bad.

—What do you mean it wasn't that bad? When was the last time you saw a pageant where a contestant goes on stage and kicks a ball using his elbows and ankles for five minutes?

—You shouldn't talk, Vince. You were getting carried away on the Casio synthesizer. You nearly broke the damn thing.

—Shit, I can't believe I allowed you to talk me into joining.

—I had to, Vince. Recruiting was part of my job as Mr. AmPIL all around, 1990.

—It was so fucking humiliating.

—Eh, it's over, ok? Besides, Mr. API is a prestigious title. It wasn't what you was aiming for, but you still won a thousand bucks and a trip to Manila.

—Prestigious, my ass. It's only prestigious because it's sponsored by AmPIL Inc.

—Look at the golden bright side of the tunnel.

—You mean the light at the end of the tunnel.

—Yeah, whatever. It all boils down to the same tunnel to you and me—

—...

—Now, where was I?

—In the tunnel.

—Oh, yeah. Look at the bright tunnel, Vince. You never won the grand prize to Queens but you still getting outta this lovely rock.

—How can it be my savior when the ticket is round-trip and has an expiration date?

—Eh, no be complaining cuz you was the one who told everyone in the audience that if you had twenty-four hours left on earth, you going spend it in the Philippines because that's where you was born and raised. Remember?

—Of course, I remember. I said it, remember? But just because I said it doesn't mean I meant it.

—How come you said it if you never meant it? Why you never just say Queens or Daly City or someplace else.

—Because I thought it was the pageantically correct response. What better answer out there can you give?

—Maybe that's the ideal answer for one immigrant, but you ain't one immigrant anymore, Vince. You are now one hundred percent pure American citizen. Besides, better two weeks in Manila than four days and three nights in Kalaupapa, right?

—Shut up.

—Vince, all I saying is that you cannot have your lumpia and eat it too. You gotta roll then fry some for others too. Besides, you always get the option of never returning.

—What the hell am I gonna do in Manila?

—Shop, what else? Or visit relatives and pretend you rich. When was the last time you saw them, anyway?

—Never went back since I came here.

—Well, that's even more of a reason.

—So what was the juicy thing you had to tell me?

—Oh, I almost forgot. Thanks for reminding me. I got a couple of juicy stuff. Which news you wanna hear first?

—Are they news or rumors?

—What's the difference?

—CNN or *Hard Copy*?

—Doesn't matter, Edgar.

—Ok, you remember Babette?

—Babette who?

—Babette Ignacio.

—The cross-eyed chick with the big tits in Mrs. Takemoto's class?

—Jackpot.

—What about her?

—Remember her first calabash cousin Johnny Lee, my ex-neighbor, the jock with the eggplant-sized cock you and me used to spy on with my binoculars cuz my bedroom window faced his bathroom?

—What about him?

—Remember his sister Chandra?

—Wasn't she the one who nearly lost it after shooting their mother's boyfriend because he used to beat their mother up?

—Wrong. She shot their mother's boyfriend cuz he raped her in front their mother. Anyways, you know that she recently got out of the correctional center, right?

—No.

—Yeah, couple months already. Some hotshot psychiatrist at Kahi Mohala, who helped her snap out of it, finally OK'd her to face the public eye again.

—Where is she now?

—Still in Honolulu. My mother just ran into her the other day, riding on the Waikiki bus. My mother was on her way to work and Chandra, who now changed her name to Sandra, was heading home. She said that Chandra/Sandra looked OK. She get one job now, working as one sales assistant at the lingerie department in Liberty House at Ala Moana. Anyways, my mother said that Chandra/Sandra said that on that day that they ran into each other on the bus, there was a so-so commotion at Liberty House because Madame Imelda Marcos was trying to close the store for a couple of hours so she and Doris Duke can shop in private.

—And?

—But the management said no way, José, cuz everyone in the entire island, except for the Ilocanos, of course, complained till thy kingdom come the last time Liberty House closed off the store to everybody so Madame could shop.

—OK.

—Then my mother said that Chandra/Sandra told her that Imelda and Doris looked kinda disappointed when the manager told them that they had to share the space with the other Liberty House shoppers. Chandra/Sandra also said that Imelda and Doris was walking around like they IT cuz they was being followed by an entourage of a hundred plus bodyguards, reporters, photographers and maids. But Chandra/Sandra said nobody bothered with them. Poor Imelda. If not for the Ilocanos, I really think she lost every ounce of her Martial Law popularity. And as for Doris, nobody in Hawai'i knows or cares to know who she is, cuz to us, she just another Haole, right? Anyways,

Chandra/Sandra was the one assigned to help Imelda and Doris shop for panties, OK?

—OK.

—So the whole time Imelda and Doris were in the dressing room talking and trying on lingerie's, Chandra/Sandra overheard Imelda telling Doris that she and her family are all packed and ready to go back Manila.

—But isn't Cory Aquino banning Imelda from returning to the Philippines?

—But Imelda said she don't care. According to Chandra/Sandra, Imelda said that with or without the green signal from Cory, she going back home.

—What about the freezer?

—Imelda told Doris that, of course, shes taking the frozen-up Ferdinand with her.

—When is she planning on leaving Hawai'i?

—Next week or so.

—Really?

—For real. I ain't kidding.

—I can't believe she tried closing off Liberty House to the public again.

—Vince, is that your call waiting or mine?

—Mine.

—You not gonna pick it up?

—No.

—Why not?

—Just cuz.

—Maybe it's Dave.

—What?!

—No act all innocent, Vince, I heard from the grapevine that Dave tried to make a pass at you at the pageant.

—What?!

—Yeah, it was all over the backstage. Maybe he wants reconciliation.

—I don't think so. Besides, my two-week relationship with the biggest rice queen in the City and County of Honolulu is enough to turn me into a sticky-rice queen forever.

—You so incestuous, Vince!

—How in the hell did he end up as the host, anyway? Didn't the program say that the emcee was going to be last year's MISS ASIAN PEARL OF THE PACIFIC?

—Yuki Velasco-Wong.

—Yeah. What happened to Yuki, anyway?

—She was supposed to be the host but Miss APP had to bow out at the last minute cuz she was offered a cameo in *Days of Our Lives*.

—So AmPIL Inc gave the job to Dave?

—Bingo. So you mean to tell me, Vince, that there's no hope of you and Dave ever rekindling your two-week romance?

—Don't even go there, Edgar.

—Too late. I already did.

—No, not a chance. Besides, wasn't it you, of all people, who warned me not to get involved with models, especially rice queen models?

—Yes, ma'am.

—I think Dave just wanted an Asian fuck buddy that night.

—And you were obviously the best candidate.

—Thank you, but no thank you. Besides, his rice queenliness is starting to gross me out.

—So are you turning into a sticky-rice queen now?

—God, Edgar, you make it sound like I never had sex with other Asians.

—Vince, when was the last time you slept with an Asian?

—Right after Dave and I broke up.

—Which was when? Six months ago?

—Right.

—And when was the last time you slept with a Caucasian?

—Six months ago.

—With Dave?

—Yeah, with Dave.

—And you never slept with any other Haole after your two-week relationship with Dave ended?

—Correct.

—You're such a liar, Vince.

—Look, Edgar, I don't know what you're getting at, but I remember vividly the guys I fucked around with. Lance Nishihara was the last Asian I slept with. And Dave Manchester was the last Haole.

—What about James?

—James who?

—Don't act all innocently with me, Vince. You know which James I talking about.

—No, I don't, Edgar.

—JAMES DANIELS!

—James Daniels?

—Yeah, you know, rice queen who's only into kung hee fat choys?

—What about him?

—I know you two spent the night together.

—Huh?

—Vince, this is Edgar you talking to.

—What?!

—Must I spell it out, Vince?

—Who told you?

—Shit, Vince, it's all over CNN.

—No, Edgar, I'm not kidding. Who told you?

—James did. He told me and everybody else in Luau's last night.

—That fucker! He promised not to kiss and tell.

—Maybe he crossed his fingers when you asked him to cross his heart.

—I can't believe it.

—How many times I gotta tell you, Vince? Next time you fuck around with somebody, and you don't want all the fags on the island to know, do it with somebody like Helen Keller.

—But even if the fag was mute, Edgar, he could still spread it around to his friends via sign language.

—Then do it with somebody who don't have hands. So tell me, is it getting serious between you and James Daniels?

—It was nothing, Edgar. Simply a one-night stand.

—You sure.

—I'm positive.

—Then answer this: How did you get him to bed?

—What do you mean?

—I thought James was strictly one hundred percent joy luck queen? I bet you gave him all that half-truths about being one-third Filipino, one-third Spanish and one-third Chinese.

—He didn't tell you guys?

—No. He just said that you and he oofed.

—And?

—And he also said that it was the longest sixty-nine he's ever had.

—Fucker!

—Just exactly how long did you blow each other off?

—What else did he say?

—That's all. So tell me, what was the ancient Chinese secret recipe you used to hook him?

—...

—I waiting, Vince.

—...

—Tick. Tock.

—You better not tell anyone.

—Cross my bra.

—I ran into him last week at Luau's. He had just arrived from a modeling assignment in Tokyo. We started chatting, or rather, he was doing all the talking and I was doing all the listening. So he talked and talked and talked the whole night; all about himself, of course. When the bartender yelled out the last call for alcohol, we had one more drink and then he invited me over to his place.

—Then you two sucked the night away.

—No, it wasn't as easy as that. We started making out first then we took a break.

—It was that intense?

—Not really. He wanted to talk more about himself and how hard it was being a model.

—What's his astrological sign?

—Leo.

—That explains it.

—He's very much like you, Edgar. A Leo who's so self-engrossed.

—Excuse me Vince, I'm not a pure-bred Leo. I'm on the Cancer-Leo cusp. Anyway; continue; please.

—We resumed our making out position on the futon, then in between the frenching and groping, he stopped to ask me what kind of Chinese I was.

—Are you pulling my L'Eggs pantyhose?

—No, Edgar, the fucker was deadly serious. He was even saying phrases to me in Chinese.

—No shit?

—So he asked me again what kind of Chinese I was, and if I spoke Cantonese or Mandarin.

—You better not be inventing this up, Vince.

—I wish, Edgar.

—Then what happened?

—I finally had to break it to him, told him I was mostly Filipino with some Spanish on my mother's side. Then he said, 'But I thought all Filipinos have Chinese blood in them?'

—And what did you say?

—I answered that not all Filipinos were Chinese because there are Filipinos who are also part Malay or part Sicilian.

—You said Sicilian?

—I did.

—Are you serious?

—Edgar, the fucking conversation was getting ridiculous, for chrissake.

—Did he buy it?

—He bought everything, and even paid for the four percent island tax.

—What made him think that all Filipinos are Chinese to begin with?

—Jeremy Castillo.

—Oxy 10-faced Jeremy?

—Yes, MR. PHOTOGENIC Jeremy Castillo the Third.

—OK, continue.

—Well, you know that I know that everyone knows that Jeremy always had the hots for James, right?

—That's why Jeremy's the island's number one potato queen.

—So when Jeremy found out from one of James' friends that James was strictly one hundred percent pure joy luck queen, Jeremy cornered him one night at Luau's and invited him over to his house to play mahjongg with his family.

—What happened after you told him that not all Filipinos are Chinese because some are part-Sicilian?

—He turned SPF-5 on me.

—What?!

—He was embarrassed, of course. And at the same time, very disappointed because he brought me home, thinking I have Szechuan sizzling in my blood. So he got up and left the room.

—To go where? Patti's Chinese Kitchen for takeout?

—No, to get a drink.

—And left you all alone in the room?

—He went to the kitchen, OK. He came back with a six pack, turned on the TV and sat beside me on the futon. He apologized and said that he could only get it up for Pake fags.

—And what did you say?

—I told him it was all right. I went to use the bathroom to prepare my mental farewell speech. When I returned to the room, the fucker pounced on me. The next thing I knew, we were fully making out naked in front of the TV.

—What made him change his mind?

—At first, I thought it was because maybe he came to the conclusion that there wasn't much difference between an egg roll and a lumpia. But I thought wrong.

—Then what was it?

—It finally made sense when I asked him if we could turn down the TV or put on some music instead because the volume was blasting my nerves. But he said, 'No, leave it on, please.'

—Why, what was playing, *Enter The Dragon* with Vanity?

—No, Bertolucci's *The Last Emperor*.

—You two were making out to *The Last Emperor*?

—Edgar, I telling you, the Haole is the ultimate rice queen. The whole time he was going down on me, he kept calling me Pu Yi.

—Pu Yi?

—The Emperor. John Lone.

—No freakin' way?

—Yes way. So I played along and went down on him too.

—How? By calling him your butterfly?

—No, Wan Jung.

—Wan Jung? Who the hell's Wan Jung?

—The Empress. Joan Chen.

—Let me get this straight: You was Pu Yi and he was Wan Jung?

—For three fucking hours.

—Nonstop?

—Nonstop. Sex-Express all the way. Until the last credit stopped rolling.

—You better write to Bertolucci and thank him.

—It wasn't all that.

—Wait a minute...

—What?

—Was Pu Yi Chinese?

—No, he was Manchu. But I was too exhausted to give him lessons.

—So there ain't nothing serious between you and James?

—Nothing.

—You sure?

—Yeah. Why?

—Thanks a lot, Vince. You just made my mission impossible possible.

—What you mean?

—I gotta go.

—Where are you going?

—To the video store.

—For what?

—To rent *Flower Drum Song* and *The King and I*.

—For what?

—I'll tell you when you get back from Manila. Make a million wishes, Vince, and hope they all come true. Bye.

SENSORY FOR NINE

I.

Freshmen Banquet, 1983, John and I,
like the rest of the boys, went stag,
but not in the face of his father's
Visa and the clerk who handed us the keys
to the Presidential Suite. Once inside,
we started a cheap dialogue scripted for
ninth-grade porno boys stranded on an
improvised island made of hard-ons and
mermaids. A bottle of half-filled whiskey
smuggled in for excuses and emptied
within minutes strategically stood
between us to perform a ritual: skin,
which required a complete revolution
before the offering of tongues to men
who have perished in that unnamable
chasm some mistakenly called "passion."
The next day, he scribbled a short note
justifying the end of a friendship. It
was signed, Always.

II.

I met David, a Texan tourist, at the municipal
parking lot between Hamburger Mary's and God.
"On business?" I asked, "or pleasure?" He said
it didn't matter because, he reasoned, (with
a twang, of course) he was here to try
something new: Asian boys. He said he
got bored of tonguing sidewinder breaths and

doing honky-tonks who smelled in Marlboro
suits. He took me to his room and rammed his
ten-inch Southwestern cock up my ass without
a lubricant. Afterwards, he said it was the
best fuck he's had in ages. "The fuck?"
I asked, "or me?" "Does it matter?" he asked.
I said it didn't. He flew back that night.
I squatted home, sore as hell. David was 47.
I was 15. It was my first time.

III.

I used to cruise Kuhio Avenue with a gold
crucifix around my neck because I'm Filipino,
Catholic and superstitious. With the cross,
signed and blessed, I could ward off the
evil eyes of fag bashers and laser testicles
of cops who patrolled my second home in golf
cars. One Sunday night, I hooked up with a
seminarian who wanted to test his temptation
and see if we spoke the same prayer of jism
to Jesus in a piss-stained alley near Saint
Augustine Church. "Just this once," he said,
and called me "my son." "Yes, Father." I
worked him hard in my mouth, the taste of
pre-confessional cum on the tip of my tongue.
He pulled my hair and guided me gently
until he shot Holy Trinity on my face and
gold crucifix that once gleamed in the dark.

IV.

Tom, a 70-year-old Veteran, picked me up
in his BMW convertible at Ala Moana beach
park. He thought I had a million tricks
up my sleeves and offered me cash instead
of cookies. On the way to his condo,

he buried his hand on my crotch and said
it reminded him of World War II; my dick,
the US flag planted in Iwo Jima. Once
we got into the elevator, he pressed the STOP
button, crouched before me, pulled down
my zipper, and sucked me red, white and
blue. I leaned against the carpeted wall,
pumped his mouth, and slapped him with stars
and stripes. Before leaving, I told him
I was Filipino, not Japanese, that he must
have meant Bataan and not Nagasaki or
Hiroshima. He apologized, said, "You all
look the same." I said, "And so do you."

V.

He threatened to arrest me, beat me with
his baton if I resisted, blow the whistle
to my parents, then leave me in a cell
to rot if I didn't bend over and spread
wide for his authorization. I obliged,
told him he could use his spit to fuck
me because all the cops I had were all
the same: all muscles, no meat. He jabbed
his three-inch badge inside me, moaned
things I heard before—"You like my big
hard cock in your ass...oh yeah...such
sweet little ass...oh yeah, oh yeah..."
I forgot his fuck, but remembered the
cologne he wore, the mole on his thigh,
the yellow thread of name sewn on his
shirt. Ten hours later, I dialed letters
on the phone, spelled out his name to
a woman (his wife?) and told her about
Drakkar, the huge mole on his right
thigh next to the little mole that wanted
to eat me alive, yet couldn't.

VI.

Bert, a handsome teenager from New York,
met me when I was high on Ecstasy and
down on Absolut shots. We cabbed four blocks
to his hotel where we swallowed more tablets
and downed more vodka in a room fit
for Persephone. We talked about traveling,
the natural high of taking off or swimming
through tunnels without a map or compass.
I leaned against the headboard and watched
the walls devour his shadow as he took off
his clothes. He said he hadn't been with a guy
before but always had the urge to have
a man's flesh buried inside him. I believed
him, did him in, made him flinch as I had
flinched. He bit his lip as I dug
deeper than I had ever gone before. I
looked at his eyes, lost as the streetlights
that filtered through the cracks of the room.
I stared at his mouth, hungry as the walls
around us, and I stopped.

VI.

When I found out Bob, an Australian, had
a dick so fat it was made for Diamond Head
crater, it was already too late. He said
he wasn't into anal or oral, had a lover
back in Perth, and only needed a local fag
to chaperone him. After a Thai dinner,
Courvoisier, and a Stryker video, I passed
out on the floor whereby he pounced on me
like a puma in heat. My rectum ripped
while the chandeliers of Hyatt rang
in my ears. Then he turned me around and
shoved his cock, thick as a baby's fist,

down my throat. I nearly gagged. It was
the first—and only—time I tasted cum
and blood.

VIII.

Gary, a haole visual artist who got rich and
famous sketching native boys, wanted to fist
me for two grand and a roundtrip ticket to
Europe. I agreed only if we did it in his
yacht while I fucked Dario, his Filipino
boytoy. He said I was asking a lot; I said
that was what fisting was for. Sail away,
Dario said, and I blew him with one hand while
I jerked off with the other. Gary watched us
with a voyeuristic contempt as he poured baby
oil on his hands. I took my time, humped Dario
like a puppy, massaged his back, licked the sweat
off his neck, bit his earlobes. Before either
of us could come, Gary pulled me away, called me
a chinky fag and told me to scram. I left
without Penny Lane in my pockets, but I had
Dario's piece of ass still fresh on my cock.

IX.

I've had and been had by enough guys
to make a quilt and keep myself warm
forever, but I go on, open past wounds
to the night, stand or kneel or spread
in the dark, lick their sweat and five
o'clock shadows. I ask for more, ask for
the smell of salt on skin, the taste
of salt in my mouth, ask for the raw flesh
wanting more, giving more, but always,
never enough. Sometimes, when I'm alone
I jerk off to their names and shoot at the

what ifs, at the possibility of a fuck or
a blowjob session lasting longer than
a moan or the face of the clock; at
the moment when a stare at the crotch, an
opened fly, or an inviting grin means
breakfast in bed or flowers in a porcelain
vase; at the moment when an embrace or
a tongue means the making or breaking
of a night forgotten.

SHABUSERS

My brother Bong is a shabuser.
Our cousins Dongdong and his sisters
Pinky and Gigi are also addicts.
Tito Bart, their father, smoked
and dealt in shabu. Still in jail
after he got caught pushing minors
into tweaking for three, four, five days.
My mother's best friend Tita Marge
spent time in rehab. Crystal meth user,
she said, since the dawn of Martial Law.
Our neighbors next door Zsa Zsa
and Tin Tin, lovers of same sex,
who once led anti-Marcos protests
and were imprisoned several times
for inciting rebellion and conspiring
with the National People's Army
are now behind bars for selling shabu

and their bodies to foreigners
and ex-pats frequenting Ermita.

Gardo "Tondo Boy" Batongbacal, action
star and rumored to be an illegitimate
son of the President, entered rehab
for the fifth time this year. Like
Maricel, the First Daughter,
who was admitted last week at the
rehab right behind Bicutan market
where fishes, fruits and vegetables
are sold fresh daily. Attorney Edwin
Romero, son of the anti-American base
Senator Rommell Romero, confessed
to smoking shabu while attending law
school. It helped me to stay up, he
remarked in a TV docu about recovered
addicts of the rich and famous.
He quit cold-turkey soon after top-
notching the bar exam then joined
the fastest growing Born-Again Christian
movement. What a goddamn liar, said
his Chinito ex-lover Stanford Tan,
a criminal lawyer himself now under
investigation for drug smuggling.
Felipe Sin, another Chinese Filipino,
no relation to the Cardinal but
is the eldest son of a retired Supreme
Court judge, was high when he removed
the brain of a diplomat's daughter
with a .45 magnum revolver. With girl
dead, he is serving his lifetime
sentence, no parole, in Muntinlupa
Penitentiary, killing time watching
VHS tapes and ordering take-outs
on his cell phone. Felipe blamed
Manong Carlos, the family chaffeur,
for introducing him to drugs, girls
and guns. But it was in fact
his personal maid, Yaya Linda,
who got him hooked. My grandmother's

cousin the Manila Matrona Socialite
Dona Maria Esperanza and her maid Lucing
light up their pipes only once a year—
during Holy Week—so they could
stay up for the week-long non-stop
reading of the Passion of Christ.
Over half of my batchmates from
the graduating class of '89 get their
kicks on shabu, return pages via
cell phones, and hang out at posh
Makati nightclubs without chaperones
and condoms. Screen goddess Love
Perez, box office queen who's known
nationwide for her two dozen plus
titillating films and her remarkable
blowjob performances onscreen,
made international headlines recently
when she was arrested for possession
of shabu and firearms at Guam
International Airport. Her father,
a congressman and crony, begged
the President to use the country's
emergency fund for bail. No way, was
the President's response, we need it
to buy pork from Thailand. A month
behind bars, she was visited by Pinoy
fans in Guam who offered her their
homes, cash, McDonald's value meals,
until she agreed to say no to drugs,
say yes to God, appear with clothes on
in commercials and use her oral talent
at anti-drug campaigns. She was received
upon her return to Manila with a bouquet
of roses and a heroine's welcome.

TAKE OUT: QUEER WRITING FROM ASIAN PACIFIC AMERICA

TIMOTHY LIU

THE RAND MCNALLY ROAD ATLAS

Boys in the back seat
jacking off, trying to hit
their favorite state.

THOREAU

My father and I have no place to go.
His wife will not let us in the house—
afraid of catching AIDS. She thinks
sleeping with men is more than a sin,
my father says, as we sit on the curb
in front of someone else's house.
Sixty-four years have made my father
impotent. Silver roots, faded black
dye mottling his hair make him look
almost comical, as if his shame
belonged to me. Last night we read
Thoreau in a steak house down the road
and wept: *If a man does not keep pace*
with his companions, let him travel
to the music that he hears, however
measured or far away. The orchards
are gone, his village near Shanghai
bombed by the Japanese, the groves
I have known in Almaden—apricot,
walnut, peach and plum—hacked down.

TAKE OUT: QUEER WRITING FROM ASIAN PACIFIC AMERICA

E.G. LOUIE

WONDERLAND

I.

I had a cat, I had a backpack, and on Sundays, I had a pocketful of money. Sunday mornings I'd wake early and leash up Andre—I'd taught him to walk on a leash the year before—and we'd go either west to Riverside Park, or south and east to Central Park, which was less safe and therefore more exciting. I'd take a book and a bagful of grapes, and Andre and I would shortcut through leaves and underbrush until we reached my favorite bench, where I'd sit down and unleash him and he'd sprint his high-haunched run up a tree. He looked like a rabbit, with his high back legs, but he behaved like a dog, and as I read he'd drop acorn shells or tulip heads at my feet, depending on the season. I'd sit there for a couple of hours, until the families and nannies started trickling in, and then I'd get up and play with Andre for a while before leashing him again and walking to the grocery store before it got crowded.

At the store, I'd tie Andre to a parking meter and hurry through my shopping. That year, a gang of neighborhood kids had taken to slicing open stray cats and stuffing them down mailboxes, and I was always afraid that I'd come back and Andre would be gone. He was a fierce cat though, with a strong, quick bite and sharp claws; if needed, he could take care of himself. I'd buy the basics—milk and bread and peanut butter, tuna and orange juice and carrots and lettuce, eggs and pasta and a good cut of fish. I had a twenty-dollar bill every Sunday, and each week there was enough left over to buy myself a snack, although I usually had to save the money to buy food and litter for Andre.

One day—I was eight—I finished my shopping and went outside. Andre wasn't there; his nylon leash had been cut and looped in a pool around the base of the meter. I had two bags of groceries, and as I ran up the hill to my apartment, shouting his name, the bags banged against my face and their brown cardboardy smell made me sick. I tried to keep myself calm—no one would do anything to Andre—everyone in the neighborhood knew he was mine. It was three blocks north and one block west to my building, and as I rounded the corner of the last block, I saw three teenagers—a girl and three boys, they couldn't have been that old, maybe thirteen, although to me they seemed very old indeed—throwing a plastic bag in the air. I could hear Andre yowling, and they were shouting with laughter. I recognized the boys from my building. The girl I had never seen before.

I shouted at them, but they ignored me. The bag was leaping into the air and shaking, and from a distance, it looked like a wonderful toy. I jumped for the bag, but the girl caught it and threw it at one of the boys. She had a strong arm and the boy almost missed.

"Stop!" I cried. "Please stop!"

"Stop! Stop!" they taunted me. "Stop it! I'm gonna tell my mommy!" Andre was back in the girl's hand, and she spiked the bag high into the air with an athletic grace.

It was still early, and there were only a few people on the street—most of them were older, and all of them, except for a very old man wearing a felt fedora who shook his head as he passed—avoided looking our way. Many of them crossed to the other side of the street. I had dropped my groceries by the side of a building and was running between them, jumping in the air for Andre, whose yowls had grown hoarse, then quiet, then had finally stopped. When I was very young, my father had told me that only cowards and idiots cried, and although I tried not to, I could feel my face growing hot, and I knew I would begin to soon, and then I would never get Andre back, and they would laugh at me besides. I was tired, I was staggering between them, and although they were growing bored, they wouldn't stop. When they finally did, I was rubbery-legged and defeated, and as they ran away, talking and laughing, I undid the knot on the bag and Andre slid out. He looked at me and yowled, and I sat down on the sidewalk and started to cry. He seemed then to recover himself, and butted his head against my leg. I held him in my lap and he purred and licked my hand and cried again.

Someone was standing over me. "Are you all right?" he asked, and I looked up.

He was a tall man, and thin, pale, with a slant of graying brown hair brushed back from a high forehead. He bent down next to me, and put a hand on Andre's back, who gave a moan but didn't move. "Ghastly," said the man. He had a British accent, and his voice was quiet, lulling. "I saw the end of it, I'm afraid. How's your cat?"

"I don't know," I told him.

"There, there," he murmured, and fished in his pants pocket for a handkerchief, which he handed me. "What's your cat's name?" he asked me. "Andre?" he repeated. "Let me see Andre," he said, and crouched down next to me, his fingers moving over my cat, prodding him gently. He finished and handed him back to me with a smile. His teeth were slightly crooked and not quite white, but it was shy, tentative, a smile to trust, one that made you want to smile back. "I had many cats when I was a boy," he explained. "Andre will be fine. Just take him home and let him sleep." I nodded, and he smiled again and stood. I saw him gather my groceries (the eggs had been smashed against the curb) and shake the paper bags open again, placing the food inside. There was something unhurried and graceful about his gestures, about his speech, about his very calmness, as if he encountered crying boys and injured cats every day. When he came back, I managed to thank him, and he held out a hand and helped me stand.

"I'm Lawrence Sterling," he said, and I introduced myself.

"Ezekiel," he said. "What an old-fashioned name." He looked nervous then, and his smile stretched out, long and thin.

"Let me help you carry these groceries home," he offered. "Where do you live?" (*Never tell anyone where you live,* my friend Peter's mother had told us.)

But I pointed toward my building anyway. "That one," I told Lawrence.

And then he beamed. "Why, that's my building too," he said, and we walked toward it slowly, me holding Andre, Lawrence Sterling holding the groceries.

When we reached the building, Lawrence unlocked the front door and handed me my groceries, and I thanked him again. "Thank you, Mr. Sterling."

"Lawrence," he corrected me. And then he did a strange thing—he bent again, so we were at eye level, and opened his mouth as if he were about to speak. (His eyes were a strange silvery gray, with pupils so dark and large and velvety they looked blurry.) But he didn't, and in the end all he did was rest his hand on my shoulder for a moment, before straightening and holding the elevator door open for me. "Goodbye, Ezekiel," he said. "I'll see you again soon." He sounded so certain, but when I looked up, he was walking briskly toward the front door, running his hand through his hair.

II.

The building was large and gray and malodorous, on lower Morningside Drive next to the undergraduate campus. Lots of professors lived there, but most of them—except the ones without tenure, whose children tended to be very young—did not have families. Those who could afford it bought houses in Westchester, apartments on the Upper West Side, or commuted from New Jersey or Connecticut, which meant our building was a collection of single women and old bachelors. I have a friend who grew up in a similar apartment complex in Cambridge, and says there was always one or two old coots, professors of antiquities or linguistics or math, who were known as the resident nuts, from whom all the building's children would run screaming with delight and fear upon encountering. My building was *all* nuts and eccentrics; even the children—clownish and fat Michael Goldbaum, weedy little Thomas Kernes, damaged (such a disappointment to her brilliant parents, people murmured) and deadened Lucille Fisk, and myself too, of course—were misfits, forever out-of-step.

We lived in a two-bedroom apartment. There was also a study with glass-paned French doors, but my father, who used this room, had hung long sheets of black butcher paper on the inside of the doors. He'd taped the edges down, so when you tried to look in, all you could see was the glow of the hazy yellow light from his lamp. My mother used one of the bedrooms as her study, and the other bedroom was theirs, although in my years in that apartment, I rarely saw either of them in there. Both of them had low-slung hard couches in their studies, and when they were tired, they were most likely to simply lie down than go to their own unused room. Still, they must have liked the idea of their own bedroom (or maybe they just forgot about it; you could never tell with them) because I slept in a strange little alcove of a room right off the dining room that at one time might have been a walk-in closet. Upper West Side apartments are always divided in strange ways; at one time, they were nine or ten-room single-family apartments, but they were chopped up and reconfigured after the war, and you would see apartments with tiny galley kitchens and huge foyers (like ours) and then, in your next-door neighbors' (the Fisks), you'd find its missing half—a sprawling kitchen, butcher blocks and picture windows, with a small wedge of a dining room. My bedroom (as it was) abutted the Fisk parents'—at night, I could hear them talking Lucille through one of her fits, their voices first gentle, then beseeching, then angry, then weary. Eventually—after minutes or hours, depending upon how they felt—one of them would be dispatched to carry Lucille off to bed. Sometimes, after one of her more animated seizures, I'd hear one of the Fisks crying. I also heard them complaining to one another, late at night. They seemed to hold parallel conversations. *I hate this place. We have to institutionalize her. There's no closet space in this goddamn room. We could try to have another one, you know. Where am I going to put this? There's no space in here. Let's move. We should. We have no money. And if we institutionalize her, we'll have less. There're state agencies. State agencies. Yes.*

I slept in the Fisks' missing closet. It was about two bookcases wide and about twelve feet long. It, too, had French doors, but the glass in the doors had been removed and replaced with squares of whitewashed wood. There was a window in the closet too, which took up most of one wall and which, ironically, afforded the best view in the apartment—a wide sweeping view of the west. Beyond some other low buildings, you could see the park, and beyond it the river, and so every day I looked out onto a mist where the gray sky met the gray water. My bed, a narrow twin, was pushed up underneath the window ledge, and there was a trunk at the foot of my bed, where I kept all my clothes—corduroys and sweaters for the winter, t-shirts and jeans for the summer. Underneath my bed I had four large brown boxes—one for papers, one for socks and underwear, one for toys, and one for cat supplies and tinned food. I kept my shoes—sneakers for the weekend, loafers for school—under the bed as well. Lying down on my bed, I could see my books, shiny spines out, arranged in gleaming rows from floor to ceiling, wall to wall. If I sat up and swung my feet around instead of shimmying to the end of the bed and hopping over my trunk as I usually did, I'd be sitting at my desk, where I kept stacks of lined paper, an old typewriter I'd found one summer, and a can of sharpened pencils. I liked things neat, which was lucky, because the space was so small only neatness would do.

What did I do in that apartment? I ate, I cooked, I slept. There was a living room but since there was no furniture in it, no one ever spent time there. There was also, for a period, a dining room table, although one day when I came home from school it was gone, and I saw it later in my father's messy study, where he was using it as an extension of his desk. Its matching chairs sat abandoned until I donated them to charity. In my parents' thinking, I didn't need anything other than food, and they might have forgotten that too had I not reminded them repeatedly, until they gave me the money directly and let me take care of my own needs. One year I saved up the dollars from the week's groceries until I had enough to buy a radio, which I put in my room and listened to at night before reading and falling asleep. I bought books with the money too, and needles and thread. I taught myself how to darn, how to knit, how to iron. Saturdays I did the laundry and cleaned the bathrooms. Sundays, as I've said, I shopped. But the rest of the week was mine.

III.

I spent most of the weekdays with the Drapers, although I tried to leave them alone on the weekends.

To an outsider, I suppose, my parents' parenting skills would be thought of as little more than neglect. I never felt neglected, though—I liked to be left alone, liked to amuse myself. It was not until I grew up and had told a few stories about my life in their house that I began to see it as something more than strange—sad, pathetic, wrong. I don't remember ever really wishing my life different, but I knew I was attracted to parents who would act like I thought parents should act—interested, involved, a presence that could be either benign or malevolent or protective. My friend at the time was Peter Draper, whom I'd met in the halls of the building, where he used to live. If you knew Peter, it wasn't hard to imagine the kind of family he was from, and you'd have been correct— his mother was tall and attractive and soft-spoken and gentle, and his father adoring, affectionate and jovial. Both of them were intelligent and patient as well as good-hearted, and both of them would have long conversations with me and Peter about whatever interested us. Whenever we went to Peter's house after school and his father was home, he'd pick both Peter and his little sister, Maia, up in a hug and twirl them around as they squealed with glee. He once asked me if he could hug me, too, and although I was too embarrassed to reply, he did so anyway, and I was grateful to him both for offering and for not making me answer. After that, he always hugged me when he saw me. Professor Draper (Peter's mother was Dr. Draper, but I usually called them Henry and Constance, their first names) I know, thought I led a strange life, and both he and Peter's mother were always asking me long strings of questions over dinner and then trading sidelong glances after I answered. They asked me what I ate, what I did at home, what I talked about with my parents, what my chores were, what I did for fun, was I lonely without brothers and sisters, what the building was like now. They didn't really care too much about the last question, but they did like to know the gossip, if anything had happened. I think they liked to hear my stories, which I always acted out, to Maia's delight. I'd save up little tidbits—the Fisks seemed to have been throwing plates at each other the night before, I saw

Professor Cooney wander into the elevator without his pants—so I could tell them and make them either smile or laugh or shake their heads. The Drapers had moved from the building when Peter and I were six, into a large brownstone apartment on West End Avenue, not far from the building. My answers to the Drapers' questions were: Whatever I cooked, whatever I wanted, nothing, everything and nothing, nothing, and no, I had Andre. And Peter, of course. And Maia and Constance and Henry. At this last they would smile and look troubled and lean back in their chairs, and then either Constance or Henry would say, "You know you're always welcome here, Ezekiel."

I was Peter's friend, but I spent most of my time with Henry. We would go into his dark study and read together, or play chess together, or Henry would play his clarinet and I would wander around the room, looking at his books, and the collection of carved African and Asian masks he'd hung in long rows on the wall above his desk. Peter sometimes played with us, but he was usually—lucky me!—watching television or baking something with his mother, or playing with the Drapers' disruptive dog, Licky. Sometimes Henry would talk to me in his deep voice and I would listen to him until I felt his hand on my shoulder and heard his voice saying, "Come on, Ezekiel, I'll take you home." It would be late at night and Peter would have long fallen asleep. "Goodness, Henry," said Constance, mildly, the way she said everything, "you're wearing that poor child out." But she didn't mind, really. She would get my coat from the closet and kiss me on the forehead, and open the door so Henry could half walk, half carry me, back to the building. When we reached the building, he, too, would kiss me goodnight. Once, Peter accused me of being his friend only so I could spend time with Henry, and it was somewhat true. Peter and Henry got on well, but Peter, in the presumptuous way of children who have always had everything, was casual with his father, casual about time spent with him, casual about asking questions, receiving answers. Peter would be naughty, would throw a tantrum, be reprimanded by his father, and then the next minute I'd see him leaning lazily against his father's knee, as if his father was a particularly reliable and comfortable piece of furniture. At those times I would feel something in me that resembled hatred, and I would tell Peter and Henry I had to leave, and go home cursing Peter's ungratefulness, his dumb good fortune. *I* deserved a family like Peter's; *I* would do everything right. But it was Peter who was the lucky one, not me.

The Drapers were black and they took me everywhere with them. I have pictures from when Peter and I were seven and the Drapers took us to Washington, D.C. over Thanksgiving to visit Dr. Draper's relatives. They were a handsome family, and I, standing with them in front of the Capitol Building, look puny, pale, ugly. We used to pretend I was his adopted brother, and indeed, when Constance and Henry introduced us, they said, "These are our children, Peter, Ezekiel, and Maia." People would smile and look confused but, being academics, didn't dare ask questions. "What a card Henry is," they'd whisper, uncomfortable. On those vacations, the Drapers' friends and relatives would look at me once, bemusedly, and then pretend I wasn't there. I didn't mind though, because I had the Drapers, and even their relatives' disinterest didn't dissuade them from bringing me along to their house in Vermont for the summers, a friend's beach party in chilly October, and once, for part of the winter holidays, London. Before these trips, Dr. Draper used to ask me if it was all right with my mother. "I'll call your mother and make sure it's OK," said Dr. Draper before a weekend visit to a friend's house in Rhode Island. "Oh, I'm sure it's fine," I told her, but Dr. Draper made me give her my phone number and then called my house. She dialed and listened for a long time and then hung up with a nonplussed expression.

"No one's picking up," she said.

I could have told her. "My parents don't pick up the phone," I said, primly.

Dr. Draper studied me for a long moment. "Oh," she said, and her voice was soft. I knew she felt sorry for me, and perplexed by my family, and I felt a flash of annoyance and pride at my parents' persistent contrariness.

Peter and Maia and I drew pictures all evening, and when Henry was putting on his shoes to walk me home (I always said it wasn't necessary, and he always insisted it was), Constance handed me a small letter in a heavy cream-colored envelope. My mother's name was on the front. "Give that to your mother, Ezekiel," said Constance. "I'd feel better if she knew you were going with us. We'll see you tomorrow then, all right?"

After Henry had dropped me off and made sure I was in the elevator and walked back down the hill and west toward Riverside, I opened the envelope. The paper was cottony and made a smooth sluicing noise as I ripped it.

Dear Elka,

We've never formally met, but I wanted you to know what a delight Ezekiel is, and how much we enjoy having him spend time with us. Indeed, I think I speak for the whole family—my children, Peter and Maia, and my husband, Henry—when I say I consider him as dear as one of our own.

I'd like to have Ezekiel join us when we go to Rhode Island at the end of the month. Henry's college roommate has a house on the beach, and I'm sure the children will have a wonderful time. I hope this sits well with you; I'll give you the number there.

I know you and your husband must be busy, but Henry and I would like to have you over for dinner sometime. Please let me know which dates work for you.

All best, Constance Jarvis Draper

I read Constance's note a few times. I wanted desperately to go to the beach. I couldn't show my mother this. She wouldn't know what to make of it. "What!" she'd say. "What is this? Why are you showing me this?" It was obvious that (meddlesome) Dr. Draper wanted a response. I knew that I couldn't tell teachers at school that my parents wouldn't sign permission slips, attend open houses, or arrange parent-teacher conferences. I learned to forge my mother's signature and to say that my parents were attending symposiums abroad. I went to a school with lots of professors' children, and the teachers there knew that professors operated in different ways. But mine didn't operate at all, especially when compared to the Drapers, who seemed sometimes to exist only as a contrast to my own.

IV.

My parents didn't like to be disturbed, and I took care to do so only when absolutely necessary. My father typed a list and stuck it under my door after I had once bothered him (I hadn't been able to reach the can opener, much less operate it). The list said: NECESSARY—FIRE, DEATH, WAR, BURGLARS, REVOLUTION, NATURAL DISASTER. EVERYTHING ELSE—UNNECESSARY. He had a wicked sense of humor, although I was too young and resentful to appreciate it at the time.

My father's name was Chong. I never knew his given name until shortly before he died, when I discovered it was Liu Bao. I never called my parents anything, but I thought of them by their names. Chong was tall and pale-skinned and had once been handsome; he moved to America from Shanghai by way of Paris in 1968, which is when, according to my mother, his looks began to disintegrate. He wore sweaters and khakis and heavy rimless glasses, which he was forever taking off and misplacing. Chong was a professor of astrophysics and never talked to me, communicating only through notes, which he typed and slid under my door. A typical note might read only: TOILET PAPER, which meant we were out or almost out and I should go to the store and get some more. I used to leave my parents their meals outside their doors, and once when I picked up my father's plate, he'd left a note on it: DELICIOUS. I was so proud—I'd made him a salsify fritter, I think—and I made it day after day, but never received another note again. (I stopped making the fritters when my father started leaving them, untouched, for me to collect.)

My mother's name was Elka Beata Rothstein, and she was a professor of medieval European history. My mother was a large woman, almost as tall as my father, and fat too. She had pale blond hair that was fading to the color of dust by the time I was born. She, too, never talked to me, and it was not until she was dying and I was once feeding her that I heard anything of note come from her mouth, but when it came, it was a chant: *I am from Prague and my family had once been rich. We owned a textile factory near the river, and when the Nazis came to Czechoslovakia, my father refused to move. My older sister, Lulu, was in boarding school in Lausanne, but I was ten and my brother Tomas was eight, and my father and mother wanted us to stay at home. My family perished at Auschwitz, all except for me. I was twelve when the camps were liberated. Lulu died the next year of cancer. I went to Paris and lived with my uncle, who'd been hidden during the war. He was kind to me, but he was always sad. And at seventeen, I ran away.* Elka chiseled money from her uncle and went to St. Catherine's at Oxford. After university, she came down and went back to Paris, where she studied at the Sorbonne. She married one of her university professors and had two girls, Anna and Marie-Sylvie, both of whom died in a boating accident with their father one year on vacation. I didn't discover any of this either until after she had died and I had read through her journals. Then there is a long, unaccounted-for gap not recorded in her journals, at least none of the journals to which I was given access. (My mother was cagey, mean like this—when she died, she left thirteen journals. I was allowed the first five, with the final eight to be doled out to me, one a year, by her literary executor, when I reached my fortieth birthday. Her executor, a fusty and dusty colleague of hers and a Sanskrit scholar, was not inclined to circumvent my mother's will and indeed, seemed to take a wheezy sort of pleasure in my initial desire to read her words and his own unwillingness to let me. After asking twice to see them—both times refused by him—I asked no more. He called me up a year after my last request and proposed that I offer services in exchange for the journals; I declined, and have not heard from him since. I wonder now if he has burned them, humiliated or vengeful after I rejected his offer, or if he is keeping them, convinced that I will relent. It will be in keeping with my mother's character, though, that if I do indeed receive the journals when I am forty, they will be eight leatherbound books of blank pages, dotted only with water and mildew spots.)

The known thread, however, continues in 1965, when my father, thin and mute from the Cultural Revolution arrived in Paris on a student visa and defected. Somewhere, he met my mother, who was now a professor at the Sorbonne. A friendship began, and in 1966, they married. In 1967, they accepted positions at the same university in New York. And in 1968, said my mother, teeth bared and eyes bright, sighing, resigned and yet still determinedly resentful, "You came."

V.

Was it any wonder, then, that a few weeks after Lawrence saved me in the street, I met him in the laundry room and, after he awkwardly, hesitantly, asked me if I'd like to come to supper, I quickly agreed? Here was what happened.

Saturday was chore day, for which I saved all the heavy tasks—laundry, scrubbing the floors, cleaning the bathrooms. I liked during the laundry because it meant I had a chance to read. I liked the laundry room too: It was next to the boiler and warm. It smelled of detergent and clean cotton, and as long as I got there early enough, there was no one to bother me. The laundry room opened at eight in the morning, and every

Saturday I'd be waiting for Michael, the super, to open the door and let me in.

It was the first Saturday in November, and it was cold and since whoever managed the building never adhered to proper building codes, there was no heat. I stood at my window and looked out to the river, which capped in gray peaks. My breath was white against the glass. I was a little late that morning, but no one in the building ever got up early on Saturdays, particularly when it was chilly, and so I was able to take my time. I used a black plastic garbage bag for the laundry, and stuffed into it my own clothes along with my parents', who'd leave spreading mounds of it outside their doors the night before. I dragged the bag into the creaking elevator and thudded down to the basement. But as I neared the laundry room, I could see someone was already there—from around the corner, I saw a leg in khaki, a black sock, the toe of a brown shoe.

It was Lawrence. "Hello," he said.

"Hello," I said.

"I couldn't sleep," he said. He looked—or rather, peered—at me closely. I turned away for an instant, and when I turned back, he was looking elsewhere and smiling, faintly. "How's your cat?"

"Fine," I said.

I realize now that I'm making Lawrence sound somewhat lecherous, or at the least, a bit suspicious. The truth is that he came across as neither. It was confusing, though, to have someone already in the laundry room before I arrived, and more confusing still to have it be the man who'd helped me on the street.

"What are you reading?" Lawrence asked, pointing at my book.

I showed him. "Ah," he said. "'Twas brillig, and the slithy toves/did gyre and gimble in the wabe…" He looked at me, smiling expectantly.

I admitted I hadn't read *Through the Looking Glass* yet.

"Oh," said Lawrence. He looked disappointed. "Well!" he said. "You will, soon." There was a silence. "Do you remember my name, Ezekiel?" he asked. His voice was quiet.

"Yes," I said. "You're Professor Sterling."

"Lawrence," he told me.

"All right," I agreed.

The timer on the drier buzzed and both of us started and then laughed. "Let me help you," said Lawrence.

"No," I said. "I can do it."

So Lawrence watched as I dragged my bag of laundry in and started throwing it into the washing machine. I made myself concentrate, suddenly angry that he was staring at me. Something fell to the ground and Lawrence, who had at last started removing his clothes from the drier, bent to pick it up. It was a pair of my mother's enormous

underpants, and he retrieved them gingerly, between thumb and forefinger, before dropping them into the machine.

I wanted to laugh. "Thank you."

"You're welcome," said Lawrence, who had by this time finished unloading the
drier and had (I noted disapprovingly) thrown everything into a plastic hamper without
folding it. "I say," said Lawrence, his voice becoming plummy and crisp; he ran his fingers
through his hair. "Might you like to come over to my house for dinner tonight? I have a
beautiful edition of *Alice in Wonderland* that you might like to look at." He said the last of
this in a rush and then blushed such a deep red that I felt sorry for him and agreed. Also—
why not admit it?—I was a bit curious.

"Really?" asked Lawrence. He beamed, as if I had somehow made him supremely happy, and seeing this, I was happy too.

"You don't have to bring anything," said Lawrence, quickly. "It's Apartment 5H.
Why don't you come over at around six o'clock?"

"All right," I said.

Lawrence smiled again, but the gentle, timid smile I had seen him wear when
he approached me on the street. "It's a date then," he said, so softly I wasn't sure I had
heard him, but when he left, he let just the tips of his fingers brush across the top of my
head.

VI.

Lawrence's apartment was not like ours, which is to say that it looked like a real apartment, with furniture and art on the walls and bookcases from floor to ceiling actually
filled with books, unlike our apartment, where the shelves held only dusty unpacked
boxes of papers and books my parents had brought with them from France.

"Welcome, welcome," said Lawrence, drying his hands on a dishtowel and smiling. "Let me show you around." He showed me the apartment, which, aside from the
kitchen, which was large, was laid out somewhat like ours, except with only two bedrooms instead of three. It was also much neater, and warm, both in color (there were
lamps scattered about) and in temperature (there were space heaters in both the hallway
and living room). The air was pleasantly hazy with heat and the smell of bread, and I
thought of the Drapers' house and felt comfortable. I started to follow him into the
kitchen, but he flapped his hand. "No," he said. "It's almost done. You're my guest tonight.
Why don't you look at my books, see if there's anything you want to borrow?"

Lawrence had a dizzying array of books. Really, he probably didn't have any
more than my parents did, but they were so nicely arranged, so accessible, that it seemed
like more than I'd ever seen. Many of the books were fairy tales: *Puck of Pook's Creek*, *The
Little Elf*, *The Merry Faerie*. There was a couch in front of one of the banks of books, so if
you wanted, you could grab a book from behind you and spend all night on the couch,

reading.

"Dinner's ready," called Lawrence. "I made an eel pie and salad."

I sat down and Lawrence cut me a slice of pie and put a large helping of salad on my plate. It was all so familiar—the dinner, the conversation that would follow, being treated like a child, as if I couldn't do or hadn't done anything for myself—I could have been at the Drapers'. Lawrence watched me fork into the pie with some nervousness; he explained that he had loved this pie when he was a boy and visiting his grandparents in Wales, but if I didn't like it, he could make me some pasta with pesto, or soup, or whatever I wanted.

"It's good," I said.

He looked relieved and smiled. He didn't seem to stop smiling: when I looked up, he was smiling, and when I bent my head, I could feel him smiling at me anyway. That, coupled with those pale stone-colored eyes, made me think that he might be a little strange.

"How old are you, Ezekiel?" asked Lawrence.

I told him.

"Ah, eight," said Lawrence. "I can hardly remember when I was eight." Then he reddened like he had in the laundry room and fiddled with his fork. "You're much smarter than I was at eight though, that's certain. Where do you attend school?"

Structurally, the rest of the conversation was very much like the ones I had with the Drapers: Lawrence asked questions and I answered them. What grade was I in? My goodness, I must be very smart indeed. He knew I was. Did I like school? He hadn't liked it much either, and now he was a professor and in school for the rest of his life, what did I think about that? My parents were professors too; was I very close to them? He had met my mother once, and knew she was very well-respected. I seemed very independent, and mature: Was I an only child? Did I always do the grocery-shopping and the laundry? How old was Andre? He'd loved his boyhood cats and was thinking of getting one now—maybe I'd like to come to the pet store and help him pick one out? In short, the conversation was terrifically dull (but the eel pie was delicious), and by the end of my second slice, my answers had, I'm afraid, become monosyllabic, and Lawrence was firing efficient and detailed questions at a feverish pace to compensate for the silence: What was my favorite book? What did I like about it? What other languages did I speak? What was my favorite food? Did I like to cook? Did I want to borrow one of his books?

"Do you have a girlfriend?" asked Lawrence, smiling his timid smile.

"I don't know," I said. It hadn't occurred to me.

Lawrence laughed softly and flushed. "I guess you're a little young for that, aren't you?" he asked. "I keep forgetting."

There was a silence. "Well!" said Lawrence, suddenly bright and animated. He went into the kitchen and emerged with a ceramic dish containing a gloppy pudding and spooned a large mound of it into a bowl for me. "Strawberry trifle," he said. "Comfort food. Another favorite." He rolled the "r" grandly, served himself some, and sat down again.

"You have a lot of fairy tale books," I told him.

"I do!" Lawrence breathed, as if I had just discovered some cache of jewels he'd never before noticed. "Yes, I certainly do!" He was so sincerely delighted that I felt insulted. "Would you like to know why?" he asked.

What could I say?

"Well," said Lawrence, and his voice dropped back into its normal register. "I'm a professor of Victorian literature. Specifically, the ways in which, um, well...." He stopped, thought for a moment. "The Victorians were fond of fairies, you see. It wasn't just because theirs was a culture obsessed with infantilization, with concealed sexuality, with...with...the appearance of innocence, although that was certainly part of it—they were morality tales, of course, but they were also an expression of wonderment, of a carefully constructed naivete. They..." he stopped. "This must be boring for you," he said, his face stricken.

"No," I told him. "It isn't." He was a good teacher.

Lawrence jumped up and went to the bookcase over the couch. He came back holding a small green book, about the size of his palm, which he opened halfway, with great care. It was a book of beautiful (almost too beautiful, I thought) illustrations: fairies, their wings so finely drawn they looked sticky, hovering over sleeping children and snoring animals. In some of the pictures, the fairies looked gentle, benevolent, but in some their smiles looked wicked, as if they were laughing at the creatures upon whom they showered sparkles of light. There was no text, only page after page of fairies. "This is a fairly typical depiction of fairies," said Lawrence (his voice had become crisp-toned and authoritative; I preferred it).

"They look evil," I interrupted. "Like they don't like children."

Lawrence looked up from the book then and smiled, and his smile, like his voice, was at once proud and sad. "Yes," he said, "You're right. Because the children grew up, you see, and then forgot the fairies ever existed. It was their fate in life to be one day made redundant by everyone they had touched."

———

Lawrence told me to leave the dishes and we sat on the couch looking at an old edition of *Alice in Wonderland* with its hand-tinted blues and lemony yellows. I yawned and Lawrence looked at his watch. "My goodness," he said. "It's ten o'clock. I've kept you up far too late. You ought to be getting home." He looked hopeful, as if I might contradict him. "Your parents will worry."

I agreed. Lawrence looked disappointed. "Thank you for having me," I told him.

"You're very welcome," said Lawrence. I put out my hand and Lawrence smiled, sadly, and shook it. "Ezekiel," he said, and his voice was whispery, almost hoarse.

"What?"

"May I…" he stopped. His face was coloring again. "May I kiss you goodnight?"

I knew, I must have known, that this was something different—the Drapers never asked; they just did it, easily, as if it was their right, because they did it every day. But I agreed anyway.

His smile trembled then, and he folded himself down on his knees, and took my hands in his, leaned in his face to me and kissed me, once, on the mouth. When he drew his face back, I saw that his eyes were shining. "One more," he whispered, and he brought his face close to me and gave me a strange sort of kiss, wet, covering my mouth with his, his tongue darting in my mouth, once, as quick and smooth as a silvery fish, before pulling back again. Then he wrapped his arms around me and gave me a strange sort of hug, rubbing his arms and palms of his hands up and down my back, sloughing instead of squeezing. I pulled away and he put the tips of his fingers to his mouth. He looked stricken again and I felt, at once, profoundly, uncomfortably, embarrassed for him.

"Well, goodbye," I told him.

He didn't get up off the ground. "Goodbye," he said, clearing his throat.

I was opening the door to leave when he called out, "Maybe you'll come back sometime?"

I could have left forever, I could have pretended not to hear him, or I could have just not answered him. But I did. "All right," I said, and as the door shut behind me, I could feel, rather than see, him rise quickly to his feet again.

VII.

I went to the Drapers' after school. It had gotten colder, and Henry had promised to teach us how to make walnut pies as soon as the temperature dipped.

"Hello, Ezekiel," said Henry. His hands were covered with dough. I dropped my bag on the floor and slid into one of the chairs. Henry stood behind me and showed me how to shape the dough into little balls before punching them down and fitting them into a tart tin. He smelled of cloves and sugar and the pipe he liked to smoke. Lawrence had smelled of something lighter, woodier, like orange almost, but not quite.

We each made three small pies, and after Henry put them into the oven to bake, he ordered us a pizza. Over dinner, Peter talked about his day—his class had gone on a field trip to the museum, and he told us about the dinosaurs, the stuffed birds, the whale hanging from the ceiling.

"I've been there before," I said.

"So?" said Peter.

"Boys," said Henry, calmly.

By the time we were finished with dinner, the pies were done as well, and Henry slid them onto a baking rack to cool. Peter and I burned the tips of our fingers trying to pinch bits of walnut off the tops. "Stop it, kiddos," said Henry. "When they've cooled, you can each have one for dessert. Maia, honey, don't touch—it's hot."

We ate our pies and drank the milk Henry poured for us. The pies were flaky and sweet, so sweet that they made my saliva thick and stubborn, and I gulped down three glasses of milk. "Karo syrup's the trick," said Henry, munching on his second pie. "When I was a boy, we used to make these with pecans." Maia had a cold so Henry put her to bed early while Peter and I played checkers in his room. We played game after game, speaking very little; we took turns winning. After a time, Constance came up. "Hello sweetheart, hello Ezekiel," she said. "It's late, boys." (It was nine.) "Time for bed, bean," she said to Peter. "Henry'll walk you home, hon," she said to me.

I went to the study to find Henry. He was reading a book and smoking a pipe. "Ezekiel!" he said when he saw me, and stood up to stretch. "Let's wrap up some of your pies; you can take them home to your parents, OK?" I didn't correct him, but followed him to the kitchen, where we wrapped three tarts in wax paper and put them in a plastic shopping bag.

It was cold outside and I had to borrow one of Peter's jackets because I had forgotten mine at home that morning. Henry carried my bag and I carried the bag of tarts.

"You're so quiet, Ezekiel," Henry said.

I shrugged. "I like to be," I told him.

Henry laughed, a low rumble. "Yes," he agreed. "But you seem different tonight. Are you all right? Is everything OK at home?"

"Everything's the same," I said. "It's fine."

"Constance and I," Henry began. He sighed. "We're very fond of you, Ezekiel. You know that."

"Thanks," I said. Henry sighed again.

We were at my building. Henry bent down and gave me a kiss on the cheek and I made myself not pull away. "Goodbye, sweetheart," said Henry. I watched him walk back down the hill.

Once, Peter had had a secret, which he made sure I knew. In the middle of walking home or playing together, he'd burst into a fit of giggles. When I asked him why, he'd grin at me: "It's a secret," he'd say. "I can't tell you." He relished it. His eyes gleamed, and I hated him. Later, I discovered that he and Constance had planned a surprise birthday party for me—they made me a chocolate cherry cake and gave Andre a little pillow with catnip in it. I was ashamed then, as if Peter had seen my resentment, my selfishness, and had forgiven me anyway. Suddenly, he seemed powerful, generous, and I felt mean, stingy, little.

And now—I had a secret too.

VIII.

I didn't know what to do with the pies. I put them in the refrigerator. I must have thought a hundred times about taking Lawrence one of the pies—should I leave one outside his door? If I knocked, would he open the door and invite me in? What would he do? What should I do? Should I borrow a book? In the end, I solved my problem by eating the pies myself, one after the other, one cold night. The radiators had finally, reluctantly, clunked into action and their hissing made Andre cock his ears and arch his back in annoyance.

I read *Through the Looking Glass*. Friday nights in the building were even quieter than usual—there were no classes to teach, or children to pick up from after-school activities, and everyone seemed to settle into a silent weekend with nothing to do but wait for Monday. I had caught Maia's cold, as had Peter, and when I went over to the Drapers' house on Thursday, Constance examined me with her cool, dry fingers and sent me home to bed with a small bottle of peach-colored pills. "We'll go to Rhode Island some other time," she told us, and Peter and I were too tired and sick to argue or care. "Go straight to sleep, Ezekiel," she told me. "And call us if you need anything, do you hear?"

But by the weekend, I was truly sick. Water roared in my ears and I couldn't stand without immediately feeling dizzy. The floor rocked beneath me. On Saturday morning, I picked up my parents' laundry and took it downstairs, running my hand against the side of the wall to guide myself.

Someone was saying my name, and I realized I'd been asleep, one of those deep, watery sleeps like an ocean with no bottom. I looked up into Lawrence's pale face.

"Ezekiel," said Lawrence. His voice was soft and made me sleepy. "Ezekiel, are you all right?"

His hand was on my shoulder. I was in the laundry room, on the chair.

"Oh dear," said Lawrence, looking worried. "Well, well." He slapped his hands against his back and side pockets, as if feeling for something and then, cautiously, as if I might bite him, lay the back of one of his hands against my forehead and then pulled it away quickly. "Oh dear," he repeated. "Have you been to see a doctor, Ezekiel? Oh, of course you haven't. I—ah—I—I'll take you, then, all right? All right? Oh dear."

"Laundry," I made myself say. I could feel myself falling asleep again.

"What?" asked Lawrence. "Oh, the laundry. I'll take care of it, Ezekiel. Don't worry."

At the time, it was good enough for me. I let myself slide under the water's surface again.

————

That was how Lawrence became my uncle. "You're lucky your uncle thought to bring you in," said the doctor. He patted me on the shoulder. "I'll have my nurse call these prescriptions in," he said to Lawrence, who thanked him.

"Can you walk?" asked Lawrence. "Do you feel well enough?" I nodded and he helped me off the examining table, his hands under my arms. "I had to carry you here." I looked up and he smiled. "You've got pneumonia, my boy." He bent down to me. "Didn't your parents notice?"

"No," I said. "They're busy." The room shook before me.

"Ah," said Lawrence, still kneeling. There was no disapproval in his voice, no warning or sternness—he did not sound like Dr. Draper did whenever she asked about my parents. "I'll take care of you," he said, his voice easing into a whisper again. "I will." He brought his face closer to me and for a second I thought he would try to kiss me again. But instead he stood, and held out his hand. I let him lead me home.

We worked out an arrangement, the two of us: Lawrence would check in on me every day, and I would let him bring me meals and medicine. The first day, I stayed at Lawrence's apartment. When I woke up, I was in his bed. I could hear him in the kitchen, humming to himself. My laundry—including the clothes I'd been wearing—was folded and stacked on a chair in the corner. I was wearing a plain white T-shirt that reached the tops of my knees and nothing else. My mouth tasted gummy and dry, but I felt clean and my hair smelled of shampoo.

"Soup," announced Lawrence, coming into the room. I sat back in the bed and wrapped the blanket around my waist, feeling suddenly ashamed.

"I'm not hungry," I told him. I was being rude. "I'm sorry," I said.

"Why?" asked Lawrence. He sat on the side of the bed and put the bowl of soup on the nightstand table next to me. "You can eat it later," he said.

"Yes. Thank you."

He smiled. "Move over," he told me.

I inched over on the bed and he stretched out next to me and lay on his side, facing me. We were silent for a while, looking at each other. Then Lawrence reached out his hand toward my face, where it hovered for a few seconds, fingers outstretched. He lowered it and ran the tips of his fingers over my cheek. "Close your eyes," said Lawrence, his voice quiet once more. I did.

I could feel Lawrence's face very near mine now, feel his breath on my eyelids. There was a rustling of fabric; the blanket lifted, and fell. Then I felt his hand on my thigh, snaking up under my shirt, pulling it away from me. I opened my eyes.

"Shhh," said Lawrence, although I hadn't said anything. His eyes were closed. I looked down to see his hand tenting my shirt. His hand moved up and down me, across my chest, not lingering anywhere. His touch was fluttery, a skim, as if I was burned and he couldn't put the full weight of his hand on me. I was naked underneath the shirt. "Close your eyes," said Lawrence, not opening his. "Close your eyes, Ezekiel, it'll make it easier." I closed my eyes, and Lawrence began to murmur, but it was an animal, not human sound, the low rumble of contentedness that Andre made sometimes when he was happy and pressed close against me. In the summertime, I sometimes slept in only my underwear, and Andre's long hair would tickle me as he shifted and sighed through the night. I thought then that I was with Andre, and asleep in my bed, and it was summer outside. Lawrence began to breathe then, in fast, short little bursts that made me, for some reason, feel nauseated. After a while he gave a great sigh and put his palm on my stomach. His hand was hot and dry.

He lay there for a long time, it seems, until his breaths grew soft and slow again, and then he laughed a little and said I could open my eyes again. But I shook my head, and I could almost feel him nodding. When he spoke, his words seemed to come to me from a great distance although, perversely, it might have been because he was so close.

"Open your mouth," he said, and I did, and this time, when he kissed me, I was used to it, the wetness, the sloppy thickness of his tongue. "Yes," he sighed after he was done. "Yes, Ezekiel. Yes."

IX.

Was Lawrence a rapist? Technically, I suppose he was, but ironically, he was the one who first defined rape for me: "Someone," he told me, "who uses force to make you have sex with them against your will." Now, of course, I know that the word has other connotations, and meanings, and that legally, too, its definition can be quite different, but back then, when I was a child, it seemed a logical enough explanation, and I was able to assure myself that I was involved in nothing wrong, and neither was Lawrence. For Lawrence was so gentle—even during sex he was gentle, at least until I got older and wasn't in danger of misinterpreting vigor, or roughness, as anger.

"Let's take it slowly," he said.

I had recovered and was back in Lawrence's apartment. I didn't know why. There was something undefinably repulsive about him, and whenever I returned from his apartment I washed and washed myself in the shower, as if I'd never be clean again. And yet I always returned. The previous spring, a professor in our building had killed himself, and as the police wheeled the gurney with his body out of the building, a wind carried the sheet off of him, and I saw his blue face, his bulging tongue. It was horrifying, and as much as I wanted to, or thought I wanted to, I couldn't turn away. Lawrence fascinated me in the same way.

And he was true to his word. He never forced me to do anything I didn't want to, not really, and gave me all the time I needed—he was patient. The hardest thing, I think, was growing accustomed to his body. Not his scent, or his taste, necessarily, but the very strangeness of looking at him—the length of his slightly yellowed teeth, the faint brown spots on his hands and feet, the spray of wrinkles around the corners of his eyes, the looseness of the skin on his chest—sometimes sickened me, and I had to close my eyes. Now, when I look back at the few pictures I have of him, I realize he was a handsome man, fit and healthy for his age, elegant. Back then though he seemed ancient, an ossifying lump of sad, weakening flesh that moved and spoke and sighed and wanted, so vulnerable that I felt sorry for it and disgusted by it both.

Still, in the end, it was my decision, I suppose. He never tried to coerce me or bully me into staying, into coming back—there were no "I'll kill your cat if you tell anyone," or "I've cooked you meals, let you borrow my books—how could you be so ungrateful?" It sounds odd, I know, but Lawrence treated me as an equal. I'd come over, he'd guide me to the bedroom with his fingertips on my back, above my shoulder blades, and after he'd finished, we'd make dinner and sit down to read, or play chess.

"Here, Ezekiel," he might say, waving a book. "You ought to read this." I'd read it, and we'd discuss it afterwards, with Lawrence arguing points with me and nodding as I defended my opinions.

"Mmm," he'd say, tamping down the tobacco in the pipe he smoked from time to time. "You may be right." Or, "Quite true, Ezekiel, I'd never thought of it that way." But I wasn't always correct, and sometimes Lawrence proved his point, either through strength of conviction, or better reasoning, or through his superior breadth of knowledge. After, we'd sit, Lawrence puffing, me drinking milk, and he would put on a record and we'd listen in silence until it was bedtime. Lawrence gave me an apartment key, and I began to do my homework there. "What're they teaching you in school these days, Ezekiel?" Lawrence would ask, picking up a textbook. He marveled at the speed with which I could solve math and science problems, and praised my writing—"Very impressive, Ezekiel." He was a skilled linguist, and helped me with my French homework, quizzed me on my German. His compliments warmed me, and sometimes, by night's end, I'd been paid so many I felt drunk with a simple, stupid happiness. Once in a great while, he'd talk about his own childhood—his beloved sister, Annabel, who'd died of leukemia when he was ten; his mother, her chilly efficiency and stern beauty; his father, a banker, who disappeared into The City at day and came back at night when Lawrence was already asleep. Sometimes he talked about his days at school—the pranks he and his friends used to play on their teachers, the boys who crept into each other's rooms at night and lay cramped in a single bed until the morning monitor made his rounds.

Once I asked him if he had ever wanted children of his own, and he lurched back a bit, as if I'd just stuck something foul-smelling in his face.

"No, never," he said. He sounded, I thought, a little perplexed by my question, even though I'd meant it as a compliment, of sorts—Lawrence was good with children, particularly very young ones. Sometimes on our walks we'd encounter babies in strollers, and Lawrence would bend down to talk to them in his soft voice. There was something about him, his voice, his sad, sculpted face, that made children look Victorian and serious—all quiet and wide-eyed—he seemed like someone you could trust, and the babies' mothers would smile and make small talk with him.

The first year after we met, Lawrence bought me a book of Greek myths for a birthday present. He'd signed the inside: "Happy Birthday, Ezekiel. With affection from your uncle who loves you."

"Is that what you are?" I'd asked Lawrence.

"Hmm, I suppose so," he said. He'd baked me a carrot cake too, with a wonderfully sticky caramel frosting, and now he licked his finger and dabbed it around the edge of his plate, picking up crumbs. "Or...." He stopped. Smiled. Licked his finger. I waited. "But you can just call me your friend," he said. I was disappointed, I somehow expected something more, a more satisfying answer, but he merely licked his finger again, dabbed up some more crumbs and leaned close, his finger outstretched. "Open your mouth and close your eyes," he said, just as Peter and I had once said to Henry before dropping gummy worms into his mouth. And just as Henry had, I did as Lawrence requested, opened my mouth, anticipating the sweetness of sugar on my tongue.

X.

The first time I had sex with Lawrence, I was fourteen and I had planned the occasion, what I would say, how I would present myself. It was my birthday and Lawrence was coming up to see me at school: He came to see me once every six weeks or so, and every time he'd get us a room at a little inn. "Ezekiel and I, we like to explore," he told my dean, who nodded and smiled and said he was glad to see such a close family connection. It was known at the school that I had a strange family, and that my parents were brilliant and eccentric and not to be disturbed, and I think it was out of pity—I was the youngest in my year, and the only one whose parents had never attended a school function—that I was allowed to take so many weekend trips off-campus with my uncle, who seemed like a harmless and responsible adult. And it wasn't a lie—we would always dutifully take an excursion—to a maple sugar farm maybe, where Lawrence and I both sampled cubes of maple syrup candy and bought sticky pale brown sugar lollipops that had been pressed by molds into the shapes of leaves, or bears, or acorns. Or we'd take a long drive to Williamstown, where he had once taught, and stroll slowly through the town, Lawrence pointing out the bungalow where he'd lived, the building in which he'd taught, the theater he'd attended for summer stock productions. Once we went to a creamery upstate, and bought glass pint bottles of rich white milk to drink the next morning. Another time we visited a glass factory and watched the blowers shape vases and lamps and bowls from shining molten lumps. In the summer, we'd go to botanic gardens, and, after I became interested in first orchids, then butterflies, then carpentry, to greenhouses, and butterfly groves, and a museum dedicated entirely to different kinds of North American woods. After we'd explored, we'd go back to the hotel room ("Will your son need a foldaway cot, sir?" "No thank you, that won't be necessary.") and lie down together and nap before evening time.

That year we'd gone to visit a sheep farm, where we saw raw wool being cleaned and combed and spun into skeins, and Lawrence had bought me a plain gray pullover, which was scratchy and warm. "It'll get softer as you wear it," he promised. That night, after dinner at the small restaurant attached to the inn, we sat on the bed and I opened my present, a beautiful and heavy cloth-bound book with watercolor-and-ink drawings of orchids. The book was old and smelled musty. Lawrence showed me how to slice through the pages with the end of a letter opener. "And I have something else for you," said Lawrence, after I'd thanked him. "Close your eyes and open your hand." I did, and when I opened my eyes, there in my hand lay what looked like a small pin—a piece of dull gold in the shape of a pheasant standing among some reeds.

"What is it?"

"It's a decorative piece from a samurai sword, very old. I bought it many years ago, on my travels, and had it made into a pin. You can wear it as a tie tack, you see. Or someday, if you have a lady friend, you can give it to her to wear as a brooch." We both smiled.

"Thank you, Lawrence."

"You're very welcome, my darling. Happy birthday."

And now it was my turn. My heart was beating so hard its rhythm seemed to fill my ears. "I have something for you too," I told him.

Lawrence was surprised. He raised his eyebrows. "For me?"

I nodded, handed him the package from my pocket. "Open it."

He smiled, as if I was joking, and opened the package, slowly, carefully, as if something might leap from it, or it might explode in his hands. He placed the last of the paper to the side and held up a condom. He looked at me, confusion, then happiness, then concern moving across his face.

"I'm ready," I told him.

He moved closer to me on the bed. "Are you sure, Ezekiel?" he asked. "You don't have to do this now if you don't want to. We can wait until later." But he was excited, I could tell, and his hand on my leg seemed to glow with heat.

"It's for you," I said, and my voice cracked.

"Dear boy," said Lawrence then, and a smile, smooth and beautiful, moved across his face. He moved his mouth to my ear. "I'll go slow," he said, and I felt myself tense involuntarily even as I nodded.

It hurt terribly, it did, and the next day I was so sore I couldn't move for hours and Lawrence flitted between the bathroom and the bed, worried and guilty, murmuring apologies and reassurances and stroking my hair. "My poor boy," he crooned, "you'll feel better soon." And then, once, so softly that I was never sure if he'd said it or if I'd dreamt it, "I am not a pedophile." His hand was on my stomach, circling against it. And although I thought I would never be able to do it again, that I would never want to see Lawrence again, and although I never grew to completely enjoy it, it grew easier each month, until I could sometimes fool myself into believing I felt nothing at all.

XI.

Where, you may think, was everyone else through this, through the years Lawrence was my uncle? Where were the Drapers? Where were my parents?

One afternoon, when I was walking around the university's campus, which I did sometimes when the weather was pleasant—I liked to watch the students walk across the square, climbing the steps to the great library two at a time—I saw my father walking across the cobblestones slowly, his head bent. I knew it was him from his shuffling walk, which made me sad whenever I saw it. There was a man walking some distance behind him, quite briskly, and every few steps he would give a little running hop to catch up. Finally, when he was only a few yards away, I heard him call "Professor Chong!" and saw my father stop and straighten and whip his head about as if someone had just called him a dreadful name. It was Lawrence. He walked up to my father, and I saw him extend his hand, and my father take it and shake it somewhat reluctantly. I could not hear what Lawrence said next, but my father looked at the ground, then at his watch, and then nodded, and the two of them turned and continued walking toward the gates of the school, my father's head bent once more, and Lawrence's bent too. I could see his lips move, but the two of them might have been ghosts, they were so silent and still, even in motion.

That night, Lawrence sat back in his chair after we'd eaten and gave me a crooked smile. "Well," he said, "I met your father. A handsome man. You take after him."

"I saw," I said. He raised his eyebrows. "I was watching," I explained. "What did he say?"

"It was more what I said, I'm afraid," Lawrence said. "I rather babbled on. I told him that I thought you were very bright and that I was sorry I had taken you away from his house so often, but I hoped he might understand that I thought you had great potential, and that we had formed a special friendship. And that I promised to take care of you." He gave a slight shrug, palms up. "It was the best I could do."

I ignored this. "What did he say?"

Lawrence paused. "He said that he and your mother thought you were terrific too, and that as long as you were safe, he was happy."

"You're lying."

Lawrence sighed. "Why would I be lying?"

"My father would never say something like that."

Lawrence looked unhappy. He stood up and began to clear the dishes. "Well, Ezekiel," he said, and his voice was quiet, "there's a first time for everything, you know."

"Thank you," I said to his retreating back, and he nodded, although I wasn't quite sure, not then anyway, what I was thanking him for.

———

The Drapers were more difficult, however. They noticed, of course, when I stopped coming to their house after school. I still went over to play with Peter, but not nearly as often as I had, and when I did, I found myself in Henry's study rather than Peter's room, with its plastic toys and bright-colored checker set, and collection of dolls and stuffed animals piled around a beanbag chair.

After his usual round of questions, Professor Draper looked at his wife and then at me. "We don't see as much of you anymore," he said to me.

"I've been busy," I told him. Peter stabbed at his peas with his fork.

"Peter, honey, please," said Dr. Draper. "Have you been doing anything fun, Ezekiel?"

"Not really," I admitted. Peter scowled; he thought I had made a new best friend.

That night, I followed Professor Draper to his study. Peter had banged upstairs to play games in his room.

"Henry?"

"Mmmm," said Henry. He put down his book and smiled.

"Nothing," I said. "Nothing."

There was a silence. "Ezekiel," said Henry gently, "sit down."

I did so. I was suddenly, inexplicably frightened—I felt filthy with secrets and my own shame—and couldn't look at him. I both feared and hoped that Henry knew about me, that he would have answers for me, that he would order me to stop. "Ezekiel," Henry repeated, and sighed. "I'm afraid I've got some news for you." I looked up at him then, and he smiled, a sad smile, and nodded. "I've been offered a position at a university in California, Ezekiel," he said. "Northern California. Palo Alto. A pretty town. Constance and I have talked this over for many weeks—months—and we've decided to move. Ezekiel?"

"I heard you."

"It won't be for a couple of months, anyway. Not until the end of the semester—no earlier than May."

"Oh."

"We'll miss you, Ezekiel." And he leaned forward then and put a hand against my cheek, and I looked up into his face. Henry sighed. "You know we'll miss you, right? Constance and I, not to mention Peter and Maia. You'll have to come visit us in California. It's not so far away, not really." He laughed then, just a bit.

"I suppose not," I said.

Henry leaned back in his chair and picked up his book again, although he didn't open it. He closed his eyes.

"I think I'll go upstairs and see Peter," I said then, and felt myself standing up.

Henry opened his eyes and smiled at me. "I think that's a good idea," he said.

———

"I understand," said Lawrence. We were walking through the park late on Sunday; it was cold and dry, and Lawrence held my hand in his. It was a couple of weeks later, I suppose, and I'd been mopey and truculent, pushing Lawrence away and avoiding Peter at school, as if it was easier to forget I'd been friends with him rather than confront his eventual departure. "You'll miss your friend, and that's normal," he said. "But you'll make other friends."

"No. I won't."

"Of course you will. You're very lovable. Who wouldn't want to be your friend?"

"*You* don't have any friends."

This wasn't true. Lawrence did have friends, tall quiet men like himself with neatly trimmed beards and mothy green and navy sweaters, all of them professors. They'd come over once a month or so and play whist or bridge and drink wine and talk in French or German. Sometimes they'd laugh, quietly. Sometimes they'd go to the theater. Sometimes there would be a young man among them, Asian or black or Latino, and he'd look from face to face with a faint half-smile, as if aware that there was some joke he ought to, but couldn't, understand. Once I'd come into the apartment, calling Lawrence's name, and the table of men had turned around to look at me. Lawrence stood up—"Ezekiel!" he said, surprised, and I froze at the doorway, wondering what he would do. But he was calm, introduced me to his friends, and told them that I was a "young friend from the building and a fierce chess player." The men looked me up and down and smiled and said hello. Then he told me he'd ring me tomorrow, and I retreated, closing the door behind me. The next day I apologized, but he waved it away, and said that he was sorry not to have warned me, and that he'd tell me next time they were over. So yes, Lawrence did have friends, I suppose. But there was something colorless, lifeless about them—even when they laughed, they seemed mirthless, and when I tried to picture their faces individually, all I could see was a blur of gray.

Lawrence sighed. "When you get to be my age, Ezekiel, all you want are people you can sit with quietly, people you can discuss things with, people who won't judge you. You want your intellectual equals." He paused, as if considering what he'd say next. "Although of course," he continued, "you're absolutely correct. There are different kinds of friendship, and you, my dear, are my special friend. I've never had a friend like you." He squeezed my hand, and, after a minute, I returned it. The park was almost empty that day—really, it was too cold to be out—and we sat down on a bench and Lawrence kissed my hand and my forehead. "Put your arms around me," he said in my ear, and I did, and then he kissed my cheek, and my ear, and my eyebrows again and again. His breath was growing heavy and fast, and I felt his hand pushing up my coat and shirt. And then he stopped, and wriggled out of my grasp.

"Lawrence?" I asked.

"Hello," Lawrence said, and his voice sounded strangled, as if from the effort of trying to keep it level and calm. "Have you lost your way?"

I looked up then to see whom he was addressing.

It was Peter.

"Ezekiel," said Peter. He was bewildered, questioning, and then he said my name again, but this time harshly, a rebuke.

Lawrence looked from me to Peter. "You know each other?" he asked. He was scared, I could tell, and at that minute I both despised him and feared for him.

"Peter, Professor Sterling. Professor Sterling, Peter," I mumbled.

"Ah," said Lawrence, dusting some imaginary crumbs off his lap and standing, extending a hand to Peter. "So this is the Peter I've heard so much about. It's very nice to finally meet you."

Peter clasped his hands behind his back and mumbled. Lawrence lowered his hand slowly. "Well," he said, after a silence. "I feel I know you already, Peter. I'm very sorry you'll be leaving the city."

Peter opened his mouth then, and I could tell he was about to say something rude, but then I heard Henry's voice: "Peter?" and then "Ezekiel!" with surprise. He was jogging up the low enbankment, and his short coat flapped around him like a cape. "There you are," he said to Peter, putting a hand on his shoulder. "Hi, Kiki," he told me. He looked at Lawrence. "Lawrence!" he said. He looked from him to me once, quickly. "I didn't know you knew Ezekiel here."

"Henry," said Lawrence. They shook hands. I couldn't tell if Lawrence was relieved or even more frightened. "Yes," he said, "Ezekiel and I are old friends from the building."

"Oh," said Henry. I couldn't read his eyes. "He's never mentioned you," he said to Lawrence, and his voice was smooth, silky. Peter hadn't stopped staring at me, and I looked at the ground to avoid his glare.

Lawrence gave a short, awkward laugh. "I heard about your move, Henry," he said. "Congratulations."

"Thank you," said Henry. "We're sad to be leaving New York, aren't we, honey?" he asked Peter. Peter didn't respond. Henry smiled at Lawrence apologetically. "He's tired," he explained.

Lawrence gave another short laugh. "Quite," he said. There was a silence.

"Well," said Henry, finally. "Ezekiel, I hope we'll see you this week?"

"OK," I told him, and Lawrence and I watched them turn and leave.

The next day at school, Peter wouldn't look at me. We were in different grades, but when I saw him on the playground during recess, he turned away and ran toward some other boys who were playing kickball in a corner of the yard, a game I knew Peter detested—it was one of the things we had in common. It was all right though, because I didn't want to see Peter either—I felt ashamed, and guilty too, and I didn't know what I would say to him. And yet I was sad as well, and angry at myself, at the distance I had moved from him, and at the way I had been treating him. I wanted to talk to him; I thought I could talk to him and if somehow he could be made to understand, it would validate Lawrence.

But of course, I couldn't articulate that then, so I took to following him around school, trying to find a quiet place where I could speak with him alone. I didn't yet know what I'd say. When I called him at home, he would answer the phone and then, upon hearing my voice, place the receiver back in its cradle, gently.

One day—it was after school, and I was there late for some reason. There was nowhere to go now but back to the building, where I'd let myself into Lawrence's apartment and sit at the kitchen table, waiting for him to come home. I knew his schedule: He had late classes on Mondays and Wednesdays, but Tuesdays and Thursdays he had only early-morning seminars, and Fridays he was free completely—he'd spend his mornings in the office at the university but was always waiting for me in the afternoon. I missed the Drapers, of course—Maia and Henry and Constance. And Peter, certainly. Lawrence's apartment was lonely and seemed, at times, a punishment—there were days when I'd sit there, watching the windows grow dark, and I thought I'd scream, times when I wanted to wreck the neat order of his house, knock the books from their shelves, throw food against the walls, smash his collection of glass bowls, shit on the floors. I'd sit, clench my fists and close my eyes, and the impulse would pass and I would feel drained and meek, and when Lawrence came home, he'd hover over me and talk to me as if I were a baby. Anyway, that day at school—it had now been almost three months since Peter and I had spoken, and his parents must have been too busy packing and preparing for their move to notice that I hadn't been coming over, that Peter hadn't—he hadn't, had he?—mentioned me of late. Peter's mother had sent me an invitation in the mail inviting me to a dinner with the family the next night ("I've been trying to reach you by phone, but no one picks up"), and I'd knitted the family long scarves—red for Peter, navy blue for Constance, a heathery brown for Henry and a bright green for Maia.

"That's a stupid gift," I could hear Peter saying, his voice high and derisive and confident. "We're moving to California. Why do we need scarves?"

"Don't be rude, honey," Constance would say. "These are lovely, Ezekiel."

"Yes, they are, Kiki," Henry would say. "And actually, Peter, California can get quite chilly, especially in the north, where we're going. Why, when I was there for college…"

"Blah, blah, blah," Peter would say, but good-naturedly, and Henry would push on with his story.

But that afternoon, I found Peter in the bathroom; he was washing his hands and already had his coat on. I called to him and he turned, his face open and expectant, then darkening and closing once he saw me.

"Get away," he told me, making for the door, and his voice was flat.

"Peter," I said. "Wait. I want to talk to you." But he pushed by me, reached out a hand for the door, and before I could stop myself, I had swatted it down. He looked up, then, his mouth and jaw set, and shoved me, hard, in the shoulder. I shoved him back. "You don't understand," I told him. "Shut up, Peter, shut up! Listen to me," although he wasn't saying anything, and although I wished he would. And then something in me wanted to see him cry, wanted to see him confused and helpless, and I reached for his face, although whether I intended to hit him or simply touch him, as Lawrence sometimes did to me, I no longer remember. But Peter was quicker than I, and he batted down my hand in mid-air.

"Stop it," hissed Peter. He was so angry the skin around his mouth had gone white.

"Stop what?" I asked. I was having fun with him. I remember that I wanted to tease him, wanted to drive him to fury.

"I'll tell my parents," Peter whispered.

"Oooh," I said, "Tell Mommy and Daddy, will you? You're such a baby, Peter. A spoiled brat." I remember thinking that I was the adult here, that Peter was a child, that he'd never understand me, not ever, that no one did. And here I was, fighting with my best friend, my best friend, no longer mine. "What are you going to tell them, exactly?"

Peter's voice was so choked it cracked. "What I saw," he said. "I saw you and Professor Sterling—that I saw you and him—you—" He lost his voice completely then, but spoke again. "It's sick," he said, and his voice was low and scary, "It's disgusting. You're disgusting. You have to stop it now."

I was so mad I could have called him names, could have hit him. We were the same height, but I grabbed his shoulders and shook him once, hard. "No," I shouted at him, "No. I can't."

He wrestled free from me and hit me in the stomach, so hard that I doubled over. When he spoke next, his voice was so level and frightening I looked up at him despite myself. "Then we're not friends anymore," he said. "Don't talk to me again." And he left. I watched his footsteps disappear.

———

The next day at the Drapers' dinner, Peter wouldn't look at me, wouldn't speak to me. I wondered if he'd said anything to his parents, but he hadn't, it appeared, since they behaved the same as they always did.

"We'll miss you so much, honey," Constance said to me, after she and Henry had thanked me again and again for the scarves.

"I'll miss school," said Maia, and her parents smiled at her.

The previous night, I came home to a note from my father at my door. "SEE ME," it read, and I stood outside of his office for a few minutes before knocking.

There was some shuffling of papers, and then my father called for me to come in.

I was never allowed in his office, but there was something reassuring and familiar about it. There was his desk, with the dining-room table pushed up against it, and everywhere—the bookshelves, the floor, the desks, the radiator, the windowsills, his chaise—were stacks and stacks of papers, books, journals. My father was sitting behind his desk, writing something on a scrap of paper. There was only one light, a deep yellow bulb covered with a black paper shade. He did not look up, and I stood in front of him, waiting for him to finish. When he finally looked up, he looked not at me, but past me.

"You're going away to school next year," he told me. "In New Hampshire. It's for the best. You're getting too old to be here." It didn't make any sense, but he said it with such confidence—my father spoke excellent English, with a French accent, and his words always sounded honeyed, smoked—that I didn't know what to say for a while.

"But," I began, but he looked back down at his paper and waved a hand. "That's all," he said.

I stood there for what felt like a long time, until my father looked up again. "Good night," he told me, and swiveled his chair away from me, toward the window. I turned and left.

Lawrence comforted me. "It won't be so bad, you'll see," he said. "I went away to school when I was a little older than you. You'll be fine. I'll come visit you every month, and we'll talk and write letters. I'll take care of Andre for you. Don't worry," he told me. It was dark, but he felt around the pillow until his hand found mine, "I'll never be far."

––––––––

The day the Drapers left for California, Lawrence drove me to the airport to see them off. He always spoke of the Drapers respectfully, was careful never to begrudge me time spent with them, but he stood off to the side as I said my goodbyes, and later I wondered if he was secretly relieved—no one would be watching him now, there was nowhere else for me to go. I said goodbye to Constance and Maia, who both cried, and shook Peter's hand, who looked at the floor and mumbled. Henry was the last to board the plane and the last to say goodbye to me, and he bent and hugged me for a long time. "You take care of yourself, Ezekiel," he said in my ear. "Don't be afraid to call us." And then he stood up and smiled and gave Lawrence a nod and turned to follow his family into the plane.

They sent me a postcard after they arrived, and Henry made me promise to write and visit—they had a great big yard, he said, and a pool, and there'd be plenty of room for Andre to roam. He never mentioned how Peter and I never talked, and he never mentioned Lawrence. But he always remembered to write to me, and my birthday too, and the next year, when I left New York for boarding school in New Hampshire, it was Henry who sent me the enormous down-filled coat I wore all through that first horrid winter. And that spring, when I was awakened by my dorm counselor shaking my shoulder in the middle of the night to deliver the news that the Drapers had been killed in a car accident while driving back from San Francisco, it was then I realized that I was really alone with Lawrence, that there was now no possibility of another life, one in California, with the sun and the warmth and Henry calling to us—"Where are my three babies? Peter, Ezekiel, Maia, dinner's on!"—from a kitchen filled with steam and the ringing sound of Constance setting five places at their dark wood table.

XI.

My current boyfriend, Clare, comes from a large family, not particularly close (or so he claims; they seem close to me) but fond of taking photographs. During that first awkward period when we began dating—when one feels compelled to tell the other all the little secrets and stories of childhood—we spent lots of time looking through his photo albums (Clare as a round-faced infant, Clare as a plump toddler, Clare as a sullen teenager, Clare's parents, Clare's brothers and sisters, Clare's family's trip to Italy; to Mexico; to Greece; to China), with Clare, not normally a voluble man, rattling on and on about the various stories behind the pictures. The first holiday I spent at Clare's parents' house (I think it was the Thanksgiving after we'd moved in together), his mother brought out a fat photo album after dinner and the entire family sat down around her, arguing over the parents' memories and making all sorts of familial allusions I couldn't, of course, understand. It was clearly a family ritual, a nice one, I thought, and touching as well; to see them poring over the pictures, you'd have thought they'd only recently been introduced to a camera.

"What did you look like as a baby, Ezekiel?" asked Clare's twin, Rachel.

"I don't know," Clare interjected, before I could answer. "Ezekiel doesn't have any pictures of himself as a kid."

"My parents weren't big picture takers," I explained, hurriedly.

"Oh my goodness, Ezekiel," said Clare's mother. "You must think we're awfully silly. We always forget that not everyone's interested in our family photo albums."

"Not at all," I said. "If I had such nice photos, I'd show them off, too."

I meant it, of course. But when we were driving home the next night, Clare cleared his throat and asked (after a longish silence; we had been singing along with the radio, listening to the station become ever fainter until the music was overcome by static) why I didn't have any pictures anyway.

"I told you," I said. "My parents didn't take pictures."

"But *none*?" he said. "I mean, you don't have any? Why don't you have *any*?"

"I just don't, Clare. Drop it, all right?"

"No need to get defensive."

"You're *making* me get defensive."

Clare sighed. "What," he continued, "were you an axe murderer as a child? A little Mary Bell?" He was joking, but frustrated too, and when he reached out a hand to pat my face, I pushed it away. We rode in silence for a while.

"I'm sorry," Clare said at last.

"I am too," I said. I had been sleepy before, watching the trees and road whip by in the darkness, but now I felt awake, exaggeratedly awake, as if I could see for miles. Clare was silent, waiting. "Look, Clare," I said in a rush, "My parents didn't take pictures. I wasn't close to them. To be honest, we hardly ever talked. I do have a few pictures…"

"With the Drapers."

"Yes, with the Drapers, but that's all I have. I've shown you everything I have—

yearbook pictures, pictures from school, but I don't have any pictures of myself as a child. And this is a dumb argument anyway—I hate it when you cross-examine me, Clare."

"No," said Clare quietly. "No, it isn't a dumb argument. But I'm sorry. I'm sorry if I upset you. I know you didn't have a happy childhood."

"I had a fine childhood," I snapped.

Clare sighed again. I sighed too. Sometimes it seemed that people spent most of their time around me sighing. We drove the rest of the way back into the city in silence.

When we returned to our apartment, Clare went to take a shower and I rummaged through our closet until I found what I had been looking for—a dusty shoebox—and sat on the bed to wait for him. He would come out of the shower, soft-skinned and trailing steam, and I'd have something to show him.

———

For reasons that were obvious to me even then, Lawrence was especially careful about photographs that showed the two of us together. Still, he was a skilled photographer, and I'm sorry to say that he destroyed most of the pictures he'd taken over the years shortly after we ended our relationship. This was a pity, because besides being a good photographer, Lawrence had a sharp eye for photographs, images, and had, in fact, made many shrewd purchases. It was from him that I inherited my love of photography, and it was also from him that I inherited something more tangible—a small, smoky early Marjorie Content photo, one of the three that Lawrence hung above his bed. (It now hangs in my study, over my desk.) On weekends, Lawrence and I used to go to the International Center of Photography, and he would bend down and tell me about the photos—the image, or the technique, or the artist—in his soft, whispery voice. Sometimes I caught other people listening, too. Afterward, we'd walk west through the park, down through the zoo, and on hot days, Lawrence would buy me an orange creamsicle rolled in crushed nuts.

When I was eleven, Lawrence bought me a camera for my birthday. It was a tiny, expensive gadget with a retractable zoom lens, and he seemed just as delighted with it as I was. The next summer, when we went to Italy, I dropped the camera on the ground and its lens shattered. I was devastated, but Lawrence didn't yell, didn't get angry, just scooped up the pieces and promised we'd get it fixed when we returned home. He had brought another camera for backup, and we took turns carrying a clunky Canon (*his* first camera) in its hard leather shell for the duration of the trip.

That was my first trip to Italy; Lawrence himself hadn't been back for years, although he had been there—to the same pensione in Florence—every year for holiday as an undergraduate. He had been helping me with my Italian in the months before our visit, and stepping off the plane into the white sun, some heaviness seemed to fall away from him as he inhaled deeply the cool, thin air.

The pensione of Lawrence's college years was no longer standing, but he had found a crumbling, cool, dark hotel near the Via Tornabuoni, with its fancy shops and bustle of tourists. Since landing, Lawrence's cheeks were pinkish and shining, and his steps, so careful and measured in New York, became long, loping strides; he wore his linen hat at a jaunty angle and stretched his neck out. Seeing this, I too felt giddy, carefree, and when we went to restaurants, Lawrence ordered extravagantly, dishes rich with oil and *funghi*, and a carafe of biting red wine he let me share. We'd return to the room late, pleasantly drunk, fall asleep instantly, wake up hot, our eyes puffy, but happy too.

We had been out especially late the night before the morning Lawrence took this picture. I remember that the shutters were closed against the morning sun but that it seeped in anyway, as if they were barely able to hold back the light. It must have been particularly hot that morning, because I'm sitting on the bed and it doesn't look like I'm wearing any clothes, although I have the sheet wrapped around my waist. When we were in Italy, Lawrence smoked cigarettes ("A terrible, filthy habit, Ezekiel," he said sternly, before lighting a long unfiltered cigarette and exhaling with a sigh of obvious pleasure. "Don't ever start.") and I'm holding one here—the liquid in the glass is water, although I was pretending it was vodka. I was trying to look urbane, and world-weary, and I remember how Lawrence laughed as I assembled the props. "You're a ham!" he cried. "You're my little ham." And see that book partially hidden by the pillow? You can't make it out, but it's *Lolita*. Lawrence had just introduced me to the concept of irony in the months before our trip, and I thought it would be funny to bring this book—of which I'd heard so much—along with me, wave it in front of the hotel clerk as Lawrence confirmed his reservation for "a single room—no, one bed—my son and I will share." The irony was, however, a little too rich for Lawrence, and he spluttered whenever I brought the book out. ("It's not funny, Ezekiel.") That morning, though, he was in a mood to laugh at himself, to laugh at my clowning, and he took roll after roll of film (some of them racy), but as I said, he destroyed them all in the end. Over a dozen years ago. This was one of our favorites though, and he made a print for me. After we had broken up, he called me four or five times a day, trying to get me to return it. I never called him back, which is why, I think, I still have it. In the end, I guess he decided he could let me keep this one: after all, if you don't know the story behind it, it's not so dangerous.

Here's the only photo I have of me and Lawrence. This was graduation day. I hadn't wanted to go to the ceremony, but Lawrence insisted. He'd come up, he said. It wasn't every day I would graduate from high school. It was a cool May day and we graduates all sat on a long stage that had been erected in the center of the main field as the headmaster read out the names and handed out diplomas. I remember looking for

Lawrence out in the crowd, squinting my eyes against the sun. I was disappointed, and angry too—where was he? What had happened? And then: *I did this for him.*

The headmaster called my name and I went up to shake his hand and take my diploma and sat back down again. And then, far in the distance, I saw a long figure running over the lawn toward the seats that had been set in front of the stage for families and faculty. As the figure drew closer, I saw it was Lawrence, but with long smears of black grease on his pants and shirt and face. He had a hand over his heart, and I stood, thinking he might be having a heart attack, but as he drew nearer, I saw he was holding his camera, which he'd looped around his neck. He stopped at the back of the last row of seats and I saw his eyes scanning across the stage. When he saw me, he gave such a smile, and waved his free arm in the air so vigorously, it looked like he was hailing a plane, and I forgave him right away.

After the ceremony, parents found their children, and Lawrence hugged me and kissed me on the forehead, not something he normally did in public.

"I got a flat," he said, still panting. "I tried to change the tire myself, you see." He laughed. "Not entirely successful. I'm afraid I missed your big moment, dear one."

"It's OK," I said. "I'm glad you're safe."

Lawrence smiled and hugged me again. We were of a height by that time. "Look at you," he whispered into my ear. "My big boy now. My big boy." His voice was thick.

My headmaster came over to shake my hand and Lawrence's. He knew him from other school events, when Lawrence had driven up. We had told him that Lawrence was my uncle, and my guardian.

"Dr. Sterling," he said to Lawrence. "Young man," he said to me. "Congratulations," he said to both of us. "You must be very proud."

"I am," Lawrence said softly, beaming. "He's one in a million."

"Are your parents here?" asked the headmaster, looking over our heads as if we were hiding them behind our backs. My parents had never come to visit me at the school, and the headmaster (who'd been trained as a child psychologist) was always asking me about them.

"They were ill and couldn't attend," I said now.

"They wanted to though," Lawrence added quickly.

"Well!" said the headmaster. "I'm sure they did. They have a marvelous son in you, young man."

"Thank you," I said. I felt childlike.

The headmaster cleared his throat. "Let me get a picture of you two." Lawrence took the camera from around his neck and handed it to the headmaster, who stepped back a few paces. Lawrence stood next to me and, suddenly aware that he had motor-oil all over his clothes, draped an arm over my shoulder carefully.

"Smile," said the headmaster, and clicked the shutter.

It wasn't until Lawrence had developed the film that I saw that he had bent his head down so that all you see is the crown of his head, the precise part in his hair. He looks embarrassed to be next to me, ashamed to be seen with me. He has one arm around me and one hand in his pants pocket, and next to him, I'm smiling so wide that my cheeks ache when I look at it. I could've been standing next to anyone, smiling like a fool. I confronted Lawrence: Why had he looked down?

"Oh dear," he said, looking tired and old and apologetic. "I chickened out, I'm afraid. Are you very angry? Will you forgive me?"

But that time I wouldn't, I was too upset, and frustrated at Lawrence's cowardice, and his hypocrisy, and I remember taking the photo out of his hand and leaving the room. And funny—here it is now, all these years later.

One last picture—I had forgotten I had this one, mostly because I never look at it. This is the only picture I have of me with my mother and father. I don't know where it was taken, or when—although judging from my face, my wide-open mouth, I must be around one, or maybe a little older—but here are my parents, my mother on my right, my father on my left. It makes me smile a little to see it now, how determinedly unhappy they look—my mother, resigned, her mouth sewn into a long, thin seam, my father, deadened, his eyes gazing somewhere into middle space, his hands clenching his knees— but when I was younger I couldn't look at this photo, it made me too depressed, for reasons I was unable to articulate but also unable to ignore. The photo is black and white, and my parents—all three of us—are dressed rather scruffily. Lawrence said it looked like we'd all just stepped off the boat at Ellis Island, three unrelated immigrants, and it's true— I'm the only one who looks happy, almost crazily happy. My hair was a pale brown when I was a baby, and it floats, a light-gray blur, around my face. I don't know when or where this picture was taken. We're clearly outdoors, but there's nothing behind us but a chalky sky. Where are we? Who took the photo? I asked my mother about it once, when she was dying for the last time, but by that time she had lost most of her language; she spoke only in the perimeters of words.

I hear Clare coming out of the shower; he's humming to himself, which means he's in a good mood again.

I can't show these pictures to Clare.

"Clare?" I call.

"What?" Clare calls back.

I look at the photos one last time. I put them in their envelope again and slide them into the bottom of the shoebox. There will be another time.

"Nothing," I say. "I'm ready for bed."

XII.

The coffee house I frequented my senior year of college was called Beasley's, and like most of the cafes in Cambridge, it lacked any sense of creativity, of innovation—the red-brick walls, the plush velvet couches, the anonymous jazz playing in the background—it was as familiar and comfortable as a film set, and its clientele—and I don't consider myself any different—was as generic as its sweet pale coffee, its dry scones, its sugary tea. The whole thing seemed to have been built and planned and peopled according to some diagram, and as embarrassed as I am to admit it, it was comforting, even desirable—a place to go where the surroundings demanded neither appreciation nor scorn.

I liked to think that I went to Beasley's because it was slightly less crowded and the coffee was slightly better than the other places closer to campus, but really it was because I was renting a small apartment two blocks away, and I was too lazy and uninspired to seek better refreshment. I'd take my books and pen and notepad there in the late morning, between labs, or in the late afternoon, when the place was quieter, and sit there for hours, grading papers (I was a teaching assistant for a class of Introductory Biology and hating every day of it) or reading, or reviewing the next day's notes. I sat at a corner table in the back, near the lavatory. The most desirable tables were near the windows, and I was never bothered. I always worked best alone, but sometimes teams of students, study groups, would come in and quiz each other on upcoming exams: I liked to hear them argue back and forth, particularly the law students, whose style of studying seemed to be as much about performance as it was proving their own comprehension.

That January was a particularly bitter one, and the snowfall was so heavy that classes were canceled for three days. Beasley's, however, remained open, and I went as usual, assumed my seat, and worked through the day until closing, eating salads and scones when I was hungry. Something about the cold, snow, has always made me sleepy, and on the third night of the storm I fell asleep. When I woke up, there was a man sitting in the seat across from me, where I usually propped my legs. I recognized him—he was one of the law students who sometimes met at Beaseley's, and the brightest, the quickest, the most intense. He delivered all of his arguments in a low, level, rapid voice, and his friends had to sit forward to listen, their brows furrowing as he delivered his point. Now he leaned forward across the table toward me.

"I didn't mean to alarm you," he said in that same low voice. He had small glasses and a fine, serious mouth and was sharp-boned and grimly handsome. His curly brown hair stood up in clumps. "But they're closing soon. And you were asleep. I thought I ought to let you know."

"Thank you," I told him.

He leaned back in his chair then and looked at me for what seemed a long moment, before learning forward again. "My name's Sionil," he said. "Clare Sionil."

"It's very nice to meet you," I said. "My name's Ezekiel."

"I know," said the man. And then he flushed, and I suddenly liked him. We shook hands, solemnly. "I'm a law student," he said.

"I know," I told him.

He smiled then, a quick flash of a smile that changed his face, and then disentangled himself from the chair and slung his backpack over his shoulder. "Maybe I'll see you, Ezekiel," he said. And then he smiled again and was gone.

———

And then it became busy, and there were finals to take and finals to grade, and I only saw Clare Sionil a few times in the next month, both of us hurrying in opposite directions, and there was never time enough to do anything but nod at one another. Once I saw him on the undergraduate campus as I hurried to turn in my class's grades. He was wearing sweatpants and an anorak and running shoes and talking with a friend, and when I jogged past him he nodded and raised his hand, and I raised mine back and nodded to him too. And so it went like this for a while—we'd see each other and nod, and sometimes see each other and wave, and soon it seemed that I was seeing Clare an awful lot around campus, around town, and I used to imagine that he'd be there waiting for me behind each corner of the twisty Cambridge streets. But I didn't think too much about it—I was still talking to Lawrence almost every night, after all, and, having only been with Lawrence, I wasn't aware that Clare, in his clumsy, bold way, might be trying to communicate anything more than mere friendliness.

The new semester began and people settled into their classes. Lawrence, who'd begun his own second semester ("the happiest time of the year, Ezekiel," he always said), came up to visit.

"Pick out a nice restaurant, for goodness' sakes, Ezekiel," he told me. "Let's celebrate the end of another ghastly semester."

I picked a restaurant (now closed) called Cucina della Sorella on the north side of Boston—it was the sort of place both Lawrence and I appreciated, with its good food, and fat Italian women (the sorelle themselves?) cooking, stern-mouthed, in the steamy kitchen, and the food served by dark, plump-lipped boys, the sons and nephews of the chefs.

"Ah," sighed Lawrence, pouring himself another glass of wine. He'd driven up from New York that afternoon, and in the candlelight, his hair looked more silver than ever, and the lines in his face soft, as if painted with watercolors. He reached across the table and patted my hand, the most affectionate gesture he allowed himself in public, but one which told me he was happy. He opened his mouth to speak, and then looked up, puzzled, and then to me.

"I'm sorry to interrupt," said someone, and I looked up and it was Clare.

"Clare," I said. "What a surprise."

"Yes," said Clare. "Do you come here often?"

"No," I said. There was a pause. "I like the food though."

He smiled then, a crooked half-smile, and I quickly introduced Lawrence, "Uncle Lawrence, Clare Sionil. Clare, Lawrence Sterling."

"Nice to meet you," said Clare. He smiled his regular smile then, that quick flash, and he and Lawrence shook hands, Lawrence looking a bit dazed.

Clare took a deep breath and looked at me. "I hope you won't think me too rude," he said in a rush, "but I was wondering if you might like to go have dinner with me sometime next week."

I wanted to look at Lawrence. I did. But something—an old fear that we'd be given away? Cowardice?—kept me from doing so. So instead I looked up at Clare, whose face seemed hidden in shadows, and whose expression I couldn't read.

"Yes," I told him.

He smiled then, again, a smile that stayed, and nodded, slowly. "Good," he said. "I'll look you up." He nodded at Lawrence—"A pleasure, Mr. Sterling"—and then again, he melted away.

———

Lawrence was angry on the ride home. We'd finished the dinner in thick silence, and he'd silently paid and then silently shrugged on his coat, and started the car all with a furious calm.

"Lawrence," I began.

"Who *was* that beastly boy?" he hissed, whipping the car around a corner. When Lawrence was angry, he never yelled; his voice dropped to a whisper, a spit, and when I was younger, I would do anything to coax him out of it, to make his voice rise. "How terribly rude," he continued. "How horridly *obnoxious*. To ask someone out while he's having dinner with someone else!"

"It was a little rude," I allowed miserably. "He didn't know though."

But Lawrence seemed not to hear me. "And you!" he said. "Uncle Lawrence? My *god*, Ezekiel."

When I am angry, I yell, and I sulk, and I am, I'm afraid, petulant. "You taught me that, Lawrence!"

"When you were a *child*, Ezekiel," said Lawrence, sounding very weary. "You're not a child anymore. We don't need to protect ourselves anymore. You're a goddamn *adult* now. An *adult*."

Suddenly the whole thing seemed very funny to me, and if Lawrence hadn't been so angry, I might have laughed. I pictured, suddenly, Clare's sharp, foxy face as clearly as if he was in the back seat, and wondered what he'd think of this, what explanations he'd form in his mind.

Once inside my apartment, Lawrence stood by the door and stared at me. I went to make him some tea.

"Stop," said Lawrence, and I did. "Do you still love me, Ezekiel?" His voice was steady, and I couldn't answer him. "It doesn't matter," he said quietly. And then: "Go to the bedroom. And take off your clothes. And lie down. And wait for me." And I would have, everything in me wanted to—but I couldn't. "Go," whispered Lawrence, and then, when I didn't move, he repeated it, softer still, "Go. Go. Go," until I heard nothing but the sound of his lips separating and closing, again and again.

XIII.

When I was in England for my first round of graduate schools, studying for my exams— just as my mother once had—my father died—hanged himself—and when I was back in the States, in graduate school again, my mother died too. Both times, Clare was the one to deliver the news, which he did tenderly. "Honey," he called me, a pet name he rarely used, his voice faint and choppy over the phone, "I'm afraid I have some bad news to deliver." I felt—what did I feel? I had never been close to my parents, and after I graduated from high school, I had all but stopped speaking to them, stopped thinking of them, really. I spent my summers between university terms with friends, or with Lawrence, or on campus. I visited my mother once after her first stroke, directly after I graduated college, and was stunned—horrified even—by the state of the apartment—garbage lay in every corner, and the hallways were fetid and stank of old soup and unwashed laundry. Roaches and silverfish crawled over the hallway carpet, and the faucets coughed water the color of clay. My father was nowhere to be seen. I had put her in a nursing home soon after, and although her death was not particularly surprising—she had been dying for ten years, after all—it left me feeling exhausted and sad, even more so than my father's death, whose suicide, I'm sorry to say, seemed inevitable, although no less depressing. There were small notices in the paper for both of them, and after each of their deaths, Lawrence sent me a note, really little more than his name signed to a piece of his heavy stationary.

After that I didn't hear from him. I met a woman in England who'd attended the university where Lawrence taught, but she'd never taken a course from him. "Victorian literature wasn't really my thing," she told me. She had hair the color of dirty water and was studying for her degree in chemistry.

At Christmastime, Clare sent me a ticket to visit him in New York, and I walked up and down Morningside Drive, staring at the building. I re-walked the routes Lawrence and I used to take, marking them by season: Summer—across the park from the ICP, Winter—downtown and west to Riverside Park, Fall—uptown and east around the northern reservoir toward Spanish Harlem, Spring—straight down Broadway to the museum. I was distracted, but Clare was too, and didn't seem to notice. He came home late from work, and I'd have dinner waiting for him, and on Christmas Eve, he put on some music and waltzed me around the living room before stopping, and bowing, and letting me take the lead. I thought, then, about our first date, our first dinner, and Clare, his serious face, the way he leaned forward to listen to me, how his eyes never moved off mine, and how he later told me was so nervous, he thought he'd vomit.

"You're how old?" he'd asked, sighed. "I feel like an old man." But then he'd smiled, tentatively, and I'd smiled back. He was young, really, and smart, and I loved to listen to him talk about his work and life and plans for the future.

But when I think of that time, I'm more confused than happy—that night that seemed to last for days, with Lawrence standing in the doorway and me against the kitchen counter, neither of us able to speak to the other, and finally, Lawrence turning and closing the front door softly behind him, and then the notes he began to send me, first terse, then pleading, then cruel, then pitiful, and how after a while I'd slip them, unopened, into my bottom desk drawer, stretching the distance between us further and further with each envelope I refused to open, each letter I refused to answer. Once, he left me a message: "Ezekiel, please call me." And then, when I didn't, "Andre died. I'm sorry, Ezekiel." And then, when I still didn't, "You cold-hearted little snake. You undeserving little brat. I've given you everything. Everything. You wretched, beastly little *insect*." He was so angry, he was spluttering his words in staccato bursts, and he sounded spent, drained, an old, old man.

For our breakup is perplexing to me even now, for its emptiness, its lack of drama, answers, events. Sometimes I thought: What made me stand there, so stubborn, while Lawrence asked me again and again? It would have been so easy to walk into the bedroom, lay down as I had hundreds, thousands of times before, let my mind drift until I felt Lawrence's hand rubbing against my back.

In the early days of our relationship, I loved to hear Clare say he loved me, and each time he said it, I wanted to hear it again, and again, and each time we fought, I'd think of Lawrence in his apartment, waiting for me, a book in his hand, his eyebrow cocked and his head turned toward the front door, as if my key was turning in his lock. So—days, weeks, months, years. Why had I stopped? My hand on the counter, Lawrence's arm against the doorframe, the orangey light from the street seeping into the dark living room.

When I was in high school, I had bounced from passion to passion, and when I went to college and settled into a rhythm of interests and hobbies (biology, botany, photography, running, chess, theater), I thought of how patient, how tolerant Lawrence had been through all my phases—the orchid farms and butterfly groves and walks through the woods, and then, one summer, how he'd introduced me to a beekeeper and had listened to endless lectures on bees, and pollen, and royal jelly. I was overcome then with love for him, and had called Lawrence to thank him. He was happy to hear from me, and gracious.

"How'd you do it?" I asked him. "Didn't I drive you crazy?"

"No, never," he'd replied. "It was rather wonderful, in fact—you were so interested in everything, so passionate about everything. I was reminded myself of being young."

"Aren't you happy I've settled down now?" I teased. "No more unpredictability. No more waste."

But Lawrence was serious. "You're growing up," he said. He sighed then, and it was a wistful sound. "It does make buying gifts for you easier," he allowed, "but you were always my surprise. You always surprised me." He was trying, I think, however clumsily, to capture, to celebrate, the recklessness of youth, the speed with which one could fall in and out of love. As an adult, I have always considered myself a fairly consistent person, a man set in my own patterns and fussy in my tastes. No one would call me fickle, and any decision can become an embarrassingly—and for Clare, who sits and sighs and begs, pleads with me to *make up your mind*, irritatingly—complicated process, so there is something thrilling in the memory of my own inexplicable assertion of whim, reassuring proof of my now-gone childish spontaneity.

XIV.

It's our anniversary, and so we go to dinner. I get to pick the restaurant and Clare promises to leave work early and meet me there. He's late anyway, but I don't mind, and when I look up from my book, he's talking to the maître'd, and then he sees me, and gives his slight smile, and walks toward our table briskly.

It's been a busy year for both of us, but busier for Clare. I got my tenure last year, but Clare made partner this year, and in the months before he did, he was terrible, and grouchy, and snappish, and I used to wake to the sound of him grating his teeth, like metal against bone. Now he's relieved, and the whites of his eyes have lost most of their redness. He's expansive, apologetic, and when he reaches me, he kisses me, lightly, on the jaw, which is not something Clare has done in public, ever, before sitting down and smiling at me.

We order—wine, salads, fish. The sommelier pours a shallow splash of wine into the glass and Clare inhales the bouquet, sips and nods. The sommelier pours again and leaves.

"Well," says Clare, raising his glass slightly. "Ten years."

"Yes," I say.

"Good years," says Clare. He looks a bit embarrassed, but then repeats himself, and this time, he sounds happy, I think. He clears his throat and says quietly, "To many more," and then we touch the lips of our glasses together and Clare leans forward, just like he used to when we first met and we were both so awkward.

We have a pleasant dinner—the food is good, Clare is relaxed: We talk about where we want to go on our next vacation (Clare votes for Nairobi, I vote for Kiribati); the bookshelves in my study Clare wants to remodel; the books we've just finished reading; the play we'd seen a few days ago but had been too tired to discuss after; and his sister, Rachel, who's pregnant with her first child, a girl. Clare's excited about becoming an uncle, which surprises me a bit. Neither of us are very fond of children. But Clare harbors a secret hope that Rachel will name the baby after him. I tease him, tell him he's becoming sentimental. He laughs and doesn't deny it and says it's a different game when it's your twin who's going to be the mother, but I know it's also because he's worried: Rachel's pregnancy has been difficult so far.

"Uncle Ezekiel and Aunt Clare," I tell him.

He grunts. "More like Aunt Kiki and Uncle Clare," he rebuts.

"Aunt Kiki and Aunt Clare," I say, and he laughs out loud.

We linger over dinner, and when we finally emerge from the restaurant, the night is clear and very cold, but we decide to walk until we can't stand it anymore. It's late, and the streets are mostly deserted, so we walk slowly, looking in shop windows. We discuss again whether we should move downtown, where Clare owns a townhouse, inherited from his aunt the previous year. There are plenty of arguments against it—we both work uptown, and on the east side, and we both like the quietness of our neighborhood, how its streets empty out at night. Now, there is only one old man walking toward us, alone, his arms crossed over his chest, his head bowed, and as we pass, he looks up at us suddenly, almost furtively, and I pause, then stop, and it's too late to pretend I haven't met his eyes.

It's Lawrence, of course, and I'm shocked, at first, by his face, which is so gray, and lined, and thin. He's not wearing a hat, and he still has his hair, although thinner, and almost all white, which the breeze lifts in a solid piece. I feel, for an instant, breathless, as if my body has forgotten what to do, and then horrified, at Lawrence's physical presence, at his age, the obviousness of his decay.

He would, after all, be seventy soon, and I supposed if I was able to look at him—he was a bit stooped, thinner, paler—I wondered if he wouldn't look the same to me, in the end.

"Ezekiel," said Lawrence. He didn't seem particularly surprised to see me, and his voice was picked up and carried away by the wind. He looked at Clare, once, and then smiled at me, just a bit. "Clare Sionil," he said to him.

I could sense Clare squinting a bit, wondering where and how and when he had met this man, how he knew his name.

"My uncle," I reminded Clare, and the word felt strange to say. "Lawrence Sterling."

"Ah," said Clare, remembering. He took his hand out of his pocket, but Lawrence made no move to extend his own, and so Clare quickly slid his behind his back. He didn't seem to know what else to say.

"You look well, Ezekiel," Lawrence told me, and I was embarrassed that I couldn't bring myself to say the same.

He laughed then, probably seeing the expression on my face, a short, brittle laugh, and then raised one of his hands, partway, as though he were going to touch me, or wave at me, or adjust the scarf around his neck. But he did none of these things, only nodded at Clare again and then at me. "Congratulations on all your accomplishments, then," he told me, but his voice was so soft I wasn't sure I'd heard him correctly. And then he shoved his hand back in his pocket and turned and continued walking downtown, down the sloping sidewalk.

Clare and I stood there for a moment and watched him go until he became just a line of black moving down the street. And then I wanted to shout after him: What are you doing on the east side? Where are you going? How have you been? Are you well? Do you ever think of me? But I didn't, of course, and after a while, Clare touched my arm and suggested maybe we get a cab, because he couldn't feel his feet anymore.

That night, we lay in bed in silence for a long time, not doing or saying anything, and then Clare took a deep, sharp breath and said, "That man. He wasn't really your uncle, was he?"

His voice was gentle, and seemed to float over me, over the room.

"He was once your lover, wasn't he?" Clare asked.

I didn't know what to say, but finally, I found the words to ask Clare how he knew.

"Just something in the way you looked at him, talked to him," Clare said.

Oh, I said.

"So," said Clare. We were quiet for a while longer. "What was it?"

So I told him. I told him of how we met and what we did and how it was that we fooled so many people for so long, and how I outgrew him and I hope he outgrew me too. There was too much to tell about the vacations he took me on, and the foods he taught me to eat, and the ways in which he taught me to think, and read, and write, the ways in which he taught me to look, to touch, to eat and drink and move—so I told him nothing. I had never said these words to anyone, and they felt strange to say, they filled my mouth like strange objects. I told him what he had said after the first time we had sex—"I am not a pedophile."

"But he was," said Clare. "He was a pedophile."

"Yes," I said, but only after a pause. "I guess he was."

There was nothing more to say after this without the conversation becoming complicated, but after Clare had told me that we'd discuss it in the morning and kissed me and turned on his side to fall asleep, I lay awake thinking that in spite of everything (or perhaps because of it), I have not been damaged. I live with a man I love, and who, I think, loves me. I have a career, and friends, an apartment, and this weekend, we are going to our house in the country, where Clare and I will lay down fresh mulch in our new, blank orchards, and plant some young pear saplings and that night we'll start a fire and our friends will come over and we'll roast vegetables. The nights out in the country are so clear and cold, and sometimes, once Clare has fallen asleep, I'll go for a walk outside, just to hear my feet crunching through the ice, and my own quiet breath.

We are very happy.

ALEC MAPA

POINTLESS

Hi. Welcome to the last show of the century here at East–West Players. Historically, I now represent Asian American Theatre at the turn of the century. A thousand years of art, and then me. Be afraid. Be very afraid. Millennium, Shmellinneum, I DON'T CARE. It's just another night. Just another New Year's Eve. I'm watching Dick Clark and then taking a pill. If the next thousand years are gonna be anything like the last thousand years, I'm gonna need a nap. Do you like this shirt? It's from The Ricky Martin Collection at Kmart. This one's called Livin' La Vida Lycra. I have no act. I don't know what you're expecting. My last show was written in response to a nervous breakdown and quite frankly, my life hasn't been *that* interesting lately. I really did crack up, though. Like *that's* hard to believe. In 1992 a series of horrendous things happened all at once. My lover dumped me, I was audited by the IRS and they took all my money, and my mother died, all within the span of six months.

No, this is a cute story, I promise you.

Three years later it looked like my life was starting to turn around. I was back in New York doing a play at the Public Theater and it was a big fat hit, which was a huge relief because I hadn't had an acting job in two years.

The big hit on Broadway that season was this play by Terrence McNally called *Love! Valour! Compassion!* and it was about a bunch of gay white guys who rent this house in upstate New York for the summer. Now, I'm not white, but I felt like I could really relate to the characters, I mean, the play was so accessible. I don't remember a whole lot about the plot. I remember that two of the characters in the play were named Arthur and Perry. I remember this because they had this scene, I think it was in the second act, where Arthur was trimming Perry's ear hair with a pair of scissors. And he mentioned that after being together 16 years, this is what it came down too. Trimming each others' ear hair. That was love.

Upon hearing this, I felt like such a loser. It was 1995 and I hadn't been on a date since Ronald Reagan was President. I hadn't been in what you'd call a successful relationship for any significant amount of time, and not only that, but up until this point in my life, when it came to love, I'd made nothing but a series of rotten choices.

My twenties were a mess. I mean it wasn't enough for me to have feelings of worthlessness, I needed *proof*. Concrete evidence. That usually meant turning my affections toward someone who was emotionally unavailable, unsure about their sexuality, or just wanted to be friends. "I like you as a friend"—are there six more humiliating words in the English language? Well, there's "I'm in love with someone else" and "get the fuck off of me." Sometimes, if you're really lucky, you get to hear all three sentences in a row. "I like you as a friend, I'm in love with someone else, get the fuck off of me."

And the guys I did end up going out with were just seven kinds of wrong. There was the Southern Baptist flight attendant. Gorgeous. Not the sharpest tool in the shed, but let's just say I wasn't dating him for the conversation. He used to pray immediately after having sex. Orgasm, prayer, orgasm, prayer.

He'd kneel and kneel again, and one time, just out of curiosity, I said, "What are you praying for?"

And he said, "For forgiveness...for what we've done."

And I said, "Well, I believe that God answers all our prayers. So in addition to forgiveness, you might want ask for cab fare. 'Cause you're going home. Don't let the door knob hit ya where the good Lord split ya."

My last relationship had been with a very famous actor. Well, he thought he was famous. Famous enough that he had to keep his sexuality a big secret, and like most closeted people, he thought nobody knew.

We know.

It wasn't Kevin Spacey. Honest. Oh, I wish it was, I'd tell you everything. This guy wasn't that famous. He was famous enough to have his own action figure from a movie he had done. Which was really cool because after we had broken up I could take that sucker out in the sun and hold it under a magnifying glass.

I can forgive, it's that whole forgetting thing I'm having a problem with.

He didn't want his friends or family to know that we were going out or my friends or family to know that we were going out, and I went along with it at first because one, I loved him very much and I thought that's what you did when you loved someone. Y'know—completely compromise your entire value system. And two, he just made it seem like he was this intensely private person. And it was kind of glamorous at first, having this clandestine affair with a person with their own action figure, but after a while I felt like I was working for an escort service. One time I flew out to visit him on location and he was staying at the Four Seasons and he wanted me to hide from room service. He ordered room service and he wanted me to hide in the bathroom. And I did. And I remember sitting on the toilet (in one of the most beautiful bathrooms I had ever seen) and thinking, This is so stupid. I mean, first of all, with all due respect to the hard-working men and women in the hotel industry, who gives a shit what room service thinks, and second of all, he had ordered dinner for two, so if room service was thinking anything, they were thinking, Well, here's your dinner, sir, and here's a cheeseburger for your imaginary playmate.

As I sat there that afternoon watching *Love! Valour! Compassion!* I thought

Arthur would never make Perry hide in the bathroom. Arthur would never pray for forgiveness after making love. And all at once I felt so ashamed and mortified by my past choices that I started to cry. And not discreet sniffly little tears, but big loud boo-hooing sobs. Sobs so loud that the woman in front of me turned around and said Do you mind? and I said, Listen old woman, I didn't say anything when you were unwrapping candy all through the first act. I don't remember much more about the rest of the play. I remember there was a lot of nudity and Nathan Lane was in it, and at one point he showed his butt and I remember being really glad I was in the balcony.

As I left the theatre, I reflected on my own life. Art makes you do that. (I'm sure many of you will leave the theater tonight, think about your own lives and sigh with relief.) For years I had been in search of The Great LTR. The LONG TERM RELATIONSHIP. I was Ahab and the LTR was my Moby Dick, this all-consuming goal that remained unfulfilled despite my relentless and dogged pursuit. But like Ahab at the end of the day, I would find myself alone. Just me. And my harpoon.

Being brought up in a very strict Filipino Catholic household, I was raised with the notion that two people were supposed to mate for life. Whether they liked it or not. I was also raised with the notion that those two people were supposed to be a man and a woman, but like most kids I only ever really listened to half of what my parents ever said.

That spring I was determined to have a healthy relationship. Even if it was with myself.

The following week on my way to the theater, I stopped by the post office to drop off my Publishers Clearing House entry form (they said I was a finalist), when I was approached by a very handsome man. For the sake of anonymity, let's call him Andrew. He said, "Are you Alec Mapa?"

I said, "Why, yes. As a matter of fact I am."

He said, "I saw you in the play next door. I thought you were terrific."

And all of a sudden I liked this man. He seemed to possess a keen intelligence. We talked for a bit. He seemed like a nice person, so I asked him out. "Listen, I'm in town for another month and I'm usually wired after the show, so would you like to go out maybe have a cup of coffee sometime?"

And he said, "Sure. Usually when I'm wired, coffee isn't my first choice, but I'd love to."

We went out for drinks the following night and it was the best first date I've ever been on in my entire life. I mean usually on a first date I'm doing my best to act like someone else, y'know, so they'll like me, but something about Andrew put me entirely at ease. I don't know what it was, his smile, his demeanor, or the gallon of red wine we consumed, but I was so relaxed.

Andrew was funny, smart, beautiful and it wasn't at all like we were going out for the first time. It was like Oh. There you are. And after that first date we were inseparable. It was if we'd been going out for years. We just got each other in ways no one else ever did. Like I never met anyone who wanted to stay in as much as I did. I hate going out. I'm not a bar person. I've seen that movie. I know how it ends. We would stay in for hours and watch Meryl Streep movies. *Sophie's Choice:* Stinko, you are looking very nice in your cocksucker...*A Cry In The Dark*: A dingo ate my baby daughter....

We'd play Patti LuPone CDs full blast and have contests to see who could hit the same notes as her, in head voice, not falsetto. We'd do the Sunday *Times* crossword puzzle in ink, stuff ourselves with Chinese food, get drunk on cosmos and dance around the living room. And we were always laughing. We never got sick of each other. Y'know that feeling when you're with someone and it's like, OK. Enough. Go home now please. Never had that with Andrew. And we'd just met.

After two weeks of seeing him I told him I loved him. By accident. I was leaving a message on his machine at work. "Hi it's me. I'm going on an audition and then I'm doing the show and then I'll see you later on tonight, 'k? I love you." SHIT. I didn't mean to say that, I mean I did, but not so soon, but Oh fuck it, I love you. There. I said it.

This was the happiest I'd ever been. I was in a hit play, it was spring, I was hooked up and I thought OK! What's the catch?

One night I turned to him and I said, You shouldn't be so nice to me. I'm not used to it. He said That's the stupidest thing I've ever heard. We're supposed to be nice to each other. Take care of each other, look out for each other, be good to each other. That's what people do when they love each other.

And I said, "Oh. Do you love me?"

And he said, "Sure. Parts of you."

And I thought OK, this is the one. Sixteen years from now, this guy's gonna trim my ear hair. I had finally landed the LTR. And I was very happy.

I spent half the year in L.A. and half the year in New York. We were able to do the long-distance thing for three years because we loved each other very much, had this amazing connection, and nobody was hiring me. I had a lot of time on my hands.

Then I started to get work. Lots of it. I worked on two different pilots (neither one of them was picked up, but I was able to buy a sweater), I did a movie, a play in La Jolla and I toured all over the country with my solo show.

I was thrilled to be working nonstop. Andrew not so much. I tried to make it back to New York as much as I could that year and it ended up being about three weeks. Andrew was miserable. He tried to be as supportive as possible but he was basically trying to maintain a relationship with someone who was never around. I had become his imaginary playmate. He'd talk about me to his friends and they'd say Oh Alec, your boyfriend....Is he in the room right now?

Each announcement of a new job or project was followed by an apology for not being able to make it back to New York. I'm sorry, I'm sorry, I'm sorry. It got to the point where I dreaded telling him I got another job. Things between us became very strained. For our third anniversary we decided to go to Disneyland and stay over at the Hotel, because we thought it'd be fun. We hadn't seen each other in four months. It was very tense. We ordered room service, and over a Mickey Mouse-shaped burger, he said I can't do this anymore. And I said I can't either, this food is horrendously overpriced.

And he said NO. Us. This isn't working. We're never together. I'm happy that you're working, I'm so proud of you. I love you, but I can't pretend that I don't need the things that I need. I'd have to be a different person.

And I said I love you too. But in order to walk away from something I've wanted to do my whole life, I'd have to be a different person.

So on our third anniversary, we broke up. At the Disneyland Hotel. The Happiest Place on Earth.

I felt like such a hypocrite. For years I thought the one thing I wanted above everything else was a successful relationship. Getting what I always wanted only made me realize that I wanted something else more.

But I figured everything happens for a reason, right? Perhaps now that I was untethered by the obligations of a long-distance relationship, I could now focus exclusively on my professional life and my career would just take off. Here's a tip: If you ever have to choose between having a relationship or a career, it's probably a good idea to actually HAVE a career.

Pilot season rolls around and my career comes to a grinding halt. It seems that all four major networks came to the conclusion that Caucasian teenagers (well, Caucasians in general) have been woefully underrepresented in the media, so they decided to do a whole bunch of television shows about them. Which is all fine and good, but that left people like me with very little for me to do except go to the gym and watch television. So I've decided to stop grousing about it and be proactive. Take the bull by the horns. In times of great stress I always ask myself, y'know, "What would Madonna do?"

Try it sometime.

So I've written my own pilot script and I'm very excited about it. It's called "GET HER!" and it's kind of a nineties version of *That Girl*. Remember on the old show how within the first five minutes someone would point to Ann Marie and say "THAT GIRL!" Well, in my script someone always points to me within the first five minutes and says "GET HER!" That's all I've come up with so far. But the network is *very* excited.

I dealt with my breakup the only way I knew how. By watching hours and hours of television. I know it's a tremendous breach of social protocol to say this in Los Angeles. "I haven't been doing a thing since February. I've been watching television."

I've been watching MTV's *Total Request Live* everyday. It's the top ten most requested videos in the country. Just videos. It's like the perfect show for me because I have the attention span of a flashcube, and I hate to say it, but I've become obsessed with The Backstreet Boys.

I didn't mean for it to happen.

I initially dismissed them as just a bunch of pretty boys, pure bubblegum, a bunch of lightweights. But then I started listening to the music.

No, *really* listening. And their music, well, it's like Gywneth Paltrow's acting.

It has so many levels.

When Gywneth Paltrow won the Oscar this year I felt like it was a tremendous wake-up call to those of us in the acting community. It was like a whole new standard for artistic excellence had been set. Forget about what you thought good acting was before. Meryl who?

One of the crappy thing about breaking up is I used to see all the summer blockbuster movies with Andrew and this year I had to watch all those crappy movies by myself. *Notting Hill*? Did anybody see this movie? *Rotting Swill*, I call it. The movie that dares you to feel sorry for a world famous actress who makes 15 million dollars per picture? THE NERVE! "…I'm just a girl, standing in front of a boy, asking him to love her." I'm gonna slap her. "Every time my heart gets broken it's splashed across the front page of every newspaper. It's just entertainment for you."

Every time my heart gets broken, I'm so used to nobody giving a shit that having millions of people finding my personal tragedy even remotely interesting just might be a breath of fresh air.

I know it sounds like I'm jealous, but I'm not. I think it's pretty clear from my present situation that being rich and famous is the furthest thing from my mind. I used to want to be rich and famous, but then I started watching VH-1 *Behind the Music* and it's like the the worst thing that can possibly happen to anybody. It's like some kind of curse, like the monkey's paw. And it's always the same story. The minute you can afford prescription drugs, your life's headed straight for the toilet. One minute you're a rich, famous, Grammy award-winning artist, the next you're the opening act for Sha-Na-Na at Knott's Berry Farm.

One Sunday on VH-1 it was Divas' Day, with *Behind the Music* specials on Cher, Madonna, Bette Midler, Aretha Franklin, Stevie Nicks, and Donna Summer. All I can say is, thank God there was food in the house.

I've been watching a lot of Rosie. You think she's gay? Or as they say in the Philippines, "Do you think she's a gay?"

I thought Rosie was a gay, but then she can't be a gay because she has a crush. On Tom Cruise. Do you think he's a gay?

Poor Tom. It really doesn't matter if he's gay or not, that rumor's been going around for so many years, it might as well be true. Like that whole Richard Gere and the gerbil story. And everybody in Los Angeles knows someone who was working in the emergency room that night. "My roommate was there! We saved the hamster claws, see?" And everyone in L.A. is so smug about it. Go to any party and ask people "Do you think Tom Cruise is gay?" and people are like "Puh-leeze!" And for all we know he could be 100% heterosexual.

Speaking of closet cases, did anybody watch Prince Edward's wedding? I thought he was a gay. Well, he was single forever, didn't have a steady girlfriend until he was thirty, and he dropped out of the airforce to go work for Andrew Lloyd Weber. Walks like a duck, talks like a duck, hangs out with ducks, must be a gay.

I watched the royal wedding on CNN and they talked about the big party afterwards, and the commentators reported that the big wedding brunch was going to be a buffet.

Buffet.

Like they couldn't even be bothered this time.

"Well, we haven't had much luck with these marriages, and he's probably a fag, so I'm thinking buffet." Can you imagine? Standing in a buffet line behind Queen Elizabeth?

"Hey. No cuts!...Excuse me? Those buffalo wings, are they terribly spicy?"

Y'know, the queen's walking around with a big plate, "Is anyone sitting here? Oh look, they're bringing out more lobster salad. I'm going back, does anyone want anything?"

In the closet, out of the closet. Do what you want, just leave me out of it.

Nothing brought me joy this year, not even the new *Star Wars* movie.

Can we talk about this for a second? Am I the only person who thinks it's strange that a long time ago in a galaxy far, far away there's all these white people walking around dressed like Japanese people and not a single Japanese person in sight? Did that strike anybody as being slightly ungrateful? 'Cause let's face it. If it weren't for Japanese people there would be no Obi Wan Kenobi, OK? Is there some nether region of the galaxy where Japanese people are walking around dressed up like Vikings? In lederhosen? And I'm not stingy, I'm all about sharing our culture. Let's just acknowledge where the shit comes from, OK? Rumor has it that Steven Spielberg came up with the idea for E.T. after eavesdropping on Filipino people at the airport.

"Home. I want to go home! BE GOOD!" That was my gramma. E.T.'s Filipino. Yoda's Filipino. Paint him brown, give him a suit and tie, he could be a security guard at Well's Fargo.

I can make fun of Filipinos because I am one. Filipino-American.

Born in America, raised by Filipinos.

Which is a lot like having a lot of boundaries but no sense of personal space.

As I get older my culture is becoming more important to me because I'm running out of things to blame on my parents. I'm starting to think that I'm fucked up because I'm Filipino. And when I say I'm fucked up, I'm not trying to be cute, I *am* kind of fucked up. If I was a well-adjusted person, none of us would be here this evening.

As a child, I was told that my Filipino family bloodline can be traced all the way back to the Spanish colonists. Now to the uninformed this would seem rather glamourous and exciting.

But any historian will tell you that the Spanish colonists traditionally weren't very nice people. Well, first of all, they were colonists, so they were basically claiming for themselves something that wasn't theirs and enslaving the natives to work their own land. And they wouldn't marry the Filipinos because they wanted to keep the property in their own families. So there was a lot of inbreeding. And when that didn't work out for them (there were a lot of farming accidents) THAT's when they started to mix and match with the local color. So this just might be speculation, but my Filipino family bloodline probably started when some unsuspecting native woman and some rich retarded Spanish guy hit it off.

This would explain a lot. My family DNA is nuttier than Crunch and Munch.

I come from a notoriously eccentric family. The Mapas are CRAZY. A lot of manic-depressive over-achievers, obsessive-compulsives, and just plain ol' pull your pants up over your head and run down the middle of the street kooky.

There was my great aunt Luz.

Maria Luz, who was absolutely convinced that every man who ever laid eyes on her wanted to take her to bed. Now this isn't eccentric in and of itself, but she came to this conclusion when she was about 87. My father used to accompany her on her errands around town and she'd say "Hijo, tingnan mo, that man over there? He wants me. That man over there, he also wants me. THEY ALL WANT ME." So I guess that's where that part of my personality comes from.

I wasn't just raised by Filipinos. I was raised by Filipino CATHOLICS.

That's 500 extra crazy points right there. OK, it's not just that Filipinos believe in God, they believe in EVERYTHING. Witches, ghosts, vampires, Bigfoot, free tickets to my show. When I was on Broadway and I'd meet Filipino people, they'd always say "I'd love to come see your show. Are there free tickets?" My response to this was always, Of course. Usually tickets to a Broadway show will run you about 80 or 90 bucks, but if you go to the box office and tell them that you're Filipino, you'll get in *absolutely free*. Just ask for the Free Filipino Tickets. My Lola (my gramma, who lived with us when I was growing up) was very superstitious. She used to tell us stories about the old country and all the unexplained phenomenon that took place in her in her village. She'd tell us stories about dwendes—little demons who lived under houses who would sneak in at night and snatch children from their beds and carry them off, never to be seen. She'd tell us stories about aswangs—real-life vampires who looked and behaved like normal people during the day but by night transformed into bloodsucking beasts with insatiable appetites. She'd tell us about mananangals, half-human, half-beast creatures who could detach from the lower halves of their bodies and fly through the night in search of human flesh to consume. She'd tell us all these stories without the slightest bit of irony and then say, All right now. Go to sleep.

Thanks a lot, Lola. Why didn't you just give me cup of coffee?

I grew up terrified of being abducted by some creature or consumed by some demon that would separate me from my family.

My father scares the shit out of me. He leaves these terrifying messages on my answering machine. He has this really heavy Ilocano accent that makes him sound like he's furious all the time. ALEC, IT'S POP. NOTHING IMPORTANT. JUST CALLED TO SAY HI. I LOVE YOU. And I'm like five years old again. Oh my God, he's gonna kill me! ALEC, IT'S POP. He always identifies himself like that. Like I'd get him confused with all the other Ilocano men who call me in the middle of the day.

Whenever my father calls, the first question he asks is ARE YOU EATING? It's the Filipino way of saying I LOVE YOU. Once when I was in college I completely ran out of money and I didn't want to write home for more. I mean I was on my own for the first time and I didn't want my father to think I was weak or incapable of taking care of myself, so rather than ask for more money, I just stopped eating. For a couple of months.

My father came out to visit me one February and when I met him at his hotel room, his jaw hit the floor. I weighed about 90 pounds. Almost. I made Calista Flockhart look like Delta Burke. And he was soooo angry with me.

My father grew up starving and poor in the Philippines during World War II, and from the time he was ten years old my father's main function in life had been to put food on the table no matter what. I mean, it was real life or death stuff. Living in this constant state of crisis kind of traumatized him, and unfortunately, when the Americans liberated the Philippines from the Japanese, therapy was not a part of the relief effort. So every once in a while when I was a kid my father would just FLIP OUT. Once when I was five years old I was helping to bring in the groceries and I tripped and dropped two dozen eggs and every single one of them broke. My father LOST IT. Before anyone could make a move to clean it up, my father grabbed me by the scruff of the neck and used me as a mop to clean up the mess.

Incidents like this when I was growing up always made things kind of iffy with my father. Being gay made things even iffier, and over the years we kind of grew apart. We weren't close for a very long time.

That night at the hotel my father took me out to dinner and I could tell he was pretty mad because he didn't say a word, and neither did I, because I was too busy eating like I was going to the electric chair.

That night, I stayed over at his hotel and right before I fell asleep I became very ill. All of a sudden I had a 110 degree temperature and the chills. My dad gave me a bunch of aspirin and bundled me up and as soon as I drifted off to sleep, I had a terrible nightmare.

I dreamt that I had a dwende living in my in my stomach. It was covered in wet black hair, had cloven hooves, and it was curled in up in a ball.

And it was like I was watching it through some kind of hidden camera.

Then all of a sudden, I saw it see me and it started to freak out.

I could feel it trying to escape from my stomach.

I could feel long sharp fingernails scratching and clawing against my stomach lining. I could feel cloven hooves clacking against my ribcage.

OW! OW! OW!

And then I heard someone praying. Someone's saying the Lord's Prayer and the Hail Mary over and over again super super fast, and as the prayers got louder and louder the dwende screamed out in agony and it started to shrivel up. But as it did, it continued to claw at my insides even more ferociously and just as it was about to rip through my stomach I woke up.

I was drenched in sweat.

I was sitting up.

The room was completely dark and my father was sitting at the side of my bed and he had this frightened look on his face like he was five years old. And all of a sudden, for whatever reason, maybe it was the expression on his face, or the rosary beads he was clutching in his hands, I got for the first time in my adult life that he loved me.

And not only that, but I loved him.

And I hugged him in a way that I hadn't since I was very, very small.

And I started to cry. I mean, huge heaving sobs.

And I kept on saying over and over and over again, Imsorry Imsorry Imsorry Imsorry.

And he said For what?

For not being who I was supposed to be.

Only I didn't say that. I just remember that night as if I did.

And all my father could say was, "Son. You gotta eat."

So I started dating again. What can I say? It's not you, It's me. I'm older. I'm crankier and I'd rather make it a Blockbuster night. And when it comes to dating I think I'm an acquired taste. Like liver and onions. It's not the most popular item on the dating menu, but it's there because there's always going to be that one person who's really into liver and onions.

And I feel like I haven't learned a thing. It's like all these life lessons have been coming up for review, like pop quizzes and I've been getting Ds.

I keep lapsing back into these old codependent patterns.

In February I met this guy after a performance, absolutely stunning.

We talked for a bit, and I found that we had absolutely nothing in common, no shared valued or interests, he didn't seem to have a sense of humor, and showed no signs of being physically attracted to me at all, so I thought: We should go out!

We exchanged phone numbers on a Thursday night. I called him on Friday during the day: "Hey, this is Alec, um, I was just wondering what your week was gonna be like, y'know, maybe we can get together and have dinner or a movie, call me!"

Nice n' easy. No big deal.

He didn't call back Friday, Saturday or Sunday.

And I OBSESSED ABOUT IT THE ENTIRE WEEKEND. Now normally I'd be like, "It's a white balloon, let it go."

I'm of the philosophy that if the train does not stop in your station, IT IS NOT YOUR TRAIN.

It's just that I hadn't been on a train in a REALLY long time.

But to me, an unreturned phone call is like Kryptonite. This toxic substance that renders me powerless.

So I'm thinking, Did he lose my number? Is he really busy, did he get hit by a bus?

And I was this close to leaving that AWFUL message. You know what I'm talking about? That AWFUL message?

"Um, this is Alec, Uh...I'm just calling to make sure I got the right machine. Um, I'm still free all next week. Call me, OK? Please?"

But I thought, no. Let's break the chain. There are times when you should not get on the phone.

Like when you're missing your ex. Don't get on the phone.

Because there'll be no way to mask your desperation.

Hi...what's up?...Nothing...I was just hanging out and I was wondering... HOW ARE YOU?

You should not drink and dial. I think there should be a breathalizer on the phone. It should just automatically shut off.

It's a dangerous instrument in the hands of the wrong person. You know what's really changed the face of dating? The computer.

My roommate and I bought an iMac and overnight I became an AOL WHORE.

I'm now Alexandria, the She-Bitch of Cyberspace. The first couple of months I was addicted to the chat rooms. I could not get out. I'd log off and it would say You have spent 700 minutes online, and the sun's coming up.

Have you tried this? You log on, order yourself up a date, and he comes to your door. It's like Pink Dot. If you'll excuse the disgusting imagery.

My first time in a chatroom I made up this profile that was all a bunch of big fat fucking lies, y'know, just for fun. I was 6' 3", Eurasian, half-German, half-Korean, and I was a business student.

I went into a chat and within the first 5 minutes I was busted on every single fabrication.

The first Instant message I got was from this guy who said: "I'm half-Korean half-German too!"

And I was like, "Um…that's nice."

And then he started to write me something in Korean.

And I was like, "I was raised by my stepmom…"

And then he started writing me something in German,

And I was like, "Uhh...my German's even worse."

And then we started chatting about our computers and I was like, "I'm really excited. I'm new to all of this cyber-stuff, I've never had a computer before!"

And he was like, "You're a business student and you've never had a computer before?"

And I was like, "Well, I'm not a very good student…." I went to dummy business school.

So I was about to leave that chat and make a clean getaway when I get this other IM from somebody who was all, YOU SOUND REALLY HOT, and I was like…You sound really hot too!?

I download his profile: 19 years old, surfer, construction worker, swimmer's build.

So we start chatting, he starts typing me all these smutty messages, trying to move the conversation into this whole cybersex thing. Which I think is just silly.

Well, first of all, I can't do two things at once, and I'm a really slow typist.

So he's like, Do you want to get together? Should I come to your place?

And I'm like, No, I have a roommate.

And he was like, Do you have a picture?

And I was like, No, I just bought this computer and I haven't downloaded one yet.

And he's like, Well, would you like to see mine?

And I was like, Uh, OK.

So he e-mails me his photo and it's downloading on the screen, blip blip blip...

...and I was like OH. MY. GOD. I CAN'T SEE YOU TONIGHT. I'VE ALREADY SLEPT WITH YOU.

My first time in a chatroom and I run into someone I've already slept with. It's like my life is God's favorite sitcom.

So now he's all like, I'm intrigued, when was this?

And I was like, It was a long time ago, it was in Soho, I was living in New York and I was really depressed, and I thought no, that's way too much information, I don't want to get into, and I was going to press delete, but I pressed ENTER instead, and the whole message comes up on the screen

And he was like, IS THIS ALEC MAPA?

And I was like, Yeah.

And he says, You are so NOT 6' 3"!

And I was like, YOU ARE SO NOT 19 YEARS OLD!!!!!

So I actually went on a bunch of AOL dates at the beginning of the year and none of them were memorable enough to be a stageworthy anecdote.

But I've come up with a couple of AOL dating tips that I'd like to share. If you'd let me:

#1: If someone describes themselves as having a swimmer's build, ask them to be more specific, because to be perfectly honest, all kinds of things can swim. Manatees, Giant Sea Bass, Shelley Winters in *The Poseidon Adventure*.

You get the picture. I'm gonna come across as being so shallow. I don't care.

#2: If you have sex on the first date, nine times out of ten, it's a sex date. Which is perfectly respectable in this day and age, just embarrass yourself by making it something that it's not. Having sex on the first date is like getting on the bus one stop before the end of the line. Enjoy the ride, just don't act all surprised when it turns out to be such a short trip.

A really good friend of mine suggested that since I'm pretty much on the rebound I should just be having hot meaningless sex. So he suggested that I go to a sex club or a grope bar. And I was like, I'm a little too vanilla for a sex club. I've been to a sex club once and it was really dark and scary. And it reminded me of one of those haunted houses that they set up at the Halloween fair where they blindfold you and plunge your hands into a bunch of different things.

"These are his brains! These are his eyeballs!"

It just wasn't sexy.

But what about that grope bar idea? What's a grope bar?

It's a bar where you get groped.

What if I don't get groped?

I mean how embarrassing would that be? Loser! I'm in a grope bar and nobody's touching me.

And he said don't worry about it, you'll get groped. There's this place in Silverlake called Cuffs. It's a leather and Levi's bar.

And I thought, cool.

So we show up at this bar in Silverlake and there's this line that stretches all the way down Hyperion, and I'm thinking this groping thing must be really popular with the kids! So while we were waiting in line I said to my friend, OK, I'm doing this but I'm a big chicken so stick close in case I change my mind and I wanna go home. And he's all like, "Will you RELAX?"

So we finally make it into the bar and I'm immediately struck by the smell, y'know, it has that old gay bar smell, y'know, like smoke and pee and it's super dark and the whole place is done up in this abandoned mineshaft motif and I'm like OK, this isn't my thing, I CHANGED MY MIND! I WANNA GO HOME!

And I turn around and my friend is GONE. I can't find him anywhere. And I'm like, Great. So I make my way into the bar and it's super crowded and dark with people just crammed up against one another, like this big leather and Levi's lobster tank. Total fire hazard. But there's really no way to get past anybody in this place without rubbing up against someone, so I'm making my way through this crowd and I'm all like excuse me, pardon me, um that's my foot…and every time I do this I get these really strange looks and I'm like, What? Doesn't anyone have any manners? It takes me about half an hour to make it through the entire bar when I've realized that I've missed the point entirely. Everyone is rubbing up against each other on purpose, and not only am I the only person in the entire bar saying Excuse me, I'm the only person in the entire bar TALKING. So I've pretty much spent the last half hour establishing my role in this place as the village idiot because as crowded and as claustrophobic as this place is, people are actually starting to AVOID me.

And I'm thinking, I'm gonna kill my friend.

So just when I thought that, I found him. He was standing on this balcony that overlooked the bar. Friend. And I'm about to say, Thanks a lot for abandoning me, when this man who can only be described as incredibly huge, I mean John Goodman huge, I mean I can curl into the fetal position and fit in this man's stomach, starts rubbing up against me. And he has no shirt on and I'm thinking, y'know, if I was into the big sweaty bear, this'd be a slice of heaven…but right right now I just feel like this tiny Filipino man about to be swallowed by a belly button and I'm terrified. So I'm looking at my friend and saying, "Move, you have to move!" And just for fun, he grips hold of the railing in front of him and pushes me against this guy, and I'm thinking, great. This is my life. It's 3 A.M., I'm in Silverlake, and I'm being dry-humped by Babe Ruth.

So I decided that I wasn't going to date anymore, that I was far better off by myself and I was pretty much going to make it a Blockbuster night for the rest of the year.

And then I met someone.

For the sake of anonymity, let's call him Joseph.

Joseph was 43, Asian, gorgeous, rich, successful, had a great sense of humor, and best of all, he worshiped the ground I walked on.

Well, the last part was a bit of an exaggeration, but I gotta have some fun.

I met Joseph at a pool party of a very close friend over a plate of barbeque pork. Very romantic.

I was stuffing my face at the buffet table when someone tapped me on the shoulder and said "Hi Alec. I'm Joseph," and I was like "Hi. AHM ARJTFCMDLEC!"

Immediately after we said hello, and I swallowed, there it was again, that feeling. Oh. There you are.

And we ended up spending the entire weekend together.

I liked him so much because he wasn't anything like me. He just was so at ease with himself, like he was already the person he was going to be and not in some place where he was figuring things out. He said he was single and dating. I told him I had been conducting interviews at Koo-Koo-Roo. He said that he was training for the AIDS ride. Very cool. He said that he lived in San Francisco and was in banking. I told him I lived in L.A. and Mastercard was suing me.

We hung out for the entire party and fell asleep in front of the television watching *Bewitched* reruns on Nick at Nite.

The next morning I woke up lying next to him, and even though we didn't do anything the night before I felt in some strange way as if we as if we had. I woke up with his arms around me, I felt really close to him, and all of a sudden I really had to brush my teeth.

That's when you know it's love. If I didn't care I would've rolled over and said Good Morning.

The following week I was up in San Francisco performing and he came with a whole bunch of friends. We all went out to dinner afterwards and I was all over him. I was holding his hand, playing footsie under the table, acting like a total goon, and one of the friends who went out with us that night was this French guy with an accent so thick,

I thought it was fake. For the sake of anonymity, let's call him Jacques Cousteau.

"So, Jacques Cousteau, where you from?"

"I'm from Paris."

And I was like, "Yeah. I'm from Paris too. Hohoho."

And the table goes silent and everyone's like, He's really from Paris, idiot.

"So, do you like living in San Francisco?"

"Yes, I like it very much."

"You have a boyfriend?"

"Yes, him."

And he points to Joseph.

And Joseph has this look on his face that says HUH?

And I cornered him during the evening and I said HUH?

And he said that he and Jacques Cousteau had to have a talk, because as far as he was concerned, he was just someone he had been dating and they weren't serious. And he was just as surprised as I was to hear Jacques Cousteau call him his boyfriend. And I believed him because during the meal I was all over Joseph like a cheap suit and Jacques Cousteau didn't bat an eyelash. And if that had been my boyfriend? I would've had to open a can of whoop-ass. Somebody once cruised my boyfriend at a party quite blatantly and right in front of me and it was like I had testosterone poisoning.

"What are you doing?"

"Wh-wh-what are you talking about?"

"Wh-wh-what the fuck do you think I'm talking about? You're cruising my boyfriend right in front of me like I'm fucking invisible, what are you nuts? You don't know me. I could be some crazy inbred Filipino Spanish person."

Jacques Cousteau didn't seem to mind, in fact later on we were at another bar and he was making a move on this African-American guy and I totally encouraged this. I was like, "He's gorgeous. Is that your type?"

And he's like, "Yes. I am not attracted to white men. He is more my type. I am with Joseph because he is a nice guy, I'm a nice guy, It's OK for now. Don't tell him I said that." So now I feel like this whole thing is this big yellow light. I'm interested, but I don't want to get all *Melrose Place* about it. Later on, Joseph and I are standing outside of the bar, and it's June but it's freezing, and I have on this navy peacoat with the collar turned up and I'm shivering. And I look so cute. And before I can say anything he kisses me.

Quite suddenly and for a really long time.

Now, sex is a tricky thing. It can mean a whole lot of something or a whole lot of nothing.

But a kiss.

A kiss is deliberate and specific. And as Joseph kissed me with the fog whipping around us and the streetcars clanging by I thought, OK, this is gonna be a great summer. I'm coming up to San Francisco, getting married, adopting two children and moving to Hawaii.

We e-mailed and talked on the phone nonstop all week. Basic getting-to-know-you stuff. Plans for the summer. At one point we discussed a weekend trip to Mendocino what kind of nightgown that would require. I suggested a shortie, 'cause it just makes you feel pretty.

And then something changed.

The following week, my phone calls weren't being returned immediately, and my e-mails, which had previously been answered lickety split, were now being answered a day later. And I thought to myself, No. You're just being paranoid. I won't let you blow this, he's an adult, he works in a bank. He can't just drop everything to call you up and write you a cute little e-mail. Get a life, go to the gym, you self-centered, high-mainte-nance, codependent pain in the ass.

It's that kind of nurturing inner dialogue that makes me the person that I am.

The day of the AIDS ride he had to be at the starting point at 5:30 A.M. So I got up at 5 to call him and wish him luck. He gave me his pager number in case I want-ed to call him while he was on the road, but I said Nah. I'll see you in San Francisco.

I fly up to San Francisco, and while I'm up there I'm not doing a damn thing but focusing on Joseph coming back. And I have the whole thing planned out.

OK, the ride was over on Saturday. I figured after seven days on a bike, he'll need some rest. So I'm not expecting a call Saturday. Sunday, he might want another day to chill, so I cross off Sunday. Monday he's driving back, and if gets in late and has to get up early for work, hasta la vista Monday. Tuesday, there'll probably be a lot of catching up to do at work, especially if it's a bank, he might have to roll some pennies or something, so Tuesday day is out, but Tuesday night'll be his first full night at home where he can kick back and relax. Tuesday night he'll call, so this is a very wide berth. Four days and I fig-ured I'd be a sensible creature. And I was. Until Tuesday night came and he didn't call. He didn't call Wednesday and I lost my mind. I turned into Glenn Close. There's no way for me to accurately describe just how nuts I became or how fast I lost it so I've decided to read to you actual excerpts from my journal:

June 16th, 1999—

I'm doubting myself and hating him with each day that passes without a phone call.

This morning I thought, well maybe he drove in and went straight to bed, he's exhausted, blah, blah, blah, but those excuses make me feel about that important. So now I'm thinking about forgetting the whole thing.

I already have plans for tonight and I'm visualizing phone calls in my head where I'm very cold and unforgiving:

Maybe.

Whatever.

Something's different now. Somebody's feelings have changed and it has to do with my e-mail or the phone or something. It doesn't feel the same. I don't feel special.

He's already got Jacques Cousteau at his beck and call, so I'm like number two or something.

I fucking got up at 5A.M. in the goddamn morning.

Maybe that was it.

And if it was, good.

It should be fantastic that I did that.

Know what I mean?

I hate this.

I hate being in a place where I'm deconstructing and doubting my every fucking move just cause he didn't call. And now I'm feeling like I was when I was dating so-and-so [the semi-famous closeted actor I mentioned earlier] making excuses on his behalf, rationalizing his behavior and minimalizing my own feelings

Well, fuck that.

I'm MAXIMIZING MY FEELINGS TODAY, BECAUSE THEY'RE MY FUCKING FEELINGS

And they're hurt.

And I don't think I'm being too judgmental when it comes to the phone— you're either thinking of me or you're not, and if you're thinking of me it takes ZERO effort to make a phone call.

Zero fucking effort.

Well, I have my answer.

He's not wild about me and I thought he was.

I mean it's not worth me feeling like this.

I've been waiting for him like Christmas,

and maybe it's just as well.

This whole phone obsession thing tells me

I'm not in such a good space right now.

I mean my life's been so up in the air lately,

I've felt my ex pulling me in one direction,

but we've discussed that a gazillion times

and work this year has been non-existent,

so maybe I was looking for someone or something

to brighten things up a little.

And maybe I'm no good to anyone right now,

especially if I'm living for the PHONE.

Nope, this is not good at all,

I take everything too personally,

and why shouldn't I—

I'M the one he's not calling back.

It's not just my imagination.

I'm not being paranoid.

And you know what?

I DESERVE that phone call.

I DESERVE to be kept in touch with,

and thought of

I'm THAT valuable

I don't know what I'm supposed to learn from this

Guard my heart, I guess,

This has been a major block to my creativity and maybe with him out of the picture, things will really start to flow.

I always get creative when I'm in pain.

That's it.

It's time to go it alone again.

And if going it alone means that I don't have to anxiously wait for someone to let me know that I'm OK, then bring it on.

He calls Friday. He hadn't gotten in until late Tuesday, he was swamped with work all day Wednesday, and then he got sick. He didn't want to give me his cold, so he stayed in bed all day Thursday but today he's feeling better and would like to see me tonight.

I'm so ashamed. He was *sick*. I went crazier than a rat in a coffee can and he was sick.

I arrive at his house Friday night and he looks fantastic. He says he's exhausted and suggests that we just watch a movie. I say Fine by me. We watch *Two For The Road*, this great Audrey Hepburn/Albert Finney romantic comedy, and during the film we discuss the summer like we're still going to be hanging out. And an hour and a half into the film I ask: "Whatever happened to Jacques Cousteau? Did you guys ever have that talk?"

"We really didn't need to. We're kind of settled now."

"What?"

"We became kind of serious while you were away."

And now my ears feel hot and I can feel my heart sinking down into my stomach.

"When were you going to tell me this?"

No response. He just shrugs and says the very words I'm dreading:

"I hope you won't exclude me from your life. I'm really glad that I met you. I hope we can be friends."

I'm stunned but the words come out of my mouth anyway:

"No. I don't see that happening anytime soon. Up until two seconds ago I was spending my entire summer with you and now I just can't see myself hanging out with you and your boyfriend."

So now I'm past shock and I'm charting a course towards denial and bargaining and

I'm sputtering "Wh-wh-what about Mendocino? What about all those things we were gonna do?"

And he says, "Yeah. I shouldn't have said those things."

And I said, "OK, I need to know one thing. That chemistry thing that happened between us, that connection—that wasn't something I made up, that was real."

And he says, "Yeah. I was a real basket case trying to figure out what to do."

And I want to shake him and tell him he's making a big mistake and that Jacques Cousteau is evil and must be destroyed.

But instead I hug him 'cause I know that my summer with him is officially over. And he hugs me back. And the minute it feels like pity I leave quickly and I don't look back.

So. What was the point of all that? What was the point of me choosing work over Andrew only to have work evaporate? What was the point of me meeting this guy that I thought was so great only to have it turn out so badly? Every move I've ever made in love always seemed to put me right back in the same confused place. It was like seventh grade algebra, this thing that everybody else was able to figure out except me.

The following weekend was Gay Pride and the entire city had this fiesta atmosphere and I just wasn't in the mood. I just had six months of useless dating culminate in my heart getting stomped on and I didn't feel like watching a fucking parade.

But I woke up Sunday morning and the weather was flawless. Just sunny and clear, no wind, the kind of sky they rarely get in San Francisco. Well, never. So I took the streetcar downtown to Montgomery Street and I got on the escalator, and even before I came up from underground I could hear the roar of thousands of people cheering.

I reached daylight.

I was surrounded by throngs of people watching this parade go by. And the first float that rolls by is for some disco and there are a million cute boys on it in tight shorts and they're dancing and blowing kisses to the crowd and throwing plastic Mardi Gras necklaces, and all of a sudden I'm like five years old, and I'm shouting "ME! ME! I WANT ONE! I WANT ONE!"

And for the next three hours the parade keeps coming and coming and it's populated with the queerest creatures of every sort.

Fairies and trolls, witches and vampires, people who could detach from the lower halves of their bodies and fly.

And after three hours of this it was like, Geez. The whole world's queer.

'Cause that's what it felt like.

Like everybody on the planet had some kind of heartbreak that mystified or confounded them.

But today not only were they were all completely over it, they were in a parade. And there was such an overwhelming feeling of acceptance and forgiveness, that the very thought of being angry and bitter about one more thing in my life just seemed so....

Pointless.

And by the end of the parade I was sunburnt and dripping with Mardi Gras beads and I felt giddy. And sleepy. And I went home.

TAKE OUT: QUEER WRITING FROM ASIAN PACIFIC AMERICA

DAN TAULAPAPA MCMULLIN

THE BAT

Once upon a time in old Pulotu there were two faafafines named Muli and Lolo.
Lolo was pretty but Muli knew how to talk.
Every night they walked the beaches looking for sailors.
In those days everyone in Pulotu was a sailor.
When they found one they had their way with him
because they never did each other:
One of those things.
Afterwards,
because the islands used to be dens of cannibalism,
one of them hit the nodding sailor with a rock,
and they devoured him.
They did this until there were no more young men left on their particular island.
In fact around this time Lolo had really learned everything he would from Muli,
and Muli was starting to desire Lolo,
so they did each other; but afterwards Lolo killed Muli
and devoured him
as people who come to one for advice will.
This act made the gods very angry at Lolo,
so for punishment they turned him into a bat.

For years Lolo flew up and down the beach at night on little leather wings.
And there were no young men
until finally the Americans landed.
Lolo's first white man, still he knew a sailor when he saw one.
Lolo sunk his teeth into the sailor's fat neck and the sailor fainted.
Then Lolo drank until he got plump and passed out.
When he woke up he was in a basket aboard ship
and ended up at University of Minnesota Medical School
where he was given a nice warm cage by a local foundation.

One day
I'm not sure how but I'll let you know,
he escaped.
It was the especially cold winter of '94;

eighteen–ninety–four.
Lolo flew above the buildings
and south over the pale Mississippi landscape.
It was snowing
and everything was white.
Suddenly far below he saw something in black leather.
Flying down he discovered a boot
that some young man had left there the previous summer
along with his glasses and a pair of shorts he had lost along the river bank
while walking to the corner store late one night to fetch a bottle of milk
for the wife and five kids.

By now Lolo's wings had frozen and he was stuck.
He was in love with the black leather boot
although it didn't speak
and he couldn't eat it.
He didn't think he could eat it
and love it.
The snow kept falling
until it covered them both like a blanket.
The end.

THE DOLL

[*Three men. Me and two others. Wrapped together in a ball. I separate myself.*]

When I was a little boy, he took me down to his basement...

[*The second man separates himself and leads me down.*]

We lay down on a pile of laundry on the bed; there was a closet door half open, someone there watching...

[*The third man there.*]

We were naked, he turned me over on my stomach and I was shaking...

[*The second man leads the third man behind me.*]

I felt a hand enter me...

[*I stand up.*]

He had put a doll's hand in my butt! I ran around the place with his doll's arm up my butt!

[*Running in a circle, the third man with his fist on my butt flailing like a doll.*]

'O KAULAIKU

Tasi	Lua	Tolu
Let's go into the forest.		
	I'm afraid.	I'm not afraid.
There are cacao trees with sweet seeds to suck. There are breadfruit trees, which means baking, of course. There are plump birds who sing so sweetly you can almost hear them say yes dear.		
There tiresome vines, and battlements. There are old land mines, with the imperialists' complements. There are shattered trees and giant stinging bees.	I'm afraid of dying. I'm afraid of arguments. I'm afraid of mailing postcards. I'm afraid of seeing treetops. I'm afraid of. I'm afraid of.	I'm not afraid of anything. Except when someone is standing in the distance. I'm very afraid of seeing someone standing in the distance. I'm afraid of that.

And beyond is an old temple.		
	I know the place.	I don't know the place.
	It's forbidden.	Let's go.
It's really just a clearing.	It's evil.	
They used to dance there long ago.	They ate people!	
That's not true. I don't think it's true.		Well, they stopped didn't they?
Oh, let's go.		Oh, let's go.
Tonight.		
	No.	No.
	We should finish shelling these nuts.	
I'm done.	I'm afraid I'm not done.	It might be fun. I'm done.
I'm done.	I'm afraid I'm not done.	I'm done.
Let's wait here under this tree.		
	It's getting dark.	
I can hear the ocean.	I can hear the ocean.	
		I can hear the flying fish.
	What's that thing there?	
It's my grandparents' tombstone. They were buried together. If you stand here at midnight, you can hear them singing hymns. They were a serious couple.		
	I don't want to hear them singing.	I heard someone singing yesterday.
It's dark now.	Let's go back.	
Follow me.	Let's go.	
		It's sort of dark up here. Darker than I thought.

We're far enough to raise a light. I brought a lamp. Where are my matches?	Where are your matches? It's awfully dark here.	Something big and wet is on my foot.
There. Now we can see the trail well enough.	The light doesn't make me feel better.	It's just a toad.
	The forest doesn't look better by lamplight.	
Can you hear the forest?		
	You say that like it was a person.	It's beautiful.
		It is a person. I can hear it talking.
Follow me.	I have to be home by a certain time.	
Quiet.		
		I can see the moon.
Let me blow out the light.	It doesn't look like it.	
Wait.		The moon is so big.
	It looks like it's falling.	
You'd almost think it was falling.		
		It is falling.
The moon is falling.	The moon is falling.	
Hold hands!		
	The moon is falling.	The moon is falling.
Hold hands.		
Circle. Circle. Circle. Circle. Circle. Circle.	The air is turning round with bats.	Here is the moon.
	There are bats everywhere.	The moon! The moon! The moon!
	Circle. Circle. Circle. Circle. Circle. Circle.	The moon!

MAIANA MINAHAL

POEM OF THANKS TO ALL THE POETS IN POETRY FOR THE PEOPLE FOR THREE NIGHTS/ONE HUNDRED THIRTY POEMS
INSPIRED BY BEI DAO'S "A BANQUET"

uc berkeley bureaucrats may say
politicians may say
the world bank may say
that
between you and the world
walks hatred
a hail of pepper spray and batons
as police beat protesters
and farmowners force strawberry pickers
to stoop with short hoes
between you and the world
slips the myth
of money as power
the almighty dollar
the whore of moral conscience
in this country
between you and the world
the love you can't claim
of she for she
he for he
or you for yourself
for your families for your peoples

but i believe
between you and the world
nothing

beyond
these three nights
one hundred thirty poems
nothing
beyond this room

and everyone here
hushed to hear poetry
nothing but the moment
you look up
and see faces listen
to each and every word
of your most precious
urgent
truth

hold that moment close
closer than the breath
you catch and suck in
closer than the fist
you form
to keep watch
closer than the world
that winds its way daily
without you
closer than this
closer than the world
waiting for your words
begging for beauty
closer than the world
closer

EIKI MORI

UNTITLED 1

UNTITLED 2

MEI NG

BEES

Mona pulls a towel around herself, cracks the door and looks down the hallway before dashing to her room. The humming of the bees is louder now. She walks to the window and counts eleven crawling around on the glass. They work their way to the top, fall back down and start all over again. Mona checks that her door is shut before she dresses, not that she thinks walking around naked is making Raymond touch her, but she can't be too sure.

Before, there were only one or two bees in the morning. Mona could live with that. She isn't afraid of them, not like some people, who jump up and start swatting at them. Instead, she opens the window, catches the bees in a cup, and puts them outside. Raymond said that was dumb, that they would only come back later.

Now that there's so many, Mona is starting to think he's right. Dressed now, she opens the door. "Ray," she calls, "the bees."

Raymond comes into the room, still in his sleep clothes, a white T-shirt and Hanes briefs. "Morning, sweetie," he says.

He holds a flip-flop and a paper towel. He kills them one by one, quietly, so the others don't notice what's going on. Mona sits on the bed and watches. Raymond wipes the window after he crushes each one. When Mona can't watch anymore, she goes into the kitchen.

She stands at the sink with her sleeves rolled up and washes yesterday's dishes. There are lots, even though they ordered from Red Hot Szechuan. Raymond comes into the kitchen. "Did you get them?" says Mona.

Raymond nods. He gives her a little kiss on the cheek and pats her shoulder. At the same time he touches her ass. Mona laughs a little and wonders if he really touched her ass.

"Going out?" says Raymond. He pours himself a glass of juice and offers some to Mona, although she never drinks juice.

"To Magda's." She presses against the wall to get past. The kitchen is much too narrow, especially with the plants growing wild. Raymond said he would cut them back but he hasn't done it yet, and the leaves are reaching out, taking over the kitchen. Mona tries to walk around them, but there just isn't any room.

Really the apartment is too small for two people who used to be lovers, even if that was years ago. When Raymond lost his job last year and got kicked out of his apartment, Mona said he could move in with her.

Their bedrooms are separated by a room they use for storage, the boxes piled almost to the ceiling. Raymond's things don't fit in his room, what with his 55-gallon tank in there.

Yesterday Mona sat in bed rubbing cocoa butter on her legs. They get dry from the cold, dusty almost. Besides, she likes to groom after a breakup. Three weeks ago, Louis left her. Just when she had been close to committing, as in you and me babe forever. But not close enough. Giving up Louis made her almost as miserable as giving up her wandering ways.

As she rubbed the oil into her skin, she thought she heard Raymond jerking off. She listened closely. The quick breathy sound was unmistakable. Not that it bothered her, but he could put music on, thought Mona as she wiped the oil from her hands and turned on her own radio.

At Magda's, Mona is so aware of being a girl in a café reading a book that she can't even read. Men sense this and come up to her, cute ones and ugly ones. The ugly ones get the briefest nod and if they still don't go away, Mona puts on her headphones and taps her foot in time to the music. The cute ones, she gives her number. They walk away, amazed it was so easy. You should see my dried-up legs, Mona thinks as they stuff her number into their pockets.

Mona hasn't fucked in three weeks, since she and Louis broke up. Her teeth are on edge. She meets a writer named Joe and gives him her number. Almost anyone will do.

Not Raymond though. Not that he's so bad looking, she just doesn't feel that way about him. In the past couple of weeks, Raymond has been touching her more. When Raymond rubs her arm, his fingers always seem to brush against her breast. Mona pulls her arm closer to her body and wonders if he's really trying to touch her breast or whether she's just paranoid. Raymond hasn't dated anyone since Mona. Once he told her that he jerked off all the time. Mona didn't say anything.

Mona and Raymond are eating dinner in her room. The chicken is good and burnt, the way she likes it. At first they don't talk, then Raymond says, "What did you do today?"

"I bought some water glasses. Did you see them? From the ninety-nine cents store. Then I went to Magda's. I met this guy, a writer, Joe."

"Another writer? What, he just started talking to you?"

"You know how it goes: He looks, I look, then someone smiles. I gave him my number."

"Was he on the make?"

"Of course," says Mona. Raymond doesn't say anything. He cuts some chicken and chews it for a long time.

"No girls ever give me their numbers in cafés." He glares at her. What can I do? she thinks.

Later they're watching TV and Raymond pulls off Mona's socks. He puts her feet in his lap and plays with her toes. Mona doesn't care about her feet; he can touch them all he wants. He bends her toes this way and that, puts his fingers between them.

Raymond isn't even watching the movie, but staring at the fish tank. The angels are chasing the other fish away from the corner. That means they've laid eggs again. They go nuts when they lay eggs, no one can get near them. But then one day the eggs just disappear. Raymond caught them one day, eating their own eggs. They're so busy guarding, not sleeping, not eating, they must get so hungry that one day they're like, Hey, let's eat these yummy eggs.

"Are you depressed?" Mona says.

"I need to meet someone," Raymond says. Mona moves her feet from his lap. She thinks of all her women friends but no one seems right for him.

"You should get out more," she says.

A couple of days later when Joe the writer calls her, she says she's too busy to get together. She always does that. Sees a guy in a café and thinks she would like to fuck him. She looks at him while they're talking, touches his arm, gives him her number, but when he calls, she's too busy. This doesn't stop her from giving out her number the next time around, even though it's more people to avoid.

Mainly, she avoids Louis. There's only one café in Blue Hills and Mona needs her tea and Louis needs his coffee. But now Louis is in Seattle with his new girlfriend. Louis is working fast; if Mona won't marry him, he will marry Melissa, even if she is anti-abortion. Mona and Louis had talked about going on vacation together, and now he's in Seattle with another woman. At least Mona can go to Magda's at all hours and doesn't have to worry about seeing him there, doesn't have to feel she's waiting for him to show up. Louis and Mona have broken up many times, but they end up meeting at Magda's; they talk a little and maybe go for a walk. Then Mona has to piss, and since Louis lives right near Magda's, they go to his house so Mona can use the bathroom. They lie on the bed like two friends talking, but then someone says something about having a naked nap and then it's all over.

He better not send her a postcard from Seattle. If he does, she'll kill him. Mona wishes she could bring herself to fuck the men she meets at Magda's. When her legs recover from the winter, she tells herself.

Mona meets Sola for tea. She wants to talk about Raymond but doesn't want Sola to think badly of him. Already, Raymond and Sola don't like each other. Raymond doesn't like any of Mona's friends.

"Those little fuckers. Guess how many of them turned in their papers. Seven.

Seven out of twenty-five." Sola rants some more about her class. Then they sit drinking their tea.

"The exterminators are coming on Saturday," says Mona.

"Good. You have to get rid of those brats," says Sola.

"I'll have bad bee karma now," says Mona. She thinks of this morning's scene in the kitchen with Raymond touching her. It has never been so clear before. "I think Raymond is touching me too much," says Mona. She can't believe she said it. It seems real now, not in her head anymore.

"What do you mean, touching you?" Sola chews the inside of her cheek.

"Touching me. Like the other day in the kitchen he touched my butt. But first he put one hand on my shoulder so maybe I wouldn't notice he was touching my butt," says Mona.

"He touched your butt? That fucker." Sola chews her cheek even more.

"Don't say that. He doesn't mean it."

"It's creepy. Did he do anything else?" says Sola.

Mona doesn't want to talk about this anymore. Sola is getting upset. "What else?" says Sola.

"Sometimes he tries to touch my tits," says Mona, wondering if he really does.

"No, Mona, he doesn't? You have to tell him to stop it," says Sola.

"But what if he isn't really? It's not like he's groping me. Maybe I'm making it up," says Mona.

"I'm sure you're not making it up," says Sola. That makes Mona want to cry.

"I'm letting it happen. Besides, he knows it's wrong, I can feel it. But he can't help himself," says Mona.

Sola sees that Mona is about to cry. "Oh, Mona," she says, and pats her on the back. Mona starts to cry, right there at Magda's. She looks down at her shoes. Last week a man on a bike came up to her when she was sitting on the bench outside. Mona had her headphones on and was reading and still he came up to her and started talking about her boots, were they comfortable, he had the same ones, they're expensive but he got them on sale. Are Mona's comfortable? She said they weren't and then the man said his weren't comfortable at first either, they only got comfortable after the heel started to wear away. Right here, he said and reached down and stroked the heel of Mona's boot. She could feel it inside her shoe and didn't know what to do. After the man finally went away, Mona got mad at herself for not slapping his hand. Who was he to come up to her and touch her shoe. A shoe wasn't a breast, but it was still part of her.

Mona thinks of telling Sola about the shoe incident but maybe Sola will think something is wrong with her. Mona decides she won't let anyone else touch her. Sola is touching her but her hand is so small it feels nice. No one else can touch her, if they do, she'll scream.

Mona gathers up the paper cups and pushes the crumbs to the floor. "Are you going home?" asks Sola.

"Yeah, I guess so," says Mona.

"I keep seeing you and Raymond in the kitchen. It's kind of grainy and I see his hand moving in slow motion to touch you," says Sola.

"He's lonesome," says Mona.

"Who isn't? I'm lonesome. I don't go around feeling up my friends," she says. Mona knows that Sola is right.

"Next time he does it, I'll tell him to stop," says Mona, and she means it.

On Saturday, the exterminators ring the bell. Four o'clock, right on time. There are three of them in brown uniforms. They carry a tool box, cans of spray, hoses. Mona moves her plants so they can get at the nest built into the brick wall outside her window. She goes into Raymond's room while he chats with the bee men.

"How many do you think are in there?" says Raymond.

"Last week we did a job over in New Hyde Park. Over four hundred bees in one nest," the head bee man says.

"Four hundred?" says Raymond, excited. The bee men drill holes in the wall and shoot white powder and gas inside. The drilling gets to Mona and she puts her shoes on and goes out for a walk. She walks around the block, thinking about the bees that aren't home, who went out for a bit and when they come home, will find everyone dead. Mona wishes she hadn't called the exterminators. After all, the bees weren't really bothering her. She walks faster.

It stinks in her room and there are a few bees crawling on the floor. There's white powder on them and they're moving slowly, like they don't know where they are.

That evening, Mona and Raymond are going over the bills. Raymond likes to pay right away, but Mona doesn't mind waiting until they threaten to disconnect the phone, shut off the electricity. Mona gets up to get the calculator; neither of them can add. She wants to finish the bills, get out of her work clothes, and have a shower. She roots around in the desk and then Raymond is behind her, hugging her, and then he's kissing her neck and grabbing her breast. Mona goes very still. She doesn't scream. She spots the calculator but doesn't reach for it.

Then she twists away from his hands, his mouth. Maybe she laughs. They don't say anything, they just go back to doing the bills. The electricity bill seems higher than usual, it must be that they're not turning the lights off when they go out. They figure what each owes, down to the penny. Mona keeps trying to remember if she laughed when Raymond grabbed her—did she?

The bills are in Mona's name and she always pays for the stamps. She just realizes this and it doesn't seem right. The post office is always crowded and the people who work there are so mean.

"We have to use your stamps this month," says Mona.

"What?" says Raymond.

"For the bills. I always use my stamps." She dares him to say something about it.

"I'll give you the stamps." He takes out his wallet. "Here," he says and places three stamps on the table. "Here, have the whole book." He pushes it across the table. Mona doesn't touch it.

"Are you mad at me?" Raymond asks and tries to touch Mona's arm. Mona jumps up and puts the bills away. Did she laugh when he touched her?

"I need a shower," she says and waits for Raymond to go back to his room.

He sighs and gets up slowly. "Mona," he says. She doesn't answer, just stares at the calculator. "Let's talk later, OK?" he says.

"Yeah," she says, but she doesn't mean it, just says it so he'll get out. Get the fuck out, she screams in her head. Raymond pats Mona's head and she sits very still while he does it. Don't fucking touch me, she screams again in her head.

Finally, he leaves. She listens to him walking down the hallway to his room. She blames the house, it's too small. She blames herself, she shouldn't have walked around naked in front of him. A powdered bee staggers across the floor. Mona thinks of stepping on it but doesn't.

In the shower, Mona holds her breast for a long time, the one that he touched. Mine, she says softly under the running water. She stays in the bathroom for a long time.

PAUL PFEIFFER

FRAGMENT OF A CRUCIFIXION

AFTER FRANCIS...

MEMENTO MORI

INSTALLATION VIEW

DETAIL VIEW

ANDY QUAN

WHAT I REALLY HATE

Chinese people, if you study Chinese history, are very hard to handle.
In normal times, they are obedient. They respect senior people, they respect authority.
Chinese people are flexible. They can suffer to an extreme
that most of the European race cannot imagine. So elastic.
But on the other hand, just like a spring,
if they get beyond the limit, the Chinese race loses all reason.

—*Chao Yao-Tung, retired cabinet minister, Taiwan government*

Sometimes they get it wrong. By "they," I mean the laughing gods, the chief scientists, the potion-mixers and spell-casters. By "wrong," I mean that by clumsy stirring, the tiniest ill measurement, a drop of sour milk, the experiment is ruined. By "the experiment," I mean, well, everything, really.

Like, why can't Chinese drink alcohol without turning red? Or, why do old ugly white men chase young Asians in gay bars? Or even, why do I have this name, Buster?

I mean, there's no short form, no nicer nickname, and my middle name is much worse and a well-kept secret. I managed to find out that Mother had enrolled in a night school literature course at some point in my pre-history. She never actually finished the course, but I got Tennyson as my middle name.

Buster, however, was incomprehensible, and I could uncover no explanation. "Huh, so demanding, so ungrateful," when I would ask my mother. Father, on the other hand, would simply smile, blankly, at a practical joke that I was not willing to identify as me. He successfully made it seem like it was all Mother's doing.

I'm not sure whether I see my name as an inheritance, per se, but I do see it as a cultural trait. Who else would have such a name but a child of Chinese immigrants? A Fontaine, Lester, Byron, Leonard, or Dexter. I feel marked by it, and am essentially too conservative (arguably another inheritance) to consider adopting something different. Although I do know of a Chinese acquaintance who dropped his original name (also top secret) and renamed himself Tony, after the lead character in *Saturday Night Live*. An aunt and her son who both changed their names to something luckier after consulting with a Chinese numerologist.

What I think I really would have liked to have as a cultural heritage is something else. A toughness, a lack of sentimentality. The Chinese are a brutal people. This is something I can admire. For example, we have none of the fondness toward animals that pervades a pet-crazed West. Dog soup, why not? Better yet, stir-fried. Who cares about endangered species? The Chinese will cut the bollocks off of any animal unlucky to have rubbed the ancient soothsayers the right or wrong way.

It's not just animals that we're talking about here. Only a generation or two ago, families would give away children to other people—relatives, perhaps, if there were too many mouths to feed, or if one family was short of a son. No hullabaloo, it was just done. Imagine the tabloid story that would make today. You could sell that to *The Star*.

Another tale: A daughter is dying of leukemia. Her father and uncles can afford the new and unproved treatment, but only if they sink a considerable proportion of the family fortune into it. They weigh the risks: certain financial hardship for the family but the girl may live; certain financial hardship for the family but the girl may die. Pragmatism ruled; you know the end of the story.

Now, I'm not saying that I'd like to be able to turn my back on the dead and dying, but I would like some of that practicality and lack of sentimentality, that kind of working with the world rather than fighting it. Thicker skin, really: the stand in the rain, water rolls off me kind of thicker skin. Instead, the words go right into me, the incidents pour inside; my internal organs have little room to do what they are supposed to do.

So what is blocking up my breathing, interrupting my heartbeat, pressing on my liver? A partial list: every time someone comes up and asks me where I'm from (where I'm *really* from) before they've asked my name; every time someone tells me I look like I'm eighteen even though the hair's going and the baby fat on my face is long gone; finding out that the person talking to you has a special interest in Asian culture; the ones who insist on approaching and talking to you when you've not made eye contact, smiled, or shown any friendliness whatsoever; the ones who treat you like you're too stupid or unassertive to order your own drinks or get your jacket from the coat check—they try to do it for you.

What's worse is the ones that come up and think they're so clever. Oh yeah? Born in Canada. You're not Chinese! You're a banana! White on the inside, yellow on the outside. OK, I suppose I should be sympathetic. I can relate to this, you've been given concepts and it's a pleasure to finally be able to match them up. Like when you first see a Tasmanian Devil in the zoo, and you get to compare it to the one in the cartoon. Or how about when someone describes what a Baked Alaska is, and when you actually get to see it. The problem is, I guess, if you think that the wallaby with rabies is the Tasmanian Devil and the oddly shaped Pavlova is a Baked Alaska. In truth, no sympathy for wrong guesses.

When it comes down to it, I think they should stand there and scratch their heads, and say "go figure." Rather than, oh, you're Chinese, you're gay, you're born in Canada: guessing what that means. In fact, I'm checkerboard. Through and through, two-tone abstract art, multi-coloured swirl painting. Plaid, baby, I'm plaid, so out of fashion I'm in fashion and so stylish I'm on my way out. I don't go with anything you own.

Anyway, what I really hate are Gay Asian clubs: They're the worst. I mean, what a bad joke: a race of people who can't handle alcohol. Sweet elixir: gin and tonic, frothy beer, the bite and softness of good red wine, bubbles-up-your-nose champagne. I would-n't want to see us as a race of Londoners, drinking at the pubs after work until we fall down at closing time at eleven at night. Or how about drunken Scandiwegian-Germanic tourists crawling through Spanish and Portuguese cobblestone streets, sangria and sherry spilt down the front of their shirts?

But at least we should be able to toss back a few brewskies. A roomful of soda waters with lemon does not ooze sex appeal.

Furthermore, why do we have a separate club night anyway? Does this put us into the category of leather night, rubbermen, underwear parties? Are we a fetish or are we a theme party? Here you can see my arms in front of you, stretched out, a movie star, a pop star, a poster child, a peace campaigner: I'm saying, "Why can't we all get along?"

But I'm being facetious. I know why there are separate nights. It's because we're supposed to share a culture, and have the opportunity to be in the majority, to celebrate what we have in common, and be together. And also because we don't fit in at regular gay bars, that we need a relief from them. If you don't know why, it's probably not worth explaining.

Or maybe what the point really is here is sex. Isn't that what it always boils down to? The fact that we can't get sex at other clubs, and don't know whether some white-black-Latino-whoever is going to just look right through us, or that guy we're interest-ed in is going to turn his back, but before doing so, snarl, as if to say, how dare you? How dare you even think about it? Since we're not sexual, not masculine, since they don't go for Asians.

So, really, what we're talking about is, yum, yum, how am I going to get some?

———

Now listen, I have tried to enjoy myself at these clubs. I've got my Asian complex of duty. In fact, I'd stayed away from the first gay Asian nights I'd heard about. It was a gut reac-tion—when I think of Asian men, I think of my weird cousins or my uncle who shakes my hand when he sees me, only as a way to grip it, and swings me around to look at the back of my head. "You need a haircut, nephew." Square black-framed accountant's glasses, his thinning hair slicked back.

So what makes me change my mind is the time I'm in this mainly white club (they're all mainly white), striding along, when I three Asian boys sitting off to my left, all kind of girly, dressed in the same flashy way. I walk straight on by, since what have I got in common with them? Am I supposed to do some hey-Asian-brother hand signal each time? That's when one turns to the others, scowls and says "Gao." Now, I hardly speak any Chinese, mostly food words like other Western-born Asian kids. But I did struggle through a few years of Chinese school where they taught us useful phrases like "The cow ascends the mountain. The moon is bright." And we also learned the animals in the Chinese horoscope (very useful), one of which is the dog. *Gao.*

So, I'm a dog, am I? Angry for a moment, but it made me think. Maybe I should get to know Asian gay guys. Not that I'd want to go out of my way, but maybe I'd been actually avoiding them more than if they were just a neutral generic Mr. Wonder Bread White.

———

So that's when I ended up at the Long Yang Party. First Sunday of the month. I get there and the guys at the front desk are, like, ultra-friendly. Have you been here before? Do you want to get on the mailing list? I get this feeling like I'm in Communist China, and we're all supposed to be this big happy family with red books tucked in our back pockets. Some Chinese people I meet, it's like they adopt you, hallelujah (except most are heathens), we can do tai chi in the park together and sing Chinese opera.

Up the stairs to check out the crowd, it's mostly Asian, the music is regular dance club beat-beat-beat, the bar-boys are white and have their shirts off. I'm scared before we even start because I've heard the rumours. Gay Asians suddenly hauling out a karaoke machine, the dancing stops, it's a KARAOKE party. Or at this club, I know it's coming. At midnight, inexplicably, they cut the dance music, and start up the Cha-Cha music. And what's worse, everyone knows the dance. Cha-cha-cha. No wonder they think Asians are geeks.

I look around for something I relate to, but it's no good. In the people, the place, the air itself. What is this idea about a big happy Asian family, like A for Asia is like a big teepee tent construct, and we're all underneath it. Granted, I've met a lot of camp Asian boys, but I look around at the crowd, and I ask: What am I supposed to share with these people? Malaysia, Indonesia, Thailand, Singapore, China, Japan, Korea, Vietnam. Hello? Different countries. I mean, Thai guys, for example. I don't get them. They giggle all the time, always happy, always trying to be nice. No wonder white guys who are into power and domination and talking about themselves all the time like to have boyfriends like them. Wallflowers.

Or OK, let's narrow it down to just the Chinese. My grandparents were villagers in a feudal countryside. Is this anything like growing up wearing Mao Blue in Red China? Or born into an overpopulated noisy cauldron like Shanghai or Taipei or Beijing, which, by the way, is still Peking to me. The language, even if I did speak it, isn't even the same, and even if it was, would a rich city boy from Hong Kong put down his mobile phone to talk to a country hick like me?

The song playing is not one I can dance to, and I know no one here. Time for a drink at the bar. None of this Campari, white wine spritzer stuff. I ask for a scotch on the rocks, try to make eye contact with the barboy when he gives me my change, but he barely glances up.

Scanning the room once more: I can recognize others who are Western-born. How we walk, how we move, the clothes, the people we're with. I can't explain it. But there's hardly any of us. What I see is dozens of twinkies, chickens, young boys from abroad, clothes and speech at too high a volume, the bulge of a mobile phone barely hidden at the waist. Demure, giggly, and oblivious.

After all, the ones who weren't born here were raised in a society where they were the majority, not the minority. They haven't been snubbed all their life; they don't expect racism so they don't see it. They're here for a good time, papa's paying for a Western education. They don't even know they're being oppressed.

And what's the big idea chasing after the old ugly white guys in the bars? That makes the oldsters feel invincible; the rest of us have to fend them off. I don't understand it at all. The theories are: Respect for elders, veneration for ancestors, no youth-oriented culture, no age bias.

But listen, at a certain age, you can't get it up. Are we going to take it as a given that adage about trading youth and beauty for age and experience? More like they're trading it for a meal ticket into the West, or a place to live, good meals, free rides. Which I can relate to, I'd like a boyfriend with a car too. But what's worse than going into a bar and seeing all these pairs of cute young teenage Asian boys with Yoda from *Star Wars*, Santa Claus, and Bob Hope? What's a self-respecting Canadian-born Chinese guy supposed to do?

A brightly-dressed short Asian guy jostles by, dragging his Italian-looking boyfriend by the hand. Cute. I catch his eye. And I hate that. Hate cruising other guy's boyfriends. Can't stand it. If he looks at me, I think, Creep! If he doesn't, I think, aren't I good-looking enough? This one looks. The next one doesn't.

I've figured it out, though. Why I do it. It's because in other clubs, I don't know if guys are looking right through me because they think I'm ugly, or because they wouldn't consider touching an Asian with a barge pole. And if someone comes up to me, I don't know if it's because of me, or because I'm Asian. Or if it's somewhere in between, what's the ratio?

So when I see a white boy with an Asian guy? The heart jumps and the other sensory organs come to life, a beast waking from hibernation. Whether I'm right or wrong in the end is irrelevant, but for now, what I smell is a gay man who must in some way be attracted to Asians. Spit forms inside my mouth, my chest and shoulders draw out bigger, and I can't stop myself, I'm helplessly without control. I cruise them, maybe even before I have a good look.

The Asian half of the pair looks over with a look of death, squints his eyes to say *He's mine*, and prances off.

I grab a handful of potato chips from a table in the corner and stuff my face. Who cares if I'm seen looking like a slob, my mouth full of food? They advertise free snacks. What have we got? Dim Sum? Prawn crackers? Canapes? No. Chips and pretzels, a bowl of peanuts, and if I'm not mistaken—no, I'm not—there's a few plates of home-made biscuits. How classy, it's like a lesbian bake-off. Asians are so cheap.

And the boorish rice queens? That night, I didn't meet any, and other nights I did. I won't go on at length. What to say about a group of people who say they were Asian in past lives, have never mastered the art of subtle cruising, and in conversations, consistently cut off their Asian boyfriends in mid-speech? And furthermore, collect art and boys in equal numbers and display them the same way: glass cases, photos, receipts, authenticity certificates, or plain old boasting. I mean, I go for certain physical types too, but it's a variety. Isn't only being attracted to Asians kind of like eating only pasta for breakfast, lunch and dinner? Or rice, more like it.

Enough of that. But I will tell you, after that first Asian night, I went back. Not every time, but on and off over the years: Red Lantern, Rainbow Room, Phoenix, Dragon, Katana. Even though I didn't enjoy myself, I couldn't keep away, each time hoping that somewhere in that room would be the person who was looking for me: a guy who happened to be Asian, and an Asian who happened to be me.

So that's really why I hate gay Asian clubs: the gold-diggers, the rice queens, the tackiness and forced togetherness. The cha-cha-cha, the chicken and dinosaur pairings, and other people's boyfriends. And I guess, really, that's why I hate gay Asians. And I guess that's why I hate myself. Buster Tennyson Chang. Nice to meet you.

CALENDAR BOY

January

It's the images. Men made into statues. Perfectly expressionless faces. Bodies like he's never seen before set in the softest edge of shadow, in the afterthought of light; amidst tropical jungles or northern forests, overexposed beaches, hidden lakes; decorated in water frozen in mid-air, in complicated patterned beads of sweat.

What fascinates him the most is the body divided into sections—like window panes or puzzle pieces or the day's boxes on a calendar month. When he focuses in on these smaller parts, he loses the bigger picture, sees new details, worlds within worlds he'd never noticed.

Like the lines dividing the body, their tension wrapping around the form. If you could somehow untie the knots that hold these lines together, would the rope simply fall away, a Houdini escape trick: the shadows of pectoral and torso and the fishing net of abdominal muscles disappearing and leaving a more formless shape? Gods become human again, arms unencumbered by large bumps and lines, a smooth flat back rather than a mountainous landscape.

Or are these lines of definition actually holding something back? If released, would the body spring out, become fat? A larger version finally free?

Gary knows that in his case, he'd be back to where he started. Shorter. Thinner. Not that he could do anything about the height. A gym buddy told him it's probably to his advantage. If he was tall, it might take forever for the form to fill out, rather than the fairly quick progress Gary's achieved: arms, chest, thighs, all expanding. But skinny, yeah, if he stopped working out, if the lines disappeared, that's what he'd return to.

So, which calendar will he choose? The black-and-white ones are more classy than the ones in colour, with their slightly lurid bright shades of flesh and swimsuits. The bodybuilder one he skips over too; Gary likes muscles but these guys are ridiculous. Another, with couples, he also rejects. Why would you want to look at two men in states of lust when you're single yourself? Salt in the wound and all that. Policemen, no. Latino men, no. A few of the models are beautiful but he doesn't want to be that limited.

He finally settles on the highbrow. Black and white, all very well defined and muscular but only a few too big for his liking. The title of this one is "Desire" and even though most of the model's body is in view in each photo, you can clearly see the facial expressions, sultry and come-hither, eyes direct into the camera, variations on a theme.

Gary pays at the counter, feeling sweaty and overheated, and hopes that his roommate won't be there when he gets back to their apartment.

February

All February, Gary works out. If he's short of time, he'll go to the university recreation centre. But mainly he goes to the YMCA in the centre of town where there are more people. He does his sets, and scans the room in between. He hopes no one notices.

It's a good month to work out hard, it's cold and damp and gray. What else is there to do? Business classes crawl along, though he's learning something at least. Setting goals, strategic planning, working toward an end result, measuring the achievements.

He uses his calendar at home to mark his progress: writes chest and arms in some boxes, legs and back in others. Abdominals are every day, they go in each box. He's bought a tape measure too, one that tailors use, although he doesn't record the results just yet. His chest seems different each day depending on how much he can inhale, and which part of the back the tape seems to rest on.

March

All month, Gary notices changes. Swelling in his body, more curve and breadth than ever before. His wardrobe changes too. He decides to stop wearing loose rugby shirts and long-sleeve business shirts. Makes space for the tight white T-shirts, which he irons to a crisp sheen. The close-fitting black Levi's 501s. He notices eyes like never before: side-long glances on the street, bolder stares in the clubs and bars.

In response, Gary walks upright, moves with a slower and more deliberate pace, and strides with legs slightly wider apart. He's even been treated like a bimbo. A himbo, he thinks, over for dinner at a friend's place. Mark's roommate couldn't stop staring at his chest, could only ask questions about his routine at the gym. Suddenly, his conversations were moving onto a different plane—guys asking him where he worked out, instead of simply where he worked. It all felt a bit easier.

Easier than the meetings he's been going to lately, the City Gay Asian group. His first meeting, Chen, the president, a doctor from Hong Kong, greeted him and asked "Do you speak Chinese?" Such a look of incredulity and pity at the answer. Also, Chen and a few others broke into a long conversation in Cantonese during the middle of the meeting. Didn't they think it was rude that the rest of them couldn't understand?

But he goes to the meetings when he can. Something inside him says that it's the right thing to do. He likes as well that the group's members are noticing his changes; no one else comes close to looking like him.

April

Gary's never approached anyone in a bar before. Men are always in tight clusters of friends; the ones who are alone usually radiate need, a dangerous energy. Tonight is different. All the compliments he's been getting lately; Gary feels desired, the glances from random strangers through shop windows, in the mirrors at the gym.

The muscular blond with cheekbones and short hair had seemed to look at him, once near the bar's entrance, once passing each other on the way to the restroom. He's not looking now from where he's leaning, but it's not an unfriendly expression on his face.

One of the guys at the meeting last month was talking about sex with body-builders. "You can never tell," he'd explained. "Two guys, both the same shape, the muscles might feel like sourdough bread, or they might feel like oak. You can't know by looking."

Bread or oak? Gary takes slow steps over. What will they talk about? At worst, polite conversation to an interested party. Or they'll talk about what they're doing, or where they're from. Or maybe they'll really like each other and just start talking. He glances at his watch and sees, with a jitter of nervousness, that it's almost closing time. Not perfect timing, but he's not going to pass this up.

Gary walks straight to the space at the bar next to him and orders a Coke. He didn't plan on doing this but he gets his drink, swings around to face away from the bar. Notices the blond glance at him, but so quickly, he can't respond. And at his face, just a general sort of double take, as if seeing if it's a barstool that he might bump into.

"Hi," says Gary and there's no response. Maybe the music is too loud. He shifts his weight onto his other foot. "Hi," a little louder, completely unprepared for the response: a slow turn of the head, a direct look into the eye, and not a change in the pose, right elbow casually against the bar, left hand flat against the front of his thigh.

"No."

"Sorry...I..." backs away too quickly, but I didn't ask a question, thinks. Sees a black space at the back of the man's throat, an illusion, since the bar is too dark to see. But still this opening, pitch black, the belly of a coal mine, the centre of a deep forest. Echoing with the round and swirling shape of nothingness. O.

No.

May

...

June

Pink is a little too obvious, yellow, a bad joke. He considers blue, but decides in the end on red. It's an Asian colour, all those red envelopes and red lanterns and tablecloths in Chinese restaurants.

Here's what it says:

Looking for hot Asian men to pose for a calendar. Masculine, athletic, straight-acting. Show us what you've got. Don't be shy.

Then: contact information, address and phone number. He's printed and cut out 200 fly-ers, a little ambitious maybe, but then again, the Pride March is the city's biggest event. The crowds have already started to form, a buzz in the air. Gary is dressed in a tiny pair of white shorts and black boots. Simple but effective, he hopes. Everyone's in a good mood, they thank him before reading the paper.

He spots another head of black hair, and then is disappointed. It's Derek, this academic type from the Gay Asian group. He doesn't trust him. Gary's arm hangs out with the flyer in mid-space, not wanting to give it to Derek, not able to hide it.

"Straight-acting, what's that supposed to mean? I bet they don't look straight when they're down on their knees."

"Don't you know what I mean?"

"No." This queeny voice. Skips off, ta-ta! No, of course he wouldn't know what it means.

July

Before the photo shoot, Gary works out extra hard, and without meaning to, skips meals, eats less. By the time he gets to Art's house and the makeshift studio set up in his living room and backyard, Gary feels lean, toned, pumped up. He's had a workout an hour before just to make sure.

Art is a friend of a friend, a photographer who usually takes photos of friends and acquaintances in grotesque poses, with fake blood and toy weapons as props. But he's tried fashion photography as a way to pay the rent, and has agreed to shoot Gary for free.

The high fence in the backyard obscures the view of neighbours—at least Gary hopes so. Though the weather is warm, he shivers slightly, his naked skin glowing white against an overgrown maple tree. "Should have gotten a bit of a tan," he thinks as Art asks him to stand, lie, kneel.

He's surprised at his comfort in front of the camera lens. It's easy to simply fol-low Art's directions, keep a neutral expression on his face, concentrate on keeping his muscles tensed. Inside, with blackout curtains over the window, Gary basks in the hot light of a theatre spotlight, Art's proud prize from a recent garage sale. With the light angled down toward him, shadows form under his chest, and in the crevices of his stom-ach. He thinks of the calendar, of himself in the calendar. No difference between him and the models in other calendars. With the boys in the gym and the bars.

———

When the photos finally come back, Gary feels explosions of excitement all over his body. He can't believe his eyes. He knows it's him in the photos, the one who did all the posing and waiting. But the lighting and shadows make his body look like nothing he recognizes. The chest is bigger, the muscles more defined, his face, too, is leaner, his chin more angular, the face that people call boyish is here more of a man's.

Photos lie. Or do they? Is this a different person or creation, is it trick photography? Or is it the best that Gary can be, the perfect man inside of him revealed on shiny paper? The men in the glossy men's exercise magazines, or fashion or porno mags: Maybe they look a bit like him in real life. Or is it the other way around, that he looks a bit like them? No matter, he's excited about this project, maybe more excited than he's been for anything.

August

By the deadline, Gary has received four photos. One completely stunning Chinese Malaysian boy: How did he get so tall? A handsome Japanese man, and a compact, muscled Thai. He also received a photo of an entirely ordinary Chinese guy. Doesn't even look like he works out. Nude, too. Agh! What was he thinking?

Four is enough to make a start, five including Gary, and if all else fails, maybe they'll have six models with two months each. Which months would Gary choose? No time to think about that, he's running through the presentation in his mind: upbeat, positive, and most of all, convincing.

———

"I've even got the title." He pauses for effect. "Fresh Blood!" Looks around at the nine guys in the room. "I know there's a market for this. Even girls that I know, white and Asian, have said they'd love a calendar of hot Asian men."

"Is that the community we're aiming at?" It's Derek, dressed in a Greenpeace T-shirt, not even tucked in. Torn blue jeans. He doesn't add any more to the question, just leaves it hanging there.

"Well, no. Yes. We want to sell all the copies we produce, and we should sell them to anyone who appreciates it." Unsure if he's said the right thing. "But of course, the primary market is gay men."

"And does it say gay anywhere on the calendar?" Him again, why doesn't someone else speak?

"No. We don't want to alienate anyone in the marketplace and limit our sales. It's evident. Who else buys these calendars? The models in the other ones are all gay too." Maybe he's reaching too hard with this one.

"Listen. I seriously think we need to consider if we would be buying into the commodification of the gay male, the reduction of ourselves to images of the body and our accompanying dehumanization in the process. Aren't we aping the misogynistic hyper-masculine values that a heterosexist dominant society celebrates?" Derek scans the room piercingly.

Gary's left in a half-smile trying to figure out if anyone else in the room understood what was said. It doesn't look like it, since there's an air of confusion, and no one speaks.

Brian, overweight with heavy-framed glasses, pipes up from the corner. "Are you sure this is a sound idea financially? I don't think that community organizations are very good at selling merchandise. Remember the T-shirt fiasco two years ago?"

Gary looks over to President Chen hoping he'll be supportive, who instead says "Let's hear from some others. Who else has something to add to the discussion?"

"I like the idea." Dear sweet Peter, a cute Vietnamese guy, with a light melodic accent. "We need more images of Asian beauty in the gay community. I'm tired of all the white men." He turns to Gary. "Can I help choose the models?"

September

He gets a phone call from Chen, thinks it's going to be about organizing next month's "Korea Night" dance. But no, Chen's the bearer of bad news, as he puts it in an overbearing paternal sort of way. A little over-caring. But also the voice of reason. Gary can picture them all "discussing" the issue and then all looking toward Chen: You're the president, you get to do the dirty work.

"It's not necessarily a bad idea," the voice intones. "And we appreciate the initiative shown and the new idea." *We*, as if it's the Communist Party or something. "It's just that we don't feel that we have the resources to fully support the project." Short pause. "And some concerns were raised about whether this is really the right message that we want to get across to the community."

October

It's rainy October, the city falling into depression. Gary is too. He's walking home from class and decides that it might help to stop in "Flaunt," the newish bookstore on Daniel Street: brightly lit, stylish, and lots of gift store items alongside books and magazines.

Gary is surprised. Only October and there's calendars for the New Year. A tiny knot suddenly at the top of his stomach, he moves closer. Long-haired Chippendales, all plastic skin and bodies; the slightly menacing but sexy Colt models, all hair and muscle and moustache; various porn star promos; shirtless firemen; a mostly clothed group of policemen, and numerous arty black and whites of identical white hairless men.

The next calendar would be a relief if it wasn't for the jealousy covering him, as if he'd set off the sprinkler system above with the heat from his anger. It's entitled "Asia." Simple name, although looking through it, it's a misnomer. One part of Asia only, the little finger deciding it's the whole hand. A benefit for an AIDS organization in Hong Kong, it doesn't say gay anywhere, as if it needed to, twelve sepia photos of Chinese models in various states of nudity, backdrops of urban jungle—concrete lines of office towers and staircases. A big calendar, professional and glossy.

He won't buy it. No. Definitely not, words filling up the space above his head as if he's suddenly been drawn into the box of a comic strip: scooped, beaten to the punch, to the finish-line. My idea. My idea. Damn those skinny politically correct geeks!

November

Classes this month focus on marketing and promotion, small business, and business plans. Gary follows them half-heartedly, still sore about the whole calendar incident. He looks at the box of photos, unused, that Art took—in the backyard against the maple tree, lying in the leaves and grass, the indoor shot with dramatic lighting bringing shadows to the muscles in his chest and stomach. Such beautiful pictures. He hates wasting things, thinks he got that from his parents, who never threw anything away. Rubber bands, stationary, nails and screws, old letters....

Greeting cards! He can get the negatives from Art, investigate the art supply store for paper stock and envelopes. By that evening, he's worked out a list with six stores to approach, the names of printers, a rough schedule, a script: "local entrepreneur...new consumer tastes...multiculturalism...tasteful...erotic."

December

From a book on Chinese traditions, Gary remembers numbers.

> *Lucky number nine.*
> *One hundred gates.*
> *One thousand poems.*
> *Four horsemen who saved China.*
> *A five-toed imperial dragon.*

> *Four auspicious events in the last month of a year.*

The first event:

"Yes?"

"Gary, it's Chen. I know you haven't been to meetings for a while but we've got a favour to ask you."

"Uh huh."

"During the last meeting Derek led a discussion on racism, media representation, and self-esteem."

"Uh huh."

"Well, the guys examined all fifty-two covers of last year's *Q Pink News* and they found that all of the cover boys were white except a black guy in March and two or three models who looked vaguely Latino, though they're probably Italian."

"And?"

"And they're protesting to the editor and have nominated you as a model for an upcoming cover. They figured you wouldn't mind...Gary?"

"Well..." Almost speechless. "You could have asked me first..."

The second: the cards are in three shops. Maybe selling well.

Third: he thinks he can get a date with someone from his marketing class, who conveniently has just joined the YMCA.

Fourth: Art stops by to pick up his negatives. He's happy because the photos of Gary in his portfolio got him hired this month for a well-paying shoot. Gary's pleased too. He and Art are becoming friends, and a friend is a good thing to have. Also, come to think of it, he can't remember the last time he had a straight male friend; his social circle is mostly girlfriends and other gay men. It will be good for him.

They're drinking beer.

Art excuses himself and grabs a package from the hallway, wrapped in angels and Christmas bells, a lopsided silver bow in one corner. "I thought you should have this." Hands it over.

It's the calendar of Asian men. Gary grins at it. What else can he do? Except thank Art sincerely, and give him a bear hug. He sees the calendar from this passing year up above his kitchen table. Takes it down. Puts this one up. Where it stays to welcome the new year.

NINA REVOYR

KENJI, 1955

Kenji Hirano was closer to Jesus than most people, so when He advised him to take up bowling as a way to occupy his hands, Kenji went down to the Family Bowl that very day. It was 1955, and Kenji had just turned thirty-six. His father Seiichi, who was suspicious of all forms of sport, had to defer to the Lord in the case of his son. It was Seiichi, after all, who had written the Bishop in Japan back in 1912 and asked if he could confess his sins—and be pardoned—through international mail. The horrified Bishop, realizing the dire situation of the tiny flock in Southern California, arranged for the formation of the Catholic church in Little Tokyo. Seiichi Hirano was, and continued to be, one of the most influential members. A cheerful, rugged man, he'd made his trip to the Land of Rice on faith alone. Denied a visa in Japan, he'd taken a ship to Mexico, fighting off heat, snakes, sandstorms, starvation and a pack of masked bandits (Catholic, so he believed they wouldn't hurt him) on his way up the bent elbow of Baja, California. Once in the City of Angels—he chose Los Angeles over San Francisco because it sounded more holy—he spent several years at the mercy of the sour-breathed labor agents who took huge cuts from his pay and lied about the nature of the back-breaking jobs they found him. Finally, he joined up with another laborer and started a gardening business. He'd never worked as a gardener before, but this didn't concern him—he was from a farming family, and knew how to grow things. Gardening was just a matter of water and balance and what you did with your tools, plus a few rocks you dragged down from the mountains. So with the help of Jesus, whom he asked to bless his shears, truck and lawnmower, he and his partner prospered.

Seiichi eventually saved the eight hundred dollars he needed in order to send for a picture bride. Noriko, the young girl who became his wife, was from one of the few Catholic families in Wakayama Prefecture. Once she got over her fear of the crowded American sidewalks and the sputtering of cars, she found a job at the orphanage on Alameda street for abandoned and homeless children—many of whom had been deposited there, it was rumored, by the women engaged in shameful work near old Chinatown. Kenji, the couple's only child, spent his early years going to church twice during the week and all day on Sunday. But by ten years after the second world war had ended, Jesus was less a distant deity the Hiranos went to church to worship, and more like a member of the family. The wisest member though. So when Jesus instructed Kenji to start in with the new craze of bowling, all the Hiranos paid attention. Especially after what happened the one time that Kenji had ignored his advice.

Kenji defied the son of God in the fall of 1942, soon after the Hiranos had been evacuated to Heart Mountain. He became convinced that he and his new wife, Yuki, should have a baby, because of the rumor that all Nisei men would soon be sterilized. His wife did not believe the rumors—the government, she knew, would never resort to such measures—but she liked the idea of having a baby. And besides, there was very little to do with all their leisure time but try. But then, one already-cold evening, as Kenji took a walk along the borders of the camp, getting as close to the fence as he dared to with the snake-like rifles sniffing his way, Jesus fell in step beside him. He was wearing a government-issue peacoat just like the internees so as not to draw the guards' attention, but his flowing beard, the bleeding scars on his hands, his limp from the wounds on his feet, were unmistakable. "It is not time, my child," He said.

Kenji didn't want to seem disrespectful, so he folded his hands together and nodded. "But the rumors," he said, not looking his Lord in the eye.

"Never mind them," said Jesus. "Wait awhile. Your child is not yet ready to enter the world."

Kenji nodded, but didn't pay the words much heed. Jesus couldn't understand such earthly matters. Besides, he and Yuki were enjoying themselves, sneaking brief, clutching moments in their barracks when his parents were out; and in the mess hall after lunch; and in the closet of the supplies office where she worked afternoons, boxes of band-aids falling down on their heads. Their marriage had been arranged by their parents, and negotiated by two baishakunin who were also members of their church. And while the two intendeds had liked each other—they were both good-looking, and educated, and very devout Catholics—they'd been shaped just enough by the country of their birth to regret not marrying for love. So when they found themselves, a year into their marriage, starting to grin and blush and shiver in each other's presence; starting to feel like it was Christmas morning every day, they knew that they were the luckiest couple alive. Yuki finally missed her period in November, and they celebrated with two rare, fresh oranges that a friend had smuggled out of the camp kitchen.

A few months later, when the recruiters came, Kenji signed up for the army. He was sent to Camp Shelby for boot camp with the other Nisei men, but allowed to come back to Wyoming for the birth of his child. When he stepped into the barracks he'd left five months before, he hardly recognized his wife. She was puffed up all over, her features bloated and exaggerated from the salt tablets the doctors had prescribed to fend off dehydration. He had never seen a woman look like this—pillow-like, almost comical—and worry buzzed around him like a fly. A few days after he arrived, Yuki went into labor. Kenji took her to the camp hospital, where they were shunted into a corner, shut off from the rest of the patients by a hanging brown blanket. A nurse came once to talk to Yuki and take her temperature; then she disappeared. But Yuki's contractions, her pain, her moaning went on for hours, and Kenji, between prayers, finally emerged from behind the blanket to ask the nurse where the doctor was. The nurse looked uncomfortable. She finally informed him that there were only two doctors capable of delivering a baby, and that one of them, a Nisei woman, had been suspended for treating—and thus endangering—the white employees of the camp. The other, the hakujin, was not in the hospital, and she didn't reveal her suspicion that he was being entertained by a certain large-busted Nisei woman who'd been given a private room. They stayed there—nurse, Kenji, Yuki—through one sunrise, one sunset, and part of another sunrise, Kenji pleading and praying, catching snippets of sleep between his wife's contractions. Finally the nurse determined that the baby could not emerge through the normal avenues, and she ran off to the Nisei woman's barracks to fetch the doctor. Kenji held his wife's hand and looked into her sweating face—the rounded cheeks, the pert but now-spreading nose. "If it's a boy," she said, "we name him Timothy, after my brother."

And although Kenji didn't like this name, he nodded and smiled, anything to bring a moment of pleasure to her eyes. "And if it's a girl?" he asked.

"Same thing."

They laughed, and squeezed hands and began to pray together, and then they heard the doctor come in. Kenji pulled the blanket aside and saw a big, red-faced man, shuffling toward their corner.

"Hello, Mack!" the man called out cheerfully when he caught sight of Kenji. "You know, I've never seen a yellow belly in a uniform before."

The nurse, who walked behind him, lowered her eyes, and Kenji decided it would be best to say nothing. As the doctor reached the side of the bed though, Kenji caught a whiff of liquor, and he looked at the man uncertainly.

The doctor touched Yuki's stomach, and then moved down between her legs, his hands huge and clumsy as two-by-fours. "Looks like this one's stuck in there pretty good." He was going to have to perform an operation, he said, but the nurse reminded him that there was no anesthesiologist in the camp. He swore, and sighed, and reached behind him, producing a long needle from a cart the nurse had brought over. "This here's a local," he informed the Hiranos as he administered the shot to Yuki's belly. They waited a few moments. Then the doctor pulled out a knife. He placed it against the dome of Yuki's stomach, and at the precise moment that the tip broke through her skin, Kenji felt a piercing pain in his own flesh. Yuki did not feel it though, even as the hakujin doctor pulled the knife downward, a bit crookedly, a path of blood springing up where the blade had cut. Kenji crossed himself and muttered. He had accidentally caught a small shark once, off the pier at San Pedro, and when he split its belly, the wound had looked something like this. Now, the doctor hooked both his thumbs in the incision and pulled Yuki's flesh apart like a loaf of bread. Kenji felt sick. Yuki couldn't face the doctor, or look at her own numbed stomach, so she stared instead at her husband's face. Kenji tried to hold his expression together. Then, the doctor put the knife down, and the nurse handed him a huge pair of forceps. He wriggled them in through the wound. He seemed to strike something, because after a few more grunts and adjustments, he braced himself against the table and started to pull. His face was even redder now, and the smell of whiskey was rising out of his pores. Kenji tried not to look too closely at the procedure, saying under his breath, "Please, Jesus, take care of them, please." He watched his wife's eyes grow wider. The doctor seemed to be yanking very hard, as if pulling a stubborn tooth. The nurse looked at him in alarm, inquired, "Doctor?" But then, with a final yank and grunt, the doctor pulled the big tooth free. Kenji saw immediately that the baby, red and slick, was very still. Its head was crushed on both sides between the forceps. Then, to his horror, he saw that the stubborn tooth had brought its roots with it; the gaping mouth in Yuki's belly was pumping blood. She screamed at the sight of it, since there wasn't any pain, although she began to feel something tugging at her chest, her legs, her arm, her heart, something pulling hard from inside. The doctor swore again and pressed towels to her stomach, one after the next, but the blood bloomed through them all and oozed and bubbled between his fingers. Kenji looked past the doctor at his wife, and her eyes were bright with comprehension. He'd been holding her hand, and now he brought his face up to hers, touching her softly with his fingers, whispering into her cheeks, her ears, her eyes, her lips, until the yawning mouth in her belly was silenced forever.

Twelve years later, Kenji didn't know what to do with his hands, which still shook from not strangling the doctor. They quivered and jumped all the way back to Camp Shelby, and then over to Italy, where the hakujin they did kill didn't satisfy his rage. They shook through the year his family lived in a government trailer in Lomita, where they were sent after the war because their neighbors in Boyle Heights, upon receiving word that they were returning, promptly burned down their house. And they shook for eight years after Kenji's parents bought the new place in Angeles Mesa. The only way he could keep them still was to give them occupation, which was why he had so enjoyed holding guns, and then his father's gardening tools. Jobs that didn't require his hands weren't appealing to him, and not useful anyway, since it took hard labor and constant pep talks with himself to keep from going after each burly hakujin he saw with flushed cheeks and cheap whiskey on his breath. Sometimes his gruff pep talks alarmed the people he passed on the street or the families he gardened for, but they didn't mind because he did do such a beautiful job on the lawn, honey, don't you think? Even if he is a bit odd. And he was even starting to learn what to do with his hands when they weren't holding a pair of shears or pushing a mower. He took up smoking, buying a pack every other day from Frank Sakai's store, even though, three years later, his father would die of lung cancer. And then one afternoon outside of Frank's store, Jesus came up to him again, dressed in his normal white robes this time. He looked at Kenji and pointed over towards Crenshaw Boulevard. "You must bowl, my son," He said. "Fill your hands with the nourishing weight of sport." Then He disappeared into the store, where Kenji was sure he was going to buy some fruit. Kenji followed, but when he got inside, there was no one there but Frank.

"Did you see Him?" he asked. "The Son of God. He was here."

Frank didn't lift an eyebrow. "No, I must have missed Him."

Kenji stared, eyes wide. He looked hard at the fruit bins, and then turned back to his friend. "Never mind," he said. "Tell me, Frank, could you teach me how to bowl?"

SHYAM SELVADURAI

PIGS CAN'T FLY
AN EXCERPT FROM *FUNNY BOY*, A NOVEL

Besides Christmas and other festive occasions, spend-the-days were the days most looked forward to by all of us, cousins, aunts and uncles.

For the adults, a spend-the-day was the one Sunday of the month they were free of their progeny. The eagerness with which they anticipated these days could be seen in the way Amma woke my brother, my sister and me extra early when they came. Unlike the school days, when Amma allowed us to dawdle a little, we were hurried through our morning preparations. Then, after a quick breakfast, we would be driven to the house of our grandparents.

The first thing that met our eyes on entering our grandparents' house, after we carefully wiped our feet on the doormat, would be the dark corridor running the length of it, on one side of which were the bedrooms and on the other the drawing and dining rooms. This corridor, with its old photographs on both walls and its ceiling so high that our footsteps echoed, scared me a little. The drawing room, into which we would be ushered to pay our respects to our grandparents, was also dark and smelt like old clothes that had been locked away in a suitcase for a long time. There my grandparents Ammachi and Appachi sat, enthroned in big reclining chairs. Appachi usually looked up from his paper and said vaguely, "Ah, hello, hello," before going back behind it, but Ammachi always called us to her with the beckoning movement of her middle and index fingers. With our legs trembling slightly, we would go to her, the thought of the big canes she kept behind her tall clothes almariah strongly imprinted upon our minds. She would grip our faces in her plump hands, and one by one kiss us wetly on both cheeks and say, "God has blessed me with fifteen grandchildren who will look after me in my old age." She smelt of stale coconut oil, and the diamond mukkuthi in her nose always pressed painfully against my cheek.

When the aunts and uncles eventually drove away, waving gaily at us children from car windows, we waved back at the retreating cars with not even a pretense of sorrow. For one glorious day a month, we were free of parental control and the ever-watchful eyes and tale-bearing tongues of the house servants.

We were not, alas, completely abandoned, as we would have so liked to have been. Ammachi and Janaki were supposedly in charge. Janaki, cursed with the task of having to cook for fifteen extra people, had little time for supervision and actually preferred to have nothing to do with us at all. If called upon to come and settle a dispute, she would rush out, her hands red from grinding curry paste, and box the ears of the first person who happened to be in her path. We had learned that Janaki was to be appealed to only in the most dire emergencies. The one we understood, by tacit agreement, never to appeal to was Ammachi. Like the earth-goddess in the folktales, she was not to be disturbed from her tranquillity. To do so would have been the cause of catastrophic earthquake.

In order to minimize interference by either Ammachi or Janaki, we had developed and refined a system of handling conflict and settling disputes ourselves. Two things formed the framework of this system: territoriality and leadership.

Territorially, the area around my grandparents' house was divided into two. The front garden, the road, and the field that lay in front of the house belonged to the boys, although included in their group was my female cousin Meena. In this territory, two factions struggled for power, one led by Meena, the other by my brother, Varuna, who because of a prevailing habit, had been renamed Diggy-Nose and then simply Diggy.

The second territory was called "the girls'," included in which, however, was myself, a boy. It was to this territory of "the girls'," confined to the back garden and the kitchen porch, that I seemed to have gravitated naturally, my earliest memories of those spend-the-days always belonging in the back garden of my grandparents' home. The pleasure the boys had standing for hours on a cricket field under the sweltering sun, watching the batsmen run from crease to crease, was incomprehensible to me.

For me, the primary attraction of the girls' territory was the potential for the free play of fantasy. Because of the force of my imagination, I was selected as leader. Whatever the game, be it the imitation of adult domestic functions or the enactment of some well-loved fairy story, it was I who discovered some new way to enliven it, some new twist to the plot of a familiar tale. Led by me, the girl cousins would conduct a raid on my grandparents' dirty-clothes basket, discovering in this odorous treasure trove saris, blouses, sheets, curtains with which we invented costumes to complement our voyages of imagination.

The reward for my leadership was that I always got to play the main part in the fantasy. If it was cooking-cooking we were playing, I was the chef; if it was Cinderella or Thumbelina, I was the much-beleaguered heroine of these tales.

Of all our varied and fascinating games, bride-bride was my favorite. In it I was able to combine many elements of the other games I loved, and with time bride-bride, which had taken a few hours to play initially, became an event that spread out over the whole day and was planned for weeks in advance. For me the culmination of this game, and my ultimate moment of joy, was when I put on the clothes of the bride. In the late afternoon, usually after tea, I, along with the older girl cousins, would enter Janaki's room. From my sling-bag I would bring out my most prized possession, an old white sari, slightly yellow with age, its border torn and missing most of its sequins. The dressing of the bride would now begin, and then, by the transfiguration I saw taking place in Janaki's cracked full-length mirror—by the sari being wrapped around my body, the veil being pinned to my head, the rouge put on my cheeks, lipstick on my lips, kohl around my eyes—I was able to leave the constraints of my self and ascend into another, more brilliant, more beautiful self, a self to whom this day was dedicated, and around whom the world, represented by my cousins putting flowers in my hair, draping the palu, seemed to revolve. It was a self magnified, like the goddesses of the Sinhalese and Tamil cinema, larger than life; and like them, like the Malini Fonsekas and the Gettha Kumarasinghes, I was an icon, a graceful, benevolent, perfect being upon whom the adoring eyes of the world rested.

———

Those spend-the-days, the remembered innocence of childhood, are now colored in the hues of the twilight sky. It is a picture made even more sentimental by the loss of all that was associated with them. By all of us having to leave Sri Lanka years later because of communal violence and forge a new home for ourselves in Canada.

Yet those Sundays, when I was seven, marked the beginning of my exile from the world I loved. Like a ship that leaves a port for the vast expanse of sea, those much-looked-forward-to days took me away from the safe harbor of childhood toward the precarious waters of adult life.

———

The visits at my grandparents' began to change with the return from abroad of Kanthi Aunty, Cyril Uncle, and their daughter, Tanuja, whom we quickly renamed "Her Fatness," in that cruelly direct way children have.

At first we had no difficulty with the newcomer in our midst. In fact, we found her quite willing to accept that, by reason of her recent arrival, she must necessarily begin at the bottom.

In the hierarchy of bride-bride, the person with the least importance, less even than the priest and the pageboys, was the groom. It was a role we considered stiff and boring, that held no attraction for any of us. Indeed, if we could have dispensed with that role altogether we would have, but alas it was an unfortunate feature of the marriage ceremony. My younger sister, Sonali, with her patient good nature, but also sensing that I might have a mutiny on my hands if I asked anyone else to play that role, always donned the long pants and tattered jacket, borrowed from my grandfather's clothes chest. It was now deemed fitting that Her Fatness should take over the role and thus leave Sonali free to wrap a bedsheet around her body, in the manner of a sari, and wear aralia flowers in her hair like the other bridesmaids.

For two spend-the-days, Her Fatness accepted her role without a murmur and played it with all the skilled unobtrusiveness of a bit player. The third spend-the-day, however, everything changed. That day turned out to be my grandmother's birthday. Instead of dropping the children off and driving away as usual, the aunts and uncles stayed on for lunch, a slight note of peevish displeasure in their voices.

We had been late, because etiquette (or rather my father) demanded that Amma wear a sari for the grand occasion of her mother-in-law's sixtieth birthday. Amma's tardiness and her insistence on getting her palu to fall to exactly above her knees drove us all to distraction (especially Diggy, who quite rightly feared that in his absence Meena would try to persuade the better members of his team to defect to her side). Even I, who usually loved the ritual of watching Amma get dressed, stood in the doorway with the others and fretfully asked if she was ever going to be ready.

When we finally did arrive at Ramanaygam Road, everyone else had been there almost an hour. We were ushered into the drawing room by Amma to kiss Ammachi and present her with her gift, the three of us clutching the present. All the uncles and aunts were seated. Her Fatness stood in between Kanthi Aunty's knees, next to Ammachi. When she saw us, she gave me an accusing, hostile look and pressed farther between her mother's legs. Kanthi Aunty turned away from her discussion with Mala Aunty, and, seeing me, she smiled and said in a tone that was as heavily sweetened as undiluted rose syrup, "So, what is this I hear, aah? Nobody will play with my little daughter."

I looked at her and then at Her Fatness, shocked by the lie. All my senses were alert.

Kanthi Aunty wagged her finger at me and said in a playful, chiding tone, "Now, now, Arjie, you must be nice to my little daughter. After all, she's just come from abroad and everything." Fortunately, I was prevented from having to answer. It was my turn to present my cheek to Ammachi, and, for the first time, I did so willingly, preferring the prick of the diamond mukkuthi to Kanthi Aunty's honeyed admonition.

Kanthi Aunty was the fourth oldest in my father's family. First was my father, then Ravi Uncle, Mala Aunty, Kanthi Aunty, Babu Uncle, Seelan Uncle and, finally, Radha Aunty, who was much younger than the others and was away, studying in America. Kanthi Aunty was tall and bony, and we liked her the least, in spite of the fact that she would pat our heads affectionately whenever we walked past or greeted her. We sensed that beneath her benevolence lurked a seething anger, tempered by guile, that could have deadly consequences if unleashed in our direction. I heard Amma say to her sister Neliya Aunty that Poor Kanthi was bitter because of the humiliations she had suffered abroad.

"After all, darling, what a thing, forced to work as a servant in a whitey's house to make ends meet."

Once Ammachi had opened the present, a large silver serving tray, and thanked us for it (and insisted on kissing us once again), my brother, my sister, and I were finally allowed to leave the room. Her Fatness had already disappeared. I hurried out the front door and ran around the side of the house.

When I reached the back garden I found the girl cousins squatting on the porch in a circle. They were so absorbed in what was happening in the center that none of them even heard my greeting. Lakshmi finally became aware of my presence and beckoned me over excitedly. I reached the circle, and the cause of her excitement became clear. In the middle, in front of Her Fatness, sat a long-legged doll with shiny gold hair. Her dress was like that of a fairy queen, and the gauze skirt sprinkled with tiny silver stars. Next to her sat her male counterpart, dressed in a pale-blue suit. I stared in wonder at the marvelous dolls. For us cousins, who had grown up under a government that strictly limited all foreign imports, such toys were unimaginable. Her Fatness turned to the other cousins and asked them if they wanted to hold the dolls for a moment. They nodded eagerly, and the dolls passed from hand to hand. I moved closer to get a better look. My gaze involuntarily rested on Her Fatness, and she gave me a smug look. Immediately her scheme became evident to me. It was with these fools that my cousin from abroad hoped to seduce the other cousins away from me.

Unfortunately for her, she had underestimated the power of the bride-bride. When the other cousins had all looked at the dolls, they bestirred themselves and, without so much as a backward glance, hurried down the steps to prepare for the marriage ceremony. As I followed them, I looked triumphantly at Her Fatness, who sat on the porch, clasping her beautiful dolls to her chest.

———

When lunch was over, my grandparents retired to their room for a nap. The other adults settled in the drawing room to read the newspaper or doze off in the huge armchairs. We, the bride-to-be and the bridesmaids, retired to Janaki's room for the long-awaited ritual of dressing the bride.

We were soon disturbed, however, by the sound of booming laughter. At first we ignored it, but when in persisted, getting louder and more drawn out, my sister Sonali, went to the door and looked out. Her slight gasp brought us all out onto the porch. There the groom strutted, up and down, head thrown back, stomach stuck out. She sported a huge bristly mustache (torn out of the broom) and a cigarette (of rolled paper and talcum powder), which she held between her fingers and puffed on vigorously. The younger cousins, instead of getting dressed and putting the final touches to the altar, sat along the edge of the porch and watched with great amusement.

"Aha, me hearties!" the groom cried on seeing us. She opened her hands expansively. "Bring me my fair maiden, for I must be off to my castle before the sun settest."

We looked at the groom, aghast at the change in her behavior. She sauntered toward us, then stopped in front of me, winked expansively, and, with her hand under my chin, tilted back my head.

"Ahhh!" she exclaimed. "A bonny lass, a bonny lass indeed."

"Stop it!" I cried, and slapped her hand. "The groom is not supposed to make a noise."

"Why not?" Her Fatness replied angrily, dropping her hearty voice and accent. "Why can't the groom make a noise?"

"Because."

"Because of what?"

"Because the game is called bride-bride, not groom-groom."

Her Fatness seized her mustache and flung it to the ground dramatically. "Well, I don't want to be the groom anymore. I want to be the bride."

We stared at her in disbelief, amazed by her impudent challenge to my position.

"You can't," I finally said.

"Why not?" Her Fatness demanded. "Why should you always be the bride? Why can't someone else have a chance too?"

"Because," Sonali said, joining in. "Because Arjie is the bestest bride of all."

"But he's not even a girl," Her Fatness said, closing in on the lameness of Sonali's argument. "A bride is a girl, not a boy." She looked around at the other cousins and then at me.

"A boy cannot be the bride," she said with deep conviction. "A girl must be the bride."

I stared at her, defenseless in the face of her logic.

Fortunately, Sonali, loyal to me as always, came to my rescue. She stepped in between us and said Her Fatness, "If you can't play properly, go away. We don't need you."

"Yes!" Lakshmi, another of my supporters, cried.

The other cousins, emboldened by Sonali's fearlessness, murmured in agreement.

Her Fatness looked at all of us for a moment and then her gaze rested on me.

"You're a pansy," she said, her lips curling in disgust.

We looked at her blankly.

"A faggot," she said, her voice rising against our uncomprehending stares.

"A sissy!" she shouted in desperation.

It was clear by this time that these were insults.

"Give me that jacket," Sonali said. She stepped up to Her Fatness and began to pull at it. "We don't like you anymore."

"Yes!" Lakshmi cried. "Go away, you fatty-boom-boom!"

This was an insult we all understood, and we burst out laughing. Someone even began to chant, "Hey, fatty-boom-boom. Hey, fatty-boom-boom."

Her Fatness pulled off her coat and trousers. "I hate you all," she cried. "I wish you were all dead." She flung the groom's clothes on the ground, stalked out of the back garden, and went around the side of the house.

We returned to our bridal preparations, chuckling to ourselves over the new nickname we had found for our cousin.

When the bride was finally dressed, Lakshmi, the maid of honor, when out of Janaki's room to make sure that everything was in place. Then she gave the signal and the priest and choirboys began to sing, with a certain want of harmony and correct lyrics, the "Voice that breathed on Eeeden, the first and glorious day." Solemnly, I made my way down the steps toward the altar that had been set up at one end of the back garden. When I reached the altar, however, I heard the kitchen door open. I turned to see Her Fatness with Kanthi Aunty. The discordant singing died out.

Kanthi Aunty's benevolent smile had completely disappeared and her eyes were narrowed with anger.

"Who's calling my daughter fatty?" Kanthi Aunty said.

She came to the edge of the porch.

We all stared at her, no one daring to own up.

Her gaze fell on me and her eyes widened for a moment.

Then a smile spread across her face.

"What's this?" she said, the honey seeping back into her voice. She came down a few steps and crooked her finger at me. I looked down at my feet and refused to go to her.

"Come here, come here," she said.

Unable to disobey her command any longer, I went to her. She looked me up and down for a moment, and then gingerly, as if she were examining raw meat at the market, turned me around.

"What's this you're playing?" she asked.

"It's bride-bride, Aunty," Sonali said.

"Bride-bride," she murmured.

Her hand closed on my arm in a tight grip.

"Come with me," she said.

I resisted, but her grip tightened, her nails digging into my elbow. She pulled me up the porch steps and toward the kitchen door.

"No," I cried. "No, I don't want to."

Something about the look in her eyes terrified me so much, I did the unthinkable and I hit out at her. This made her hold my arm even more firmly. She dragged me through the kitchen, past Janaki, who looked up, curious, and into the corridor and toward the drawing room. I felt a heaviness begin to build in my stomach. Instinctively I knew that Kanthi Aunty had something terrible in mind.

As we entered the drawing room, Kanthi Aunty cried out, her voice brimming over with laughter, "See what I found!"

The other aunts and uncles looked up from their papers or bestirred themselves from their sleep. They gazed at me in amazement as if I had suddenly made myself visible, like a spirit. I glanced at them and then at Amma's face. Seeing her expression, I felt my dread deepen. I lowered my eyes. The sari suddenly felt suffocating around my body, and the hairpins that held the veil in place pricked at my scalp.

Then the silence was broken by the booming laugh of Cyril Uncle, Kanthi Aunty's husband. As if she had been it, Amma swung around in his direction. The other aunts and uncles began too to laugh too, I watched as Amma looked from one to the other liked a trapped animal. Her gaze finally came to rest on my father, and for the first time I noticed that he was the only one not laughing. Seeing the way he kept his eyes fixed on his paper, I felt the heaviness in my stomach begin to push its way up my throat. "Ey, Chelva," Cyril Uncle cried out jovially to my father, "looks like you have a funny one here."

My father pretended he had not heard and, with an inclination of his head, indicated to Amma to get rid of me.

She waved her hand in my direction and I picked up the edges of my veil and fled to the back of the house.

That evening, on the way home, both my parents kept their eyes averted from me. Amma glanced at my father occasionally, but he refused to meet her gaze. Sonali, sensing my unease, held my hand tightly in hers.

Later, I heard my parents fighting in their room.

"How long has this been going on?" my father demanded.

"I don't know," Amma cried defensively. "It was as new to me as it was to you."

"You should have known. You should have kept an eye on him."

"What should I have done? Stood over him while he was playing?"

"If he turns out funny like that Rankotwera boy, if he turns out to be the laugh-

ingstock of Colombo, it'll be your fault," my father said in a tone of finality. "You always
spoil him and encourage all his nonsense."

"What do I encourage?" Amma demanded.

"You are the one who allows him to come in here while you're dressing and
play with your jewelry."

Amma was silent in the face of the truth.

Of the three of us, I alone was allowed to enter Amma's bedroom and watch her
get dressed for special occasions. It was an experience I considered almost religious, for
even though I adored the goddess of the local cinema, Amma was the final statement in
female beauty for me.

When I knew Amma was getting dressed for a special occasion, I always positioned myself outside her door. Once she had put on her undershirt and blouse, she
would ring for our servant, Anula, to bring her sari, and then, while taking it from her,
hold the door open so I could go in as well. Entering that room was, for me, a greater
boon than that granted by any god to a mortal. There were two reasons for this. The first
was the jewelry box which lay open on the dressing table. With a joy akin to ecstasy, I
would lean over and gaze inside, the faint smell of perfume rising out of the box each
time I picked up a piece of jewelry and held it against my nose or ears or throat. The second was the pleasure of watching Amma drape her sari, watching her shake open the
yards of material, which, like a Chinese banner caught by the wind, would linger in the
air for a moment before drifting gently to the floor; watching her pick up one end of it,
tuck it into the waistband of her skirt, make the pleats, and then with a flick of her wrists
invert the pleats and tuck them into her waistband; and finally watching her drape the
palu across her breasts and pin it into place with a brooch.

When Amma was finished, she would check to make sure hat the back of the
sari had not risen up with the pinning of the palu, then move back and look at herself in
the mirror. Standing next to her or seated on the edge of the bed, I, too, would look at
her reflection in the mirror, and, with the contented sigh of an artist who has finally captured the exact effect he want, I would say, "You should have been a film star, Amma."

"A film star?" she would cry and lightly smack the side of my head. "What kind
of low-class-type person do you think I am?"

One day, about a week after the incident at my grandparents', I positioned
myself outside my parents' bedroom door. When Anula arrived with the sari, Amma took
it and quickly shut the door. I waited patiently, thinking Amma had not yet put on her
blouse and skirt, but the door never opened. Finally, perplexed that Amma had forgotten,
I knocked timidly on the door. She did not answer, but I could hear her moving around
inside. I knocked timidly on the door. She did not answer, but I could hear her moving
around inside. I knocked a little bit louder and called out "Amma" through the keyhole.

Still no response, and I was about to call her name again when she replied gruffly, "Go away. Can't you see I am busy?"

I stared disbelievingly at the door. Inside I could hear the rustling of the sari as it brushed along the floor. I lifted my hand to knock again when suddenly I remember the quarrel I had heard on the night of that last spend-the-day. My hand fell limply to my side.

I crept away quietly to my bedroom, sat down on the edge of my bed, and stared at my feet for a long time. It was clear to me that I had done something wrong, but what it was I could not comprehend. I thought of what my father had said about turning out "funny." The word "funny" as I understood it meant either humorous or strange, as in the expression "That's funny." Neither of these fitted the sense in which my father had used the word, for there had been a hint of disgust in his tone.

Later, Amma came out of her room and called Anula to give her instructions for the evening. As I listened to the sound of her voice, I realized that something had changed forever between us.

A little while after my parents had left for their dinner party, Sonali came looking for me. Seeing my downcast expression, she sat next to me, and, though unaware of anything that had passed, slipped her hand in mine. I pushed it away roughly, afraid that if I let her squeeze my hand I would start to cry.

The next morning Amma and I were like two people who had had a terrible fight the night before. I found it hard to look her in the eye and she seemed in an unusually gay mood.

The following spend-the-day, when Amma came to awaken us, I was already seated in bed and folding my bride-bride sari. Something in her expression, however, made me hurriedly return the sari to the bag.

"What's that?" she said, coming toward me, her hand outstretched. After a moment I gave her the bag. She glanced at its contents briefly. "Get up, it's spend-the-day," she said. Then, with the bag in her hand, she went to the window and looked out into the driveway. The seriousness of her expression, as if I had done something so awful that even the usual punishment of a caning would not suffice, frightened me.

I was brushing my teeth after breakfast when Anula came to the bathroom door, peered inside, and said with a sort of grim pressure, "Missie wants to talk to you in her room." Seeing the alarm in my face, she nodded and said sagely, "Up to some kind of mischief as usual. Good-for-nothing child."

My brother, Diggy, was standing in the doorway of our parents' room, one foot scratching impatiently against the other. Amma was putting on her lipstick. My father had already gone for his Sunday squash game, and, as usual, she would pick him up after she dropped us off at our grandparents'.

Amma looked up from the mirror, saw me, and indicated with her tube of lipstick for both of us to come inside and sit down on the edge of the bed. Diggy gave me a baleful look, as if it were my fault that Amma was taking such a long time to get ready. He followed me into the room, his slippers dragging along the floor.

Finally Amma closed her lipstick, pressed her lips together to even out the color, then turned to us.

"OK, mister," she said to Diggy, "I am going to tell you something, and this is an order."

We watched her carefully.

"I want you to include your younger brother on your cricket team."

Diggy and I looked at her in shocked silence, then he cried, "Ah! Come on, Amma!"

And I too, cried out, "I don't want to play with them. I hate cricket!"

"I don't care what you want," Amma said. "It's good for you."

"Arjie's useless," Diggy said. "We'll never win if he's on our team."

Amma held up her hand to silence us. "That's an order," she said.

"Why?" I asked, ignoring her gesture. "Why do I have to play with the boys?"

"Why?" Amma said. "Because the sky is so high and pigs can't fly, that's why."

"Please, Amma! Please!" I held out my arms to her.

Amma turned away quickly, picked up her handbag from the dressing table, and said, almost to herself, "If the child turns out wrong, it's the mother they always blame, never the father." She clicked the handbag shut.

I put my head in my hands and began to cry. "Please, Amma, please," I said through my sobs.

She continued to face the window.

I flung myself on the bed with a wail of anguish. I waited for her to come to me as she always did when I cried, waited for her to take me in her arms, rest my head against her breasts, and say in her special voice, "What's this, now? Who's the little man who's crying?"

But she didn't heed my weeping any more than she had heeded my cries when I knocked on her door.

Finally I stopped crying and rolled over on my back. Diggy had left the room. Amma turned to me, now that I had become quiet, and said cheerfully, "You'll have a good time, just wait and see."

"Why can't I play with the girls?" I replied.

"You can't, that's all."

"But why?"

She shifted uneasily.

"You're a big boy now. And big boys must play with other boys."

"That's stupid."

"It doesn't matter," she said. "Life is full of stupid things and sometimes we just have to do them."

"I won't," I said defiantly. "I won't play with the boys."

Her face reddened with anger. She reached down, caught me by the shoulders, and shook me hard. Then she turned away and ran her hand through her hair. I watched her, gloating. I had broken her cheerful facade, forced her to show how much it pained her to do what she was doing, how little she actually believed in the justness of her actions.

After a moment she turned back to me and said in an almost pleading tone, "You'll have a good time."

I looked at her and said, "No, I won't."

Her back straightened. She crossed to the door and stopped. Without looking at me she said stiffly, "The car leaves in five minutes. If you're not in it by then, watch out." I lay back on the bed and gazed at the mosquito net swinging gently in the breeze. In my mind's eye, I saw the day that stretched ahead of me. At the thought of having to waste the most precious day of the month in that field in front of my grandparents' house, the hot sun beating on my head, the perspiration running down the sides of my face, I felt a sense of despair begin to take hold of me. The picture of what would take place in the back garden became clear. I saw Her Fatness seizing my place as leader of the girls, claiming for herself the rituals I had so carefully invented and planned. I saw her standing in front of Janaki's mirror as the other girls fixed her hair, pinned her veil and draped her sari. The thought was terrible. Something had to be done. I could not give up that easily, could not let Her Fatness, who sneaking to Kanthi Aunty had forced me into the position I was now in, so easily take my place. But what could I do?

As if in answer, an object that rested just at the periphery of my vision claimed my attention. I turned my head slightly and saw my sling-bag. Then a thought came to me. I reached out, picked up the bag and hugged it close to my chest. Without the sari in that bag, it was impossible for the girls to play bride-bride. I thought of Her Fatness with a triumph. What would she drape around her body? A bedsheet like the bridesmaids? No! Without me and my sari she would not be able to play bride-bride properly.

There was, I realized, an obstacle that had to be overcome first. I would have to get out of playing cricket. Amma had laid down an order, and I knew Diggy well enough to know that, in spite of his boldness, he would never dare to disobey an order from Amma.

I heard the car start up, and its sound reminded me of another problem that I had not considered. How was I going to smuggle the sari into the car? Amma would be waiting in the car for me, and if I arrived with the sling-bag she would make me take it back. I could not slip it in without her noticing. I sat still, listening to the whir of the engine at counterpoint to the clatter of Anula clearing the breakfast table, and suddenly a plan revealed itself to me.

I took the sari out of the bag, folded the bag so that it looked like there was something in it, and left it on the bed. Taking the sari with me, I went to the bedroom door and peered out. The hall was empty. I went into Sonali's room, which was next to my parents', and I crouched down on one side of the doorway. I took off my slippers and held them with the sari in my arms. The curtain in the open doorway of Sonali's room blew slightly in the breeze, and I moved farther away from it so that I would not be seen. After what seemed like an interminable amount of time, I heard Amma coming down the hallway to fetch me from her room. I crouched even lower as the sound of her footsteps got closer. From below the curtain, I saw her go into her room. As she entered, I stood up, pushed aside the curtain and darted down the hallway. She came out of her room and called to me, but I didn't stop, and ran outside.

Thankfully the rear door of the car was open. I jumped in, quickly stuffed the sari into Sonali's sling-bag, and lay back against the seat, panting. Diggy and Sonali were looking at me strangely but they said nothing.

Soon Amma came out and got into the car. She glared at me, and I gave her an innocent look. I smiled at Sonali conspiratorially. Sonali, my strongest ally, was doing her best to keep the bewilderment out of her face. By way of explanation, I said, with pretend gloominess, "I can't play with you today. Amma says I must play with the boys."

Sonali looked at me in amazement and then turned to Amma. "Why can't he play with the girls?" she said.

"Why?" Amma said and started up the car. "Because the sky is so high and pigs can't fly."

Amma sounded less sure of herself this time and a little weary. Looking in front, I saw that Diggy had turned in his seat and was regarding me morosely. I was reminded that the sari in the bag was worth nothing if I couldn't get out of the long day of cricket that lay ahead of me.

All the way to my grandparents' house, I gazed at the back of Diggy's head, hoping inspirations would come. The sound of his feet kicking irritably against the underside of the glove compartment confirmed that, however had the consequences, he would follow Amma's orders. The sound of that ill-natured kicking made me search my mind all the more desperately for a way to escape playing cricket with the boys. When the car turned down Ramanaygam Road, I still had not thought of anything. Meena was standing on top of the garden wall, her legs apart, her hands on her hips, her panties already dirty underneath her short dress. The boy cousins were on the wall on either side of her.

As we walked up the path to pay our respects to Ammachi and Appachi, I whispered to Sonali to keep the sari hidden and tell no one about it. When we went into the drawing room, Her Fatness, who was as usual between Kanthi Aunty's knees, gave me a victorious look. A feeling of panic began to rise in me that no plan of escape had yet presented itself.

Once we had gone through the ritual of presenting our cheeks to our grandparents, we followed Amma outside to say goodbye.

"You children be good," Amma said before she got into the car. She looked pointedly at me. "I don't want to hear that you've given Ammachi and Appachi any trouble."

I watched her departing car with a sense of sorrow.

Diggy grabbed my arm. I followed reluctantly as he hurried across the road, still holding on to me, as if afraid I would run away.

The wickets had already been set up in the field in front of the house, and the boys and Meena were seated under a guava tree. When they saw us come toward them, they stopped talking and stared at us.

Muruges, who was on Diggy's team, stood up.

"What's he doing here?" he demanded, waving his half-eaten guava at me.

"He's going to play."

"What?" the others cried in amazement.

They looked at Diggy as if he had lost his mind.

"He's not going to play on our team, is he?" Muruges said, more of a threat than a question.

"He's quite good," Diggy answered halfheartedly.

"If he's going to be on our team, I'm changing sides," Muruges declared, and some of the others murmured in agreement.

"Come on, guys," Diggy said with desperation in his voice, but they remained stern.

Diggy turned to Meena. "I'll trade you Arjie for Sanjay."

Meena spat out the seeds of the guava she was eating. "Do you think that I'm mad or something?"

"Ah, come on," Diggy said in a wheedling tone. "He's good. We've been practicing the whole week."

"If he's so good, why don't you keep him yourself? Maybe with him on your team you might actually win."

"Yeah," Sanjay cried, insulted that I was considered an equal trade for him. "Why don't you keep the girlie-boy?"

At the new nickname "girlie-boy," everyone roared with laughter, and even Diggy grinned.

I should have felt humiliated and dejected that nobody wanted me on their team, but instead I felt the joy of relief begin to dance inside of me. The escape I had searched for was offering itself without any effort on my part. If Diggy's best team members were threatening to abandon him he would have no alternative but to let me go. I looked at my feet so that no one would see the hope in my eyes.

Unfortunately, the nickname "girlie-boy" had an effect which I had not predicted. The joke at my expense seems to clear the air. After laughing heartily, Muruges withdrew his threat. "What the hell," he said benevolently. "It can't hurt to have another fielder. But," he added, as a warning to Diggy, "he can't bat."

Diggy nodded as if he had never even considered letting me bat. Since each side had only fifty overs, it was vital to send the best batsmen in first, and often the younger cousins never got a chance.

I glared at Muruges, and he, thinking my look was a reaction to my new nickname, said "girlie-boy" again.

Diggy now laughed loudly, but in his laugh I detected a slight note of severity and also relief that the catastrophe of losing his team had been averted. I saw that the balance he was trying to maintain between following Amma's orders and keeping his team members happy was extremely precarious. All was not lost. Such a fragile balance would be easy to upset.

The opportunity to do this arose almost immediately.

Our team was to go first. In deciding the batting order, there was a certain system that the boys always followed. The captain would mark numbers in the sand with hyphens next to each and then cover the numbers with a bat. The players, who had been asked to turn their backs, would then come over and choose a hyphen. What was strange to me about this exercise was its redundancy, for when the numbers were uncovered, no matter what the batting order, the older and better players always went first, the younger cousins assenting without a murmur.

When Diggy uncovered the numbers, I was first, Diggy was second. Muruges had one of the highest numbers and would bat toward the end, if at all. "Well," Muruges said to Diggy in a tone that spoke of promises already made, "I'll take Arjie's place."

Diggy nodded vigorously as if Muruges had read his very thoughts.

Unfortunately for him, I had other plans.

"I want to go first," I said firmly, and waited for my request to produce the necessary consequences.

Muruges was crouched down, fixing his pads, and he straightened up slowly. The slowness of his action conveyed his anger at my daring to make such a suggestion and at the same time challenged Diggy to change the batting order.

Meena, unexpectedly, came to my defense. "He is the first!" she said. "Fair is fair!" In a game of only fifty overs, a bad opening bat would be ideal for her team.

"Fair is fair," I echoed Meena. "I picked first place and I should be allowed to play!"

"You can't," Diggy said desperately. "Muruges always goes first."

Meena's team, encouraged by her, also began to cry out, "Fair is fair!"

Diggy quickly crossed over to Muruges, put his arms around his shoulder, turned him away from the others, and talked earnestly to him. But Muruges shook his head, unconvinced by whatever Diggy was saying. Finally Diggy dropped his hand from Muruges's shoulder and cried out in exasperation at him, "Come on, men!" In response, Muruges began to unbuckle his pads. Diggy put his hand on his shoulder, but he shrugged it off. Diggy, seeing that Muruges was determined, turned to me.

"Come on, Arjie," he said, pleading. "You can go later in the game."

"No," I said stubbornly, and, just to show how determined I was, I picked up the bat.

Muruges saw my action and threw the pads at my feet.

"I'm on your team now," he announced to Meena.

"Ah, no! Come on, men!" Diggy shouted in protest.

Muruges began to cross over to where Meena's team was gathered.

Diggy turned toward me now and grabbed the bat.

"You go!" he cried. "We don't need you." He pulled the bat out of my hands and started to walk with it toward Muruges.

"You're a cheater, cheater pumpkin-eater! I chose to bat first!" I yelled.

But I had gone too far. Diggy turned and looked at me. Then he howled as he realized how he had been tricked. Instead of giving Muruges the bat, he lifted it above his head and ran toward me. I turned and fled across the field towards my grandparents' gate. When I reached it, I lifted the latch, went inside the garden, and quickly put the latch back into place. Diggy stopped when he reached the gate. Safe on my side, I made a face at him through the slats. He came close and I retreated a little. Putting his head through the slats, he hissed at me, "If you ever come near the field again, you'll be sorry."

"Don't worry," I replied tartly. "I never will."

And with that, I forever closed any possibility of entering the boys' world again. But I didn't care, and just to show how much I didn't care, I made another face, turned my back on Diggy, and walked up the front path to the house. As I went through the narrow passageway between the house and the side wall that led to the back, I could hear the girls' voices as they prepared for bride-bride, and especially Her Fatness's ordering everyone around. When I reached the back garden, I stopped when I saw the wedding cake. The bottom layer consisted of mud pies molded from half a coconut shell. They supported the lid of a biscuit tin, which had three mud pies on it. On these rested the cover of a condensed-milk in with a single mud pie on top. This was the three-tiered design that I invented. Her Fatness had copied my design exactly. Further, she had taken upon herself the sole honor of decorating it with florets of gangaphana flowers and trails of antigonon, in the same way I had always done.

Sonali was the first to become aware of my presence. "Arjie!" she said, pleased.

The other cousins now noticed me, and they also exclaimed in delight. Lakshmi called out to me to come over and join them, but before I could do so Her Fatness rose to her feet.

"What do you want?" she said.

I came forward a bit and she immediately stepped toward me, like a female mongoose defending her young against a cobra. "Go away!" she cried, holding up her hand. "Boys are not allowed here."

I didn't heed her command.

"Go away," she cried again. "Otherwise I'm going to tell Ammachi!"

I looked at her for a moment, but fearing that she would see the hatred in my eyes, I glanced down at the ground.

"I want to play bride-bride, please," I said, trying to sound as pathetic and inoffensive as possible.

"Bride-bride," Her Fatness repeated mockingly.

"Yes," I said, in a shy whisper.

Sonali stood up. "Can't he play?" she said to Her Fatness. "He'll be very good."

"Yes, he'll be very good," he others murmured in agreement.

Her Fatness considered their request.

"I have something that you don't have," I said quickly, hoping to sway her decision.

"Oh, what is that?"

"The sari!"

"The sari?" she echoed. A look of malicious slyness flickered across her face.

"Yes," I said. "Without the sari you can't play bride-bride."

"Why not?" Her Fatness said with indifference.

Her lack of concern about the sari puzzled me. Fearing that it might not have the same importance for her as it did for me, I cried out, "Why not?" and pretended to be amazed that she would ask such as question. "What is the bride going to wear then? A bedsheet?"

Her Fatness played with a button on her dress. "Where is the sari?" she asked very causally.

"It's a secret," I said. I was not going to give it to her until I was firmly entrenched in the girls' world again. "If you let me play, I will give it to you when it's time for the bride to get ready."

A smile crossed her face. "The thing is, Arjie," she said in a very reasonable tone, "we've already decided what everyone is going to be for bride-bride and we don't need anyone else."

"But there must be some parts you need people for," I said and then added, "I'll play any part."

"Any part," Her Fatness repeated. Her eyes narrowed and she looked at me appraisingly.

"Let him play," Sonali and the others said.

"I'll play any part," I reiterated.

"You know what?" Her Fatness said suddenly, as if the idea had just dawned on her. "We don't have a groom."

That Her Fatness wanted me to swallow the bitter pill of humiliation was clear and so great was my longing to be part of the girls' world again that I swallowed it.

"I'll take it," I said.

"OK," Her Fatness said, as if it mattered little to her whether I did or not.

The others cried out in delight, and I smiled, happy that my goal had been at least partially achieved. Sonali beckoned to me to come and help them. I went toward where the preparations were being made for the wedding feast, but Her Fatness quickly stepped in front of me.

"The groom cannot help with the cooking."

"Why not?" I protested.

"Because grooms don't do that."

"They do."

"Have you ever head of a groom doing that?"

I couldn't say I had, so I demanded with angry sarcasm. "What do grooms do then?"

"They go to the office."

"Office?" I said.

Her Fatness nodded and pointed to the table on the back porch. The look on her face told me she would not tolerate any argument.

"I can't go to office," I said quickly. "It's Sunday."

"We're pretending it's Monday," Her Fatness replied glibly.

I glared at her. Not satisfied with the humiliation she had forced me to accept, she was determined to keep my participation in bride-bride to a minimum. For an instant I thought to refuse her, but, seeing the warning look in her eyes, I finally acquiesced and went up the porch steps.

From there, I watched the other cousins getting ready for the wedding. Using a stone, I began to bang on the table as if stamping papers. I noted, with pleasure, that the sound irritated Her Fatness. I pressed an imaginary buzzer and made a loud noise. Getting no response from anyone, I did so again. Finally the other cousins looked up. "Boy," I called out imperiously to Sonali, "come here, boy."

Sonali left her cooking and came up the steps with the cringing attitude of the peons at my father's bank.

"Yes, sir, yes sir," she said breathlessly. Her performance was so accurate that the cousins stopped to observe her.

"Take this to the bank manager in Bambalapitiya," I said. Bowing again, she took the imaginary letter and hurried down the steps. I pressed the buzzer again. "Miss," I called to Lakshmi. "Miss, can you come here and take some dictation."

"Yes, sir, coming, sir," Lakshmi said, fluttering her eyelashes, with the exaggerated coyness of a Sinhala comic actress. She came up the steps, wriggling her hips for the amusement of her audience. Everyone laughed except Her Fatness.

When Lakshmi finished the dictation and went down the steps, the other cousins cried out, "Me! Me!" and clamored to be the peon I would call next. But before I could choose one of them, Her Fatness stormed up the steps.

"Stop that!" she shouted at me. "You're disturbing us."

"No!" I cried back, now that I had the support of everyone else.

"If you can't behave, go away."

"If I go away, you won't get the sari."

Her Fatness looked at me a long moment and then smiled.

"What sari?" she said. "I bet you don't even have the sari."

"Yes, I do," I said in an earnest tone.

"Where?"

"It's a secret."

"You are lying. I know you don't have it."

"I do! I do!"

"Show me."

"No."

"You don't have it and I'm going to tell Janaki you are disturbing us."

I didn't move, wanting to see if she would carry out her threat. She crossed behind the table and walked toward the kitchen door. When she got to the door and I was sure she was serious, I jumped up.

"Where is it?" I said urgently to Sonali.

She pointed to Janaki's room.

I ran to Janaki's door, opened it, and went inside. Sonali's bag was lying on the bed, and I picked it up and rushed back out onto the porch. Her Fatness had come away from the kitchen door.

"Here!" I cried.

Her Fatness folded her arms. "Where?" she said tauntingly. I opened the bag, put my hand inside, and felt around for the sari. I touched a piece of clothing and drew it out. It was only Sonali's change of clothes. I put my hand inside again and this time brought out an Enid Blyton book. There was nothing else in the bag.

"Where is the sari?" Her Fatness demanded.

I glanced at Sonali, and she gave me a puzzled look.

"Liar, liar on the wall, who's the liarest one of all?" Her Fatness cried.

I turned toward Janaki's door, wondering if the sari had fallen out. Then I saw a slight smirk on Her Fatness's face and the truth came to me. She'd known all along about the sari. She must have discovered it earlier and hidden it. I realized I had been duped and felt a sudden rush of anger. Her Fatness saw the comprehension in my eyes, and her arms dropped by her sides as if in readiness. She inched back toward the kitchen door for safety. But I was not interested in her for the moment. What I wanted was the sari.

I rushed into Janaki's room.

"I'm going to tell Janaki you're in her room!" Her Fatness cried.

"Tell and catch my long fat tail!" I shouted back.

I looked around Janaki's room. Her Fatness must have hidden it here. There was no other place. I lifted Janaki's mattress. There was nothing under it, save a few Sinhala love comics. I went to Janaki's suitcase and began to go through the clothes she kept neatly folded inside it. As silent as a shadow, Her Fatness slipped into the room. I became aware of her presence and turned. But too late. She took the sari from the shelf where she had hidden it and ran out the door. Leaving the suitcase still open, I ran after her. The sari clutched to her chest, she rushed for the kitchen door. Luckily Sonali and Lakshmi were blocking her way. Seeing me coming at her, she jumped off the porch and began to head toward the front of the house. I leapt off the porch and chased after her. If she got to the front of the house, she would go straight to Ammachi.

Just as she reached the passageway, I managed to get hold of her arm. She turned, desperate, and struck out at me. Ducking her blow, I reached for the sari and managed to get some of it in my hand. She tried to take it back from me, but I held on tightly. Crying out, she jerked away from me with her whole body, hoping to wrest the sari from my grip. With a rasping sound, the sari began to tear. I yelled at her to stop pulling, but she jerked away again and the sari tore all the way down. There was a moment of stunned silence. I gazed at the torn sari in my hand, at the long threads that hung from it. Then, with a wail of anguish, I rushed at Her Fatness and grabbed hold of her hair. She screamed and flailed at me. I yanked her head so far to one side that it almost touched her shoulder. She let out a guttural sound and struck desperately at me. Her fist caught me in the stomach and she managed to loosen my grip. She began to run toward the porch steps, crying out for Ammachi and Janaki. I ran after her and grabbed the sleeve of her dress before she went up the porch steps. She struggled against my grip and the sleeve ripped open and hung down her arm like a broken limb. Free once again, she stumbled up the steps toward the kitchen door, shouting at the top of her voice.

Janaki rushed out of the kitchen. She raised her hand and looked around for the first person to wallop, but when she saw Her Fatness with her torn dress, she held her raised hand to her cheek and cried out in consternation, "Buddu Ammo!"

Now Her Fatness began to call out only for Ammachi.

Janaki came hurriedly toward her, "Shhh! Shhhh!" she said, but Her Fatness only increased the volume of her cry.

"What's wrong? What's wrong?" Janaki cried impatiently.

Her Fatness pointed at me.

"Janakiii! See what that boy did," she replied.

"I didn't do anything," I yelled, enraged that she was trying to push the blame onto me.

I ran back to where I had dropped the sari, picked it up, and held it out to Janaki.

"Yes!" Sonali cried, coming to my defense. "She did it and now she's blaming him."

"It's her fault!" Lakshmi said, also taking my side.

Now all the voices of the girl cousins rose in a babble, supporting my case and accusing Her Fatness.

"Quiet!" Janaki shouted in desperation. "Quiet!"

But nobody heeded her. We all crowded around her, so determined to give our version of the story that it was a while before we became aware of Ammachi's presence in the kitchen doorway. Gradually, like the hush that descends on a garrison town at the sound of enemy guns, we all became quiet. Her Fatness stopped her wailing.

Ammachi looked at all of us and then her gaze came to rest on Janaki. "How many times have I told you to keep these children quiet?" she said, her tone awful.

Janaki, always full of anger, now wrung her hands like a child in fear of punishment. "I told them," she started to say, but Ammachi raised her hand for silence. Her Fatness began to cry again, more out of fear than anything else. Ammachi glared at her, and, as if to deflect her look, Her Fatness held up her arm with the ripped sleeve.

"Who did that?" Ammachi said after a moment.

Her Fatness pointed at me, and her crying got even louder.

Ammachi looked at me sternly and then beckoned me with her index finger.

"Look!" I cried and held out the sari as if in supplication. "Look at what she did!"

But Ammachi was unmoved by the sight of the sari and continued to beckon me.

As I looked at her, I could almost hear the singing of the cane as it came down through the air, and then the sharp crack, which would be followed my searing pain. The time Diggy had been caned for climbing the roof came back to me, his pleas for mercy, his shouts of agony and loud sobs.

Before I could stop myself, I cried out angrily at Ammachi, "It's not fair! Why should I be punished?"

"Come here," Ammachi said.

"No. I won't."

Ammachi came to the edge of the porch, but rather than backing away, I remained where I was.

"Come here, you vamban," she said to me sharply.

"No!" I cried back. "I hate you, you old fatty."

The other cousins and even Janaki gasped at my audacity. Ammachi began to come down the steps. I stood my ground for a few moments but then my courage gave out. I turned, and, with the sari still in my hands, I fled. I ran from the back of the garden to the front gate and out. In the field across the way, the boys were still at their cricket game. I hurried down the road toward the sea. At the railway lines I paused briefly, went across, then scrambled over the rocks to the beach. Once there, I sat on a rock and flung the sari down next to me. "I hate them, I hate them all," I whispered to myself. "I wish I was dead."

I put my head down and felt the first tears begin to wet my knees.

———

For a while I was still. The sound of the waves, their regular rhythm, had a calming effect on me. I leaned back against the rock behind me, watching them come in and go out. Soon the heat of the rocks became unbearable and I stood up, removed my slippers, and went down the beach to the edge of the water.

I had never seen the sea this color before. Our visits to the beach were usually in the early evening when the sea was turquoise blue. Now, under the midday sun, it had become hard silver, so bright it hurt my eyes.

The sand burned my feet, and I moved closer to the waves to cool them. I looked down the deserted beach, whose white sand almost matched the color of the sea, and saw tall buildings shimmering in the distance like a mirage. This daytime beach seemed foreign compared with the beach of the early evening, which was always crowded with strollers and joggers and vendors. Now both the beach and the sea, once so familiar, were like an unknown country into which I had journeyed by chance.

I knew then that something had changed. But how, I didn't altogether know.

The large waves, impersonal and oblivious to my despair, threw themselves against the beach, their crests frothing and hissing. Soon I would have to turn around and go back to my grandparents' house, where Ammachi awaited me with her thinnest cane, the one that left deep impressions on the back of our thighs, so deep that sometimes they had to be treated with gentian violet. The thought of that cane as it cut through the air, humming like a mosquito, made me wince even now, so far away from it.

I glanced at the sari lying on the rock where I had thrown it, and knew that I would never enter the girls' world again. Never stand in front of Janaki's mirror, watching a transformation take place before my eyes. Nor would I step out of that room and make my way down the porch steps to the altar, a creature beautiful and adored, the personification of all that was good and perfect in the world. The future spend-the-days were no longer to be enjoyed, no longer to be looked forward to. And then there would be the loneliness. I would be caught between the boys' and the girls' worlds, not belonging or wanted in either. I would have to think of things with which to amuse myself, find ways to endure the lunches and teas when the cousins could talk to one another about what they had done and what they planned to do for the rest of the day. The bell of St. Fatima's Church rang out the Angelus, and its melancholy sound seemed like a summoning. It was time to return to my grandparents' house. My absence at the lunch table would be construed as another act of defiance, and eventually Janaki would be sent to fetch me. Then the punishment I receive would be even more severe. With a heavy heart, I slowly went back up the beach, not caring that the sand burned the soles of my feet. I put my slippers on, picked up my sari, and climbed up the rocks. I paused and looked back at the sea one last time. Then I turned, crossed the railway lines, and began my walk up Ramanaygam Road to the future that awaited me.

TAKE OUT: QUEER WRITING FROM ASIAN PACIFIC AMERICA

SVATI SHAH

GRASS

Life is dark on the subway. Sometimes, it's mean. "Who are you?" they ask with their eyes. I'm not sure which they see first—boots, crew cut, breasts, tattoo, girlfriend? Girlfriend, breasts, tattoo, boots? "What are you?" they ask emphatically with their faces and hands. Sometimes, I shut my eyes and answer them silently. I am an adult role model and a child prodigy with all the answers. I am queer in search of family, asked constantly about mother father sister brother husband wife, looking for a reflective surface, making it up as I go. Sometimes, before I open my mouth, I close my eyes and grip tighter to the horizontal steel bar that holds me steady, remembering what I think I can know. Places, people, my street address before I was born. Sometimes, I open my eyes and my hands are sliding on the square metal handle of a lawnmower.

———

It was 1980, the year of Reagan, puberty, and the smell of sweet grass clippings in Orange Park, Florida. I lived with my mother and my grandmother, my Motiba. Our first day in the neighborhood, I'd met Angie. I saw her hair first. Long, dark hair and olive skin, living with her two older sisters and her parents in the big house across the street.

"What does your dad do?" she asked as she checked out my storybooks, my miniature animal collection from India, and the knitted doilies Motiba had begun making for my room. "My dad's an engineer," she said, as if she were describing herself. I wondered if I should come out with another fable about growing out of the earth and getting plucked by my mother, or adapting that story about the Greek god whose daughter popped out of his head because he had a migraine.

"I don't have a dad. My mom's a doctor. She's stationed here."

She should have heard it before. I mean, it was a Navy town, and mostly all the heads of the household wore the same uniform to work. Whenever I asked her, Ma insisted she'd joined the Navy on a whim. "I just wanted to learn how to fly helicopters, beta," she said simply. I pretended to believe her, even though I'd feigned sleep through enough family conversations about medical school and exams and getting a residency in America to know that Ma had joined the Navy to change her career the only way she could. It was six years after her divorce from my father, and I knew that she had Weighed Her Options and was now Starting Over for the Sake of Her Babuli (me).

It didn't take long for sessions with Angie to get more usual. We'd both just outgrown our training wheels, and we went to the same school up the road. It's enough reason when you're eight. Once we'd gone out berry-picking on our bikes; it was an excuse to be outside and scratch up our shins, to be boys together. These adventures rarely involved much talking; being outside in the quiet was usually enough. Once, when Angie asked, "So how can you not have a father?" I stared at her. For a minute, I wasn't sure if she had asked me, or the silence itself. The reason for the divorce was still "untold" to me, meaning I was too young to remember and no one had filled me in. "Why make her suffer even more?" Motiba would say when she and Ma thought I was asleep in the back of the car. "After all this, it's God's blessing she doesn't remember." I would hear my mother' sigh and look up at the telephone wires weaving themselves against the sky like traces of a giant charcoal pencil going on a road trip. I pulled out one of a handful of memories from our time as mother father child, stopped car by the side of the road, Ma crying, his face screaming over the seat, threatening to set free my blue helium balloon for something I have never been able to remember.

"He lives in Michigan," I said, since that was pretty much all I knew. Angie looked back at me for a minute and then, satisfied, started popping our harvest into her red, puckered mouth.

If no one had asked. I wouldn't have cared. I mean, if I hadn't been surrounded by mothers fathers children, by visiting grandparents and people who spoke English all the time, my life would have seemed plain and uneventful. School, home, Motiba, TV, Ma, bed. It would've rolled on and on. The questions and the British novels my cousins brought me from Bombay spurred my own Harriet the Spy investigation into the Why I Was Growing Up in My Maternal Family. After school, while Ma was at work or on call and Motiba was making dinner, I would go through Ma's books and files, looking for some proof that I was dropped on their doorstep by aliens or really related to Indira Gandhi. I found medical books, insurance files, a framed picture of the helicopter Ma had learned to fly on and, once, a book on how to have sex stuck between stacks of paper and some wooden elephant bookends. The book was yellowed and fraying, dated from 1962 or something. I was shocked, until I realized it was just full of words. I stuck it back in its hiding place after I got bored of reading one long section after the other on how to make a penis go into a vagina in every situation there is—naked, dressed, on a ski lift, while the guy has his leg in a cast, while the woman is pregnant, upside down, inside out. No one would've known about my discovery if I hadn't gotten curious and asked Ma after work one day, "So, did Daddy ever have a full length cast on his leg?"

"Why, beta," she asked, changing from her khakis and black leather dress shoes to her cotton house-kaftan.

"Because then maybe you wouldn't have just had one kid, if he hadn't broken his leg."

She looked at me from a place between love and exasperation and explained that No, Daddy had never had his leg in a full length cast, and Yes, the book had been a wedding gift from my aunt, and No, I wasn't allowed to go through her office like that whenever I wanted. From then on, I was much more careful.

I never did find proof of my extraterrestrial or noble birth, even though I eventually started insisting that we had Indian maharajahs in our family tree. Ma said No without even thinking. "But how do you know?" I pressed. "Don't we have to look it up or something?" I was thinking about the Angie's most recent school project, when she took a big poster of a bush with branches to school for Show and Tell. She said it was her family tree, and claimed she could trace back her ancestors to Sicily. It had names and pictures of people's faces at the end of every branch. Each face was wearing a different kind of hat to indicate the historical period, and it made me think that maybe it really is possible for people to pop out of other people's heads. Most of the people on the poster had beards or swords. I asked "Is this your mom's family or your dad's family?" She looked at the pictures again, the bark sprouting from each hairline, and shrugged like it didn't really matter.

"I just know," said Ma. "In India, if you have maharajahs or politicians in your family, then you become a maharajah as well." Then she laughed. "If there were any maharajahs in our family, I think we would know by now."

I thought about our family in India, all the mothers fathers sisters brothers who worked as school teachers, postmen, bank tellers, and bond writers. I guessed there weren't any maharajahs or Gandhis, even though all the mothers sisters fathers brothers in America were doctors or engineers. I had some vague recollection that my own father was one of these because he'd brought ball bearings from his factory on his last annual visit to Florida. "I want to you know what I do every day," he said, his face pained and a little small as he tried describing his office, his apartment, his drive to work. I'd nodded then, because it seemed important to him that I understand something of his life, even though I couldn't even pretend to imagine a world of factories and apartment complexes and cold weather. I looked at the little mechanism in my hands and thought it resembled my roller skate wheel. "Do you make roller skates?" I asked, trying to connect. "Sort of," he had said, and showed me slides of himself, smiling and waving in front of frozen ponds and piles of snow.

After a couple of years in Orange Park, our lives settled into a kind of rhythm, punctuated by summer visits from our family in India and winter visits from Michigan, and the occasional adventure with Angie. Ma, Motiba and I found a division of labor that seemed to work: Ma learned how to fly, Motiba took care of me and Ma, and I took care of the yard. If our family structure had never changed, if Ma had never remarried and Motiba had never gone away, I may well have begun to emulate middle-aged men whose pride and joy is a well-kept yard. I may even have aspired to a life that affords a "yard" in every sense of the term. In 1980, I thought of the lawnmower as mine. I loved cutting grass because it was the loudest, sweatiest, most public chore my family life could offer. I loved every part of it—hanging a dirty rag out of my back jeans pocket while I filled the gas, yanking on the starter cord with a foot propped up on the engine, and assuming the position required to do the job—knees bowed, arms akimbo, pushing along a big, bad, loud machine.

Motiba, bored of cooking and watching ESL classes on PBS, tried to come out and help once. She took the mower's handlebar in her large hands and held it still while it was sitting in the garage. She waited while I finished with the gas, and casually asked how to turn it on. I don't know why; maybe the sight of her sari and her graying hair behind heavy equipment was too out of place with the Motiba I needed when I came home from school everyday. Maybe I was possessive of the machine, or my role. Maybe I decided that the sight of my grandmother in her pastel cotton sari pushing the lawnmower along in our front yard was too much for the neighborhood to handle. Whatever the reason, I flashed her an angry look and forbade her to ever touch it again, chastising her for being foolish with a dangerous machine. "Do you want to hurt yourself or something?" I snapped. Her face closed up then, and she went back in the house to reread the Gujarati newspaper someone had brought back for her that spring.

———

The first grass-cutting of the year was always the best. It signaled the summer, the end of school, end of mother father sister brother questions, and the beginning of marathon TV sessions interspersed with meals and weekly yard-trimmings. Mint grew wild out front. Thinking it was weeds, I ran it over on the first go. When I described the smell coming from under the blades, Ma and Motiba looked shocked, as if I had thrown a stack of fresh rotis into the garbage disposal.

"Fudino che? Fudino kapi nakhiyo?"

So, then, on some Saturdays, they picked the weeds and the mint while I cut the grass. The post-mint-discovery version of "cutting the grass" involved hauling the middle aged mower over the hills and gullies, and avoiding the large patches of fudino they put in tea and made chutney from. I understood the significance of this some years later when I realized there were no Indian or Arab groceries in Orange Park in 1980, and no fresh mint or coriander, either.

I took a special pleasure in doing my chore when the summer family visits would start. With more mothers fathers sisters brothers around, the small local Indian community would come over more frequently for dinner parties and beach trips. In a pack of my uncles and aunts and cousins, me, Ma, and Motiba looked a little less out of place. In July, when both the Florida heat and family attendance at the house was peaking, I decided the grass needed a desperate trim. Pushing the machine down the drive, I looked across the street and saw Angie through a window sitting up in her room, idly staring at the street, the sky, and me. I positioned myself at the head of the first row of grass with my elbows out even further than usual, and started in on the grass as if I'd been ordered to march. As I bumped and slipped along over the little dips and hills of earth, I slipped into a daydream about Angie and my family, about trees and TV and the future.

By about halfway through the yard, I was oblivious to the work. Without really watching in front of me, I managed to run over a patch of yard which, between then and the last time I'd cut the grass, had been occupied by a nest of ground hornets. I ran right over their new home with my prized machine. They retaliated in force, flying enraged from their hole. Angie later said I looked like I was either yard-dancing or having a screaming fit, like those snake-people in West Virginia. It felt like hot lead pellets on my bare arms and legs, or bullets.

Minutes long as hours later, when the hornets had gone, when the mower was retrieved and my cousin-brother had pulled the last stinging worker from my flesh, the aunties descended with their tavethas. The traditional remedy for bee stings is to rub them vigorously with a roti-flipper to friction out the stinger. This species of bee, as it happened, wasn't a bee at all but was, in fact, a species of hornet. Hornets don't leave stingers behind. The aunties essentially succeeded in rubbing my legs sore and released me to my mother's care. Ma's approach was more direct—two Tylenol, some ointment, and bed. The pain faded as I slipped into a real sleep. Just before it went black, I though I heard Angie's voice downstairs.

"Is she OK? We saw it through our windows. My parents wanted to know if she's OK."

"Don't worry. She's sleeping."

———

Eventually, the relatives left, the season wore on, and the grass grew. By late-August, it had grown past the too-lazy-to-cut-it stage, past the shaggy dog stage, until it resembled an old forest clearing. More grass, more hornets, my logic said. It was a foot high before Motiba decided to take things into her own hands. She must've noticed me filling the mower with gas, just to leave it for another eight hours of TV. She may have remembered the many hours we'd spent outside together harvesting the mint. Or the dirty rag hanging proudly from my jeans.

I'd noticed that, that summer, almost everyone was suddenly interested in my romantic future. Even Angie's mother had an opinion, asking Ma whether I ever wore dresses, and was I allowed to date boys at school? Ma replied by asking after Angie, thinking about the rag the whole time. Whenever my aunts started speculating about the kind of boy they'd someday find for me to marry, Motiba would get quiet and distant. Everyone else's grandmothers would come visit from India with fistfuls of Prospective Photos, biodata and all. Motiba just sat, and, when we were alone, told me stories about leaving my polygamist grandfather the year India became free, about going to an ashram with my four-year-old mother in tow and teaching kindergarten to tidy indigenous children whose families had never known how to read. The aunties decided Motiba was just getting too old to care about the world, "even about her own granddaughter's marriage," but I knew better.

Motiba said that all bees—even the hornet kind—are afraid of smoke, and that she had a plan to cut the grass, bee-free. She convinced me to turn off *Gilligan* and step outdoors. We walked around the yard and found a long, fat stick. To one end, she tied a long skein of old, kerosene-soaked rags made from her cotton saris now too tattered to wear. She told me to strike a kitchen match, and light it. It burned with a thick, black smoke and a dull orange flame. It looked like a volcanic sunset. She went out ahead and started beating the first row of high grass with her torch. She lifted it high with both arms and brought it down with her whole body, as if she were pulling streams of smoke down from the sky. I watched her do this up half the first row before I started following behind with the running mower, reassured that any bees lurking beneath were either dazed asleep or frightened away.

In this way, we did the whole yard—her ahead, beating the weeds in a regular rhythm, row by row, me following to cut it down by tilting the mower to the sky and bringing it down, patch by patch. By then, it was too high to simply roll over. After the first half-hour, Ma pulled up in her Buick. I didn't hear the engine under the whine of the mower, and only noticed her when I turned to start another row. She was sitting on the porch in her uniform, her head resting in the palm of her hand, watching us make our way through the yard as if we were performing a large-scale, animistic puja. It took the better part of the day, and several changes of rags.

With every whiff of kero and exhaust, I knew I'd never, ever forget this. Motiba never expressed her I-love-yous with affection and speech. Ma's long hours meant more and harder embraces and saying-out-louds when she was home. Motiba was simply our ritual of life, our haven. I watched her in front of the household gods, and ate her ketchup-flavored dal and rice, and could not imagine my life without her presence in it. Watching her soaked back as she raised the torch up and down, over and over, I felt our truth in the smell of fuel and sweat, and knew it was enough.

RICCO VILLANUEVA SIASOCO

SQUATTERS

Veracia Gabales

We are close to Boston and I can smell the salty air. Outside the window, an army of pine trees stands at attention beside the road. Their formation reminds me of the palm trees beside the highway from Manila to Visayas—except that these trees are lush, designed to withstand the New England winter. The trunks of the palm trees were thin and delicate, their palms outstretched like lovers. These trees are proud, unforgiving. Much like everything I know that is American.

The ride has been long, almost three days, and the bus driver—his name is Thomas—stopped our bus in Ohio and I slept in an air-conditioned room. I sit directly behind Thomas in his driver's seat and say, "Thank goodness for Cleveland! I don't want William to see me for the first time in four years with bags under my eyes."

Thomas smiles up at me, lifting his single dark brow in the horizontal mirror. Our bus is moving cautiously in line to pay a toll. The covered plaza ahead looks like my new dentures, with rows of automobiles like dental floss.

I remove a banana from the large, hand-carried bayong at my feet and unpeel it. A small automobile outside my window is full of young people. They are loud and merry, with assorted limbs hanging outside their car. An arm here, a bare foot there. They're laughing to rock and roll music, which reaches my ears through Thomas's open window, and I wonder: Could my William know them? I hope he has made friends with other Filipinos.

Last week, William called home from Boston. I could hear the shouting of his friends and a stereo in the background, though I couldn't understand how this music was enjoyable when I could not make out the words. "It took forever to get the couch Teresa gave me through the hallway," he said, in a booming voice. Someone in his apartment was also talking with him, and he spoke to the two of us at the same time. "I can't wait for you to visit, Mom."

My next-door neighbor Francine was seated on a tall stool in my kitchen. I held the telephone a few inches from my ear while William continued to brag and Francine flipped through an old photo album on the counter, pointing at photos of herself and that awful football-helmet hairdo she used to wear. Francine is a good friend; she baked cashew muffins for my family when we moved in.

"I'm still here, William. Your sofa did not fit." In his new tirahan it sounded like a man was screaming and the electronic guitars were screaming, right into my eardrum.

"How many others are there?" I asked, but he would not explain. He snapped at me with his ordinary response, Don't worry, Mom, and when the voices became persistent he quickly closed our conversation and hung up.

Francine closed the padded cover of my photo album and pushed it across the counter, next to the Fry Daddy and a pile of credit card bills in the corner. "Boys will be girls," she said, blowing a stream of cigarette smoke through her mouth, and we laughed in the quiet afternoon hour before our grown boys returned from their jobs. "How long's your visit to Boston?"

Thomas drums his fingers on the steering wheel, waiting for the slow line of automobiles to shrink. The mid-day sun finds its way through the glass and makes me sweat beneath my arms, the mixture of outside heat and cool air reminding me of the air-conditioned buses I used to ride to Baclaran on Wednesdays, to afternoon Mass, and then to shop for fruit and romance komiks in the crowded markets.

"I'm not certain. I am surprising William for his birthday." I want to escape this boring bus and run between the car lines, tapping on windows and waving to the strangers inside.

Above my head, in Thomas's wide mirror, only the top half of his face is visible, his rosy cheeks and clear blue eyes, and I want to reach over his seat and take what is good from his expression and save it for another time.

"Lucky kid," Thomas says.

"Lucky Mama!"

Thomas grips both hands on the extra-large steering wheel and maneuvers our bus into an outside lane. Is "Lucky Mama" my automatic response? Yes, I want to know if my William is eating well and working, if he arrives home safely on his nights out, but unlike my boys believe, I do not care about every small detail of their lives. Do I bother to tell them every activity in my day?

A few weeks ago, before I retired from my position at Bates Elementary, my staff held a send-off party for me in the school library. I did not tell Johnny Boy or Raymond, for I knew they would not bother to attend.

That afternoon, after all of the students ran screaming out of the building to their real homes, my principal and staff drank blue Kool-Aid from an Igloo. Mrs. Steppuhn, the school nurse, brought cheddar cheese that squirted from a can, and when our principal, Mr. Smith, held a cracker underneath, I squirted cheese all over his fingers. Everyone laughed so hard, we were next to tears!

Later, the teachers presented me with a book by Annie Dillard, who had given a special assembly to our third-graders. I have read one hundred and forty-three pages of her book on this bus ride, and this morning, as I underlined a sentence in the book, I looked up to see the sign indicating we were entering Massachusetts. "Experiencing the present purely is being emptied," I underlined with a ballpoint pen.

Am I always filled-up with the trials of my anak, and my other girlfriends?

I fold the slimy peel of my banana in one hand and stow it in a plastic Baggie inside my bayong. Pressing my forehead on the cool inside of my window, I notice the boys in the automobile shaking it from side to side. These young men look like America. The pale one, the driver, has a red bandanna tied around his scalp and curly locks that poke out of a knot in the back. Their automobile is like a tarantula, wiggling in the same place with all of the arms and legs dangling outside the windows. William looks American like them, perhaps; he is the tallest in the family and he has big bones.

Is this only my perception? To the girls he looks like another Asian boy, I'm sure. I want to say to them, he is guapo, my son, can't you see? His nails and his hair grow fast (he always eats rice) and he has dark eyes that do not lie. But this is another of his differences—William does not look back at the girls.

When William returned from college the first time, a December when the snow formed a ramp all the way to the roof of my garage, he did not eat anything at the dinner table, even though I made his favorite—menudo without garbanzo beans. I made a small bowl especially for him; for his kuya Johnny Boy and kuya Raymond, the meat and garbanzos I mixed together.

"Where's your appetite?" I asked him.

"I ate on the plane, Mom."

"Hoy naku, you eat again." I spooned his bowl of menudo on a plate of white rice.

Johnny Boy, my first-born, finished his menudo with garbanzos and gestured to me for William's without. Johnny Boy drove thirty-five miles from his dormitory to pick William up at the airport, so I decided to give him what was left of William's dish.

None of my boys talked as they ate. Was my family extra hungry that night, or, as always, did they have nothing new to say?

I stood and walked to the refrigerator to prepare dessert—vanilla ice cream with coconut shavings, tiny cubes of gelatin, and sweet beans in syrup. From the dining room, I listened as Johnny Boy asked William questions about his university. William was quiet, answering simply: "It's windy," and "I don't get out much."

As I scooped ice cream into individual bowls, I remembered asking Johnny Boy why William chose Boston University. He said it was for the quality of the education. And then one evening, when Raymond returned from a date with his girlfriend, I asked him the same question. Raymond covered his small moustache with his hand and yawned.

"Maybe he just wanted to get out, Ma," Raymond said, then went down the stairs to his room.

I carried the desserts to the table, along with more Pepsi Cola. William's menudo was still untouched, no longer steaming. Suddenly he touched my wrist and stopped me pouring pop into his glass. He hadn't touched me in this way for years, not since he was a small boy and would swing from my arms with both hands while we waited for the merry-go-round at the Iowa State Fair. Yes, he hugged me when we said goodbye, but not with this closeness.

"Mom, please, sit down."

And after I took my side of our octagonal table and my sons were all quiet, he told us that he was now a gay. "I've known for a long time," he said.

His large hands trembled in his lap.

Did this come from Boston? I wondered. Would William never get married? I don't know much about being a gay and thought before anything else, What did I do to make this happen? I watched William look up at his brother Raymond, who smiled at him across the table.

Johnny Boy lowered his head and said nothing. Raymond was also silent, but in his tight purple lips I saw that he already knew William's secret. And so it was my moment and I took my William's hand and said, like I think Meryl Streep would say in a dramatic movie, "You are my son," and "I love you no matter who you are."

"Get the hell out of the bus lane!"

Thomas is sweating through the back of his short-sleeved shirt, yelling out his window at the automobile with the rowdy young boys. The driver with the pale features puts his arm out his window, gestures at Thomas, and then speeds through the toll booth. Which university do they belong to, the Massachusetts Institute of Technology or the New England School of Art and Design? I learned so many names when William was studying the beautiful college brochures.

I bend to gather Annie Dillard's book, my cinnamon night cream, a small disposable camera, and the half-read issues of *Filipina*. As I collect the runaway ballpoints on the sticky floor, I listen to Thomas talking with the toll man like they are good friends. The toll man's voice is high-pitched, like a bird, and when I raise myself again, I realize that the toll man is a woman.

As our bus continues through the mouth of Boston, I remember the previous journey I made on this road.

That first trip, we drove from Iowa in one whole day, Johnny Boy in the driver's seat the entire time. "The sidewalks in Boston are paved with cobblestones," William would say from the backseat beside Raymond. Or later, from an expensive guidebook I had given him, "There are over eighty universities in the area." At a Burger King drive-up in the Berkshire Mountains, my baby said: "Jack Kerouac was born in Massachusetts." Jack Kerouac was an author who wrote books about traveling, Johnny Boy explained when I asked.

Was Jack Kerouac attracted to other boys like my son? William doesn't talk about being a gay. I think he shares these details with Raymond on the telephone, who shares with me only small bits. Once I asked Raymond if there was a chance William might marry a nice Filipino girl. "Maybe a boy," he answered, smiling like a cartoon character while he waxed his skateboard in the garage.

Another time, when William entered junior high school, he came home with his face all red and his fists tightly clenched. What happened? I asked, clearing unfinished letters on my bed to make room for him. He sat on the edge like a fisherman, waiting on a dock. In front of his entire P.E. class, he explained, Mr. Woodson announced he could not play soccer without a jock.

"Skinny Billy Tripp told all the girls in the other class!" Even at that time, his hands were always nervous in his lap.

This was when my Dominic was still alive. I took Dominic aside that evening, and gave him twenty dollars and sent him with William to Midwest Sporting Goods. I knew William would not go with me. But my Dominic, he was athletic and used to practice his hoop shot long into the night, until the shadows from our garage stretched all the way to Francine's back porch. I knew if Dominic asked, William would go.

When they returned, William stormed by me in the living room without a single word. "They didn't have his size," Dominic said, returning the crumpled bill in my hand.

When we traveled to Boston that first time, I remembered this story while William was unpacking his damit in his dormitory room. "Did you remember your jockeys?" I asked him, seated on his naked mattress. "You want to fit in with the other boys." And that time we laughed.

Our bus exits the interstate and drives beside a curving river of glass. Thomas tells me we're a few minutes from the South Station bus terminal. I recognize the square electronic sign of a triangle positioned on top of a building, and when we pass this sign it grows smaller and looks to me like it might be a better advertisement if all of the light bulbs were alive instead of dead.

In South Station, Thomas skillfully steers the bus into a slanted parking space and the bus bumps to a stop. Through a large glass wall, many passengers are rushing, pulling their suitcases behind them on wheels. A woman with a bright scarf tied around her head holds her boy's hand, hurrying him along. She seems to know exactly where she's headed, her destination clearly in mind.

Before he opens the door, before he allows any of us to step off the bus, Thomas turns in his seat and asks me if I need directions. He is a polite young man with a wife and two girls at home.

"Open the door," I say to him. "Let's be on our way."

Will Gabales

Paul hadn't settled in my apartment when my mother knocked on the front door, her bayong in one hand and Dom's long-forgotten Super Friends backpack in the other. Paul and I were hesitantly certain that living together was the next step in our relationship; somehow his intuition, or my unspoken fear of commitment, had cautioned us to move one pair of his satin boxers at a time.

We lay on our backs, necks wet in the humid afternoon, ignoring the interruption at the door. The knocking grew insistent and finally, on Sunday time, I donned a pair of jeans and left Paul half-asleep on the mattress.

"Honey, I'm home!" she cried, her short arms outstretched in the hallway. A good foot smaller than me, I saw patches of scalp visible through her thinning, black hair, and drops of sweat collected on her forehead like the outside of an icy glass. She reminded me of an elderly actress I'd seen peddling greeting cards or adult diapers on TV once— not my mother, but a shrunken, more animated version of a woman in her seventies.

"My baby," she said, embracing me. She stepped back, then reached out and pinched my love handles. "You look taba!"

"Mom! You're here?"

"Let your Moms see your new tirahan!"

Mom, or "Moms" as she often referred to herself, stepped into my skinny hallway, handing me her bags and kissing me on one flushed cheek. Wasn't it customary to make an announcement before an occasion like this? Pick up the phone and reach out to someone you love? I imagined a monotone voice overhead, as rehearsed as a stewardess, or the driver of a subway train: The performance will begin in five minutes; please return to your seat. Then you'd gather yourself in the back of the room, tuck in your ragged shirt tail, spit your hair back in one of those giant gilded mirrors. Thank you for waiting, the guide would then say, the show will now begin.

Never do they plop you in a hard-backed seat and say, Hey buddy, move it along.

"How? When? Did you leave Des Moines?" I asked, my mother dwarfed by a mountain of unpacked boxes. I held her thin arms in my hands.

"Hoy naku, you have a head cold?"

"It's just, you're here, right here in my living room!" I thought of Paul, naked in my bed thirty feet away. Was he still napping, dreaming of our earlier consummation in the midday heat?

"Surprised, hah? I have surprised my baby on his first day as a man!" The unnatural whiteness of her dentures filled her mouth like correction fluid. I felt a small hair lodged in the back of my throat and coughed loudly into my fist.

"And you answer your door like this, not wearing a scrap of clothing? What kind of job do you have, where they don't pay you enough to purchase a new shirt?" She squinted. I figured she was studying how much wider I'd grown since the last time we'd seen each other, in her home for Christmas a few years earlier.

Paul emerged from my bedroom with a long, calm stride. One side of his blond, sun-bleached hair was flattened against his head and he wore one of my loose T-shirts and his own worn jeans.

"So the shelves are all set up," he said, winking in my direction. "I thought I heard you talking."

I dropped my mother's luggage on the floor.

"Paul, this is my mother Vera." I ushered him into our circle, my hand on his back. "Mom, this is, um, Paul."

We'd been dating for more than a year, but Paul and I still disagreed on introductions. He introduced me as his boyfriend or his partner no matter whether the person was a colleague or close friend.

My mother smiled politely, taking her two-handled bayong from my hand. She knew I was gay, and in her well-wishing, had told me in overly enunciated Tag-lish that it was "poor-feckt-ly OK naman." She ate up that bullshit from her television altar, weepy soap operas like *Loving* and *The Love Boat* (anything with the "L" word in its title). When I broke the news to her, she had proclaimed I love you no matter what you choose, and You will always be my baby boy. That was back in school, a couple spring breaks ago. We'd spoken little about it since, focusing when we talked on the weather, her mall-walking club and the various plights of my brothers.

"Excuse me a second," I said, hustling into my bedroom. "T-shirt," I shouted over my shoulder.

In the still room, I kneeled beside a heap of dirty clothes beneath an unscreened window. Someone threw a heavy object into the dumpster several floors below, clanging against the dumpster's rigid metal sides. How did my mother find my new place? And how long was she planning to stay?

A ragged green polo, my favorite, was tucked in the center of the small mound and I lifted several pairs of jeans and removed the shirt from the pile. After all, any shirt would be acceptable; I was a grown man. I pulled the polo shirt over my head and looked at myself in the long mirror mounted on the back of the door. Smoothing my short, tousled hair with one hand, I remembered Paul was wearing the same BU T-shirt my mother had given me as a gift before I left home.

I walked barefoot into the hall again, the cinnamon smell of my mother's night cream surprising me in the narrow passage. In my peeling kitchen, Paul poured my mother a tall glass of orange juice.

"Vera says you never separate your whites and darks. Maybe that explains the pink underwear," he said smugly.

I breathed through my nose, nostrils flaring, as I took the brown plastic pitcher from his hand and returned it to the refrigerator. When I turned back to my mother and boyfriend, Paul's haughty, tightly pressed lips formed a small "O" as he realized the intimacy of his flippant revelation.

———

Later, frying eggs with crisp edges, I asked Paul if we were keeping him from his other commitments for the day. Beside me, on the counter, the rice cooker my mother had mailed me hissed and blew a miniature geyser of steam.

"Nope," he said, mopping the yellow of his fried egg with his toast and placing it his mouth, "what other commitments?"

"I don't know; I hear the radio station is hiring."

My mother, silent since Paul had greeted us from my bedroom, stared at her bleeding eggs and rice and pretended not to understand.

———

Four years earlier, on the occasion of my twenty-first birthday, my mother had mailed me a bookmark with a length-wise illustration of a giant sperm whale on one side, and a description of its mating habits on the reverse. I proudly showed my prize to Teresa, my best friend and housemate at the time. She asked sardonically if my mother was aware of the connotations associated with this offering to her virile young son.

My mother, Veracia Migdalia Santos Gabales, happened to be neither liberal-minded or extraordinarily blasé about the comings and goings of her four misguided sons, of which I am the youngest. I would debate she has always been involved—eerily intimate even—with the careful lives we lived amongst the landscaped cul-de-sacs of sub-urban Des Moines. Between the melodramatic crises of girlfriends and best friends, and our chauffeur-necessary jobs at Hy-Vee Food Store and the Gap, she's managed her children more efficiently than her fluctuating accounts.

Skinny Billy Tripp, the kid who lived next door, had the kind of mother who'd buy him industrial-size chocolate bars and 1000-piece constrictor sets. While fourth graders at Bates Elementary School, Billy's mother—Francine was her real name but Dom and I nicknamed her Fran-Clean—Fran-Clean threw her son the most rocking of roller-skating parties. She invited every kid in our class to the extravaganza, pick-up and delivery included. However, Fran-Clean could only do so much; when we hit puberty, nature took a sadistic turn on Skinny Billy, who appeared on the first day of middle school with unwieldy tufts of hair masking his elbows and knees, and most repugnantly, the wide expanse of his back. Crazed tangerine hair sprouted everywhere, sneaking out from his shirt sleeves in P.E. class and bathing him in an odor my brothers and I worked to avoid.

Vera Gabales organized earnest get-togethers for her Number One Son. On wooden platters, she offered my playmates affection and homemade chicharron. The latter, rinds of pork roasted and dried in our kitchen, were served with a vinegary dip seasoned with black pepper and garlic, which my pals—unbelievably—scarfed like squares of semi-sweet chocolate.

Vera knew all of my friends' parents, and the ways in which they provided for their children; her day job was as the Vice Principal of Elmore Bates Elementary School. When these parents arrived to pick their children up from our house, Mom had prepared praise or small bits of advice for them. She would take the moment when my trouble-adapting-with-others friend was pulling on his rubber boots to escort the unsuspecting parent aside—eager Mrs. O'Neill, let's say—to pull eager Mrs. O'Neill aside and whisper with unnerving directness, You know, you might spend an extra hour or two with Jamie while he completes his homework—he needs more attention, don't you think?

But with her kaibigan she took a more familiar approach. Laughing with Tita Cyntia and Tito Ned, Claro's parents and family friends, she'd slap their backs warmly and declare, Read with Claro more, puede ba? For your kid's sake, naman! And then she'd wink, her crow's feet smiling with concern.

She knew everyone's business, but most distressingly, the ins and outs, the triumphs and melodramatic tragedies, the supposedly "private" moments of her own troop of little men. Among the Privates I surely occupied the most prominent space in her heart. I was her "magandang baby," a laugh-getter she'd exclaim to kaibigan during potlucks on our insulated back porch. Her kaibigan howled through wet cheeks, and my Mom hit them with the one-two-punch, screaming I was "God's Blessed Reason" for even bothering to remain in the States.

And though I'm certain every mother loves her child in a way that is known only to her and that afterbirth of genes, my mother's and my bond was unique. Dad? Before Frances moved out of the house, his responsibility was to guide my older brothers from misanthropy, to keep them from strangling each other with a pair of dirty jeans.

Mom, my Mom, she belonged to me.

In those young moments with her, atop that bedspread embroidered with the Islands of my mother's youth, I was babied by her, read to from Dr. Seuss and Carlos Bulosan and Ziggy, and whispered to in ticklish tones. *Who's my magandang baby? How much does William love his nanay?* Her effort was unlike the effort she gave to my siblings, or her acquaintances here in the States. It surpassed the expansive heart-sickness she felt for her family overseas.

Will is a Mama's boy, my brothers teased me. When I moved to Boston, I admitted to Ray late one evening that I missed Mom's doting, her reassuring whispers, the touch of her fingers on the back of my arm. Then why did you leave? Ray asked. It was a question I couldn't answer.

For my twenty-third birthday, this time in a heavy FedEx box, her gift to me was six pounds of heart-shaped rocks she'd collected during her dusky walks through the fields behind our house. The fields were poised between the edge of our suburban neighborhood and the patchwork of cornfields to the north. Each of the pebbles had been weathered by nature, possessing the shape of a swallow-tailed valentine.

Teresa signed for the delivery and before I opened it, swore up and down that my mother's present was potting soil for the clumpy square of dirt and refuse behind our triple-decker. She recalled my mother's long-distance advice when we'd moved in. "You could grow carrots and cabbage and all kinds of greens in your yard," my mother said to her immediate friend, "and Will could cook for all of your friends fresh lumpia."

Teresa was from Berkeley and embodied the laid-back attitude of a typical West Coast transplant. (Could I have distinguished between an East and West Coast sensibility before I moved out here?) Her puffy face wilted as I removed one of the stones. "Where does your Mom get these fucked up ideas?" she asked.

Teresa took one of the larger rocks and cracked open a walnut on our unfinished pine table. She joked that my mother could never top a gift of such "enormous gravity."

One year later, approaching a quarter of a century and finally stepping up to an apartment of my own, I proved Teresa wrong, receiving the largest, most unexpected surprise of all. My mother forgot to mail a present. Instead, she moved in.

———

The evening she arrived on my doorstep, Johnny Boy sent a terse e-mail indicating his wish for our mother to stay in my care as long as humanly possible.

"Mom needs her Magandang Baby," my kuya Johnny wrote, "and the rest of your brothers just won't do."

I sat at my round table, alone in my apartment save for my mother's bestsellers and a spacious living room cluttered with newspapers, purchased but unread DeLillo and Denis Johnson novels, and a pile of one-act plays from the office. My mother wanted Bufferin and other last-minute items for her sudden sabbatical, and Paul had offered to show her the local CVS on his way home.

I turned the power strip off beneath the table and phoned Ray to confide in him Johnny Boy's message. The roar of small, coordinated wheels on pavement and his skater friends' raucous cheers drowned out his voice.

"Johnny Boy thinks Mom's running away to avoid him," Ray said, projecting his voice over the skittish skateboard noise. Our older brother had asked her to subsidize another of his degrees—this time a doctorate in some subject Ray didn't have a clue about in the fall. I heard Rebecca, his bland girlfriend, shout across the room: "Asian American Studies."

I peeked through the thin blind covering my bay window. A streetlight hummed to life. On the crumbling stoop of my brownstone, Paul waved goodbye to my small mother and she disappeared into my building. What revelations had Paul made to her? And how much of his babble had the First Lady retained?

"Shit, Will, I swore she was leaving next week," he apologized, a safe distance from our mother and her willful path. Ray hadn't separated himself from his workshop long enough to notice the First Lady and her luggage on their merry way.

It had been almost four years since I'd seen him. Ray was a year older, but was often mistaken as the younger one; the teaching staff at my mother's school had a tendency to pinch his fat, dimpled cheeks. The last time we'd seen each other was the morning after Christmas when he brought me to the airport. I remember he bought me two prime-cut steaks from the gift shop.

"You're running away from home," he said, handing me the steaks and a crisp two-dollar bill—his totem for luck. He hugged me, then gave me a familiar shove.

I waited for liftoff in the cabin of that nasally 747, surrounded by a group of Eastern-bound strangers. Fidgety, I glanced at the plane's Emergency Instructions and remembered the rest of his sentence: "And the First Lady knows."

One of my brothers, Dom probably, had secretly christened her the First Lady of Iowa's Filipino Nation because her knowledge of her family was absolute. She could rattle off our immunization records, off-color remarks we'd said and forgotten—a detail as impossible as the date Johnny Boy first learned to spell the "Philippines" correctly—as nonchalantly as the time of day. From the way we squeezed Crest on our toothbrushes (Johnny Boy, left to right, Dominic, right to left, Ray, when he was forced into personal hygiene, directly into his mouth, and me in a hurried squish) to how many times each of my brothers masturbated in the privacy of the bathroom or our shared rooms, my kuyas were convinced she kept a mental notebook of the secret goings-on in her house.

She found Dom getting off in the metal toolshed once. I stood in the kitchen nuking green bean casserole for our afternoon merienda. The First Lady's hissing was as concise and threatening to me, eavesdropping through the patio door, as I learned it was to Dom seated on the riding lawnmower, his white gym shorts limp around his calves, and a copy of a Victoria's Secret catalog beside the stick shift.

"*Hoy naku!*" she yelled. "If your Lolo and Lola could see their apo now! They would say you'll go blind, that you'll never grow up, but of course all that is not true! You know what's going to happen, hah? You're going to use it all up and have nothing left for making babies! Hoy, hindi puede maganak. You keep that up—I know you and your brothers are touching your tetes at all hours in this house—and you'll be sterile! Hoy naku, what would the neighbors say?"

She was the unfortunate mother of mortals. The First Lady had birthed four human, incorrigible sons. Three of us made it to adulthood, Dom run off the path in the middle.

The First Lady had given us her milk and sweat to ensure there was menudo on the table. But despite these outwardly human qualities, each of us sensed our mother was omniscient. We swore.

———

A garbage truck hunkered through the alley behind my apartment. Ray droned on about Johnny Boy's e-mail, the nuances of his message, its subtle implications. He was convinced that like me, Johnny Boy was gay and in a cosmic show of force, my mother had given birth to two twin sets of sons, one set identical in their orientation (me and Johnny Boy), the other in their impulse toward delinquency (he and Dom).

I picked up the base of the telephone and walked to the waist-high counter that divided the kitchen from the living room. My mother had placed a shrink-wrapped basket of fruit on top of the divide.

"Johnny Boy will never come out," Ray lamented, "he's on the fifty-year plan. You know, get married, have a couple kids—then after half his life is over, he'll discover he's just a normal schmoe like the rest of us, not the brainiac he thinks, and come dancing out of the closet."

I sized up Vera's new arrangement of my furniture, accumulated over the years by upwardly mobile friends. Teresa's coffee table was shifted 90 degrees; a pile of CDs were stacked in a column on top. My mother had arrived a few hours earlier. When had she had time for a face lift?

Ray uttered something to his girlfriend. He continued, "Then all Johnny Boy's gonna have left is slim, slim pickings, Will. He'll have to choose between that flaming florist in the strip mall or our old swimming coach at the Y."

"You're full of shit, Ray."

"Can't you see it, Nightslug? Johnny Boy's a closet case. You've noticed that little wrist thing of his when he gets upset, and dude, the way he darts his eyes when one of Mom's friends mentions her daughter."

I selected a firm green apple from my mother's basket and took a bite. "Maybe he's not ready for a commitment."

"A commitment to who? A man or woman? Can you imagine Ma's face if he came out too? Dude, you don't give a shit cause you don't live with her anymore."

Where was our mother now? How quickly my work-a-phobic brother forgot.

"I'd never hear the end of it. Everyday the First Lady'd be, 'Sus mariosep, first my baby and now Johnny Boy? What have I done to deserve this, Raymond? Hah? Come now, are you a shoky too?'"

His calm voice had grown to an all-out shrill. I laughed as Vera entered the kitchen and placed Dom's Super Friends backpack on the stove. In the glow of the open refrigerator, she turned to me with one of her patented who-are-you-talking-to-now? faces. It was difficult not to love her.

"*Hoy naku*, Raymond," my brother continued in his high pitch, "I am cursed to have no grandchildren! None of my boys will part with their precious child-bearing seeds! I should never have allowed you boys to touch yourselves so much—you've turned into a bunch of perverts!"

All of us loved her to death, though we'd be hard pressed to be the first to admit it. In her tireless wisdom and painful, loving drills, she had managed to cultivate healthy doses of humor in us. And despite a chasm in ideologies and pursuits, my brothers and I shared a common understanding: The First Lady would never change a bone.

TAKE OUT: QUEER WRITING FROM ASIAN PACIFIC AMERICA

MOHAN SIKKA

ALPHA HYDROXY

My mother greets me with nervous eyes, clutching, unclutching her purse, touching my shoulder.

"My son, my son."

My father gives me one of his massive hugs. When I was smaller, I would be enclosed by his arms, crushed, unable to breathe. But now his head comes to my chest—we are a small family you see, and I am the tall freak at 5'7"—and our greeting is less burdensome to me. I am amazed to see how old they look, and my eyes rudely mark each unfamiliar fold and crevice on their faces.

My father points to the cavernous reception area: imitation marble floors, fluorescent lights, a sign that reads "greeting hall–namaste–hello–welcome to the land of hospitality."

He says: "India is not so bad, after all, new, modern airport, impressive, isn't it? Just like San Francisco."

We load my suitcases in the car. They watch me, silently.

"So many gray hairs," my mother finally says, as we sit together in the back seat, and the car begins to move. "You must be working too hard, and no one to look after you."

I swallow, and try to deflect the conversation: "How is your school doing, Mummy? How many students do you have now?"

But my father, sensing some tension, says: "I think he is looking very good, not as dark, slim and fit. Must be clean air, good water in America."

———

"Get up, my baby boy," she says on a smoky winter morning. "Time for cleaning-up." I had been bathed the night before, to mitigate the morning bathroom rush. Still, Mother isn't about to send me out on the streets without some ritual ablution. I dive into the sheets, pulling the comforter over me. It's no use; I cannot escape her firm hands. I am pulled from beneath the covers, my face twisted and grumpy. She sits herself down on her petite, four-legged stool, and stands me up between her petticoats. My thick, unruly hair is pushed back into a rubber headband. "Like a girl," she says, laughing. Several cotton wads appear with Anne French Deep Cleansing Lotion, a precious, milk-like fluid. Each part of my face receives its mandatory attention. Forehead; cheek; nose (carefully); an almost abrasive pressure on the neck, front and back; the skin around the eyes (lightly).

"Now cream, beta, so my baby boy's face will remain fair and lovely for a long, long time." *And ten fingers with little spots of lotion appear, miniature puppets with white faces, playing a soft beat on my dry, chubby cheeks. The stuff is smoothed into my face. She beams at me, satisfied, and pinches my glistening cheeks. "Now run and catch your schoolbus," she says, "and don't get into any fights." As if. As if I would just let some grubby hands touch my perfect skin. I thought many little boys had their faces cleaned and moisturized by their mothers each morning. When I was old enough to begin sleeping over at a friend's house, I learnt that I alone was enrolled in this special skin-care program.*

————

In a discount store in New York, I am shopping for presents four hours before my departure. Salim refuses to be persuaded by my sense of urgency, carefully examining each bottle to see what the stuff inside is made of. I am walking down the aisle, grabbing plastic bottles of shampoo and conditioner without heed for brand name or price. I am clutching my mother's last letter, page after page of familiar tones, looking for the relevant instructions.

Bring something small for everyone. After all, it's been so many years since aunts and uncles have seen you. Naturally, they expect that you earn enough for at least a token gift. I get to where she finally mentions what she wants for herself. *For me, just one small thing beta (so sorry to cause trouble for you). Face cream. Not hand-and-body lotion, not intensive-care lotion. Face cream. Preferably the anti-wrinkle variety. I am sure the people in the store can point you in the right direction. Or ask one of your girlfriends!*

Salim walks up to me with a small, white box. "Daahling! How about this? Neutrogena Healthy Skin—Face Lotion—Vitamins A, C, E—Pro-Vitamin B5—Alpha Hydroxy Acid—a daily facial treatment to improve the texture and appearance of skin."

I sense the end of the rainbow. I kiss him on both cheeks: "Thank you, Salim darling. Let's get several." I pay up, we drag my bags and bundles to a taxi, and I make my Delhi flight. In the plane, I read the rest of my mother's letter.

So long since you have been home. Terrible anxiety when we don't hear from you. We are not sure what your plans are. We are very open-minded people as you know. If there is something you want to share with me alone, write to my school address. I am not the same person as your father, never pressured you to do anything, but everything has its time and place. Consider your choices carefully, and, beta, treat me as your friend.

————

In my parents' TV room, my suitcases are opened. This time I am prepared, and anything of a sensitive nature went into my carry-on bag, which is with me at all times. On a previous visit, my father, rummaging through my luggage with his customary sense of entitlement, came across a packet of condoms. He didn't say anything to me, but he said quite loudly to my brother-in-law: "You know, men in our family are very virile. But these days, with AIDS and all, sex within marriage is the best choice. I am concerned he is having uncontrolled life with those white women."

I wanted to tell him he had it all wrong, that I was just being a good scout like the brochures said, but the explanation got terribly complicated in my head so I was quiet.

The chocolates, and lotions, and cheeses are spread everywhere in the room, as if a dollar store truck had had an accident outside my parents' house, and we picked up things at random and brought them inside. My mother's eyes meander through the pile, then stop and turn away.

She says, softly: "You must have been so rushed. We are very demanding people, sorry! It's OK, I can use this other, Vaseline stuff you've brought, or even buy from here. Everything is available in India now."

I smile. From my closely held carry-on bag I take out one bottle of face lotion for my mother and one bottle of Johnny Walker for my father. And for one instant, I sense they are relieved that I am still paying attention.

———

The boys in New York are such cosmetic queens. Richard is twenty-five and worries about dark circles under his yes. Salim tells me: "Daahling, I know my skin is flawed. No one says anything, but I notice people glancing at my face when I go inside a bar. I've seen a dermatologist, but he wasn't much help. Kept harping about diet and regular sleep. Didn't even want to talk about chemical peels."

Every time I'm in New York, we find ourselves at the Clinique counter at Macy's or the MAC store in the Village. It's nice to be in a city where I can ask to see cosmetics and the counter lady doesn't say: "Present for the girlfriend?" And where the guys I meet know everything there is about cleansing, exfoliating, toning, and moisturizing. Such a relief from growing up feeling ashamed about stealing my mother's makeup.

———

My mother is sitting on her four-legged stool in front of her dressing table. There is a long mirror, which is warped along a diagonal. She says it makes her look thinner, so she never had it replaced. I'm sitting on the bed, which the dog defends as a fortress, so I must perch myself on only one buttock, at the very edge of the mattress. My heart has long since given up at trying to regulate a rhythm, as I begin the unfamiliar task of initiating a conversation with her.

"Mummy, I know you've told me many times that I never confide in you. I just wanted to tell you I don't say much because I'm afraid of your reaction.... if I share too many details of my life with you."

"Ohhh....Is there something you want to tell me? Is it about a girl? Rest assured, I am not going to shout and scream. Whatever it is, we'll talk about it like two adults. I've always told you to be open with me."

She's cleaning her face, as she does each morning, with Anne French Deep Cleansing Lotion. And I'm watching her, as always. She follows up with the face lotion I brought, and then her moisturizer (a local, Indian brand—American stuff saved for special occasions). This is not usually a seamless operation. Before she gets to foundation and lipstick, there may be several tasks to attend to: the arrival of the laundry woman, a request for money from the cook, a telephone inquiry about a new admission at the school. But today, her only distraction from managing her face in the mirror is me.

———

Delhi today is a mass of traffic and fumes and honking cars and buses. The air is so thick and dark in the evening, you can taste it, feel its weight. People rushing home on motorcycles wear white gauze masks around the nose and mouth, as if thousands of hospital workers were fleeing a sudden infectious outbreak. The *Times* of India prints a distress index every morning, and writes about plans for a new subway system that will solve "the problem," and be the envy of the third world. I hear about new car factories being built everywhere, with Japanese-style calisthenics and motivational exercises. My father points with pride to advertisements for smashing, new models: "Can you believe it, cash down, no waiting list even?"

The older women in my family say my mother's complexion was ruined by asthma drugs. I empathize so much with her on this. I'm prepared to do everything I can to help her feel she isn't powerless, or alone, in the fight against diminishing skin tone. Bringing her stuff is the smallest compensation.

———

My friend Vinay e-mailed me before I left the States.

i'm concerned about your decision...i've come to see my own coming out as a very American form of delayed adolescent rebellion...at the time, i was full of the rightness of it...i thought i had everything figured out…in hindsight, i was too young and unprepared…i should have waited…my parents….uuuhhnn….well, let's just say you know what to expect…i encourage you to find other ways to tell your folks, perhaps by being non-committal about marriage.

When Vinay was a teenager, he and his mother were best friends. In a large, demanding family, they supported each other in a way that no one else had access to. She taught him all her recipes, and they would cook, clean, and read stories together after everyone else had gone to bed.

She would say: "I must have done good karma in my previous birth. I am a blessed woman. While other boys are playing rough sports outside and teasing girls, my Vinnu is assisting me with knitting, crochet, and darning his Appa's socks. Yes, yes, I am a blessed woman."

But when Vinay told her he was gay, she broke apart.

she lay in bed…whimpering slowly…not eating or drinking for days…until I came to understand what I had done was wrong…when she spoke, she said… 'you used to be my favorite, good and gentle, but now you are mean, cruel and bad.'

————

Thankfully, my modern mother didn't whimper. She seemed mildly distracted for a few days, as if there was an equation in her head—some multi-variable conundrum from her class in school—that she needed some focussed thinking to resolve. Then one morning she simply told me that I was the most selfish person she had ever met. Her face seemed to relax a bit when she said this. I rose to protest, and she quietly dismissed me. We never discussed the subject again. I was relieved, in a sense, that any disruption seemed minor, and that she appeared to go back to her life quite seamlessly.

I went back to mine.

We communicate about once a month by telephone now, and seldom by letter. There are no more gushing appeals for closeness. I get a card on my birthday, with a Hallmark greeting like "Birthday Wishes to a Son We Can be Proud of," or a syncopated rhyme. There are few words in her own hand. I wonder sometimes if I was responsible for the fact that she didn't break down, that there were no tears, minimal drama. Perhaps I tricked her out of such recourse by pointing out that she had insisted on the importance of sharing; that the consequence of asking questions is that you sometimes get an answer. But it could be just that a casual coolness is more my mother's style.

She has, however, stopped asking me for lipsticks and face lotions. She tells me that her interest in her school project has begun to wane, and that she's come to dread attending the weddings of her friends' children. And when I visit now, she puts on her make-up in the bathroom, out of view.

———

I've become more practical now, about my own skin. I've worked hard to understand the limitations of my body, and that the exposed face is where the signs of damage will first begin to show. I've smoked my share of cigarettes, and in this way, I've evened some of the odds with my mother. As I grow older, I grow less desperate about whether people stare at my flaws in bars. I clean my face every night, though. I exfoliate, I moisturize, I put my faith in alpha-hydroxy acids. I swim regularly; I worry about what the chlorine does to my skin. I eat my fruits and vegetables; I try not to think about cancer and dying alone in an apartment in a far-off land.

I want my mother to be careful of the stuff they put in Indian cosmetics, I want to tell her about the new colors in MAC lipsticks that Salim showed me the other day, and how fabulous he looked. I'm afraid, though, that she will see my reaching out in this way as further evidence of my strangeness, rather than the way she used to see me: a nice boy, who didn't stare at girls, and loved his mother.

NATASHA SINGH

FOR ALL THE INDIAN GIRLS I'VE EVER LOVED

When a white boy is coming over, play your Indian bhajans real softly. Make sure you put out your library books on Hinduism and reincarnation all over your desk. Borrowed especially for this occasion. Ask your Ma to lend you her copy of the *Bhagavad-Gita*, even though you'll never read it. Light some candles and burn some incense. You know you'd better stock up because he'll expect atmosphere. Constantly. If he asks if the music you're playing is Ravi Shankar, nod—even though it's not. Scent your skin with jasmine or sandalwood, and comb out your hair long and loose. You know how they like that. And during dinner, when he says, I really love eating with my hands, put down your knife and fork and say, me too.

If it's Indian boy, put your books away and keep the lights on. He'll be more interested in your music collection. Play bhangra or hip hop and make sure your hair has some curl in it cuz you don't want to remind him of his mother. You'll need to have some beer around because he'll want to drink to impress you, but don't embarrass him by offering hard liquor. You know he can't hold it. Make sure to let him know that even though you're down with the music, you can still make samosas from scratch. Tell him you've been baking all morning, even though you've really ordered from the Jackson Diner. Offer him some gulab jamun and burfi, and then smile demurely when he asks you if you made them. Hide your meethai box in your neighbor's trash.

Over dinner, nod your head when white boy begins to tell you how Indians are the most spiritual people on the planet. It's the polite thing to do. When he lowers his voice, and bashfully tells you that he feels close to all Indians and most likely was one in a previous incarnation, try not to laugh. You know how defensive they can get. When he takes your hand and begins to talk repeatedly of karma and dharma, nod your head sagely and say, yes, yes. And the moment he begins to expound on his (better than yours) knowledge of South Asian studies, defer to everything he says, even though you're beginning to think he's a jackass. When you see him staring at the mehndi designs on your feet and hands, prepare yourself for the following questions: Are those tattoos? Did it hurt? And even after you explain the origins and its spiritual significance to you, get ready for his next question. Can you tattoo me too? At this point, don't even think about asking him if he's ever heard of cultural appropriation. Just tell him you'll tattoo him all right, and kick him right in the ass.

With Indian boy, talk about race politics. You know for sure that he'll be into the we are sister and brother bit. When he begins referring to all Indians as Apnas, don't get uncomfortable. He's trying to find his way. Refrain from making a face when he begins to make fun of F.O.B.s. You won't want to offend him by reminding him of who his parent's parents are. And whatever you do, don't tell him you've had sex before. You know that in spite of his progressive bit, he'll still want his Sita. So just sit still with your legs securely crossed, and let him talk about the plight of the desexualized, victimized Indian male and the snobbery of Indian women. And as his mouth turns mean and he puffs out his pecs, just nod your head sympathetically the way only Indians can, and say, Chee chee. When he tells you that he's independent, act impressed. Whatever you do, don't let on that you know his Ma still washes his underwear.

When you're with black boy, make sure to connect on issues of race and violence against men. You know that that's where it's at. If he asks you if you even identify as a person of color, don't tell him that you grew up with rocks through your windows, and your nickname was paki or nigger. In this country, you know that Asians are seen as white, so don't be angry, but don't do anything to try to prove yourself either. You don't have to. When his friends get pissed at him and tell him he should only be dating in the race, don't get your back up. You know that your community is just as full of shit. When you talk about race, make sure you don't include gender, class, or sexual orientation. This is not the time or the place. You know that if he catches on that your politics are different than his, he'll call you a sellout. Later, after you've strolled down Broadway hand in hand, keep your mouth shut when he gets bitter, and insists that all Indians are rich. Just don't ask him if he noticed who's driving the taxicabs.

If Latino boy is coming over, put on your red lipstick and matching dress. You know how he'll like that. Just don't balk when he tells you your long black hair and shapely ass makes you an honorary Latina. Blush and look as though you feel it's a compliment, even though you're beginning to have your doubts. When he tells you he loves his women smart, make sure to list all the books still sitting on your shelf, even though you've never read most of them. He'll appreciate the effort. But when you actually get into a debate, refrain from interrupting him. You know how he can't stand that.

When Indian boy comes over in a rage, and tells you that you should be dating him, tell him politely that your life is none of his business. When he starts shit about how he's better qualified than any of your other lovers, look him squarely between his legs, and tell him you doubt it. And after he has left, and the ringing in your ears has stopped, hold your head in your hands, and try not to be reminded of your father.

One night, when black boy is running his hands through your hair, and telling you all Indian women are hot, make sure not to flinch. You're sure he ain't like all the rest, so give him the benefit of the doubt. He deserves it. Even though you're beginning to think he's hooked up with someone else on the side, leave it alone. After all, he's told you he'll never hurt you. When he's pressed up against you at some club, his eyeballs all over the Indian woman beside you, tell yourself it's the last time. Ignore the shock on his face when you pull away because you know how he thinks he's the best thing you've ever had. But baby, he'll say. You're so uptight. What's got you so upset? And between your stupid tears, tell him you don't know. Because you really don't.

When Latino boy finally takes you into his neighborhood, try not to notice the way he holds you like a trophy. He just wants his boys to know you're his. When you're introduced to his friends, try to pretend you're not Indian. He doesn't want to be called a sellout either. At least just for now. Be patient. Things will change. But months later, after you've taken your lessons in Spanish, and met all of his family, try to hide your disappointment when he still doesn't know Hindi from Hindu, and Kali from Kahlua. Even when he tells you he's interested in all of you, try to believe him though he never asks you a single question. And one day after you've woken up feeling empty again, leave his place and close the door softly behind you. When he calls out *mami* from his doorstep, take a deep breath, toss back your long black hair and say, *it's woman*. And keep on walking.

———

Years from now, when you're tired and still sexually unfulfilled, call up the lesbian who moved in across the street and take a chance—you know, the one with two cats and the great Nina Simone collection. Subtly let her know you think she's cute, and suggest a date at the local café. Let her know you'll go out of your way to meet her. Wear whatever you want and don't bother trying to be something you're not. Except if she asks you if you're a lesbian. In that case, lie and say you've been around the block a few times. You know that if you tell her you've only been with men, she might get up and leave. Not everyone wants to take a chance with a het girl.

Remember to take some of your favorite books with you so you can loan them. That way, you have a reason for dropping by to pick them up later. When she actually asks you a question about yourself, try to keep the shock from creeping into the curve of your mouth. When she talks about all the things you care about, keep blinking. You don't want to make a fool of yourself by crying on the first date. While you sip from your coffee, agree with her politics—you've heard that in the lesbian community, it's the thing that matters most. Nod your head when she bemoans the fact that everybody is essentializing identity and community, race, class and gender. Tell her you think she's right. About everything. And if you're brave enough, hold her hand under the table and don't let go. This is as great as it's going to get. And you know it. You just do.

TAKE OUT: QUEER WRITING FROM ASIAN PACIFIC AMERICA

SERIES 1: LOVE IS NEVER SAFE, BUT SEX CAN BE

LOVE IS NEVER SAFE, BUT SEX CAN BE

Girl 1: I love you!

Girl 2: I love you too!

Girl 1: I know, Let's go walk our dog, Kali–Sappho.

Girls 1 & 3: Hey, she's cute!

Test Results: Love is never safe, but sex can be. Call me! 212-620-7287

DON'T LET BEING EXOTICIZED TAKE AWAY YOUR POWER

Boy 1: So, which one you fly dragons wants to take me on the Orient Express tonight?

Boys 2&3: It's exhausting to be exotic!

SERIES 1: LOVE IS NEVER SAFE, BUT SEX CAN BE

LOVE IS NEVER SAFE, BUT SEX CAN BE

Boy 1: Ali and I never use condoms.

Boy 2: Why not?

Boy 1: Because I love him and I know he's the one.

Boy 2: Isn't that what you said about your *last* boyfriend?

DRAWING ON YOUR CULTURAL PAST CAN HELP FORGE A COMMUNITY IN THE PRESENT

Girl: I can't believe that there is nothing under "lesbian" in the card catalog.

Girl: Hey!

Sakhyani Entry: **Sakhyani**–Sanskrit word for erotic bonding between women.
Yoni–Sanskrit word for female sexual organ.

Girl: Ahh!!

Illustrative woman: *Sakhiyani*. Suck *yoni* safely.

SERIES 2: WHEN YOU LOOK AT ME, WHAT DO YOU SEE?

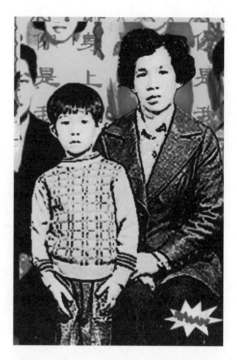

I am a femme South Asian dyke, in a world telling me that my femininity, my queerness, and my South Asian self contradict each other. I am a fearsome mind-fuck, fearsome because I make no sense to the closed. I will continue to fuck their minds and one day they will open up and come.

I was expecting the sky to fall when I came out to my mom. But it didn't. She simply said, "You've got to love yourself. I learned to love myself. You're a piece of flesh from my body. How can I not love myself? I really, really love myself." She still does.

TAKE OUT: QUEER WRITING FROM ASIAN PACIFIC AMERICA

SHARON SOOKRAM

SEARCHING FOR LOVE IN NEW PALTZ

I never thought I would fall in love with a woman. Or if I did, it would have been an Indian woman. Not a 39-year-old Jewish woman living on the Upper East Side. We met four months ago. Bjorn casually introduced us at his 28th birthday party in Montauk. His father's rich and arrogant client. I guess she thought I was from India, because her first question was "Aph ke naam?" For such a sturdy woman, she had a hauntingly soft voice. The type you would want to sing you a lullaby. Without correcting her, I replied, "Asha" and calmly returned the question in Hindi. "Lauree," she responded, in the most flirtatious voice I had ever heard. "Married girl?" she questioned and, without a warning, reached over and touched the tattooed tikka on my forehead, the one Rampeer gave me when I was nine. She had such strong, masculine fingers, but her touch was so personal and feminine that I felt it all the way to my inner thighs. In a proud voice, I replied, "No!" but didn't know whether I was responding to her question about marriage or to her touch. She smiled, and her brown eyes twinkled mockingly. Bjorn droned dimly in the background as I thought about the strange creature who so nonchalantly disrupted my serenity. With an aura of fierce awareness and macabre chaos, she was like those ancient Indian iron gods. The type you never know whether to destroy or worship. The type that can drive you to madness.

My invitation to New Paltz was extended a few weeks ago on a lazy Saturday afternoon. I was in the backyard admiring the bhaji plants Shantie Mamee smuggled from Guyana, hidden in her curlers, when Lauree called. I started to explain bhaji and daal and was on the verge of promising a home-cooked meal when she casually remarked, "Jan, my ex-partner of sorts, and I are grilling mahi-mahi and acorn squash. And I would like you to visit us in New Paltz."

Lauree called again at promptly 10:00 A.M. last Saturday morning to remind me about her invitation. I was in the shower massaging the spider veins on my thighs with the new aloe vera soap. Mementos of my $3.35 per hour cashier job in downtown Brooklyn. The answering machine took her call. It was a good thing. I didn't want her to think I was anxiously waiting. Although I was. Since Thursday afternoon. Her message— "Hi! I'll see you this evening!"—was said in such a confident New England voice that I longed to tell her I had already made plans. Even though my bag was packed since Friday night. Two shirts and my Vitamin E cream. I also contemplated her invitation. Besides, Suneeta had already warned me, "You are pursuing her too relentlessly. Challenge! That's what she needs. Not readily available coolie girls." Suneeta's cautious warning, along with all my rational declinations, faded as I promptly returned her call. She gave me directions: "Take the Adirondack Trailways at Port Authority, and I will be waiting for you at New Paltz bus terminal." I obediently followed her instructions. "And if you are late, call me," she reminded as she abruptly hung up.

She was at the terminal at exactly 9:00 P.M. I saw her from the bus window. And besides, she is very hard to miss in a crowd: tall, androgynous, athletically built with an attitude. She looked like a feminine 20-year-old male rather than a 39-year-old female. She saw me and waved frantically. Her strong arms were stretched wide, ready to embrace me, and when they did, they caressed so playfully the back of my neck that I felt uncomfortable with desire. She quickly assessed my upper torso with her right hand and confidently placed a kiss directly on my lips. I self-consciously accepted it. The college students stared in our direction and Edna, the secretary who sat next to me on the bus, was right behind my heels. We exchanged telephone numbers. She showed me photographs of her kids—Jacob and Adele—and wanted to know about mine. She was attending a family reunion. I turned around and responded to her verbal goodbye with a short wave as Lauree singled out Jan's double-parked blue convertible.

Lauree reminded me whom to expect at the house: Jan and Wendy. I nodded half-heartedly in acknowledgment. I had secretly hoped I would have her to myself. The car top was down, and the black night stared mockingly back at me. Fat and heavy mosquitoes whizzed by, defeated by the wind. She placed her broad right hand over mine. It was cold. I wanted to tell her to stop the car so I could hug her really tight and show her how much I needed to see her. But I couldn't. Instead, I rhythmically stroked her cold palm. An intense concentration masked her face. I longed to ask what she was thinking but was afraid she might give answers I did not want to know. As the cold wind created havoc with my hair, I felt so much love and primal desire and jealously and dissatisfaction. Driving along that endless stretch of road in black silence with her, I felt frustrated knowing how readily she could evoke those feelings from me. Her palm was warm by the time she pulled into the driveway.

Jan, the English ex-partner of sorts, was in front of the house. And—yes!—she looked exactly as she did in those photographs on Lauree's dining table: shoulder-length silver hair with a wide mouth and darting blue eyes. Her "how do you do?" was said in a brutal British accent, but all I thought about were her breasts and if they were still the same as in those photographs: arrogantly tilted, with the pinkest nipples I had ever seen. Before I allowed myself an answer, Wendy, a short woman with a mass of disarrayed dark curls, greeted me.

Lauree guided me upstairs to the attic while Jan hugged Wendy on the front porch. It was just as she described: comfortable chaos. Cool hardwood floors, crammed with Hebrew books and plants but without the claustrophobia. Three large black-and-white photographs of Mt. Everest separated the bookshelves. A small marble table dominated the side room, where heavy flowered English curtains were suspended from wooden rails. The ivy plants around her bookshelves were parched. Their brittle leaves were crumbling. "This is our quarter!" she exclaimed, and, as we reached the other side of the attic, she turned around and quietly took me into her arms. I could feel her tight muscles through my plaid cotton shirt. She leaned forward and stroked my right ear lobe with her lips and whispered softly how glad she was to see me. With those simple words, all my doubts about New Paltz faded. I sat in the reclining chair. She joined me, loaded down with green archive boxes, and patiently showed me gritty black-and-white photographs of Arab kids clinging to chadored women.

With her arms still around my shoulders, she guided me toward her Eye on Asia retrospective hanging on the side walls. My eyes were immediately drawn to a life-size photograph of a three-headed baby. Still in its fetal position in a big bottle of formaldehyde. She fondly referred to it as Ghidrah, her three-headed monster. Result of Agent Orange. I saw another photograph of a blind Vietnamese man staring directly into the camera. His tired, age-lined face jumped out so vividly I could almost feel his presence. Finally, against the long stretch of side wall, was a four-foot rectangular photograph of a young Vietnamese girl. Not more than ten. Standing upright and surrounded by an aura of uncertainty and abandonment in a vast forest barren from Agent Orange. She seemed to quietly sum up all the solitude and isolation Lauree talked about constantly. In a strange sense, and without the need for spoken words, I felt it too. Lauree rested her head against my shoulders and wrapped her arms tightly around my waist. I gazed into the young girl's wide, black eyes, and a feeling of security and warmth flooded me.

Jan and Wendy set the table with swirls of organic pasta and Chablis. Lauree suggested I freshen up. I did, and by the time I returned, she and Jan were already seated at the head of the table. Out of the corner of my eyes, I saw Jan stealing glances in my direction. I turned, caught her gaze, and smiled. Lauree served a generous portion of pasta into my deep bowl while she talked about the cute girl from the local bakery. The cute girl's foot size was nine. I wondered if she knew mine.

After dinner, we went to the mud porch and sat on the wooden bench. Roy, the next-door neighbor who was in love with Lauree's muscles, made it for her. Lauree lit a joint. "An organic one," she reminded me in a low, matter-of-fact voice and placed her right arm around my waist so tightly that I wanted to get up but was quietly pulled down. Jan took the first big draw and passed it around to me. I refused. "Such a good girl!" Jan scolded. Lauree retorted, "I told you so!" But somehow I didn't feel like a proper Hindu girl. Or, if that were how proper Hindu girls feel, it wasn't good. My mother would have been proud, but I felt dull and cautious. Jan took the roach in for Wendy, who was loading the dishwasher. With her right hand still clutching my waist, Lauree cushioned my head against her shoulders, and all the anxious feelings were wrenched from me. I felt a closeness only New Paltz could offer on a warm night. We sat and watched the moon as it drifted between the silver maple leaves. Jan and Wendy shouted good night. I smiled at the thought of finally having her to myself. I put my arms around her for the first time, pulled her close to me, and kissed her exposed neckline, leaving a trail of Ultima II lipstick on her white shoulders. She moaned, "Goose bumps! Your kisses are giving me goose bumps."

"That's good!" I muttered and mentally added, "At least they're doing something!" Somewhere far-off, an insect repellent buzzed. Probably killing the moths of New Paltz.

It was after midnight when I decided to shower. She handed me a green towel and cautioned, "Use the olive oil soap; it keeps your skin soft."

By the time I removed my earrings, she was already in the bathroom brushing her teeth with organic toothpaste. She has such strong, white teeth. As I examined the English bath oils on the oak cabinet, she matter-of-factly asked me to undress in front of her. Without shifting my gaze from the chamomile lotion bottle I pretended to be reading, I ignored her and pushed the clear plastic curtains aside and fussed with the hot and cold taps. "Be careful. The hot water comes suddenly," she said, and without a warning, pulled her black T-shirt over her head. She wasn't wearing a bra; she didn't need one. I instinctively looked away. But not before I noticed her taut nipples. She noted my reaction with amusement. "Shy girl," she chided, while stroking my neck with a strong forefinger. "Take your shower," she reminded me. I closed the bathroom door behind her.

As I undressed, I noticed an intricately carved silver Om hanging from a black cord on the towel rack. Shoba and I used to practice scrawling *Om* after school at Canje Mandir on Main Street. She is now married with four kids and no time for Om these days. Too busy battling the husband. The last I heard he got her from behind with a cutlass. Twenty stitches at the back of her head and four pints of blood. Just because the daal did not have enough salt. That was last Christmas day. She has a twitch on her right hand now. That could have been my fate had I stayed back. Rudy promised running water and gas burners. His wife died mysteriously last year. "Suicide," he claimed and remarried two weeks after the funeral. I hung the silver Om around my neck. It dangled between my breasts. I asked Lauree if her Indian girlfriend had given her the Om. "You're my first!" she replied without any further explanation. But I already knew from the inscription that the Om was a gift from Jan.

Over the warm water, I heard Lauree laughing on the telephone. Fire Island. That's where she wants to take me next week. "Bring a sarong if you are modest; you can always cover your lower torso," she advised. I wanted to confide about those unconscious patriarchal forefingers I still see wagging at me to cover my head and my knees and get married to that decent Hindu boy. But didn't know how. The hot water pelted my back. Shira once told me that extremely hot showers do the trick. Five years ago and three months pregnant. I used to squeeze my eyes until my face hurt while the hot water pounded my spine. I would open them flushed with hopes of seeing a bloody mass floating around the soapy suds. Nothing happened though. Eventually went to an old Chinese woman on 34th Street. $350. I cried so hard on the gurney she got scared. The green olive oil soap had a sterile smell. It didn't give a lot of soapy suds. Lauree got it in Greece. She was in Lesbos with Madeline, the one who blew kisses on her answering machine. The one who is ten years younger and broke her heart. A white T-shirt was neatly folded next to my green towel. She must have put it there during my shower. "It's my favorite," she shouted as the water trickled to a stop. I wanted to protest that it was too small but instead murmured, "Thanks." It was indeed too small. My heavy breasts hung shamelessly.

She was already in bed when I got up the stairs. From beneath the cotton blanket, she reminded me of an Enid Blyton pixie with her tousled hair, mischievous grin and dark eyes. The types that cast spells. She saw me and stood up confidently, shamelessly exposing her full nakedness while the blanket fell around her ankles. I pretended to fuss with the damp towel around my lower midriff to avoid staring, but she snatched it and pulled me close to her. Standing next to her lanky frame, I felt so safe and secure. She quietly guided me to the skylight alongside the photograph of the lone Vietnamese girl and nudged me to the foreground so I nestled in her embrace. This time we saw the moon as if it shone only for us. She told me again softly how glad she was that I visited New Paltz. At that point, I didn't care whether she meant it or not. I pulled her toward the bed, a flat king-size mattress on the floor, and hugged her tightly. I cushioned my head upon her shoulders, but she pulled me closer yet.

Roy's barking dogs woke us promptly at 7:30 A.M. Sunday morning. My eyes were red and raw from contact lens overtime. I had forgotten my saline solution. From the sunlit angle where my head rested, Ghidrah looked like an enlarged female genitalia without the pubic hair. Lauree's arms tightly wrapped my waist, her fingers cupped my breasts. I wanted to remain in that position forever, but she shifted her weight. Above the barking were sounds of chopping. "That's Jan working in the yard," she said as I propped myself on my elbows. I pretended I didn't understand and rolled closer toward her. In the morning sunlight, her nipples glowed the softest shade of pink. Almost like Jan's. I wanted to impulsively stroke them and make her forget Roy's barking dogs and Jan's chopping. But she was already half-crouched with her right hand extended to assist me.

Wendy acted as my tour guide. Lauree asked her to while she and Jan prepared to chop and stack wood for the fireplace. My tour commenced at the compost heap where acorn squash and cantaloupe saplings fought fiercely for sunlight space. I knew

Wendy wanted to ask me what was I doing in New Paltz. I saw that question burning in her eyes. Besides, I wanted to ask if New Paltz had been kind to her: Had it fulfilled its warm promises of love and security, and how did Jan's breasts feel in those dark nights? Instead, I systematically explained the art of propping up string bean vines with dried bramble. The third-world method my father used in Guyana. She talked top soil and Norwegian Evergreen; all the while, her eyes fluttered reluctantly below the brim of her beige hat in Jan's direction. I followed her gaze. Jan and Lauree were laughing. There were no signs of firewood. Even from afar, my eyes focused immediately on Jan's pink breasts in her flimsy white blouse.

Wendy took off with a wheelbarrow in Jan's direction. I opted to read in the white rope hammock Lauree had positioned between the pine and maple trees. "It's from New England," she reminded me, "Not the canvas type you have in Guyana where your ass grazes on the ground." I lay on my back and allowed myself to be rocked by the wind while I gazed idly into the distant Adirondacks. Patches of bloated clouds filtered lazily between the brown ends of the maple and weeping willow trees, brown from cicadas, the small, ugly creatures who hibernate for seventeen years. I wondered where I would be in seventeen years and sadly realized although I had known her only a few months, I already want to be her perfect wife. The one to comfort her always, feed her beets, and share deeds and bank accounts with her. My reason for visiting New Paltz never seemed clearer: I came in a desperate search for love and permanence. I came even though I knew she would never offer me those qualities. She doesn't even believe in them. Thomas is the one promising a wooden house by the stream with Prince, the white Persian cat, and Simo, the black Labrador.

Thomas is this French guy I met three years ago in my English 295 class. We used to stroke each other in the library till my crotch would get wet. He was the first white guy I met with such smooth skin. I thought I wanted him then. But that was before I met his mother, Ana. She was a radical lesbian who rendered me senseless with her charm and masculine looks. She took me to exotic queer readings in the East Village, gay bookstores at St. Mark's Place, and fed me saffroned basmati rice with almonds. She even played Beethoven's "Moonlight Sonata" for me on her big Baldwin piano. Then she decided to move back to France. At the beckoning of her lover. The one four years younger than Thomas. Ana nonchalantly told me late one night while I pretended to wait for him. I remembered crying all the way home on the F train. I also remembered how I prayed for days that her flight would crash.

Lauree joined me in the hammock. She wore a white tank top, jeans, and brown clogs. She nestled her head deep into my neck and whispered she would like to take me back to bed as she tried to unbutton my shirt. I didn't resist. Wendy pretended she was examining the tomato plants. They were six feet tall and loaded with nitrogen. Lauree massaged my exposed midriff slowly. Her fingers felt callous and masculine as my crotch got wet with unorthodox thoughts. I self-consciously pulled my shirt together as her fingers reached for the waistband of my pants. It was only when she muttered, "We have to change her!" that I realized she was talking to Jan, who stood silent nearby.

It was about 2:30 P.M. when Wendy shouted, "Lunch." I went to wash my hands. The bathroom door was opened. Lauree stood in front of the mirror, naked as she applied my Vitamin E cream around her shoulders. I instinctively wanted to close the door and confide all my primal fears to her, but resisted. I waited, half-hoping she would notice me. She didn't, and I went upstairs to change my shirt. From between the maple leaves, I saw Roy methodically mowing his back lawn. By the time I came downstairs in my new blue shirt, Lauree and Jan had positioned themselves at the head of the table. Again. This time, though, Lauree was topless. Her pink nipples glowed, but no one else seemed to notice. Jan's grilled salmon and Wendy's green salad lay next to the crisply steamed green beans my mother sent from our garden. Lauree poured two bottles of cold Guinness: one for her and one for me. Jan, in the midst of sharing a Rolling Rock with Wendy, looked over my glass and murmured how glad she was that Lauree found a Guinness girl. "Guinness girls are scarce these days," Lauree said and nodded in agreement as she beamed brightly in Jan's direction. I felt invisible.

Lauree suggested a tour of New Paltz after lunch. I sat in her car while she vigorously wiped the windshield with Windex. A collection of Victoria's Secret catalogues were strewn carelessly in the back seat. She probably saw the direction of my gaze because she immediately remarked, "Entertainment for highway traffic. I'm dying to order some of the girls." I feigned ignorance while I calmly flipped each page and carefully scrutinized the models. She poked her head through the side window and asked who my favorite was. I smiled. Jan playfully tousled Wendy's hair as they stood idly by the grill. As we pulled out, Jan waved. Lauree blew kisses in her direction.

Lauree drove through Central Avenue. "Jan and I eat here on weekends," she said, and parked in front of Rosendale Café. Our next stop was the park. The one next to the Gonks, the rock-climbing terrain where yuppies parked their Range Rovers and roamed around in Timberland sandals and J.Crew T-shirts. She took my hand. We felt like a couple. An Indian family strolled by. The old man with stern lips and thinning gray hair focused on my tattooed tikka. I could only guess his dark thoughts. She took me around the boat house, where we sat on the glacier rock and watched the sunset. Happy sounds of families picnicking echoed across the lake. As she placed both hands behind her head and reclined on the rock, the frilled edge of her black tank top shifted dangerously close to her breasts. I reached over and kissed her. My lips were cracked and dry. She placed an arm around me and smiled, her lips so close to mine I could almost taste her Guinness breath. She responded to my kiss but quietly shook off my embrace as young voices approached. And then I impulsively blurted the question: What was she looking for in our relationship? "Something casual and someone in my bed!" She responded so quickly I think she didn't even realize she had said it aloud. At that moment, I hated Suneeta for being so correct.

Lauree talked during our trip back to the house. But it was one of those distant talks where there was nothing really to say but I felt that she felt she had to say something to avoid that heavy awkward silence between us. Although my hands rested softly at the base of her neck, I sensed she was at least ten thousand mental miles away. She talked about her meat-eating days. Now she eats only macrobiotic foods, swims forty minutes daily, and takes tea with soy milk. I nodded in the dark. I doubt whether she even noticed. It was good anyway. I could not successfully relate. All I thought about were those hot Sundays after church when I would run among the coconut trees hoping to catch the heaviest white fowl. My mother would wring its neck and divide it into seven equal portions: one for each day of the week. Only with my father's permission, though. When the chickens were finished, my mother introduced us to salted shark fillets. She tried to convince us that it was flavorful. But we knew better. It was just cheap. Lauree talked about her father. Owner of a large meat-packing plant in the Bushwick section of Brooklyn. I wanted to ask if it was kosher, but too many dark images of the words "Mako shark" floated around my head. Images of me boiling those salted fillets thoroughly to wash away the slime, while the kitchen reeked. Rudy would sit patiently on the back steps. He never questioned the smell. By the time he gathered the courage to, I had already learned to make it secondary: fry crisply in garlic and fresh coconut oil. I wanted to tell her about my world. One where favors were asked and bargained daily by my mother in the Berbice market. One where we silently ate those late-night dinners without asking questions.

Lauree continued to talk about her father. Sidney Goldman. She is fond of him. I could hear it in the way her voice dipped. I thought about my father, and I was sure if I talked about him, my voice would rise uncontrollably with lots of emotions. But fondness would not be one of them. My first thought would be groceries. Lack of. His salary was budgeted the same as all my friends' fathers: one-quarter supported the family, while the remainder supported Mohabir, the guy who owned the local rum shop. Lauree talked about the dynamics of the finest cuts of meat: rib eye and shank. I thought about my mother. In New York five years already but still stretches a chicken four days. "It's America, Ma," I argue, even as I coached her to throw an extra piece of meat into the pot, "You can cook a whole onion and use a tea bag once." But she still refuses. Stretching. It is still simply a way of life for her. My father, on the other hand, has adapted quite nicely. He uses two tea bags.

He told me the other day he is now more a liability than an asset. I wanted to correct him—he was never an asset—but he was too drunk. A 45-year-old illiterate man when he married my mother, a 19-year-old deaf virgin. Arranged marriage. It's a norm. Love just comes later. Sometimes never. Five years in New York and still a helpless invalid. A sex-crazed one obsessed with a penile implant, clinging to youth by massaging his face with Pond's Cold Cream and overdosing on Vitamin C pills. Displaced yet permanently planted in a beige chair with his dazed eyes glued to the television, totally oblivious to the Spanish infomercials. His concentration on those big, busty Latina women as they fluttered around, gyrating all the right body parts while their mounds of brown breasts shook. It's been years now since my mother refused to sleep with him. Mia Mucho spun lazily around my head. The fleshy mounds of the Latina women jiggled even faster. I wished one of them would haul his face between their brown breasts and drown his heavy breathing. Forever.

It was about 10:30 P.M. when Lauree arrived home. Jan was lying on the sofa in the living room. Her blue eyes darted above her reading glasses toward my direction. "Wendy left on the 8:25 P.M. bus," she volunteered, and offered me a cup of tea. I declined. Lauree talked about her purple velvet curtains, but I continued up the stairs. "They are English," she called after me. "What isn't?" I wanted to ask, but didn't. I switched on the lamp and as I glanced at the side wall, I felt like that young Vietnamese girl: isolated and vulnerable. Between the maple leaves, I saw Roy's hazy outline shadowed by the moonlight. He sat stiffly on his back porch looking up at the stars. I am sure he too felt my loneliness. The fireflies buzzed against the skylight, tantalized by the glow of the lamp.

I was reading my Asian women's anthology when she came to bed an hour later. She turned off the lamp, lit a citronella candle and unbuttoned my shirt. I closed the book and helped her unhook my bra. She asked about my bath. I explained my ritual: five minutes of hot water on my back, five minutes of soaping, and five minutes of a cold rinse. I asked her what she was thinking. In the simplest monotone, she replied she wanted me to fuck her. I laughed, pretending she was joking although I knew she wasn't. She asked me to undress fully. I blew out the candle and removed my pants. The moonlight through the skylight lent a silver sheen to the room. I positioned myself on top of her. She grabbed my nape and pulled me even closer. "I wanted you the whole day," she whispered. But all I thought about were the purple curtains. I turned her over, parted her thighs and viciously probed for a switch, the one I could flip to make her love me the way I was starting to love her. She writhed her slender body and was about to scream when I placed a pillow over her mouth. "You wouldn't want Jan to know, would you?" I hissed. Although a part of me secretly wished Jan could hear. I wanted her so badly but just as she moaned, "Don't stop!" I withdrew my gloved hand and smiled. In the distant night, the fireflies were still buzzing against the skylight.

Jan left on the 6:30 A.M. bus that Monday morning. I heard her rattling dishes. I swore it was done purposely. Later, Lauree took me to tea at the local bakery where she flirted with the young cashier. The one with the size nine Doc Martens. The girl smiled coyly. I sipped my hot ginger tea in the white wicker chair on the front lawn while Lauree sat indoors, high up on a bar stool, long legs crossed as she faced the road with a look of casual expectancy.

The roof of my mouth was badly scorched, almost peeling, when Lauree ordered a second cup of tea and talked about her third-world parasites: *blastocystis hominis.* They dance around her lower gut. I wondered whether they felt my right hand as I caressed her ovaries last night. She contracted them in Morocco. Along with Hepatitis A and B. That's when she ate cat stew with the peasants from the montas. Dark Mohammed skinned the cat. Dark Mohammed also stole her Nike sneakers. She has an appointment with Mr. Patel next week at the new lab on Third Avenue. He wants her to shit in a petri dish. I wanted to tell her about senna pods and worm oil, but Jan had already cautioned her about those third-world Indians and worms. My mother's face drifted around my head, gently chiding, and I recalled drinking those dark senna pod dosages early Sunday mornings. I would sweeten it to a thickness to blunt the taste. By midday and with the help of fish-head soup, the worms would crawl out. Once my mother had to take a black sage stick to my brother's ass. By the time she was finished, a thick, bloodless one was coiled so comfortably around the stick that she didn't know what to do with it. She threw it, stick and all, in the backyard latrine.

We went to Andy's Nursery after tea. Lauree was taking an azalea propagation class at the Bronx Botanical Garden in her spare time. $650. My father wanted to know if it was U.S. dollars and said, "White people are too serious. All we did was add cow shit, and the plants were climbing to the sky." She got two azaleas for Jan. Afterwards, we went shopping at the local farm for fresh vegetables. She stroked the top button of my shirt and asked what would I like for dinner. I was about to say, "You!" when her cellular phone rang. It was Jan. For the third time that hour. She left me standing without realizing she was due an answer and sat on the bumper of her 1995 Volvo. I pretended I didn't mind. Although I did. Out of the corner of my eyes, I saw her looking and swung my ass even more vigorously.

I asked the blond girl with the denim overalls behind the counter about the white corn. She explained the chemistry of sucrose. "Good for the crop if the days are hot, and the nights are cold. They are sweeter than yellow corn," she insisted. "But then again, you don't need sweet corn. You are sweet enough." With that corny remark, I caught myself giggling a few decibels louder than usual. Before I knew it, Lauree stood behind me, slowly massaging my nape. A grin was planted on her tomboyish face. She was agitated. She didn't have to say anything. I just knew by the way she erratically shifted her feet and grabbed my hand. Her strong fingers easily overpowered mine. Her fingers, by this time, had started to twitch.

Back at home, Lauree raced into the shower. "Look around; keep yourself occupied," she encouraged. I did as I prepared dinner: orzo, fish, and vegetables topped with cilantro. Her mother stared non-judgmentally from a black-and-white photograph high up on the bookshelf. I looked away guiltily. It's another era, I wanted to say. One where I am free to fuck whom I want to—even if it meant her daughter. Lauree sang a Janis Joplin tune in the shower, trying to raise her voice above the water. She wasn't successful. I used to sing Janis Joplin's songs when I first came to New York. But, then again, I did a lot of crazy things when I first came to New York. My first taste of freedom from family, taboos, and customs. My chance to become an American as defined by those outdated *Rolling Stone* magazines Ann, my pen pal from Wisconsin, sent. Drugs, sex, and rock and roll. I fulfilled those requirements at a reggae concert featuring that funky Jamaican group from England. I forgot the name of the lead singer, though. And, besides, I doubt whether he remembers mine.

But the craziest thing I ever did in America was kiss a woman. That's another story altogether. I had gone with Caroline, my cousin, to a gay bar on Avenue C. Neither of us was gay—or at least, at that time. Looking back, my closest encounter was with the woman who ran our local drugstore. She was always referred to as "he" by my mother. I was intrigued by the way she flattened her breasts and bossed around the truck drivers. Anyway, Caroline left to get us drinks. I sat and as I looked up, I gazed into the most intense eyes I have ever seen. She asked if I wanted to dance; I said no. Caroline said I should. I did. It was a fast song but she held me close. Then she kissed me. Right there on the dance floor while we swayed to Prince's "Purple Rain." And I just knew I would never be the same contented person who came searching for the New York accent and the white husband.

Of course, my family doesn't know. Or if they do, they are pretending to be ignorant. They all closed their eyes last June when Roxanne visited. We went to high school together. I saw her last winter after eight years, when I visited Canada. Before leaving, she kissed me full on my lips and called even before my plane touched down at LaGuardia. It didn't work out, though. She wanted kids. She got married in May to a Chinese man who has his own grocery business. My mother is still clinging to the notion there will be a double wedding next year. My sister is getting married in July. I have a year to find a rich, Hindu dulahah. Shouldn't be a problem. I am an American citizen now. Lot of dulahahs are out there waiting for green cards.

Green card? That's another story. Got mine the capitalistic way: $2,000 U.S. and my virginity. My father warned me when he got the news from Aunt Vera that she found a nice "white" boy for me. The telegram came early one Saturday morning advising us to clean the house and keep the chickens and ducks in their coops. It also cautioned, "He might be interested in a real marriage if Asha behaves herself." He arrived on the afternoon of Dera's flight. I was still dressed in my black pants and toweline top. My ass never looked so good. Or at least that's what he told me later. We weren't expecting him until the weekend, but he couldn't wait to see the woman who was going to be his wife. At least on paper.

My father's insistence on impressing the "white" boy was no surprise; images of blond Harlequin heroes danced in my head. Instead, the "white" boy turned out to be a Puerto Rican from Valentine Avenue in the Bronx. Short and dark, with a crooked nose perched over a well-trimmed mustache, and a body so muscular it was apparent he considered physical exercise a full-time job. His name was Tony Rosado. His Aunt Milagros was fucking Tom Mamoo's son, Dewan, a 26-year-old illegal alien pumping gas somewhere out in Queens.

Tony looked and smelled so foreign with his lime cologne, well-pressed shirts and corduroy pants. I later learned they were bought with Uncle Jago's Visa card. Additional incentives for him to appreciate me. "Talk Spanish," my father encouraged. My grandmother nodded. She warned, "Too shy, and he will think you don't like him. Americans are different." "Como esta usted?" I muttered obediently. My mother had a questioning look on her face as she tried to read my lips. My father smiled in accomplishment. I knew what he was thinking. Years of selling chickens and eggs and cleaning chicken shit from the pens those early mornings to send me to that new high school in New Amsterdam were finally paying off. The Puerto Rican smiled. "Tu!" he said, "Tu! I am going to be your husband." He seemed so forward. He even took my hand in front of my parents and kissed my inner palm. I swore I felt his tongue.

My grandmother talked about the time she lived in New York: "Chicken: $.22 per pound. Too much to eat. And on Sundays, those rich white people throw out good stuff. New chairs and tables right there in the street." Without pausing, she reminisced about that cold winter afternoon she and Aunt Jankie found their green sofa. My mother gasped uncomprehendingly. She was already planning mental menus. My father shook his head, "What about rice?" Tony proudly replied, "$2.99 for ten pounds, and you don't even have to wash it." I knew my father was thinking about those early morning lines at the local co-op and his one-gallon allotment. Tony looked at me. I felt his lustful gaze. Glancing sideways out of the corner of my eyes confirmed it. He was busy scrutinizing my exposed shoulders in such a blatant manner I wanted to run inside and chaddor myself.

Lauree asked about dinner. "In fifteen minutes," I promised and remembered the time my mother invited Tony for dinner. He was late. The curry got cold, and the daal puri got hard. When he arrived, he boldly announced he had chicken in the ruff at Lim

Kang's Café with Rupan. My mother said it was OK, but in her eyes, it was not. He sat stolidly in the red leather chair. The one my grandfather made before he died. A growth in his stomach killed him. He was like a swollen plum in the coffin. My sister and brother counted stars on the verandah while my mother packed away her elaborate dishes. The ones Pastor Bone, the English missionary, gave her. My father drank the Banks Beers he bought for Tony. Then the lights went out. Without any warning. The house plunged into total darkness, save for some thin strands of moonlight that slithered through the jalousie windows. I scrambled for the candles. The $100 ones the hagglers got from Venezuela. Tony complained. These things don't happen in New York. Blackouts, however, were a way of life for us.

Tony filed my green card application a week after Uncle Jago wired $2,000 U.S. It was at Palm Court in Georgetown where he raped me. The next day, as we waited at the American Embassy, he insisted I sit on his lap. Masquerading terms of affection were necessary. Had to show those smart, white consulates we were in love. I felt the hard curve of his cock as his hands circled my rib cage and rested below my breasts. I knew he could feel my heart beat. My mother, seated opposite, pretended she was reading the newspapers, although I knew she was illiterate. He whispered in my ears about New York, "Fast life! People do this all the time. On trains and buses and in dark street corners. Get accustomed to it."

Lauree's rendition of Janis Joplin was reduced to a mere hum as she joined me in the living room. I could feel the warmth from her bath. She kissed my bare back as I laid the table. Over dinner, she talked about Schiller the Killer. He took her to Belgium, but she left him for Morocco. It was the summer of that year she consciously realized she was a lesbian. Women turned her on; men no longer did. She was three months pregnant with The Killer's child. Me? I started Multilateral School that year. Rudy, my stuttering neighbor, was in love with me. We met secretly after my father left for his night job at Taharally, the rich lawyer on Coburg Street. Back then, I never thought I would have to travel to New Paltz for love and permanence. I thought I found those two elements in my backyard.

Lauree guided me to bed after dinner. I removed her red Chinese robe and watched as the green hue of the candle light flickered over her face. Her lips found mine, but somehow I couldn't feel a closeness. I felt her fingers inside me, violently and chaotically probing until the latex gloves turned pink. I felt sore between my thighs, and a heavy feeling settled in the pit of my stomach. It was the same feeling when Dera left Guyana. As Lauree positioned her head on my shoulders, I looked at the alarm clock: 1:10 A.M. I asked her to come on top of me. I didn't have to ask twice.

Without any warning, warm tears started to trickle across the bridge of my nose. I tried to wipe them before they dripped on her white English blanket but couldn't. I closed my eyes and smiled. I knew my eyes were bloodshot. They always get bloodshot when I cry. My tears flowed faster, and my breath got shorter. She tried to conform her warm frame to the curve of my back, but I quickly escaped to the bathroom. I sat on the acrylic seat while the hot water flowed at full force. She asked if I was OK. "Yes!" I replied as I gazed at myself in the mirror. My face was flushed, and my neck felt hot. I thought wildly about the summer I was 16. Rudy had spitefully promised I would never find love after I rebuffed him for Dera.

I washed my face and thought about Dera. It was the summer of 1982 when she graduated from University of Guyana and went to Bartica with Arlene, her cousin. Then I received an unexpected letter from her. Unexpected because she is the older sister of my best friend, Shamie. Dera and I would exchange books occasionally. Once she lent me *Children of Kaywana*. It was a good thing my mother is illiterate because reading it aroused so much mature desire that I masturbated violently on every page while thinking about her.

During college, she lived with Brenda, an Amerindian girl, on Croal Street. But we always saw each other every summer when she returned home. We played cricket together: I was the fast bowler; she was the wicket keeper. We made such a good team even the boys wanted us on their side. She taught me how to swim in Berbice River where we recklessly raced all the village boys. She won every race. In the cool evenings, we took showers together in the makeshift zinc bathroom next to the pond. We took turns scrubbing each other's back with the rough nenwah.

I saw her during Easter vacations. One year she made a big kite for me. It was the first time anyone made a kite for me. We went to the nearby savannah, the one next to the cemetery with all those old British names. She tied it around my waist and laughed as I swayed in abandonment. At the end of the day, though, while everyone was reeling in their kites, she cut the string, and mine flew away. It got tangled among the coconut branches. You can't box a good thing, she told me afterward, and promised to make another. She did the following year. A bigger and brighter one, and again she let it go.

When she came home after graduation, she couldn't believe how tall I had grown. But to me, she was still Shamie's older sister. The one who taught me how to fold makeshift sanitary napkins from old rags when my mother couldn't afford to buy those belted types. Then her letter from Bartica arrived. It didn't even ask how I was doing but rather, told me she missed me. We wrote back and forth, and by my tenth letter, I realized I couldn't wait to see her. I told her, and two days later, a blue car pulled up in King Street. It was an early morning when I heard my name. And there she was on the verandah, bags around her ankles.

Lauree knocked on the bathroom door. "I'm OK!" I insisted, and continued my mental trip. Dera is the tallest girl I know: a confident six-foot frame that intimidated many easily. She had straight black hair, neatly parted in the middle of her forehead. We fell into a routine relationship. She visited me during the hot days and taught me how to cook daal and roti. In the afternoons, we picnicked behind the power plant where I lazily rested against her flat bosom. I slept in her bed at nights with my mother's blessing. The simple pleasures she taught me are still so fresh in my mind. All those hot nights she lazily brushed mosquitoes off my bare back, slowly kissed my neck and stroked my dark nipples while her parents slept in the adjoining room. Then they found Ramesh, an Indian lawyer obsessed with the *Kama Sutra*. He is, according to Aunt Indra, a proper Hindu man: doesn't drink or smoke and was not ashamed to sing Bajans at those week-long jags. Dera is now in England. "Family keeping me busy," was all she said the last time I spoke to her.

My breathing subsided into a regular rhythm as Lauree welcomed me back to bed and quickly pulled me toward her. She hugged me tightly from behind. Just the way she knew I like it. I knew she was sobbing from the short rhapsodic breaths she took in between pauses. Dark thoughts twisted around my head as I turned toward her. The wrinkled corners of her eyes were wet and soggy. She made no effort to hide herself. For a flickering moment, her eyes unveiled such heavy vulnerability I wanted to pull her close to my breasts and lull her to sleep.

Without asking any questions, I wiped her warm tears. I looked into her eyes; I knew mine were still bloodshot but I no longer cared. I thought about Suneeta. It was too late for her lethargic warnings anyway. No one wants readily available coolie girls. Above my shoulders, Lauree's jaws chattered. I cradled her and gently massaged them. She looked so peaceful and joyous as a semi-conscious smile spread lazily across her face. Her fingers reached for my left breast. "So soft!" she muttered dreamily as they circled my brown nipple. Her chatter halted, and a peaceful sleep enveloped her.

As the gray light of dawn flickered over my angular nakedness, I pulled her closer to me, conforming her contours to mine until we were no longer divisible. I scrutinized her face for signs of consciousness only to be confronted by relaxation and liberation. Damn her! How could she be so immune to the world's sleeping sickness! How dare she withdraw into a fetal balloon when there were others, like me, awake, mentally pacing and waiting. She stirred; her sweet, dry breath in my face like a flimsy curtain in the afternoon breeze. I wanted to shake her back to consciousness. I wanted her to dip her magical wand into my bottomless well and drown every pain I had ever felt. I violently positioned my face between her breasts, secretly hoping she would notice me, hoping she would wrap her hands around my nape and tell me she would never leave me. But she continued to sleep. The birds were already up singing on the maple tree. Their songs sounded so hollow in the early morning silence.

ANDREW SPIELDENNER
GEORGIA RED DIRT

Looking back, I realize my logic may have been flawed. I met him while he was involved so I figured he had to be faithful, stable. I had decided it was time to have something to call love. I chose him.

"On a scale of 1 to 10, he's a 12," were his first words at me. He said the words the way he looked; thick, short, evenly shaded. Like he would be there after the dust settled and the bills came due.

He seemed less confident than I.

I was most struck by his combinations. Short and well-muscled. A baby face and a fade tall enough to be out of style and show his age. A smile that stretched up to high cheekbones, eyes that stayed even, revealing little. Friendly and tongue-tied with awkward cuteness, the hair and fashion just a touch tacky; it made me think of low-key evenings, laughing at *The Simpsons* on syndication.

Eddie has the body of a worked-out short man, each muscle finely shaped and proud. The first time I saw his lover I decided the relationship was false, shallow, easy to break. Why would a body-beautiful black man choose a ratty, thin white guy? And an ugly white guy at that, one searching for a black man, any black man, to fill him for whatever reasons—guilt, ownership, shame, hate, street credibility, an interest in hip-hop or African culture or jazz, a need to feel the rhythm or blues, love? Eddie's lover dealt drugs and lived under the tyranny of Mother. They fought, Eddie and his lover, throwing fists and screaming into the morning. They lied to each other. They got drunk together and over each other. I saw all this and thought it would be simple to break.

Our first date, Eddie walked me to my car and we sat down in the front seat. To talk.

"I didn't think we'd ever be alone."

"That makes two of us," he spoke with a subtle accent, one you have to concentrate to figure out.

Our fingers touched, our hands the same size.

"This has been some trip. It's very different down here away from cities." I imagined I sounded worldly and big-hearted.

"I'm glad you came. I been wondering if you'd ever manage the trip." His grip tightened. "You're very pretty."

I flashed a quick smile, stared directly into his eyes. "Thanks. You're fine yourself." I let his other hand find the back of my neck and pull me into his face. The kiss was tentative and thin, even clumsy. Eventually, I came to recognize this method—all from men familiar with accommodating white men's lips. Then I simply tried to ride through it, groping at his chest, letting him discover how easy it was to push past baggy jeans and explore my smooth ass. I squirmed against his hands and tickled his neck. My fingers brushed his hard stomach.

"Wait. The backseat is better," I said this plainly, as an order. We climbed over the front seats, caressing as much as we could. In the back, we faced each other without the stick shift obstructing us. Before he could move, I lunged forward, pushing him back, mouthing his crotch through his jeans. He throbbed. I undid the buttons with some assistance. They were tighter than I expected. I sucked and licked. He shoved and pushed. He grabbed my ass, held it as I tried to hold him inside my mouth. I made my lips tighter, carefully keeping teeth away. My fingers ringed around his base. I slurped. He groaned.

He came faster than I expected. He bucked against my face, trying to pull out. I held on, swallowing, sucking madly. He moaned as if a weight had been released. We looked at each other. I grinned, wiped my face with a cloth. I was erect and still horny. We had to get back to the club and his boyfriend.

Eddie and I had three more weekends over the course of two months. In one unremarkable petty squabble, I paused before abruptly announcing my love. Without missing a beat, he responded in kind, with all the quick pride of a beaming new father. Our sex was constant, thirsty, with a hint of aggression and lots of tenderness. It kept us together longer than it should have. That tenderness was a blanket against empty nights. The hint of aggression was, perhaps, more honest between us.

My apartment at the time looked just like a trailer home. A ground-floor pad, it had horrid cream and brown paneling for walls, an old beat-down mud carpet; three bedrooms for $750 a month. That place was big to me even though friends have since joked otherwise. It was my first real bedroom and I remember it fondly. I have since returned to that apartment. I never see how dumpy it is. I gave Eddie a key, complicating my affairs.

I never liked ground-floor apartments: hearing complete strangers or neighbors chat and stroll nearby like any one of them could reach through the window and become intimately involved with little effort and no approval from me. There should be some distance between my bed and its myriad events, and outside.

The night Eddie broke off his other relationship, it was raining—a long, even winter rain. He appeared without calling. I was making spaghetti, my trademark experimental homemade sauce simmering on the stove. Eddie was dripping. He had on a drab olive army zip jacket, a black T-shirt and blue jeans which cupped his ass. When I opened the door, he stepped through and carried me to my bedroom. The door closed somehow. The sauce burned. After, we spoke.

"I moved into the barracks today," he began slowly.

"You left him?" I responded, perhaps too eagerly, "It's over? I mean really?"

"Of course. You're my baby. You know I only stayed this long to straighten out everything." He grinned again.

At 20, I was lost, convinced this was love.

I threw away the sauce. We ended up running to Wendy's for dinner and staying in until he went to work early Monday.

His white lover stopped calling eventually. For the first few years, we got weeks of sporadic hang-ups. Always I knew, could almost smell his beer breath through the receiver. When I thought about that wretched and wrecked, man for too long, I had a hard time touching Eddie. Their bodies still remembered each other.

————

Our first trip back to Georgia disrupted my understanding of what Eddie and I shared. I had thought we were similar: American, ethnic, and gay. How could I know, never having seen this land? We were to meet his younger sister, his closest relative. As our plane landed, he gazed out the window and in a hushed tone uttered, "Georgia red dirt." I asked a question with my eyes but his profile remained silent. I became jealous.

His sister met us at the gate. She saw Eddie first. I recognized her by the way her face lit up. It made her gorgeous, showed off her gold earrings and bracelet, set off the blue dress that billowed from her thin boyish frame. Her hair was trapped beneath a large white hat. She had barely a hint of some reddish-gold lipstick, and her eyes were surprisingly large, far larger than Eddie's, and round. Her skin was freckled and almost brown. She reminded me of late spring and the promise of summer.

Then she saw me and only for an instant did her face shut; Eddie ran to her, smile matching hers, and lifted her. She loosed a laugh that struck the air and hung there, happy. They whispered in each other's ears before turning my way.

"This is..." Eddie began.

"I know who this is, Eddie," she cut him off, "from your letters I have a pretty good idea of who your...friend is."

She paused slightly, only long enough for me to catch it. Then she grinned, politely at first, then it opened up and she added, as if just realizing, "Thank you for bringing my brother home. He's been so very far away."

Eddie, helpless between us, missed or overlooked the messages.

————

The weekend passed pleasantly. I stayed out of the way as much as I could, trying to be small. Eddie and his sister were radiant together, especially in everyday acts. In the kitchen, they were a marvel, anticipating the other's needs and movements. They laughed when they bumped into each other; loud, clear bells of human relief. I tried to entertain myself in the living room or the guest room I didn't share with Eddie. His sister had been precise in her house rules. Eddie slept on the couch or in her bed with her, but never with me. I could hear them whispering late into the night.

Eddie's sister lived twenty minutes from Atlanta and in a different world. There was a porch, an entryway, a living room, her bedroom, her eight-year old son's room, a guest room, three bathrooms, a back yard, and a massive kitchen and pantry. It was an old house, left to her by a crazy aunt whom no one else bothered with. There was breakfast and coffee each morning, sandwich and salad stuffs ready in the refrigerator for lunch, and a full dinner each evening. She did everything without a trace of effort, smiling at her son and Eddie constantly, more rigid when facing me. She was resplendent as the master of her home. It was hard to endure her distaste.

I read for most of Friday and Saturday, tried to prepare work reports when books bored me. I did not take the car nor venture out without Eddie. We chose to stay out of Atlanta proper for this trip. Gay life was the same in any city and the family time was more important. By Saturday, I was a little frustrated. I met some of the neighbors on a walk that afternoon. At the end of the creeping day, all I wanted was a cocktail surrounded by boys looking at other boys, to roll my eyes at the queen in the corner loudly reprimanding every man passing her up. Gay life may be the same all over, but sometimes it's the only life I want.

On Sunday, Eddie took his nephew out without us. They had chosen to do some male bonding movie-and-a-pizza afternoon, leaving his sister and me alone. She fixed an impressive lunch for the two of us. We ate lunch on the porch—sweet raspberry iced tea and thick-sliced tender roast beef on whole wheat with honey mustard, crisp lettuce, tomatoes, a little salt and pepper and Miracle Whip. Baked salt and vinegar potato chips and fruit salad rounded out the meal. We ate slowly, gazing at the cars gliding by, enjoying the sun and still air from shaded porch chairs. Occasionally, children biked by or neighbors walking their dogs shouted a greeting.

"I hope you're enjoying this little part of the world," she began.

"Oh, definitely. I haven't seen Eddie this happy in awhile."

"I haven't seen Eddie in years..." she murmured, then said louder, "I can tell he's happy. I was asking about you."

"Well, this is a lot more pleasant than other places I've lived. I mean, it's nice here. Not that I was expecting anything else. People smile a lot and seem to like you. Your home is wonderful and so is your son. You've really made this trip fulfilling."

"I appreciate the politeness, but please don't bother hiding your boredom. It 's just you and me."

I paused and stared. I had the distinct impression of wandering into a trap.

"I'm not bored," I began, and she looked away. "Not really anyway. It takes some time to get used to the pace, that's all."

She turned back to me and smiled, "If you were at home, what would you and Eddie have done this weekend?"

I took a moment, looked enviously at a group of six pre-teens strutting past on the street. Desperate, I clung to the fantasy she and I were family. "I'm not sure. Maybe we would have gone to a movie, or over to a friend's place. Sundays, we go to a show at the neighborhood bar."

"What kind of show is that?"

I winced. "Well, it's a—drag show. I have lots of friends in it. I mean, a lot of the people I grew up with perform now."

"A—drag show. Where men dress up like women?"

"Yes. But that's not the whole show. Folks lip-sync and act out to favorite songs, and the audience gives a dollar if they like the performer."

"A dollar if they like the performer," she mimicked. "We have shows like that down here. We call it indecent."

"I call it a living myself. I never said they stripped or performed sexual acts. Those are other bars I haven't been to, in a couple years at least. This is just a neighbor-hood bar where the folks come to hang out from whatever part of the world they live."

Silence settled. She picked at crumbs on her plate. I closed my eyes and listened to the day. Birds sang through the sudden welcome gusts. There was no traffic, no sirens, no screaming. Hearing a conversation five blocks away seemed possible. The quiet and the sun almost lulled the crackle of conflict. I wondered how we appeared to the side-walk, like two friends, an odd married couple, or, worse yet, landlord and tenant? I tried to say softly, "You know, I have learned something over the years; it really does take all kinds, no matter where you are."

"That's nice. I've learned some things too, and none of them account for your relation to my brother."

We glared at each other before turning to the street. I carefully sipped the iced tea, now slightly sour. I thought about Eddie, how painful this was for me and, probably, for her. I sighed heavily.

"It's not your brother's relation to me that's the problem. I can't imagine you minding that he loves someone and someone loves him. I know too much about your family..."

"You don't anything about our family!"

"I know too much about your family to believe you would begrudge anyone love. Eddie is the older brother and remembers more than you. He does love me and I do love him. No, the real problem is you can't account for your relationship with Eddie. My relationship with him has very little to do with that."

After a long, murderous moment, she smiled. She really smiled at me, if only in surprise.

"Eddie must love you," she began, "and even my son likes you. Even he doesn't understand your part in his uncle's life." I glowed. "But I don't like you." My heart plummeted. "I knew what you would be like before you arrived. I am overjoyed at Eddie's visit. Why did you have to accompany him?"

Another long pause. A car rode by and honked. She smiled and waved. The corners of her mouth were too tight at the edges, but only I could make it out. I stared at her, shocked and slightly happy she had finally told me the truth. She was someone everyone liked and she desired nothing more than my complete removal from her world. I could handle that.

Fuming, I attempted to be calm. "That doesn't change your relationship with Eddie. Tell me, when did you know he liked men?"

Her eyes widened, and she blushed. She took a gulp of her tea, the ice having long melted away.

"No one told me. No one had to. I knew when we were teenagers. Eddie was involved with this girl, a stupid plain girl I couldn't stand. She was thin and her only appealing mark was her shade—a bronze tone that shone brightly in the summer. Her name was Martha or Maggie. She was nothing to me. I thought Eddie was worth so much more than this girl. Our mother doted on her future daughter. Eddie and the girl planned on getting married. I thought the girl was with Eddie to be with our mother. The girl was devoted to my mother. They both loved baking pies and gabbing about every little sin they imagined people were doing. I couldn't get far enough away from that horrible cackling. I was the only one who realized Eddie couldn't love her."

I made a motion as if to ask a question and thought better of it. I reached for a handful of chips and munched. While she was talking, she revealed her teeth and it seemed the more honest she was, the more teeth showed. I tried not to appreciate her white, straight teeth peering out from between her lips.

"Eddie had this habit of going for an evening walk after dinner. Rain or shine, hot or cold. When he was gone, Mama and this girl started up. They always wanted me to join them, but I was more interested in books. They would warn me books never did any favors to girls but I didn't pay attention. I was fascinated by books, especially ones with maps and charts. I could think about the people there. That was where life was for me. Being locked in the house with those two and their gossip about small towns and small ways drove me crazy. One evening, I followed Eddie. They never noticed.

"Eddie wandered for about half a mile. He seemed aimless. Then he started hiking through the woods. I had to be careful so he wouldn't hear. I didn't need to worry. He was in such a rush, he didn't notice when I stepped on a branch. Eventually, I don't know how long, he made it to a large tree in a small clearing. I almost called out to him to warn him someone was there. I didn't think he saw. But the person turned into Eddie and they stood there, closer than I had seen two men stand. Then I saw the other boy's face. The moon reflected off his features, the shock of blonde hair and the smudge of freckles on his face. It was the son of the grocery store owner. I had seen him all my life and never looked at him till that night. I could barely breathe. My mouth wouldn't work. I watched in silence."

I had been told about Eddie's first boyfriend of course, but not from an outsider's view. I knew the kid was troubled, had problems with the law and school. That the kid's contempt for others had landed the kid, and Eddie, in a number of fist fights over two years. I wanted to tell her all this but she hadn't asked. I knew she didn't want anymore of this experience than she already had. She absentmindedly crunched on some chips and sipped her tea.

"I hated that boy. He wasn't friendly to any of us. His father was cruel and cold. Still, everybody had to buy from him. He offered credit. The kid threw rotten vegetables at small animals and little children. The kid enjoyed following younger girls on the trails. He called me 'bitch' three times before I was fifteen. He was a rotten boy and my brother ran to meet him every night.

"I started to have dreams about Eddie with white skin on him, white skin coating him, white skin choking him. I couldn't tell Eddie why I woke up shaking, calling his name. He would sit next to my bed for the rest of the night, until I fell back to sleep. He was my truest friend and he was gone. We were separated by that kid," she looked my in the eyes, "You remind me of him." Another pause. "Don't get up. Please."

She stopped suddenly. It took me a full minute to realize she was finished. She took the dishes inside, leaving me alone. I wondered if she was coming back. Her story twirled in my head. I certainly didn't identify with that kid. I could see she was stronger than that kid and that moment. While she didn't approve of Eddie's lovers, she had figured out how to keep Eddie in her heart regardless. And because she had, she was able to have me in her home, able to resent my presence and keep it solely between us. I sat mulling about her comparison. The heat had cooled some, and more people were out. They looked at me strangely. She returned with a fresh pitcher of iced tea, spared a "hello" for the neighbors and laughed softly.

"What am I going to tell the neighbors about you?"

"Excuse me?"

"At least if you were black, I could just say you're Eddie's friend. Even if you were white, I could say the two of you work together. But since they have to ask exactly how you got that skin and hair, I have to explain it. They probably won't even know if you speak English. And no one will believe something as frail as you is a regular guy. Oh well, the neighborhood had to go sometime."

My nostrils flared before I could stop them. I grit my teeth. "Is that what you meant when you said I remind you of Eddie's first boyfriend? I'm white to you?"

She smiled again. I was fairly sure I should be afraid, but I was tired and she had made it clear she would never be my sister.

"Did Eddie ever tell you about the only one of his—friends I met? No? I can't understand why..." I refilled both our glasses and tasted my own. The sweetened chilled raspberry accentuated the mid-afternoon perfectly and I had to grin. She looked at me oddly.

"I went to visit Eddie about six years ago. He was still in Kentucky then. I was nervous about Eddie. We hadn't seen each other since I gave birth and then it was all hospitals. We didn't spend much time together. I wanted this time to be different. We were adults and I thought we could regain our closeness. That's what I told him before I flew up to see him.

"At least Mitchell wasn't at the airport with Eddie. We had lunch at a small restaurant and it was almost like we were kids again. The woman at the counter knew Eddie and went out of her way to make sure we had large portions of everything. Eddie cheerfully dug into his fried chicken, picking the bones apart first before chewing each piece. He got that goofy grin of his, the one where you know for sure he's sitting on top of the world."

"Yeah," I agreed, the memory warming me.

She paused and stared at me as if for the first time. "I should have known whatever idea was making him so happy was more than lunch with his sister.

"We went to his apartment, a nice sized one-bedroom. I could tell immediately someone else lived there too. The shoes and jackets in the closet were bigger than Eddie's. More importantly, the place didn't smell like Eddie, it was some combination I never grew up with. Oh, meeting Mitchell was a treat.

"He entered with dinner. Mitchell's arrival broke through our conversations detouring around the one large bed. Yes, Mitchell may have released us from the secret, but then he spoke.

"Mitchell's voice was like crumbling plaster, rotten with water and insects. He commented on Eddie and my complexion awkwardly, made racial jokes often and laughed at them with a wheezy, forced, cough-like noise. He became angry if Eddie didn't at least smile. Mitchell was an accountant and he cooked wonderfully exotic dishes.

He had a goatee, dressed smartly and had a college degree. He drank wine and enjoyed shoving his knowledge on anyone."

Her bile raged in her elegant manner. I was taken aback. There were men in Eddie's life neither she nor I liked. I was afraid to be them for her. She didn't understand: I hated them too. I refused to be them for Eddie.

"He never asked me a question and waited for the answer. I never met a man so convinced of his own importance. That was a long weekend. Eddie and I never spoke of it again, not even when he called to tell me Mitchell was gone.

"Later, I thanked Jesus." She drank her tea.

"Oh," I muttered. "I figured Mitchell was an asshole. You should have seen the last guy he was with. Ugh. One of those white boys who want, need, and dream to be black." I shuddered.

We rolled our eyes at the exact same time. We paused. And began laughing, hard and full. The afternoon sun started setting, orange-burnt on the edges. We looked at each other in the softening light, calmly sipping tea.

I jumped into the quiet, and asked, "What happened to all your books anyway?"

She turned away, put down her glass, returned to her previous position.

"Like I said, books showed me other places I had never seen. I even thought up ways to get there, what to bring, people I'd keep in contact with. Those were wild days and nights, no matter how small my mother's gossip or my job. I had plans.

"Pregnancy changed all that. As my son grew inside me, I knew this too was the world. I created life and both of us formed a new branch to an old tree. I read. This world, tiny as it is, is still full of wonder."

She smiled sheepishly. "You know, no one has ever asked me about my books."

We sat there, till the sun set and went down and Eddie returned with her son, radiating their own day.

———

Eddie and I stayed together for two more years, five total. His sister and I never became closer than that first visit. I moved across the country for a new job; Eddie had started wandering again. He found someone younger, a white kid, more vibrant, less concerned with careers. I still send Christmas cards, but don't call.

In my new job, I travel one week a month. Atlanta is one of my assignments. Each time, I am still surprised on the plane.

I am returning to the land, on my way back to Georgia, but I am not—him.

OSCAR E. SUN

THE HORRIBLE OTHER

9:30 P.M., I walk through the chipped piss-yellow painted door of the Asian dance club where I strip down for the green. The stairway down to the viewing floor, which looks out on the dance floor and the go-go stage, is mirrored. I glance at my eyes, which are dry from the cold wind against my contact lenses.

The stairs themselves are brown tiled and matted with dirt from the soles of patrons who think they might have a shot at my ancient Chinese secret. Turning the corner at the bottom of the stairwell and toward the bar, Lester, the white manager, is stretching his hefty pink pachyderm leg on the bar. Fortunately, he still has his shoes on. Smile, kiss, kiss on the cheek.

"Hello!" Lester says, looking straight into my face. "You have such gorgeous eyes!" he says for the umpteenth time, followed by, "Have I told you that before?"

Smile. Eyes roll.

"And you have a fabulous smile!" he continues, grinning.

Smile, kiss, kiss on each cheek of Frank, the sweet middle-aged bartender who is also white, and Edgar, the habitually unshaven and adorably short Latino assistant manager, gets a peck on the lips and a hug.

"You're the first one here, you're the first to dance," Lester informs me. Thank goodness—the earlier I dance, the earlier I get out, but for now I must schmooze and charm for dollars.

Most of the regulars are already sitting at the bar. Most of them are fat, old, white men with glasses, receding hairlines, and waists two and a half times the size of mine. They are immediately in spirit when the go-go dancers arrive. One particular fan of mine is a skinny, not-too-old white guy who greets me with an early evening semi-drunken smile and "Hi!"

Unlike the other patrons, this one is actually interested in what I have to say. So I tell him about my "genteel poverty" status, hoping he'd get the hint that I need more paper. He nods as if his tipsy head were attached to the rest of his body with a chain link. No matter, at least he wants to listen, even if the conversations are consistently filled with my financial loathings. Most of the time, the random and mostly white patrons whom I chat with cut me off mid-sentence and stare at my lips. Fuckin' exoticizer, I think to myself. Or, like most "dialogues" begun by these men, they ask through their coffee-stained teeth, "So where are you from?" What happened to "What's your name?"

"Manhattan," I say evasively, anticipating the next question, "No, that's not what

I mean…where are you *from* from…?"

"Somewhere between French Indochina and the Dutch East Indies…"

A look of confusion.

"I'm Chinese."

More confusion. How I enjoy it. Fuckin' fetishizer.

In some idiotic attempt to save face, they begin telling me of all their travels to Asia and their admiration for Asian cultures. I give them one of my "sure-I'm-paying-attention-to-whatever-you-are-saying" nods which they interpret as being impressed; meanwhile, I imagine them in Bangkok, buying sexual favors in the red light district from a boy named "Antonio." I should get paid extra to listen to this shit. Do I care that you paid only 1,000 baht to plow some kid you only consider a tight sphincter with slanty eyes? No!

"You know, you Chinese are so smart. You invented gunpowder, kites, printing…" No kiddin'—and the historians give all the credit to some European thousands of years later. Oh yeah, we invented water torture too, did you forget? "…so intelligent, so beautiful!"

"Thanks…"

And then the ultimate compliment: "You have such good English!"

"Well, I've lived in the States most of my…."

"You're really cute." He cuts me off. Great! Thanks for listening, dick-neck.

Tonight though, the gods of good taste are with me, and no one has started one of these exchanges with me. Usually, to escape such an encounter, when a substantially long pause (5 seconds) surfaces, I excuse myself and walk into the staff room behind the black "curtain" on the opposite side of the bar. I plop down on a stained Chinese restaurant chair and open my book bag, which contains queer theory texts, for a respite.

Lucky me, the citizens of the gay white geriatric ward don't have the gonads to approach me on this chilly night, and in this nipple-erecting cold room. I flee untouched.

———

Rory, a tall, muscular, pale skim milk-skinned ballerina, treads in for his after-hours dancing. I don't understand why he ever dances here because he doesn't get tipped well because a) he's white, b) he dates the ugly stick, and c) he's a bad go-go dancer. Now, I'm sure he's a graceful prima ballerina in the morning and afternoon, but on the go-go stage, the boy has no moves. Rory throws his backpack on the table, announcing his presence, but I keep my face in my book. He sits down in the chair directly in front of me and asks mid-paragraph, "What are you reading about this time?" while gazing at the half-naked man lying on the cover.

I lift my eyes and say, "public sex," deadpan à la Christina Ricci as Wednesday from *The Addams Family*.

A deformed smile seeps through his face. "Really? What about it?"

"Well…about how public sex and public spaces have been important historically in the formation of queer…." I've lost him. What he really wanted to hear was "cream in my G-string" stories about public sex. Oh well, I said queer theory, not gay porn.

Rory walks out of the staff room to get a drink and just before the black dividing curtain settles, Edgar peeps his head through and half-asks, half-announces, "Five minutes, OK?"

"Aiight," I say, coupled with a yawn. It's time to change outfits.

————

For the first set of dancing, I usually wear red go-go shorts, a tight white tank top, black velcro-side pants, and a midnight blue G-string underneath it all. Understand that it's all about the strip tease. You shouldn't just come out to the stage already down to your skivvies, otherwise you leave no room to make 'em want it. Make 'em want to touch, for to touch is to tip. My rule is the entire first song with clothes on and occasional lifting of the shirt to expose the abs. Midway through the second song, the shirt is off and I'm running my hands all over my sweaty pecs and torso. The key is seduction and gyration. Every time I close my eyes, run my hands through my hair, and part my lips with the slow drag of my finger means another dollar.

The regulars are in their normal positions. Fred, a "big-boned" fellow, jiggles his way down from the viewing floor, his small table next to the stage. My skinny number one fan, fittingly named Marvin, turns around on the upstairs barstool and leans over the balcony to see me land on stage and slowly begin my strip tease. Every week, without failure, Marvin descends down the stairs toward the stage and stuffs two dollars down the front of my shorts within the first two minutes of my dancing. Oh reliable Marvin!

Most of the new white patrons oscillate between watching me and chatting with their friends, except for two surprisingly young white fellows who cascade down the stairs closest to the stage to sit on some bar stools in the corner. The sandy blond-headed one who wears construction worker gear immediately begins sipping his Budweiser and whispering to his bland-looking, dirty blond friend. Eyeing the dollar bills "Sandy" folds into his right jean pocket, I dance toward the corner of the stage closest to them and swivel my hips in ways that would scandalize even Ricky Martin fans. I capture "Sandy's" stare, and he watches me like a TV addict. Hoping a little more exposure will inspire him to give me a Lincoln, I collect my articles of procreation with my left hand, pull down my go-go shorts to my knees with my right, and gyrate a little more. Instead of his pockets, he reaches down to his crotch with his right hand and begins stroking his erection down the side of his denim leg, while his friend sits semi-attentively across the high table. I've gone too far to gain the appropriate and desired monetary reward, but I have to admit that being the masturbatory fantasy of a semi-attractive man is a bit exciting. Noticing myself getting hard, I turn around and dance so everyone can view my ass and I can hide my wood. Antidote: if I had to see one of the old horrible others jerk the chicken while I danced, I think I'd wretch. My dick settles down.

It's strange to be worshiped as a masturbatory aide. One snow-haired grandpa (Father Time) says to me every week between sets, "I want to take you home for a private dance. Do you do private dancing? You're heaven…you know that, right?"

Smile. OK…why!?! I wonder if he would have said these same words a few years ago when I was 35 points heavier, hardly the lean, smooth body he desires. Even so, reverence is better than this greasy-rat-eyed-bespectacled-blue polyester pant-wearin' dinosaur with a moustache who waddled up to me once, stuffed two dollars in my shorts, shoved his finger in my left armpit, scratched me, lubed his finger with my sweat and then said, "Thank you," as he licked his finger, turned around, and walked away. Was that homage or what? OK, certainly the weirdest thing to happen to me while dancing, but if he enjoys it, forks over the bills, and respects my limits, then it's fine by me.

It truly must be my lucky night because for the second time ever, I was tipped by an Asian man. And not just any kind of Asian man, but a young Asian man. I generally don't like dancing in front of the younger Asians. They watch with a critical eye—so snide, so bitchy. As if they could do better! Most nights, however, the Asian viewers watch and enjoy, but never tip. Cheap bitches. I hate it when someone watches and drools but doesn't dish out the dough. These men don't seem to understand that there is an economic exchange that is supposed to occur. As one visually consumes my body, he must pay. If one isn't going to participate in the economic exchange, don't watch. If I am going to expose up to 97% of this body to help get granddaddies' rocks off, then there better be a bunch of Georgies in my panties. The logic and math are plain and simple, and you don't even need an abacus to figure it out.

It's even weirder when the other dancers watch me. I can never tell if their own slanty eyes watch with criticism, jealously, or desire. But then there are the white roses twisted out of drink napkins, which one particular dancer throws on stage while I dance. A sweetie, truly. Too bad he doesn't realize that white symbolizes death to the Chinese. "You want me to die!" my Grandma once shouted at me in her "extra-caustic-with-battery-acid-on-top" Cantonese, when I lit a white candle in her presence. I smile at the memory. White roses…I don't think he wants me to die. Smile. He smiles from the top balcony. I wink at him. Smile. He smiles. The horrible others smile, and with that, money in the bank, or rather, to the credit card company.

My first set is done and I scramble back barefoot (I always dance barefoot) into the dusty staff room. 1, 2, 3, 4…10…Ooo! a Lincoln…15, 16, 17, 18…20…another Lincoln…28…35 dollars. 35 dollars in tips alone. Not too bad. In fact, it's pretty good. I straighten out the sweaty bills and stuff them in my wallet. I change into a white cotton-lycra 2Xist jockstrap, a pair of red lace-front football shorts, fleece sweat pants and black tank top. I walk out of the staff room and head to the bar for a bottle of water. I then lean over the edge of the viewing balcony and watch Rory show off his non-moves. The third dancer, the white rose maker, chats with a customer I've never seen before…he too is older than The Big Bang, but he wears his money in his Armani suit. I glance over, but old man is far too focused on dancer three. No room for me to schmooze. Resigned, I return to the dust den and open my book. Chapter 8, "Self Size and Observable Sex" by Stephen O. Murray.

———

The third dancer, Pedro, hurriedly breezes in and says in a fake, helium-inhaled, ultra-femme voice, "Shit! I have two minutes before I'm on!" Quickly, he rummages through his bag and pulls out a bright blue thong. Turning his back to me, he unbuttons his Levi's and pulls them down to his knees where he stops to kick off his black boots. "Argh!" he moans, his asscheeks clenching together in frustration. Pedro finally gets his thong on and wraps around his waist a sarong. Another angry gasp and he begins putting on his boots.

"Thank you Rory…next on the stage is Pedro!" Edgar announces on the microphone. And with that, Pedro runs out with one boot tied as I say, "Good luck!"

Rory trudges in and drops his four dollars on the table. "Ack! Tough crowd tonight," he whines. I feel sorry for him, but at least he'll get the sad base salary that bare-ly makes the night worthwhile.

"Yeah, tough night…" I say.

"Thank you Pedro…and returning to the stage, we have Oscar!" Edgar chimes.

The music is almost the same as in the first set I danced to. In what is supposed to be continuous go-go sounds, Edgar always forgets to play the next CD or replays the discs. Often, during the middle of a set, the music ends and the regulars shout, "Edgar! The music!" while I break out in mock ballet with a smile and a laugh. No interruptions tonight, but I do get another round of Cher, Amber, Pet Shop Boys and Enrique Iglesias remixes. Of course, the patrons don't mind, they just wanna see the go-go boys dance, so I dance, a bit annoyed by the repetitive beats.

Soon my petty annoyances give way to yet another old man—a newcomer—this time in a beige trenchcoat. He sits where "Sandy" and his Budweiser were and grins meekly. Detecting his timidity, I flash a smile at him and wink. I press the right button; he reaches into his trenchcoat pocket and pulls out some bills that he folds in quarters. Shyly, he walks over to me and extremely cautiously pulls the waist of my undies, making sure not to touch me, and hesitantly drops in a twenty with another unidentifiable president folded inside. "Thank you," I whisper. He blushes and turns back to his original perch.

This rest of the set goes on unnoticed as I ponder who is beneath the trenchcoat guy's Andrew Jackson. It's my biggest tip yet and discovering its full value is like opening up leihsih during Chinese New Year. When Rory comes back on, I rush offstage to count my tips.

Thirty dollars. Trenchcoat guy tipped me thirty dollars. And with the other tips, I made $62! Excited, I change my clothes for my final set, cram $55 in my wallet, go to the bar and order from Frank a gin and tonic with lime juice, breaking my rule of no alcohol while working. Noticing my energy, Frank asks, "What's with you?"

I lean over the bar and whisper, "Some guy downstairs tipped me $30!"

"Nice!" Frank affirms and pats my hand. He's so sweet, I tip him even though the drink's free. I decide to watch Rory and see if he's making anything. Pity gets the best of me so I march downstairs toward the stage while rolling three dollars into a skinny roll.

Gliding to the stage, I cock my neck out to Rory, and, taking the cue, he gets on his knees in front of me to bob for the money with his mouth. After dodging his first three attempts at the green cigarette, Rory grabs my head between his hands and successfully snatches the money. I laugh as he gets up and shoves his ass in my ass, giving me the opportunity to spank him in front of everyone. As I walk back up the stairs to the staff room, Rory dances with a red hand imprint on his ass.

Once I sit back down on the nasty Chinese restaurant chair, I open my book back up, only to close it again, for I can no longer concentrate. Instead, I leaf through the latest *Next* and *HX* magazines, spotting a couple of familiar faces in the local "paparazzi" photo spreads. Again, Pedro sails in and changes frantically for his next set.

Amidst his disrobing, I ask, "How's the night been for you?"

"Not bad."

"I don't know if he's still there, but there's a guy in a beige trenchcoat downstairs who tipped me 30. If you work it for him, maybe he'll drop some coins your way too."

"Really?"

"Yeah!"

"Thanks!"

That's right! You gotta help your Asian bruthas and sistas out!

"Thanks!" says Rory, entering the room as Pedro runs out.

"No problem."

———

Set three begins with different music. Yay! The crowd is pretty thin but trenchcoat guy, Fred, and a sprinkle of other regulars stick around. Old tricks for old customers, and the tips trickle in. $2, $1, $1, $2, $2…and this time around, $10 from trenchcoat guy. I make $28—a fair share considering it's 1:30A.M. on a weeknight. I think I've milked the horrible others as much as I can within the limits of the law and the club. With the prospect of heading home, I count my earnings in record time. $125 in tips alone! Pretty good for only one hour and a half of actual dancing. Sloppily put on my jeans, wrap my red scarf around my neck, and don my black pea coat.

"See ya Pedro…are you working next week?" I say between long squinty blinks. My contact lenses are dry and have tinted my eyes pink from irritation.

"I don't think so."

"Then I'll see ya later!" Kiss, kiss.

At the bar, I say to Frank, "Pay me baby!" and he opens the register to distribute my base salary of $50. "Thank you, Frank baby!" Kiss, kiss.

Napping with his head down on the bar, I come up behind Edgar and tweak his nipples to wake him. "Bye Edgar!" Kiss, kiss.

From the top, I blow a kiss to Rory and wink. He waves back and continues his "dancing."

Now finally ascending the exit staircase, I think about the $175 in my wallet. Maybe, with the right price, the horrible others aren't so horrible.

SEG SUN

A DELICATE MATTER

The men were holding meetings in bar taverns; some were sporting bright colors instead of the usual dark solids. Books were being read and talked about. One book, *The Cowboy From Down Under,* and another, *The Fabulous Fables of Paris,* were explored in these literary circles. One wife reported that her husband had asked her if she found him overweight, and when she playfully teased in return that he was quite pudgy around the middle, he began emitting tears.

The secret meetings continued nevertheless. It broke up marriages. Wives were complaining their husbands were never home, were no longer intimate. The men questioned themselves. They began recognizing others who were like them just by eye contact. They began recognizing themselves as "drolyags." Their first literary society fathered dozens of other clubs, which scattered and began communication with one another. These groups comprised young and old "drolyags." One day, as they conjoined into their circles and shared historical scandal, one asked if anyone had ever noticed the subtle delicacy of members of the regime—the judge was like a flower, being attended to by his gardener, the corporal. The young drolyags began questioning their deans and seniors of that historical scandal.

———

Everybody in West End knew who Truman was. He was the little "battering ram" of the Kittyhawks; not for his sportsmanship but for what he had done to Clancy. It was about five in the afternoon after the great soccer game that was played at Wendels Arena. On this day, Truman had tackled Clancy for no apparent reason at all. It was in the second half of the game when the Kittyhawks duped the Wildfires on one side of the field, while on the other, Truman laid on top of Clancy and remained there for 66 seconds. They had first noticed each other a few months ago at the eight o'clock service. Truman, at his thirteenth Ash Wednesday, was sitting beside his older brother, Thurber, and his younger sister, Kelsey. He noticed Clancy sitting with his older sister in the third row from the front. When Clancy turned around, their eyes locked tight as if they were thread and hem. Clancy could feel the needle of those eyes plunging in and out of him. It was a revelation. Clancy was a Wildfire; a wildfire that Truman was trying to snuff out—right there on the field.

When Clancy and his family were invited for roast barley and salad toss, Truman would sit at the table, mean-spirited and sulky, while Clancy looked bright and whole-some as he bit into his ricotta quiche. Both Clancy and Truman would play secretly the staring game. Eventually, Truman would retreat and march right up to his room and lock the door. He would listen to them speak about Clancy. He would listen to them laugh at him. This reminded Truman when Kelsey caught him doing the "carpet rub." Kelsey, in a swinish matter, swished her curly tail down the stairs and reverberated to his mother that he was at it again. Truman's old routines. It wasn't much later when his father found out and threatened to whip him with a gooseberry vine the next time he was caught with his pants down. And then there were the kidney-exploding horselaughs from his rel-atives. His aunt told him to soak it in cold water after he does it in order to keep it "small." Truman would never forget how self-conscious he became afterward. He, absolutely, would not allow Clancy to be the biggest pomp circus of West End. Truman was, after all, the leader of the Kittyhawks. When the Clancies had left, he took his rose-colored sham, his mother of a pincushion, and attacked it with his closed fists and mouthed Clancy's name, every breath bursting in a pink lint haze.

Three days before the game, Truman caught Clancy looking at him flexing his orbs on his biceps. Truman glared straight at Clancy like a pussy at his mouse. Clancy turned away feverishly when Truman addressed him as "little peninsula," out into the middle of Ms. Prime's postulates and theorems. He was immediately reprimanded. She would knight him her "cavalryman" and have him pack up the art supplies the other chil-dren had waited for in earnest. In the middle of social studies, when the children were making tipi models, Clancy walked past Truman and his forces of nature, and called him "quisling." Truman rushed Clancy against the supply cabinet. It was the biggest hair-pulling event of Attenburrough's Boys Middle School. With Truman ramming Clancy against the wooden supply cabinet and Clancy moaning like a waning daisy…

It was five in the afternoon at the soccer game when the attendees witnessed the tempest on the other side of the field. The paperboys pointing their fingers. Truman's father grunted, stood up and positioned his backhand to smack a heckler. Truman's moth-er sobbed in her hands. Thurber, inattentively, cheered the goalie that caught the soccer ball. Truman laid over Clancy, their eyes locked on each other. The Clancies scouted to the outfield and grabbed Truman off their son, frazzled and worn. Truman's father leapt over three benches at a thunderous pace, charged after Mr. Clancy and shoved him. Truman's father called Clancy "little Clancy." He exclaimed through a bullhorn that the Clancies lost his trust in deceiving his Truman pride. Mr. Clancy shoved back as if he had been henpecked. His distance from Truman's father was no more than the thickness of a pin, yelling that imminently, Truman's conduct would distress the supreme order of society. Some went sssshhh, and another did the same as if they heard the stampeding of the brigade. The crowd became maddening. They joined in the fury. They ordered for the punishment of drolyags. They broke bottles over crowns of anyone who they thought were drolyags on the field. Mothers shoved one another in retaliation. The Wildfires were hosed. Others were trampled. The young boys pulled off Clancy's shorts. Some shoved balloons under their shirts and paraded around as women. Hideous names were being thrown. Fists were being sent. Breasts were being pinched.

It was ordered by the judge that Truman and Clancy be arrested and that they would be executed publicly without a trial, for it was declared "no tolerance for drolyags." Truman was sent to the guillotine and Clancy was hung. The men of West End hid their books between their mattresses and took jobs in construction.

One nightfall, in an old wooden shed behind the West End Chapel, a secretive act shared between two men was so turbulent that it caused an uproar in the prime minister's kingdom. When the prime minister heard this, he called the male population of West End for an interrogation. Citizens were shaken out of their sleep. Some were dragged out of bed with their wives screaming. The soldiers forged through the tenements, arresting the men, young and old, and forcing them onto the hummers. Those arrested were imprisoned in the dungeons. Confused, they awaited to be called on by the prime minister. In the master conference room, the prime minister, the corporal and the judge, and all his associates gathered around a veteran mariner. While the prime minister sat upon his throne, the judge admitted to the mariner that two drolyags were seen together in an obscene activity in the wooden shed behind the chapel. Because it was dark, the two drolyags' identities were concealed. The mariner denied that he was one of the drolyags. He added that he was not a drolyag himself anyway. They were watching his movements, gestures and the manner that he spoke. He did not move, gestured nor spoke like a drolyag.

The veteran mariner was released. They watched him walk across the room, seeing if he had any hitch to his walk. They saw that he had no swinging motion of the hips and concluded that he was not a drolyag definitely. The next called upon was a barber. The judge and the corporal would begin their tactics once again while the prime minister and his associates watched. The prime minister, baffled, did not know that these tactics existed. He had entrusted the province of West End to the authorities of the judge and the corporal. He saw them in his vision. A vision of a society where a drolyag did not exist, nor his ideas. They did not conform to the ideology of true humanity. The barber was asked to his whereabouts on the night when two drolyags were observed—their silhouettes barely distinguishable. The judge decided to cunningly scare him. If he emitted a high ecstatic voice, then he was, indeed, a drolyag. But when the corporal fired his pistol, the barber merely shuttered at the sound. And neither did he use words such as "exquisite" or "radiant" or "blazed" in his speech. It seemed he was not a drolyag.

The interrogation continued until every man that was held captive was observed. Their efforts were unfruitful. The people of West End waited for the prime minister's message. It was delivered by the judge and the corporal. The judge reminded the people that drolyags or anyone acting in the manner of a drolyag would be sentenced to death, for the Creator has made only two separate beings, man and woman, and each is to fulfill their role as the church has fulfilled its mission in delivering that message to them. The corporal shot his pistol into the open air and warned the people of West End that the sentence for nonconformity was either by hanging or beheading. The former was to expel the "demon" and the latter to liberate the "demon" from the body. And the men of West End swore this very plausible.

But even as the corporal slept soundly at nights, no one was able to subdue the flames of passion that plagued the main chapel's quadrangle. In order for the judge to sneak back from the wooden shed, he needed to step over the wild dogs that were guarding the foot of the door. He would have to step over quietly, letting only his foot descend slowly and his toes touch softly with the fringes of the rug that was deported from India and was spun with the finest silk thread in all of the Himalayas. Any sudden sliding motions upon the surface of the cloth would wake the wolves disruptively to hunger. He placed one foot over and then the next, quietly setting one foot in front of another. He was thinking of the young private and how much their meeting this evening had invigorated him. To reach the front gate of the hotel he was residing in, he had to walk through the gardens of Hathaway where the prime minister's officials would interrogate those who trespass the curfew. This was a system based on the assumption that drolyags began all their festivities at dusk, and they preferred to converge in one particular public meeting place to settle their businesses with clients. The judge began to organize his appearance as he made his way across the bridge that passed over the running stream. In the opposite direction, two officials approached him with their rifles cocked and perched about them. One began a general conversation with him, passing amicably by him while the other stood in front of him. They asked him about the weather, the messages from overseas and the drolyags. The judge was preoccupied and anxiously replied with quick one-worded answers. He hoped that they had suspected nothing of him.

The two inquired of him if he had enjoyed his bass fishing or bison hunting or broad stroll. The judge self-consciously answered directly and forcefully that he was merely observing Orion and how the star points of his broad shoulders converge into the shaft of his arrow. The judge was content with himself and his eyes fell before those in front of him. An intensity sparked between him and the young official. The judge was aflame; the young soldier roused. The young soldier widened his eyes, broke the familiarity and acted up with urgency. He called to his superior and tried to repeat what he had wanted to confide to him. That the judge was one of them. The other official became alarmed with the young official's jolting nervousness that with a swift maneuver, the rifle was lowered and pointed directly at the judge.

The sudden shift was met by the judge's reciprocated motion in which he grappled the young soldier by the arms, and with his own supreme weight and size, flung him over his superior. The young soldier was, surprisingly, a delicate matter, like a dandelion. The judge fled off the bridge, not looking back behind him. He heard the rifle fired once or twice, sending overhead, rampant wild geese. The mulberry bushes were so thick and lengthy that his moonlit path was no longer bearably identifiable. He flopped and fumbled before he relentlessly gathered his preoccupations. The judge was confused and frantic. The path to the hotel could no longer be distinguished between private and industrial. The two soldiers armed with fiery torches, wild dogs, rallying horsemen galloping over water—these were the noises that echoed not too far off.

The judge was striving to find sunlight. He saw that the windows of the tenements were open. He saw the men in their boxers, holding up their crying infants and their wives, tireless over the hot stove. He apparently was in the lower side of West End. Walking along the sidewalks, he could see the fuming smoke stacks of the factories. He tasted the burned ashes in the air. The carbon sulfur of the charcoals condensing until he felt faintness. It was humid and he leaned against the brick structured tenements to ease his painful joints, his old pipes, but the walls radiated so much heat that he had to continue with his search for a hiding place.

He continued walking down the street. He did not hear the noises of his pursuers. Perhaps, the wild dogs lost his scent, or that it was too shadowy to search the gardens of Hathaway, or that they had been detained with the execution of other drolyags. The judge sighed, lessen his pace and continued walking. It was a foul-smelling place. He noticed a person walking up the street. When he passed, the judge did not look directly at him. He, instead, lowered his head to watch the pace of his feet. He had left his slippers in the wooden shed in order to pass quietly over the wild dogs. He had hoped that the young private had been more trusting. He had hoped that they would have woken up together. Two other men passed him by and he almost caught their glance when he strained to look downwards once again. His motions daunted; his neck strained. It was as if he was walking along the streets with a wooden crucifix over his shoulders.

He was afraid to look at them staring at him, pointing at him as he passed under the windows left askew; women turning up the blinds; men parting their curtains. He wondered which ones were drolyags. He would give the order to execute them all. He was infuriated with the cobblestones-his feet was flapping against them like they were flyswatters, drawing more attention to his disheveled appearance. Then he heard the galloping of horses and the barking of dogs, which stiffened him. The glowing torches reflected in his eyes; his orbs broadened; his mouth agape. One pointed at him and then another. Another urgently signaled the horsemen and another followed and then another. Each acted with urgency that there was a drolyag present; they wanted a conviction. And when he looked around to see their faces, he recognized the same intensity that had drew himself to the young private; a vulnerability, a purity that emanated like angelic cherubs, as if he was standing in a garden of Greek statues of stone; their physicality immaculate; a delicate matter. These were the drolyags. These were the epitome of the supreme spirit of evil; the diaboloses pointing at him, confirming his identity.

As the horsemen engaged with their nets; the crowd pushes forward; their incessant demands roughen the fire of the torches; the gas chambers billow smoke from its smoke stacks; the charred taste of human flesh in the air; the judge runs into a narrow court-yard between two tenement buildings. He thought it a great barrack; he thought to utilize the staircase but it was too narrow; he thought to utilize the fire escape but it was too flimsy. He barricaded the door with broken furniture; useless boxes and bales—there he remained in the damp and foul-smelling place. And he remembered when he had prepared Echinacea tea and Shanti rug for his meeting with the young private; their arms brushed against each other. And when the young private took off his shoes, rolled up his pant legs and sat cross-legged exposing his thighs and feet, the judge turned away from beauty and remained in the safe reflections of the windowpanes. And when the young private reached for the cup he was holding and felt his course backhands with his delicate fingers—and then he shuttered away with a look of fever and putrid. He fingered the judge in contempt; smashed the hot kettle upon the crown of the judge. The judge could only speculate that he was caught unconscious; the young drolyag leaving his dogs to guard him; and running exhaustedly back to the estate to find his superior.

And all this surpassed of his memory while flaming torches were thrown through the open windows. Some had to be bombarded first with bricks, shattering the glass while the judge ran in and out of the rooms ostracizing those jeopardizing his integrity. He was not a drolyag. He was not a drolyag. And that was all he could claim. And when the curtains caught fire; and old books were smoldering; the judge proclaimed in his defense that the whole system was designed for them. And when the heat consumed the tenements and reached the airshaft in between, the men, women, and children of West End entered the prime minister's kingdom, in which the women violated the corporal's resting quarters and hacked apart all that was valuable. And the men, both young and old, took fast and furiously the prime minister, outdoors; in the open; in his own courtyard.

CRAIG TAKEUCHI

THE BREATH AND THE BODY

I: *Forms*

I set the table for two now instead of three. One for myself and one for Amelia. Her set-ting is so tiny. A tiny bowl, a tiny spoon, a tiny cup. All the right size for her tiny fingers to pick up and hold. Everything about her is miniature. Even her fists, the ones she makes when I ask her to sit at the breakfast table.

"*Ou est mon papa?*" she asks. She says this many times to send me on a wild goose chase, to make me think of different ways to explain his absence when actually she does know where he is. She knows that Stephane's gone away on tour with his dance troupe. She intentionally forgets why he isn't here. She wants to irritate me, to frustrate me and to make me the powerless one. Simply because she can. And it's fun. She does this because there are so many big things in her life, big things that don't accommodate her smallness, and this is the only way she can make the rest of the world smaller than her.

———

She is a miniature Stephane.

She inhabits so little of the space her father does, but she does her best to claim it like he does.

"Zoubidou, zoubida, pouliboum, pla pla pla," she sings around the breakfast table, and refuses to sit down. She jumps and dances around the house like every day is one perpetual festival.

Just like Stephane. Empty space is irresistible to Stephane. He has an arsenal of movements he uses to dominate the spaces of this house. With his ballet repertoire, his flirtatious tap dances, his improvisational t'ai chi moves ("Horny Monkey Tickles His Aloof Lover"), he always tries to insert himself into the spaces of my life I try to keep him out of.

He would slink into my den on feather feet while I sat at the computer.

"*Mon petit boum boum,*" he would say, wrapping his arms around my stiff shoul-ders. "*Joue avec moi*…please, come play, Aki." His lips would press into my hair and he would breathe me in. The warmth of his touch would be tempting. But years of self-imposed isolation taught me how to block out all distractions. Even him. And so effort-lessly too. I concentrated my fingers on guiding the mouse across the architectural floor plans on the computer screen, thinking about imaginary walls, and lighting, and where the client thought structural supports would suit the building best.

"I'm not a good babysitter," I said to him.

His arms withdrew. "Un jour," he said. "One day and night with her will not be killing you. Or her. And who has cares if Madeleine will finds out? *Mon Dieu!*"

"I have a lot to work to do," I told him. Which prompted a blast of hot air from his nostrils on my neck.

"Ah merde, I give up. Tell me something I don't already know, mon petit patate." He hoisted himself up onto an empty shelf and sat there, sullenly, like an addition to my collection of ornaments. He took a decorative fan out of its stand and twirled it in his hands. "Eh *bien*, tell me something about yourself why this is so? Why you feel this? You tell me not very much, *non*? Keep it all inside yourself. Greedy boy."

I let the mouse reply to him, clickety-click, clickety-click. The keyboard went tickety-tap. The computer hiccupped a beep.

"What bore you are, eh?" he would frown and assume his Japanese warrior stance, feet abreast, his hands in fists at his sides. "Hai, so desho, ne!"

He would leave and there would only be the moist sound of bare feet running down the hall. A pause, and then a sudden inhale. The soft whip of his arms against the air, a footstep, a ballet leap through the doorway, into the kitchen, the screech of a bare-foot twisting on the hardwood floor, a pirouette. Another breath, the whip of air again, his body through the air in a silent arc, the spongy impact of feet landing upon the hard-wood floor, and then the final exhale.

"Aki-kun," he would say in a sing-song voice. "Come play with me…"

But I would not allow him to enter the space of my thoughts. Because I was greedy.

II: *Functions*

His presence infiltrated every room when he moved here after leaving (as he told it) Amelia's mother, Madeleine. Or after Madeleine took control of her life and kicked him out (as she put it) when she found out about Stephane and me. The divorce process was messy enough but short-lived. Both had had enough and there was no need to draw it out.

When the shock and hurt passed, Madeleine took pity on Stephane. Perhaps she still loved him. She still doesn't acknowledge me, though. She only offers me a thin smile when she comes to drop off Amelia on weekends.

This is the first time Stephane is on tour with his dance troupe at the same time Madeleine is away attending a conference. To Stephane's surprise, when he told her a female friend of his would babysit her in his absence, Amelia asked for me. And she threw a tantrum for two days until he gave in to her request.

Yes, she is such a miniature Stephane in so many ways.

III: *The Rest of the Body*

Small things.

Her blue toothbrush.

A coral pink plastic bracelet.

Three beige pebbles she collected from the lane.

She leaves these objects throughout the house, tiny reminders to me that she's still here, drawing my attention to the small places I overlook—the unused corner of a stair, the wooden rungs of a screen. I used to collect these objects from their hiding places and put them back into her room. But the next morning, they would magically reappear in the same places, making my efforts pointless.

She enters the kitchen on busy feet, moving dutifully, with purpose, across the kitchen floor, shuffle-shuffle-shuffle.

"*Bon matin, Mademoiselle* Amelia."

Her mouth remains sealed, her eyes focused on the table with determination.

"*Ohaiyo gozaimasu,*" I repeat.

She seats herself without responding.

"Good morning."

She rejects me trilingually and drives a spoon around on the table as if it were a toy car. She makes little roaring noises and screeches as the spoon car races around the peanut butter jar and the butter container.

"Which would you like—cereal or toast?"

She acknowledges me with a lift of the chin, her lips pursed, her eyes peering over her nose tipped horizontally at me.

"*Le céréale ou le toast?*" I ask.

She stops the spoon car's mad dash to meditate on this question. She scrunches her face. "A zing boum boum!" she squeals, and resumes her spoon car action scene. I make up her mind for her and put two pieces of bread in the toaster.

"*Voila.*" She presses her thumb into the buttered toast I've placed before her. She pulls it out, examines the crumbs stuck to it. She's not happy because it's not her father doing these things for her but she tolerates me because she enjoys being insolent toward me. She relishes in the idea that I'm not her real authority figure and she can do whatever she wants to me. Wickedness is brewing in her little mind.

She starts singing: "... and in the morning, morning, morning, we dance, dance, dance, to the tune, tune, tune of the big ol' BA-NA-NA— "

Shocked, I grab her shoulder and stop her and glare at her. Her eyes widen with terror. Where did she learn that song? Stephane made that song up, it was the morning song he used to wake me up with. A song for me. It was supposed to be a song only for me. Her faces expresses guilt, shock and uncertainty, and her body wilts under my firm grip.

I look away, and reprimand myself by shaking my head. "Sorry, sorry...*Excusez-moi, s'il te plait.*"

But it's not enough. She banishes herself to the other side of the table, sits there rigidly to punish herself and to punish me and make me suffer. Stephane must've taught her that song. I'm surprised.

I pray he didn't teach her the intimate actions that accompany those lyrics.

———

I am thinking incessantly about Stephane now that he's gone. More than I expected to. More than I do when he is around. I wonder if the things he says are true, that I am only capable of loving someone at a distance. I sit unproductively in my studio, my fingers resting upon the keyboard, my mind ten steps behind my body, wondering if I should comb my hair or turn off the lights in the kitchen. I can't even remember if I finished eating breakfast or why I was looking at the magazine sitting in front of me. My mind is a fish I can't catch.

Distracted, I wander from my office into my bedroom and rediscover the garden of his clothes. Aromas. Textures. Colors. I weed through them, dragged onward, pulled by the gravity of his memory, into deeper layers of the closet. I'm curious to see if I can find something still alive. I trace the masculine cut of his charcoal-grey blazer with my fingers, fondle its tender silk lining, inhale its light mint aroma and diluted traces of smoke. His odor is there alongside it: a stale, heady mix of cigarettes, leather, giddy testosterone. From the fabric, his mustard hair arises, erupting from the black jacket, his rugged grin of a devil, and the pointed goatee on his narrow chin.

I catch Amelia watching me from the doorway. I flush a hot red, a wordless signal for her to turn away and leave. She closes the door behind her. I stand there, with the sleeve in my hand, wondering how much she truly understood.

———

Sometimes in the mornings he would rearrange the furniture so the light would enter the house in a more "organic" path than the "constipated" way that I had set it up. Of course, I was not aware of such "humanistic" things. Now, I sit in the morning awaiting the soft spread of light across the floor. I'm trying to see what he saw. These spaces that he left me to fill once again.

I hear the soft pad of stocking feet behind me. Amelia has entered the room and is sitting as quietly as I am on the floor beside me. She turns her head to one side and peers into my face with an exaggeratedly inquisitive expression. Her features are cute, even when she is a caricature of herself. She rises from the floor in a dramatic flourish and runs to face the window. With the potted plants around her as her audience, she begins The Dance. She lifts her arms, curls them left, she lifts her arms and curls them right, and sweeps them up, and sweeps them down, and up and down, and up and down, in smaller and smaller and smaller movements, until all is done. She curtsies to her green patrons, who give her a potted standing ovation.

"That's a nice dance, Amelia," I tell her.

She puts her hands on her hips impatiently. "I know."

"How do you do it?"

She takes up her stance once again. "Move like this. *Comme ci. Comme ci. Comme ci.*"

"That's really good, Amelia."

She rolls her eyes.

"I know."

Stephane's royal bloodline lives on.

IV: *Motion*

In the afternoon, Amelia sits on the couch and spits French vowels at me.

"Would you like a drink?" I ask as I make sandwiches for our lunch. Her eyes glaze at my intrusive question.

"…!" She jumps up and uses her head as the catapult and the silence as the missile that rams into my ear and sticks there.

"How about cookies? Do you want the peanut butter ones? Or the oatmeal ones?"

"A! A! A!" she shrieks. My head is peppered with French A's stuck in my scalp. She maintains her poker face but her eyes sparkle with curiosity.

"Have you brushed your teeth from breakfast?"

She stares at me. "I!"

Massive in its conception and delivery, "I" lodges in between my eyebrows. The impact makes me shudder, and I drop my knife, but I pick it up again quickly and resume my food assembly line. The muscles in her cheeks twitch, trying to keep the prim line of her mouth from curling into the curves of a smile.

———

We drive up the road, headed toward the gargantuan clouds on the film screen of the sky. We sit in the park on a blanket beneath the flowering cherry trees. A picnic of fruit spritzers and plum jelly sandwiches for two. She munches on peanut butter cookies, hoarding the rest of them as if I am about to steal them from her. The sandwiches remain untouched. She continues to munch on her cookie, staring intently at the air because it is infinitely more fascinating than I am to her.

"How about I tell you a story about a line?" I suggest.

She stops, rubs her finger under her nose. I've snagged her interest against her will. "What about a story about a triangle?"

I push a sandwich across the blanket toward her. "No, this is a story about a line. Tomorrow we can have a story about a triangle."

She goes back to munching on her cookies and ignores the sandwich that has crashed into her thigh.

"But I like triangles. *Pourquoi pas?*"

"Well, because I've already thought about a line. It was a line that wanted to be a circle."

"Well, maybe the line wanted to be a triangle," she suggests.

"Well, this line was part of a box and boxes can't really do much of anything except to just sit there. So it wanted to become a circle because circles are more interesting. Circles can roll around and move and bounce and leap."

She drives the sandwich back to its original parking spot. "Well, how did the line become a circle?"

"It didn't. It only dreamt of being a circle. That's all it could do because it couldn't leave the box. The rest of the other lines were dependent upon it to make the box. If it left, the whole box would collapse. So as long as the line stayed as part of the box and only dreamt of being a circle. The line was very, very sad."

She starts on a new cookie. Her eyes are wide. She is entranced.

"But the line knew that he could no longer remain just a line. Inside, he knew was more than just a line—he was a circle. So one day, he got up the courage to leave the box and connect his two ends into a circle and finally he happily joined all the other circles rolling along through the world."

She crawls on her knees, dropping the cookies onto the blanket, and sits up close to me as if she can hear better. "And then what?"

I smile. "And he was so much more happy and free as a circle than he ever was as a line."

She waits for a moment. "And then what?"

I push the sandwich back to her. "And then, well…that's about it."

She stares at me. "That's a stupid story. You suck."

Before I can reply, a wind blasts through the park, sucking the breath out of my mouth into a snowstorm of cherry blossoms.

HO TAM

SERIES 1: MATINEE IDOLS

PETER/JOHN

SERIES 1: MATINEE IDOLS

RAY/CALVIN

SERIES 2: FLOWERS

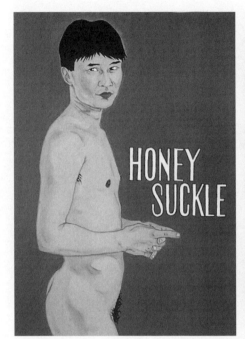

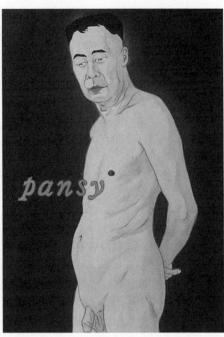

SERIES 2: FLOWERS

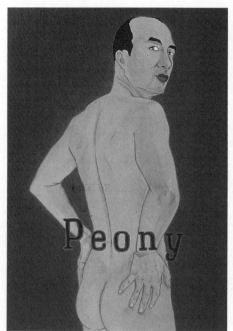 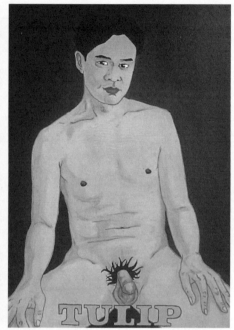

JOEL BARRAQUIEL TAN
PAPA JUN AND ME
AN EXCERPT FROM A FORTHCOMING NOVEL

Papa Jun raced his Camaro around the last of Laurel Canyon's trickiest curves. Red light. Papa Jun hit the brakes hard and I grabbed the sides of the bucket seats so I wouldn't fly through the windshield. The car hummed impatiently and Papa Jun drummed his fingers against the steering wheel. From the top of Crescent Heights the city lights twinkled and glowed like a star map to other worlds. Green light. Papa kicked the gas pedal and we went speeding down the Sunset Strip until we reached the valet roundabout of the Sunset Hyatt. He took the turn into the narrow driveway fast and sharp like a rock star, jumped out and tossed the keys happy-go-lucky-like to the aging parking attendant. Moving past the revolving doors, Papa Jun cracked a smile, one which meant big money.

We took the elevator up to the penthouse to be greeted at the door by a man with orange skin—the kind of orange that tries to pass itself of as a well-earned tan. Shirtless and sweating, he led us into the parlor of the suite. His torso revealed musculature reminiscent of something that was once alive but now mummified under a thin wrap of sweaty slick skin. Wiry hairs sprouted randomly from his nipples like wild poisoned weeds and a crooked line of black hair like a trail of gunpowder spilled into his blue and white Dolfin shorts. He was wearing baggy jaundiced-colored socks with Reeboks. He looked like a serial killer attempting to disguise himself as a harmless aerobics instructor. Sensing that he was part of the deal, my hands and feet went cold.

Another white man, rotund and sweating, was packed tightly into a big vinyl armchair in the middle of the living room watching porn from a giant-sized TV screen. One wall was a window with an awesome view of Sunset Boulevard's twisted spine that eventually spilled out into the limitless expanse of the Pacific Ocean. The breathtaking drama of sky and ocean made me wish I could both fly and breathe underwater.

The TV monitor ran a scene with two white men dressed as police officers double-fucking a black girl with blond hair. Without taking his eyes off the action, the fat guy addressed Papa Jun. "Have a seat, Junior."

"Yes, Brother Bill." Papa Jun answered nervously. "I have your order ready." Papa handed a paper bag to the aerobics instructor.

The aerobics instructor poured out the contents of the bag. Six clear diamond chunks of crystal meth, as big as babies' fists, rolled onto the glass table like Vegas dice.

"I trust that I have don't have to weigh this right, Junior?" asked fat Brother Bill. Papa arranged the chunks on the table and answered, "It's all there, and I wanted to introduce you to my son, Wesley." Wesley? Last week I was Raul, the week before that Sean, before that Tomas, before that Joel. Papa pushed me closer toward Brother until I could feel the steamy stink and heat of the fat man's gaze. Papa Jun continued, "Wesley is going to handle your deliveries from now on. All your needs, Brother Bill."

The fat man's averted his attention from the semen and saliva drips of the woman's mouth to me. Brother Bill's reptilian eyes traveled the length of my body, stopping occasionally to study my face and my crotch. His gaze was like a pizza cutter scoring my skin.

"Is he real friendly?" Brother Bill asked Papa Jun.

"However friendly you need him to be," Papa Jun answered.

"Is he 18?"

"Sure, Brother Bill, sure." Papa answered with a smile.

When Brother Bill ordered the aerobics instructor to unzip my jeans I worked quickly to push myself out of my skin. I concentrated on my breathing and focused out over the canyons, past the candy glitter of buildings and into the deep cold plunge of the expansive Pacific. I arrived at a familiar distance from my body and was relieved that I was out of harm's way. From my safe place, I saw my naked body and the aerobics instructor pushing his gray member, as big as a child's forearm, wherever the fat man fancied. The fat man barked orders. Wordlessly, the aerobics instructor obeyed. The connection between the aerobics instructor and the fat man was as obvious as falling in love, and it was easier to forgive them. They might have been lovers in a past life, or father and son, but in this life it was clear that the fat man was master and the aerobics instructor, his dog. I hovered above myself and watched my flesh tear, expand and finally submit to the aerobic instructor's cock and the fat man's will. I thought about Papa Jun, no doubt sitting on the toilet behind the bathroom door, and what he might be thinking as his only son gets fucked for money.

I was dressed by the time the aerobics instructor gave Papa Jun the OK to come out into the living room. The aerobics instructor, still naked and sweaty, handed Papa Jun a stack of bills across the laminated oak coffee table littered with the chunks of meth, a jar of hand lotion and soiled wet naps. When we got to the car, Papa Jun turned to me with one of his Hollywood smiles and asked, "Dinner, hijo? Would you like your Papa Jun to get you a nice juicy steak?"

I've done jobs before and Papa Jun always made it a habit to take me out to dinner, or ice cream, or sometimes we'd go to the bookstore but the only thing I could think about was Kimi.

"No thanks, Papa. Can you drop me off at the Denny's on Sunset?"

"Denny's? Why not Sizzler or the Old Spaghetti Factory, hijo? The food is much better there!" He pulled out of the Hyatt driveway.

My ears were hot. "I do not want to eat, Papa Jun. Could you just please take me to Denny's? I would like to go out with some friends tonight!" I was as surprised as Papa Jun at the fire behind my words.

Papa covered his face as if he were ducking blows. "All right, all right! Don't have a frikkin' heart attack. Here…" Papa Jun handed me a twenty from the fat roll with a reconciliatory grin. We moved past the billboards and lights of the westside toward East Hollywood and Silverlake. We drove the rest of the way in silence and the only thing I could think of was a world that existed outside of Papa's smile.

———

Papa Jun called it companion services but it didn't take me long to understand that he was pimping me. The way he explained it, we were simply businessmen. The law of supply and demand. Old fags liked young boys. Simple. So Papa Jun supplied what the customers wanted and the customers had what we needed to survive: money.

Four years ago, Papa Jun showed up at the residential facility of Child Protective Services like a delivery stork dressed in an Adidas running suit. "I have come to claim my baby boy." Papa Jun showed up only after a few weeks after Mama's death and up until this time I never knew I had a father. Papa Jun produced a few papers, including a certified copy of my birth certificate, and after an hour of polite conversation, an awkward introduction, and some quick packing, I was in the passenger seat of Papa Jun's pumpkin-orange Camaro, waving goodbye to a social worker who was back inside the house before we even pulled out of the driveway.

Before he turned the engine key, he leaned over slid his palm over my forehead and said tenderly, "I am your Papa, Armando. Your Papa Jun. It's you and me now and I am frikkin' never going to leave you again, hijo. Never."

The broken neighborhoods of Arleta were reduced to a blur inside the cab of Papa Jun's speeding pumpkin machine. "Let me tell you about me and your mom, hijo." He never told the same story twice, especially about him and Mama, but it never bothered me that Papa Jun could never tell the same story twice, since I felt like I didn't know the simplest detail about my mother's history. No matter how fantastic his stories were, I was just grateful that his words conjured Mama back into someone beyond my recollections of a strange, frightened woman who could never bring herself to do what seemed automatic to almost any mother: a kiss, a stroke, a warm hand on my back. I don't remember a time the word "love" ever escaped her lips.

Mama was all whispers and conspiracies. She swore that our neighbors were watching her, talking about her, wishing harm on the both of us. We moved from one rented house to the next, kept our doors double-locked and our blinds drawn. I transferred from school to school so often I eventually gave up trying to get to know any of my classmates or teachers.

Shortly before she killed herself, she landed a bookkeeping gig in one of the accounting backrooms of the Pallmore Casinos in the city of Bell. She kept her position there for almost two years. She took me there once. The air was thick with cigarette smoke, while all the bookkeepers worked the calculators and ledgers in the privacy of their tight little cubicles. With the door locked behind her, and the tight-carpeted wall that hugged the sides of her desk, Mama finally felt safe. She never complained about the Pallmore. I had high hopes we might actually stay in one place, but Mama, true to her nature, left again, and this time for good.

One fall afternoon, just two weeks shy of my thirteenth birthday, I found Mama blue and slumped over the steering wheel of our avocado-green Pacer. I came home to find thick curls of smoke pushing up under the right corner of our garage door and just knew from that moment that she was dead. The only thing Mama left for me was a Salisbury Steak dinner and that black exhaust pushing up to meet October's stormy sky.

"We first met in Santa Fe. Your Mama was the dancing girl on a horse looking for love and any excuse to leave her circus life…" or "I was working a great party in the hills of Switzerland as a chauffeur and Mama, a restless daughter of a South American diplomat, wanted to flee to America to hear jazz…" or "…during a union strike in Stockton, your Mama, the daughter of a ruthless landowner, fell in love with me while I was leading a labor strike with one fist in the air and the other holding a loudspeaker shouting justicia, justicia, justice now!"

No matter how out of control each story was, they all shared a common thread. Mama was always the pretty girl waiting to be saved from herself and Papa Jun was always the one to save her. I guess he wasn't able to save her in time when she decided to leave this world in a cloud of poisonous smoke. But maybe that's why he came looking for me. Papa Jun wanted to save me.

———

I knew what Papa Jun asked me to do wasn't right, but he was convinced that nothing could crush a man's spirit faster than a regular nine-to-five. "Let me tell you something, Armando. There is nothing that will crush a man's spirit faster than some manager or foreman breathing down his frikkin' neck. Ask me hijo, I know. Back before I met your Mama, I was picking fruit in Stockton and, union or no union, you couldn't get me back there if Saint Peter himself came down and said 'Junior, go back to Delano and pick those grapes.' I would have to say, 'St. Peter, out of all respect…there is no gosh darn frikkin' way I'm gonna go back to farm work.' Not that I talk back to saints, hijo, because I am a good Catholic, but Saint Thomas himself could not send me back to that kind of dirt and heat. It is hell on earth. Believe me. Besides, our life isn't so bad, is it? Papa Jun is always here to protect you, right? You know that Papa Jun is always just behind that doorway whenever you're with a customer. I will never let anything happen to you. I swear in front of Saint Joseph, the son of Jesus Christ and God, the father himself." These promises always led to Papa's dramatic ritual of crossing himself with his eyes cast toward heaven. I guess Papa convinced himself that the saints would pardon hustling as a practical and necessary means of survival.

Papa wasn't firmly invested in formal schooling either, but he strongly believed in education—particularly books. If he did anything at all for me, he bought me books. He said that books were almost as good as money.

"Hijo, let me tell you something about schools. Schools are crap! I've been like to ten different universities and even got a Ph.D. once and where did it get me? Believe me, the smartest people in history didn't go to school. Gandhi, George Washington, Donald Trump, President Ronald Reagan, Monty Hall, Martin Luther King, Merv Griffin…some of them ain't even got a high school diploma. But you know what, hijo? Every single one of them graduated from the school of frikkin' kicked in the ass. The school of frikkin' kicked in the ass, hijo! Trust me. I know what I'm talking about."

The worse part of moving around from apartment to hotel, to another apartment to another hotel was lugging *Little House of Prairie*, Hardy Boys, *The Hobbit*, Agatha Christie, Louis L'Amour, *The Star Wars* paperback series, *The Chronicles of Narnia*, *A Wrinkle in Time*, and the illustrated Bible in a huge box taped and reinforced beyond recognition. "That," Papa would say, "is the heavy burden of education, hijo."

Papa eventually got mixed up with two Korean ladies—Gretchen and Stella—who ran a crystal meth kitchen at the edge of Pacoima. He said that we were going to be making enough money so I wouldn't have to work with clients anymore. He had plans for me to go to medical school. Papa Jun disappeared for days, sometimes weeks, for work. He always left me enough money to scrape by but when I ran out, I had plenty of uncles—loyal customers who always had more than enough work for me.

I liked high school. Unlike other seniors, I was in school for six entire periods, mostly to finish required math courses I missed from moving around. Nevertheless, my counselor reassured me that my scores on the placement test guaranteed high SAT scores. I was placed among the college-bound. I had never even thought about college. Despite Papa Jun's hatred of farm work or manual labor, I always hoped to get my high school diploma, find decent work in some quiet countryside, and live a simple life with Papa like the Ingalls family.

I met Kimi at the Sherman Oaks Galleria. One Saturday, I took the 420 line to my house down Ventura Boulevard to go where everyone (who was anyone) always talked about going. I went upon invitation of a friend, Jermaine, who had latched himself onto me the first day I arrived at N.H. High.

Jermaine stepped off the bus wearing wraparound shades, Cavaricci balloon pants, and a green and orange shirt held together with safety pins and buttons that read: Anarchy in the U.K., Sex Pistols, Crass, Nina Hagen, Nunsexmonkroc—among others. He wore a string of tiny plastic babies around his neck and his lips shimmered from a thick layer of lip gloss. I didn't mind that he was dressed so outrageously, but the annoying thing was that he had a bad habit of trying to make it look like we were boyfriends.

"What do you think?" Jermaine posed and twisted his top lip into an exaggerated Billy Idol sneer.

"Creative. How come you don't dress like that at school?" I asked.

"And waste all this fashion magic on those boring gorillas? Aww…hell no! Come on, I'm gonna take you to my favorite boutique!"

Village Mews was like no other store I've seen before. An Asian girl wearing blue lipstick (that matched her blue hair) was popping gum near the cash register while a Chicano guy with a mohawk was glaring at the customers from behind the counter. When Ms. Blue Bob saw Jermaine walking through, she lit up and called "Hey Jermaine, what'd doing, Mr. Cool?"

Jermaine grabbed my elbow and pushed me toward the counter. Jermaine, in a voice that filled the boutique, announced flirtatiously, "Hey Kimi, this is my FRIEND-friend…AR-MAN-DO!" She put out her hand and I was mesmerized by the countless silver and black rubber bracelets she had on each arm.

"AR-MAN-DO. Hmmm, sexy. Why don't we just call you Manly like Almanzo from *Little House on the Prairie!*" she said excitedly. "My name is Kimiko but everyone calls me Kimi."

I never thought in a million years that this girl—who looked like she was from outer space—would be into the Ingalls family drama. She turned to Jermaine and said, "Hey Jermaine, your FRIEND-friend Manly here looks exactly like Roland Gift—you know, from the Fine Young Cannibals and that English movie."

Annoyed, Jermaine retorted, "YES, I know the Fine Young Cannibals, Ms. Kimi. Like, I also have every record they've ever put out, including imports? And the movie is *Sammy and Rosie Get Laid*. And I never thought about it, but I guess he does look like Roland. He's half-Korean."

"Filipino and Mexican," I corrected.

"Whatever," Jermaine said. Aside from the fact that Jermaine was already starting to annoy me by letting this girl think we were boyfriends, the shift from his usual

South Central slang to his new Valley Girl talk was creepy.

"I'm sure, Jermaine, not whatever. We aren't all alike. I'm Japanese, yonsei—fourth generation," Kimi explained. Not having an appropriate clue as to what an appropriate response might be, I nodded my head. I stared at her blue lips and longed to run my finger along the soft surface of what appeared to be the petals of an alien flower. I wasn't aware I was staring until Kimi said, "Anyway, Manly, look around but don't lift. The manager already suspects that I'm the kingpin of some new-wave shoplifting crime ring."

Jermaine led me to the back of the store where there was a sale on a rack of purple Fiorucci Angel shirts. Jermaine pointed to a pair of red and blue plaid pants adorned with buckles and straps.

"Those bondage pants are too expensive. I'm fixing to sew some up myself because you will not catch me paying $200 for those girls."

I looked through the prices and was shocked to see that a plastic shirt with green polka dots all over it was $75. I knew I couldn't afford anything here, and even if I could, there was no way on earth I could see myself asking Papa Jun for that kind of money. I was looking through the display of silver skull and bat jewelry when I felt the glare of the Chicano mohawk guy burning a hole in my back.

"You gonna buy anything?" Mr. Mohawk asked.

Before I could answer, Jermaine stepped between us. "Step the fuck off, you fairy poser. He's with me." Jermaine grabbed my hand and headed out the door. I heard Mr. Mohawk calling after us.

"Faggots! Don't come back!"

We were halfway up the escalator when Kimi pushed up and through the crowd.

"Hey Jermaine, I have free passes to the 'O'. What are you and Manly doing tonight?"

"Going with you, Ms. Kimi-KO." Jermaine answered.

"Cool. Call me after seven," she pushed a Village Mews card with her phone number into my hand.

The 'O'? I didn't know what that was, but guessed I was going. Jermaine found a booth at the food court, and when he felt that the coast was clear, he dumped a handful of buttons he swiped from Village Mews. He sorted through them and found a button for me: FYC. Fine Young Cannibals. Excitedly Jermaine announced, "You know Ms. Kimi has a car!"

The 'O' turned out to be the Odyssey—a nightclub on Beverly Boulevard. All the coolies went, as Jermaine put it. It sounded fun and I kind of wanted to see Kimi again. The plan was to meet at the Denny's on Sunset at around 10:30 and Kimi would drive us the rest of the way. By the time we got back on the bus to get ready for the big night, I was exhausted. The bus dropped me off at Victory and Laurel Canyon and I left Jermaine on the bus, who was on his way home to transform for the evening festivities. Walking home, I looked to the sleepy setting sun and felt, for the first time, somewhat normal.

I didn't expect Papa Jun to be home so soon, but I smelled the Lysol and the carpet freshener coming down the apartment hallway. When I opened the door, he was scrubbing the kitchen counter like a crazy person. He was high again. Since Gretchen and Stella found a new recipe, they went from cooking hydro to glass. Which meant a better quality drug, higher prices and higher profits. Papa Jun had gotten into the habit of sampling the goods, but he professed that he dipped in the stock solely for the sake of quality control. This was not the first time Papa Jun came home tweaked out and when he did, I could rest assured that the our barely furnished apartment was going to get a scrubbing worthy of a surgical room.

"Hijo, Papa Jun is home." Papa stood like a messiah, arms stretched out and open.

"Hey, Papa Jun," I said, trying to make it past him and into my room.

"Hijo, no hug for Papa Jun? Come to me, my only boy." And before I could think, I was trapped in his sweaty, warm clutch. Papa Jun was pungent with the smell of cleaning products, sweat, cologne, and the unmistakable tang of crystal meth. From the feel of things, Papa Jun had lost some more weight. It didn't look bad on him, but it had me kind of worried. Papa Jun looked younger than most 37-year-old men. He could have easily passed as a man in his twenties. Papa Jun and I were the same height—5'10"—and it was clear from our heavy brows, the hard curve of our jaws, the slight tightness of our eyes, and the dangerous flare of our nostrils, that we were father and son.

Papa Jun was wearing his customary T-shirt that clung to the hard brown definitions of his naturally muscular body. He wore the muscles on his shoulders and his neck like a yoke, and his smile was too bright to be legal. Women and men fluttered around Papa's web like carefree, love-struck flies.

"Son, how would you like to drive with me to San Bernardino tomorrow?"

"I got school, Papa. Can't."

"No, it's not all right. Let me tell you something, hijo. There is nothing like the school of life. And there is nothing better than traveling. When I was your age I went to Europe. Been all over frikkin' Europe!"

From the corner of my eye, I saw the glass tube, the burnt sheets of foil, and the lighter that explained everything. From a drive to San Bernardino to Europe. Here we go.

"Yup, the Eiffel Tower in Paris, the ruins in Rome, the Big in London. Why, when I was out walking around, I passed a parade, and sure enough, the Queen of England even winked at me from the crowd, hijo. I'll have to tell you more about it later. Listen, we got a gig. You want to warm up the car for me?"

"How long is this going to take?" I asked.

"Why, hijo? You got somewhere to go?" he chuckled.

" I got plans, Papa Jun. I'm going out to Hollywood with some friends later tonight…dancing."

"Dancing? Friends? Well Mr. Dancer, that crap can wait. I need you to help me with a job. We got to run something over to the Sunset Hyatt. An order for a couple of queers. Take a shower, get ready, we're leaving soon." Papa Jun had that tone in his voice that meant no fucking around.

———

I spotted the already familiar blue of Kimi's hair through Denny's huge glass windows as Papa Jun whipped around the corner and into the Sunset Mini-Mall. I jumped out with a quick goodbye and closed the door behind me. The deafening screech of Papa Jun's tires against the parking lot blacktop sounded like a thousand wailing widows.

Kimi spotted me from the booth and waved me over. She was smiling big despite her macabre appearance. She had her hair teased into what looked like a spiked war helmet. She was dressed in a black lace dress, lace gloves, and torn fishnet stockings that completed her Elvira get-up. She had countless rosaries around her neck. I was sure that every priest from Los Angeles to Rome at that very moment were looking for their rosaries. Her nails matched her blush and lipstick perfectly—all jet black.

"Manly! You made it." Kimi squealed. She threw her arms around me and I was confronted with her hot breath against my neck, the smell of patchouli, the scratchy lace of her death gown and the soft smash of her breasts.

"Uh—hey, Kimi. What's up? Where's Jermaine?" I was never going to be able to outdo her hero's welcome.

"Oh, he's in the bathroom putting on the finishing touches. Are you going to order something?" she asked.

An old Chinese woman who spotted Jermaine coming out of the bathroom gasped. When she saw him walking up to the booth, she nudged her husband so that he wouldn't miss Jermaine's entrance. And what an entrance it was. Jermaine's skin sparkled like a hooker's prom dress. Random cherry-red streaks flashed against the closely cropped sides of his flat top. He was wearing black wraparound shades; his lips and nails were painted purple-brown. He was wearing a black fitted blazer and falsies, matching tight slacks that came to the ankle, and four-inch stilettos.

"Hello, Manly. I trust that you arrived safely." Jermaine slipped in the booth; I was still shocked. "Close your mouth, Manly, it is not flattering." Jermaine then turned to the Chinese couple and yelled "BOO!" Embarrassed, the old couple went back to stirring their hot chocolates and had to settle for stealing glances at our private carnival.

I had to ask. "Jermaine, why are you dressed like a girl?"

"A girl? I am not dressed like a girl, I am dressed like Grace Jones. You know—fashion model, recording artist, performance diva, legend? And I would prefer it if you addressed me as Grace this evening. I am known at the 'O' as Grace."

Kimi jumped in. "Oooo…Jermaine—I mean Grace, what are you performing tonight?"

"I think I shall treat you all to 'Pull Up to the Bumper' tonight."

And at midnight, treat us he did. The DJ stopped the music and called the crowd's attention to the stage. "Freaks and freakettes…MISS GRACE JONES!" The room went dark and a path was cleared in the middle of the room. A spotlight illuminated Jermaine, who was growling and clawing at his audience through the bars of a cage propped on wheels. When the assistants rolled the cage close enough to the stage, the music started and Jermaine jumped out, resplendent in a cheetah-spotted body stocking, hip-high latex stiletto boots, and a bull whip. He was lip-synching to the music. The crowd was cheering as Jermaine walked back and forth, spitting and kicking at people like a rabid drag queen in the middle of a cosmetics war. He was a hit, and as Kimi said he would be, a treat.

Shortly after Jermaine was wheeled back offstage in his cage, Kimi grabbed my hand and led me outside to the patio area. She pulled out a cigarette and offered me one. "Clove? They're kutas. The best." I took a hit and felt my knees buckle. "You catching a rush? Now lick your lips." In my haze, I did what I was told. My lips tasted like a sugar bowl. "Cool, huh?" Kimi grinned.

The patio crowd once again parted for Jermaine, who was now dressed in his original blazer outfit. He came toward us, seething. "I could kill that fucking bitch Todd. She thought she was going to show me up and take the midnight spot with that played out Siouxsie and the Banshees routine! I practically had to suck the DJ off to keep my spot. You watch…I'm going to fix that toothless drag queen." And just as quick as Jermaine started cussing, he was cooing. "And oh my GOD, guess who is here…'Should I, Should I Love You' Cee Farrow. THE Cee Farrow, also a model, also a recording artist, and also my future husband!' And as quickly as Jermaine came, he left, no doubt, to hobnob with the groom to be.

Looking around the patio, the 'O' seemed to be a haven for minor celebrities and superstar stunt doubles. Boy George was smoking a clove cigarette with the Go-Gos near the booths. Four incarnations of Madonna were sipping cocktails with George

Michael. Three Chicano dudes dressed like Bananarama were sniffing amyl nitrate out of a bottle. Prince was making out with Billy Idol while Wendy and Lisa watched. A seven-foot creature with a white mohawk breezed by wearing sheer butterfly wings and a glitter wand. A fat, bald black man wearing nothing but body glitter and a G-string whizzed by on roller skates. The DJ was playing music I'd never heard before.

I felt out of place with my flannel shirt and 501s but the clove buzz made me forget and heightened my excitement. Kimi and I danced until the DJ announced the last dance at around 4 A.M. We finally spotted Jermaine amidst the crowd gathering in front of the club. He asked us if we wanted to join him and three Boy George look-alikes for eggs and coffee at Norm's.

"Quick. Get in the car. We have to get home before the sun comes up!" Kimi grabbed my hand and we ran to the car, laughing and exhausted with the smell of cloves and cigarettes trapped in our hair, skin, and clothes.

Once we were on the road, Kimi couldn't keep her mouth shut. She lived with her folks in Van Nuys and she was a senior at Grant High. She was already taking classes at the Fashion Institute of Design and Merchandising to pursue a career as a designer. She talked about eventually living in Paris or London. She hated America, American music, and American designers. Her favorite designer was Issey Miyake and she was working at the Village Mews to get "boutique" experience. By the time she got to naming her favorite bands, we were already pulling into my apartment complex. She stopped the car and before I knew what was happening, the cool wet of her tongue pushed between my lips. Her tongue, like a small fish, swam in the warm, shallow caverns of my mouth and sent electric shocks across my lap, making breathing difficult. She released me from her suction and said, "I think I like you, Manly."

"Uh. Me too." I was still reeling from her kiss.

"I'm working the noon shift. Will you come by and visit me today? I get off at six and if you want, Fabian's happening tonight. I can drive."

She reached over and opened the door and as I was getting out, I said, "Uh…sure. I'll see you. Fabian's sounds fun. Let's go—"but before I could finish, Kimi was already turning the corner at the end of the block. I didn't move for a few seconds. I watched the sky go from blue to lilac, as if to congratulate me on my first kiss.

When I opened the door, I found Papa Jun hunched over, studying the liner notes of his old Maze album. On top of being high, he'd been drinking; he always said that his favorite thing was Frankie Beverly over a glass of gin. Papa Jun was sprawled across the carpet singing the background chorus to Frankie Beverly's lead: "…feel that happy feelin'. Happy feelings…" Papa wore countless days of sleeplessness on his face.

I turned down the record player and called Papa Jun's attention. "Hey, Pops. I'm home. Come on. Let's go to bed."

Papa Jun looked up from the living room carpet and smiled, "My hijo, he is home to put his Papa to bed. What a good boy he is. Come here, hijo, let me tell you something." I hesitated. "…Come here. Come on, hijo, Papa has got something pretty frikkin' important to tell his son."

Cautiously, I sat next to Papa Jun and he grabbed my face and planted a delirious kiss on my cheek. "I'm sorry, hijo. Papa is so very frikkin' sorry for leaving you with those animals. Papa Jun is so sorry…" He was stroking my head into his chest and I felt his tears roll along my neck. "But don't worry hijo, look under the bathroom cabinet, I've stashed a frikkin' crapload…for college. A crapload, hijo…so you can be a doctor."

"Come on, Papa Jun. Sssssh. Time for a bath and bed," I propped his arm over my shoulder and started to drag Papa's leaden body into the bathroom. I ran a bath for Papa, and while waiting, Papa lit a joint. He pointed to the medicine cabinet and ordered me to hand him his Valium. I fished out two tablets and poured a glass of cold tap water from the bathroom sink. He swallowed the pills and chased it with a swig of water and a king-sized toke. I undressed Papa and directed him to the tub. By the time I got through scrubbing his back and shampooing his hair, he was already asleep. It took every ounce of energy I had left to drag Papa Jun out of the tub, dry him off, and push him onto the queen-sized futon mattress we shared. I covered him with a blanket, placed a pillow under his head, and planted a goodnight kiss on his cheek.

I cleaned up a bit in the living room while Papa's snores bounced against the walls. I couldn't help but think about how brilliant Jermaine looked last night, the disco lights that came down from the ceiling, the boys in make-up, dancing, clove cigarettes, and the deep, deep blue of Kimi's hair. Outside, the sun was climbing up the March sky, and I swore I saw Mama's smiling face peeking through the clouds.

JIMM TRAN

SELF IDENTITIES SERIES

AFRO-MERICAN

SELF IDENTITIES SERIES

BEDSPREAD

SELF IDENTITIES SERIES

BROKEN AMERICAN DREAMS GIRL

SELF IDENTITIES SERIES

FARHEEN WITH PEPSI

SELF IDENTITIES SERIES

PHO GIRL

MATT UIAGALEILEI

LETTERS

g

In the old days before PageMaker
it was scripted out or
Smith Corona'd.
It makes no sense today,
letters handmade,
those little beetles.
It belongs in the basement.
The g in Algonquin.

h

It's so unfair
I never got to kiss
Natalie Wood.

v

No.
Not allowed.
Put out your cigarette
immediately, Miss Hellman.

x

Megan's talking.
Giving me the
eye-earring-hair move
with finger snap motion.

And I count them.
This is the 4th.

Next is the perfume-
hairspray-mirror dance
at 8. Better than
a kiss from Paloma.

y

tertiary
cello trick
the fieldhand's lament

z

pierced nose
African drums
BJs in Boston

This is the house
This is the edge

LOVE POEM

flight path & search light
south shore   motorbike
tidepool & floodlight
thoroughfare
      palm frond
lighter fluid & harbor light
parchment shade   wicker chest
Bombay gin & porch light
velvet shirt
      shoulderblade
earlobe

ribcage
fingertip & diving knife
knucklebone & fishing lure

eyelid & surface light

A PARTY GOES ON

The clouds gather around the moon
in the highest cover
over Kaneohe Bay.
Weather here is unpredictable.
Storms can roll off the ocean without warning.
I'm on the lanai. The windward mountains,
cut and black
against the night.

Now the clouds are streaked high,
lit by the moon, barely there.

People at this party
talk about the comet
visible earlier with the naked eye.
Others face the north shore
and point off across the dark bay.

Now the clouds disappear into a film.
A ring circles the moon.

I keep thinking about a place on the island
where there is nothing.
And I am thinking about you.
Your wonder at such a place,
at such a night as this on the bay.

How you would come out to the lanai
to take in the view. How only now I can feel that.

Now the clouds are antique-patterned,
changing each time I think to look.
I should have paid more attention
or told you what I was thinking.

At this party tonight,
I am sitting on the railing of the lanai,
looking down on the bay
where nothing moves.

If I could only,
I would climb out of my clothes, my skin,
out of myself
and push off hard
to begin the swim into the sky,
kicking up to a place
that I have not known.

When I surface, wet and strange
and new, you will be there,
above the clouds, above the houses,
above the lights. Silly moon and funny stars,
goodnight.

ERIC C. WAT

FROM VEGAS, WITH LOVE

I

Sam's plane had arrived almost an hour ago, and I was still sitting in my station wagon waiting for Mario in Bell, a good twenty minutes away from the airport in modest traffic. I was parked across the street from Mario's house, at a distance I carefully measured (at his request), so when his mother peered out from behind the curtained window, she would not make out who I was exactly. I honked again. The curtain was lifted from the side just enough to accommodate a curious eye. The eye lingered for a moment. The curtain dropped. Faintly, I could hear Mario's name called. The eye had seen things in the neighborhood that worried a mother, but I was safe enough.

Mario emerged from behind the screen door, smiling and waving, still shirtless. I wanted to yell "hurry up," but I was too tired. I'd give him the guilt trip later: We would miss Sam. He would probably not wait for us, even though he had a four-hour layover. He would go back to Malaysia and remain forever pissed at us because he'd think we were just a couple of faggots who had only been pretending to enjoy his company so that we had someone to show us around San Francisco a few months ago. He'd think he meant nothing to us. Faggots. Sam wouldn't think that word, not exactly, but Mario hated it. The word would get to him.

I was just beginning to enjoy strategizing when Mario ran around the front of the car and slid in from the passenger's side.

"Sorry," he said.

I put on my seatbelt.

"I tried to call you to tell you I'd be a little late," he said, twisting his hand behind his back to find his seatbelt, "but they said you left already. I think it was your grandmother who picked up the phone. She always sounds so sweet when she tries to speak to me in English."

Ignoring him, I turned on the engine and pulled out.

"What's bothering you?" he asked. His body cocked to the right side, and he fished out a lighter and a pack of cigarettes from his shirt's pocket.

I didn't answer him immediately. He lit a cigarette. "Nothing," I said. "Why?" I opened the ashtray, still not looking at him.

"Nothing, then."

"I hope his plane is delayed because we're really late," I said. For emphasis, I tapped at the digital clock on the panel. It read 8:03. Sam's plane was scheduled to arrive at seven.

"He has a four-hour layover. Where is he going to go?" He said, the cigarette in his mouth. After he took it out and exhaled, he continued, "He called me last night. He sounded pretty depressed." He paused, perhaps for effect, perhaps contemplating. "I think it's me."

"Don't flatter yourself," I snickered. After all, Mario had only been seeing him that week when we were in San Francisco.

"What's the matter with you? Are you still jealous?"

"Of you?"

"God, you act like a virgin sometimes."

"Well, don't let me have all the fun. You should try it sometimes."

"Really, what is wrong with you?" He turned toward me in his seat, putting his left foot up at an angle. He was getting serious. I just hated it when he refused to play along.

"Nothing is wrong."

"Yes, there is," he insisted.

"A little bit tired, that's all. Besides, I've been driving all day at work and now picking you up to the airport. You live so damned far away."

"So this is another hint for me to get a car," he sulked.

"No, I'm just stating the facts: I hate driving, I drive a lot, and you live very far away from me. And to top it all off, tomorrow morning I have to drive my whole family to Vegas."

"Again? I wish I could go places on long weekends."

"It's only Vegas," I said, more mocking than consoling. "Besides, I took you to San Francisco."

It was easy for Mario to get excited about family trips, for they didn't come often to him. He and his four brothers and sisters took turns every year, and his luck had not been too good. He'd been to camping at Yosemite and down to San Diego where one of his mother's good friends lived. One time he was to go to the Grand Canyon, but his mother decided to take his older sister instead. That summer there was this boy in the neighborhood that they thought she should stop hanging out with.

"It's not all that. I'm just chauffeuring them," I said.

"If you're tired, I can drive," he said, looking away as if conceding. His lips had not touched that cigarette since he started talking serious.

"No, thanks. Have you forgotten why you don't have a car in the first place?"

"It was a hit-and-run." His breath was getting shorter. I knew that when all else failed, the accident would get to him. It was always an opportunity I hated to miss. It reminded him how he depended on me and my car. "It wasn't my fault."

I nodded and smiled. "Sure, you got any eyewitnesses?"

"You always do this to me. First you don't say anything. Then when I ask you what's wrong, you start throwing this shit at me. What the hell are you trying to do?"

"All right…"

"Just shut up and never mind."

I turned on the radio, and Mario faced forward again. I finally found the freeway. But after a mile or so, I saw all the brake lights light up. "Shit, traffic," I mumbled. That was all I said. I didn't want to make Mario more upset.

He tuned the radio back and forth, looking for the two adult contemporary stations that played love songs at night. But both were airing commercials. He turned the volume down. After a while he turned it off.

"I'm really worried about Sam. What would I do if he decided to stay here and wanted to live with me or something?"

"He's not going to do that. He's got a one-way ticket to Malaysia. He's under a lot of pressure, that's all."

"Do you know something I don't?"

"He didn't tell you?" I asked. I could already gather from the conversation over the phone with Sam earlier that week that he probably had not told anyone what he had been telling me. Still, I liked the upper hand.

"Tell me what?"

"I'm surprised he didn't tell you."

"What did he tell you?"

"I promised him I wouldn't tell anyone. Besides, if he wanted you to know, he would've told you.…Wait. That didn't come out right." I was sincere about that.

"Maybe to him I was just another piece of ass," he concluded, dejected.

I couldn't help laughing. "Look! You know he likes you a lot. He's gone through a lot of trouble to get your phone number."

"He called you first," Mario countered immediately.

"He called me to find out your number," I corrected him just as quickly. "I'm listed; you're not. Look, Mario. What I'm trying to say is that when he called me up a few days ago, he didn't plan on telling me anything. It just happened, OK? It just happened, the way the two of you happened. He just needed to tell someone, I guess, and I'm Asian, and he's Asian. Maybe he thought I'd understand."

"Understand what?"

"That's not the point. I was there, that's all I'm saying. I was convenient. If you were on the phone that day instead of me, we probably wouldn't be having this conversation right now. Anyway, if you want to know, you just have to ask him. In fact, I've probably said too much already."

Mario was quiet. He stretched out his arm as if it were his own agent. He fingered a small dent on the cheap plastic front panel in front of him. I had no idea how that dent got there. My parents bought this station wagon used, two years ago. They had no intention of driving a car as huge as this, but they liked station wagons because they were ideal for family trips, to Vegas, to the Bay Area, to anywhere. I was the only one who could handle the car, since my parents, having only learned how to drive after they immigrated, would be nervous driving a car this big. Mario's fingers fit the dent perfectly, like he knew my car better than I did.

I thought his concentration was utterly consumed by it until I heard him say, "I'll tell you what happened between me and Sally if you tell me what Sam told you."

I stopped him. "I don't want to hear about you and Sally unless the two of you are breaking up." He put his hand back on his lap. "It's dishonest."

"Oh, I forgot. I'm sitting next to the pillar of integrity. You never put up fronts."

"Not like this. How can you stand yourself?" I hadn't wanted to push it.

"Maybe I can't." He looked away. We had looked away from each other quite a lot already. Little was left unsaid between us. Sometimes I didn't know how to hold this friendship together. "How can you stand me?" He didn't say this sarcastically at all, and that shut me up.

We were still sitting in traffic. The needle that indicated the temperature of the engine had been slowly rising. *Need to check the liquids tonight*, I thought. It was all right now. The traffic would let up soon. After you spend so much time on the freeway, you start to have a feel about these things. He sat silent, hoping against hope that we'd forget what we said if no more words were spoken.

II.

It was my brilliant idea to go to San Francisco. For once, I wanted to go there without my parents. Mario was a perfect travel buddy. I couldn't drive there by myself; I'd fall asleep on the way. At that time, Mario and I were not always antagonizing each other. Mario said once that sometimes two people could become lovers in a matter of one night; sometimes they could get too stuck in a friendship stage that they couldn't be anything more than that. In retrospect, Mario and I could've been lovers from the beginning, but instead we got stuck. I didn't think we could be lovers anymore, and as with most people who wouldn't know what to do with sexual tension if they found it naked in bed together, we probably wouldn't even be best friends unless we cursed each other out so damn much.

Mario had never been to San Francisco, and for all intents and purposes, neither had I. Sure, I'd been there with my family, but there were so many places that I couldn't go to with them around. The first night, Mario and I found a dance club in Castro. That was where we met Sam. Actually, I saw him first, but he saw Mario. They were dancing all night. When the club closed two and a half hours later, Mario hopped toward me and asked if I minded going back to the motel alone.

I was incredulous. "Our first night in San Francisco and you're doing this to me already?"

"But..."

"Are you forgetting who drove you here?"

"Fine," he said. He went back to tell Sam the bad news. We didn't say a word to each other in the car back to the motel.

The next day Mario went to some museum and I went shopping. When I got back to our room, Mario was already there watching TV with Sam.

"You remember Sam?" Mario said without moving. Sam stood up to extend his hand.

"Yes." Both of my hands were full with shopping bags, so I shrugged. Sam took back his hand.

"Sam said we could stay with him," Mario said, his eyes still glued to the TV. I sensed that there would be no room for disagreement. "I'd say that wouldn't be a bad idea since you spent most of your money buying half of San Francisco."

Back then, Sam was a San Francisco State student living in a one-bedroom apartment all by himself. His father, who had a successful export business, paid for all of it.

"There's a price," he said one night during dinner. "I have to go back to help him when I graduate."

"You like America?" I asked.

He nodded.

"Yeah, I guess there're no gay clubs in Malaysia, huh?" Mario said.

"There are, but it doesn't matter," Sam said. "My parents found me someone to marry."

"You mean an arranged marriage?" Mario asked.

"It's not so surprising. A lot of marriages are arranged. I'm the oldest son. They expect that of me. People will talk if I don't get married and have kids. Not just about me. They'll say things about my mother too."

The last night in San Francisco, Mario surprised me. He had been sleeping with Sam ever since we stayed there, and I'd been on the couch. That night, he kissed Sam goodbye and sent him to his bedroom alone.

"Don't tell me you're pitying me," I said.

"Just a little guilty," he said, taking the other end of the sofa.

"Good," I said.

"I've never dated a college guy before. Can you imagine how our lives would be different if we had gone to college?"

"We took a couple of classes."

"It's different. That's J.C.," Mario said, kicking me under the blanket. I didn't respond and he was silent for a good minute. "It's too late for us now," he said. I could feel him turning. I pretended to have fallen asleep already. I wanted to say, "College? College hasn't changed that much for Sam." But I let it go.

It was another two months or so before I spoke to Sam again, this time on the phone. He had graduated already but had, until then, postponed going back to Malaysia. But his parents had an argument the week before about another woman, and his mother threatened suicide. He had no choice but to go back; the oldest son was expected to restore order in the family. Once he was back in Malaysia, he said, he would probably stay there for good. His mother needed him. He wanted to see Mario one last time. Could I help?

III

We were two hours late. When we checked the arrival screen, Sam's flight was no longer listed. We scrambled up the stairs, passed through metal detectors. The airport was full of people. Maybe because it was a long weekend. I managed to find an airline employee who was not busy with the real paying customers and who kindly informed us that Gate 36B was what we should be looking for. We dashed toward Gate 36B, skillfully avoiding contact with the zombies who just arrived. Tired and unattractive, they carried more luggage than they could manage. Their arms were long like those of apes. They walked slowly, but they looked like frozen statues as we breezed past them like two ninjas, hoping the two minutes we saved would compensate for the two hours of tardiness.

When we reached Gate 36B, we found Sam without trying. He was sitting in one of those bright-colored chairs they always had in airport waiting areas, reading *The Wall Street Journal*. When he looked up and saw us gliding along the wall toward him to avoid the traffic, he didn't look surprised.

Mario and I took turns hugging Sam. He asked us how we were, and we asked him if he had a nice flight. Then, standing in a circle, we let out a communal breath.

Sam picked up his big carry-on and off we wandered into an airport cocktail lounge we had passed earlier. It wasn't too far from the other gate which Sam would disappear behind later. His bag seemed to be quite heavy, and he limped through the crowd. We offered to relieve him. He shook his head. Mario took *The Wall Street Journal* under Sam's arms, and that was all we had of him. Sam turned and looked at him. His face was at once gentle and solemn, and his mouth curled in what almost qualified for a modest smile.

We chose a table in the center of the lounge. I didn't like the table. Cigarette smoke welled up above it, and when the soft lighting shot through the smoky air, there was something sinister about it, like we were on stage, being watched. But it was the only table available.

Our waitress floated on the smoky air to our table and took our orders. Mario had a Bud Lite; Sam, a Coke.

"I'll have a White Russian," I said. Then she floated back to where she came from.

"Ooh," Mario mocked my order. He always had the same reaction.

Ignoring Mario, I turned to Sam. "So why aren't you drinking? It's your last night here in the States."

"We can't drink," he replied curtly. His sentences were always efficient.

"Malaysians don't drink?" Mario interjected.

"No, Muslims. Well, not us anyway," Sam shook his head.

"Not even a drop? Not even on religious holidays or weddings or something?" Mario persisted.

Sam shook his head again, smiling as before.

"Lay off, Mario," I said.

"Weren't you a least bit curious what it tastes like?"

"It's no big deal," Sam offered finally, lowering his head as if he had said too much.

"You never had a hangover before." Mario concluded.

"You have to excuse us, Sam," I stepped in. I was afraid we were embarrassing him. "We have never known a Muslim before. Anyway, hangovers are overrated," I added as the waitress put down our drinks.

Mario and I talked and talked. I tried to sound sophisticated, and Mario kept telling tasteless jokes. Then we argued a little and Mario would break it up with another joke. Sam occasionally offered a sentence in agreement with either one of us; sometimes with both, in his own way. Most of the times, however, he just nodded, nursing his glass of soda. It was like in San Francisco. Then I ordered another drink, something that I heard a man order before, someone who had seemed like a drinker. As if on cue, Mario and I started to talk about the economy, a subject neither of us knew much about. Sam, a finance major, had no opinions to offer.

After his second beer, Mario got up and left the table. A liver problem, he explained ever so politely. Sam and I watched him disappear out of sight.

With Mario gone, our eyes had no place to fall but on each other.

"So when are you coming to visit me in Malaysia?" Sam asked. I didn't remember if he had ever initiated a conversation with me. For some reason, I felt like a witness on the stand who had his hand on a Bible.

"What's there to see in Malaysia?"

Sam looked up, perhaps trying to remember if Malaysia had something like a celebrity rodent. Then he said, "Me." He was smiling, maybe a little wickedly. But who could tell with him?

I looked down in my half-empty glass. I hoped it was the alcohol that was turning me woozy. It was nice to see him smile. After more than an hour of goading, any voluntary word, I must admit, was refreshing. But I almost wished equally that he had not spoken, for his voice, hoarse and unattractive, disarmed me. I could not offer even one volley of wit or banter to deflect his stare.

"How's your mother doing?" was my best return.

"My mother..."

I nodded to encourage him.

"I think she's going crazy. I didn't have a chance to talk to her since I called you. I called this morning before I left San Francisco. My dad said she wasn't awake yet. But I knew she was probably too upset. It breaks my heart every time I think about it. I keep thinking if I were there, she would not be taking it so hard." Sam blurted all this out in less than ten seconds, as if he were waiting all day to say it. His head turned down a little, his face flushing either out of embarrassment or exhaustion. I used to be frightened of words too, when they formed little sentences that betrayed my thoughts. Sam, however, had not learned to use them to cover his.

"She should not be hurt like this," he continued. "Especially not by someone she loves, someone she has invested so much of herself in. It's just not fair."

I sat there, not knowing what to say. I had not said anything real that night. He deserved more and better than I had to offer him.

Mario came back and we resumed our conversation before he left. I put up my best face. I played along. I wanted Sam to remember us this way, just as I wanted to remember his wicked smile, those two seconds of our lives. Mario and I kept on talking, and Sam listened. When I paid closer attention, though, I discovered that Sam was silent because he was looking at Mario all this time, hanging onto every word he uttered. He would never see him again in less than an hour. Then I had found something real to say to him. I had found a connection. I wanted to tell him what it was, but Mario never got up again. His liver was quite accommodating the rest of the night.

We hugged before Sam disappeared behind a new gate. He held me, heads touching each other. This was our last chance. But what was I to say in that brief instant? That we were in love with the same man and neither of us knew how to love him? At least he had a legitimate excuse. He would be the only one I could say those words to, but he was leaving for good.

IV.

After Sam left, there was little to say. Mario and I sat in the car, looking right through my dirty windshield. I wished it would rain. Then, remembering my long trip the next morning, I changed my mind. The radio was not even on. The silence was only broken by the sound of engine as the car stopped at a red and as it revved up and proceeded through a green. I was thinking about Sam, and I had a good idea that Mario was doing the same.

Sam's suffering was my own, but Mario had no idea. Even if Sam told him why he had to leave the country, he would've been blind to it, as he had been blind to his own situation, hiding himself in the dark havens of West Hollywood or Silverlake. Or San Francisco, bouncing from one bar to the next.

At a red light, I looked over to Mario and he received my stare. After a while, the car behind honked.

"He talked to you more," Mario said.

"That's not true," I denied it as feebly as I was pushing the pedal.

"No, I'm not being jealous or anything. It's just an observation," he said softly. And indeed, his voice did not carry any jealousy. Neither was his tone accusatory. I didn't know how to respond. That it didn't mean much? That would be a lie. "I'm glad," he continued. "He looked like he needed to get something off his chest. And you're a good listener."

I still did not know what to say.

"I was afraid he had become too attached to me," Mario said.

I chuckled. "You know, Mario. Now that Sam is out of our lives forever, I'm going to tell you everything you've been dying to know. I'm breaking a promise, I know, but someone has to stop you from masturbating with this delusion. It's getting embarrassing." I stole a look at him to detect any sign of protest. But nothing. He was listening. I thought for a brief moment that it was his way of making me tell him all those secrets that I had promised Sam that I wouldn't reveal to a living soul. Never mind. Sam was out of the picture and no one was going to get hurt. "Sam's mother is having a nervous breakdown because his father is taking another wife."

"They are getting a divorce?"

"No, they don't get divorced. He's just taking another wife. I guess it's okay over there."

"Jesus," Mario yelled. Then he sighed. "You should've told me. I almost asked him about all that bigamy stuff in Muslim societies, just to get him to say something. God, that would be embarrassing."

"Yes, that would. Anyhow, the new wife is someone Sam's father had an affair with for a long time now. Sam's mother is going to lose her place in the family and there's not much she can do about it."

"Jesus!"

"There's more." I figured Mario might as well know the whole story. "Sam is thinking about getting married."

"To a woman?" Mario almost screamed.

"Yes, to a woman," I snapped back. "To this pre-arranged fiancée back in Malaysia.

He was engaged to her even before he came to the States. The sooner he starts a family, the easier it is for his mother to hold her place in the house. Otherwise, she would just lose everything to that new wife."

Mario was silent for a while. Then he said, "That's sad."

"Yes, it is," I said.

"It's downright primitive." He shook his head again.

"Yeah, whatever."

"What's wrong with you? Don't you feel bad for him?"

"What did you think being gay means, Mario? Did you think it's all about going dancing in clubs and marching in parades? Yes, I feel bad for him. I feel bad for me. And I feel bad for you."

"Then why are you acting this way? How the hell did you get so damn cynical?" He was practically shouting.

"Well, for some of us, cynicism is an instinct." After that we didn't say anything for a while. We needed to cool down, maybe change the topic, find something we could agree on. But I was too tired. I couldn't think of anything else. "At least now you know how I feel."

"What do you mean?"

"You think you're better off than Sam?"

"If you're talking about me and Sally, it's an entirely different case."

"Please, Mario. No rationalizations. Not tonight."

"Look, I'm not you, okay? I'm happy that you could imagine your life a different way. Sometimes your life is set for you and you just have to deal with it. Look at you, you hate driving. And what the hell are you doing tomorrow? Driving your family to another state like you do twice a year. And in a car that they don't even know how to drive. You let them buy you a car so they could order you around. And what do you do for a living? You're a fucking courier."

"Except I know I won't be a courier forever."

"How do you know that?"

"Oh, fuck you."

"No, I'm not backing down this time. How long has it been since we got out of high school? And how long have you been saying you're going to quit?"

"Just shut up, Mario."

I realized how those words had sounded so familiar lately. I didn't know how much farther I could take this friendship. We knew each other like brothers, but we had not figured out a way to make the other feel better. Lately, our encounters had always ended in silence. Automatic words hurt deeper because they usually rang true.

V.

I could not get much sleep. When I came home around midnight, there was a note on my desk. It read that we would be leaving at around three in the morning. They liked leaving early. My grandmother could not tolerate even the mild morning sun. Three hours—that was all I had, and I had not even packed yet. I didn't want to think anymore. I crashed on my bed, and, like a baby who had just been breast-fed, sleep came so fast that I didn't remember slipping into it.

The alarm clock blared in the middle of my dream. I couldn't remember what the dream was when I was jolted awake. I used to have interesting dreams. I turned to look at the alarm clock. 2:30. My father, it had to be him. He always wanted to leave on time. It took him half an hour to get from his bed to his car every morning. He'd like to take care of details.

I sprang up from the bed, still wearing the same clothes last night. When I looked out the window, the outside was just as dark as I left it two and a half hours ago. It was like time had not elapsed.

When I came out of my bathroom, my father was ready. He yelled at me. It sounded like a curfew lecture, and all I was thinking was *twenty-six*. I was twenty-six years old, and it sounded like a curfew lecture. My mother came to the kitchen and told him to hush. Grandma is still sleeping. You'll wake her. Father yelled some more.

We were in the car and ready to leave at 4:30. They fell asleep at 4:33.

After all that was said, I liked leaving in the wee hours of the morning. It made me feel like a fugitive. The streets and the freeways were mine. With all of them asleep, I fancied myself a mysterious stranger. The fantasy was necessary. There were no breathtaking sights to keep me awake. Even the early sun seemed tiresome after a few minutes. I almost dozed off a couple of times before we reached the McDonald's at Barstow. I wouldn't let my family know, but the car was on automatic pilot for a good part of a minute. They went in and ordered breakfast. Grandma ate slowly. I put my head on the table while they were finishing breakfast. By the time we set out again—a little bit before nine—the sun was already harsh on those below it.

Getting out of the car and stretching helped me to stay awake for the second half of the trip. There were other thoughts that kept me awake the rest of the way. I thought about what Mario said the night before, and I seriously considered the possibility of seeing less of him. Sometimes we hurt each other like family.

The ride was smooth until the last fifty miles or so when we were going uphill. That was when I remembered the fluids. I didn't check them before the long trip. The station wagon was not in the best condition to begin with; adding to it the weight of my whole family, their baggage in the back, and almost five hours on the road, it was not surprising that the temperature needle was rising. Driving had always given me such anxieties. I hated the whole trip. I put all the negative thoughts in the back of my mind. We would be in Vegas in thirty, forty minutes. My optimism, however, did not stop the needle. It was stable when I went downhill. As soon as the road showed the slightest incline, the needle shot up at an even sharper angle. We finally reached the strip, but the traffic got worse. Cars were barely moving. Some people took advantage of the stalled cars and forced their way to make a turn, paying no mind to the traffic lights. Some of them were left stranded in the middle of the intersection, blocking the traffic and exacerbating the problem.

My needle went wild at this point, and I was as frustrated as my car was heated. I was holding this all inside. Who could I share this with? My family didn't know their way around cars. All they could do, especially Grandma, was to nag me and ask me what I planned to do or offer suggestions that even I knew would not alleviate the problem. I prayed to the car. I made promises to wash it, to take better care of it, to feed it gas well before the needle reached "E". When we reached the parking lot of one of the smaller hotels off the main strip, the temperature needle was pointing beyond 200 F.

When I got out of the car, I heard noises under the hood, like there was a fight. Green liquid was all over the ground. Only then did I tell my parents about the unstoppable needle during the last fifty miles. They decided not to worry about it. Maybe it would get better by itself. We just needed to remember to put fluids in before we'd leave. Mother even quipped about winning one of those jackpot cars.

Grandma was worried. While my parents were hitting the casino, Grandma and I checked into the rooms. She too was tired, after sitting in the station wagon for six hours. It had been a long day for her already, though we had not had lunch. She asked me a lot of questions about the car. After exhausting the theories of why the car overheated she concluded that this could only be a "one-time thing." I tried to explain to her that it was never a one-time thing to have green fluid gushing out beneath the car like a waterfall. It was hard to break bad news in Vegas. She decided to take a nap.

At around one Mom called and told us to meet them in one of the restaurants in the hotel. I woke Grandma up and we walked down together. The car was no longer in her mind. She was ready for something else.

After lunch, I was supposed to look after Grandma as she tried her luck in the casino. She liked the nickel slots, cheap excitement. Amidst the crowd, she disappeared into nowhere. I looked and looked, but people looked the same to me, all standing next to blinking lights. They were everywhere, gambling: in the bar, next to the elevator, by the snack counter, rows after rows of slot machines. Grandma could be anywhere.

I walked down the side of the aisle of slot machines, like looking for something in a supermarket. I looked down at my wrist but could not find my watch. I had left it upstairs in the room. I gave up looking after a while and sat on a stool in front of a broken slot machine. A few seats away a couple was depositing coins into narrow slots, hoping happiness would come out from the bottom. They looked like newlyweds. The groom stood by a stool, still in his tuxedo, though without his bow tie. It could get rather hot standing between rows of wish-making machines. He pressed the button on the panel instead of pulling down the lever. His bride was sitting next to him, in her wedding gown, a shocking white amidst the blinking lights. The veil was pulled back and off to one side, her sleeves rolled up, and her forehead was sweating. I wanted to wipe her face to protect the gown. She stared at the rotating wheels with an intensity that could almost will the three red sevens to magically appear across the payline.

Suddenly the siren ran off above them, and a stream of nickels fell between the bride's legs. The sound of the coins hitting the metal tray made the nickels sound heavier than they actually were. The bride screamed and clapped, and her groom lowered his head to kiss her. His left hand reached around the overflowing gown to pull her closer. Without any effort, they locked for a long moment, and I felt sick. My head was spinning. I saw cherries, diamonds, and magic sevens. Perhaps the lights and the noise were finally getting to me. I held on to the out-of-order lever in order to stand up again. I wanted to go back to the room and lie down. As I passed by the couple, I noticed the hand that the man used to embrace his wife. The fingers were dirtied by the coins, and they left fingerprints on her shoulder. The bride was scooping the mountain of nickels into a plastic container. No words exchanged between the two.

I wanted to run upstairs, but I knew I would faint if I did. So I walked slowly, my hand shielding my forehead. I had not forgotten Grandma, but I knew she'd be all right. This was Vegas. I would take a nap first, perhaps Then I'd write to Mario and tell him everything. I had not thought about how to start the letter; I would think about that later. But in the middle I'd tell him I'd take him to Vegas to make up for the lost years when he had to stay home. I'd tell him I'd be his chauffeur. Let one leg grow longer than the other if that had to be the price. In the middle of the letter, I'd tell him if he'd seen love in Vegas he would learn to recognize mine and appreciate its violence and patience. Hell, if that couple with the jackpot deserved it, then we all deserved it. I'd write the letter on the hotel stationery. No—on a postcard. For all to see. And I'd end it with "from Simon, with love." And everyone in his house would hold the postcard up by the light and wonder who I was. Meetings would be held in the kitchen after dinner to discuss the potential problem. Curious eyes shot across the street behind the window would hold up the curtain a little higher and longer.

I'd write the postcard exactly like that. Somehow I thought it'd be just as easy and painless as it was for the gambling couple. Maybe we were a special breed. When I walked into my room, I didn't do what I had planned. My head was spinning out of control, but nothing went dark for me. I could see as clearly as the day after a storm. I hadn't looked for the bed; I was afraid I would fall asleep and forget. But I ended up there anyway, flat on my stomach, gazing at the wall, waiting for all around me to stay still. I wasn't being lazy about the letter. I had figured out the middle, I had figured out the end, but I still hadn't found the words to begin a love letter.

VIN G. WOLFE

MY AUNTIE

I.

Coffee with very little
milk in it is the color of my skin
and I can't help it. I got this
from her brother whom everyone called Negro
so she called me Negrita.
The horror of sun-browned skin!
Hay! naku! maitim ka na!
Muka ka pang lalaki!
Sometimes she would look at me,
an 8-year-old skinny girl, knock-kneed
with the Beatles' haircut
and insisted on putting earrings on me each time
we went to church
so I would not look like a boy.

She would also bunch her lips together,
shake her head from side to side
and feel sorry for my flat nose
Hmmmp! Wala kang ilong!
I really wished I didn't have one,
each time she said this
so I would not have to breath
her perfume whenever she came near me
Pag-laki mo ipa pa-nose lip natin 'yan!

Nose lift. Eyelids fixed
even her name
from Rafaela to Felicidad
she had all the alterations.
My grandmother said you need
a lot of money to do all that
but she had Tito Arthur,
who had a wife and owned

a mango and pineapple plantation in Davao★
he kept her in Manila
in a three-bedroom house
she designed herself built with separate maids'
quarters, a two-car garage, a wide Bermuda grass lawn,
and a rose garden where she kept
her collections of lovebirds.

★*Southern part of the Philippines*

II.

Every Christmas, the smell of sweet ham,
queso de bola, apples, grapes and oranges
on top of her massive dining table
would drift through the walls of that house
along with the song of Bing Crosby's
"White Christmas," while all of us cousins
competed in egg races, apple-eating contests
and struggled next to each other
in wriggling a dies centimos
from our foreheads to our mouths
as fast as we could
using only our facial muscles.

She had a driver although she drove
her own Mustang
a gardener who kept the grass
well-trimmed on the edges around her red palm trees
and a nanny to look after her three children
while she went to the parlor
to get her fingers, toenails, and hair done every Saturday.

One of her three maids usually cooked
except when Tito Arthur was at home
which was not very often.
Most of the time, her five white poodles
that needed grooming once a week
sat next to her

while she drank her morning coffee
in front of her artificial fishpond.
Each night with a wet towel wrapped
around her head
her face covered with Pond's Cold Cream
she would bend down to offer one of her ears
for me to kiss goodnight.
And sometimes, instead of saying goodnight
she would look at me
her face would slowly crumple, buckling
the glacial smear, forming crevices
on the bridge of her nose and say
Hmmmp! Did you wash your flower already?

III.

If not the fumes from down there,
she would smell my head
and say Hmmmp! Amoy sako ang ulo mo!
This always made me wonder
what sack of rice could emit
such stench,
the way she contorted her nose and lips
and yelled at me to wash my flower
and shampoo my hair before I went to bed.

Her house was always a dark castle
and it became even darker
when Tito Arthur packed
all his clothes one day and left
for his wife found out about their affair.
I was already in fourth grade when this happened.
So in the afternoon, I would sneak, walking past
the living room, the windows and sliding glass doors
hiding behind those thick long draping curtains
Olivia Newton-John or sometimes Helen Reddy
sang from the turntable. There in the corner
of her melancholic couch

I would see her blowing cigarette smoke
in the empty air
her eyes staring so far away.

She stopped noticing my smell,
she did not care anymore if I had a flat nose
and my skin, even though
I stayed outside all day long
she did not care whether I turned charcoal.
All of a sudden I was running free
until the following school year came
I was unpacking my little bag
and putting my clothes away
inside another new closet
this time at her sister's house.

KATHRYN XIAN

THE PROBLEM WITH BEING (EXCERPT)

SYNOPSIS

After her academic advisors critique her dissertation ("The Lesbian Phenomenon") as too conjectural and recommend she bolster it with primary documents and first-person testimonials, Emily Irving, whose fiancé, Rick, is a political strategist for the Democratic Party, decides to go undercover as a lesbian.

But what begins as an innocently intended yet exploitative attempt to identify with lesbians as an oppressed minority soon becomes something more personal and profound; even as Emily finds herself moving away from the supposedly tolerant world of her mother (a renowned forensic psychologist and sociologist) and fiancé, she is unable to engage fully in her adopted lesbian subculture (where several women notice and remark upon her secrecy and nervousness). To complicate matters, she finds herself growing closer to one of her new friends, a woman named Sam who bartends at a club called Mama Love's.

Perplexed and increasingly suspicious of Emily's friendship with Sam, Rick gets Emily's best friend, Jessie, to divulge the name of the bar. Introducing himself as Emily's friend, he invites Sam to a surprise party in celebration of the completion of Emily's dissertation.

At the party—to which everyone has been invited, including Emily's professors—Rick positions Sam at the back of the room. When Emily walks in, Rick applauds her success and trumpets her unorthodox research techniques, commending her gay persona as "a clever hoax in the name of higher learning." Sam moves to the forefront and Emily, rendered speechless, can only watch Sam leave, upset and betrayed.

Emily finally tracks Sam down at her job, where the latter remains aloof throughout most of Emily's apology. Emily tells Sam she cancelled her engagement to Rick, but Sam remains unmoved. Finally, after a heartfelt explanation, Sam forgives her.

ACT ONE
Scene One

(One light rises on EMILY IRVING CS.
She sits on a chair facing the audience. She is casually dressed.)

EMILY

Lesbian identity is a state of being some women may claim is exclusively theirs, exclusively female. Its impetus is born from patriarchal

443

society rather than from an aberration of morality. Lesbianism threatens the establishment solely because it re-distributes all property into the hands of a woman herself, that property being a woman's own body. This is not to say that heterosexual women are inherently exempt from a free state of being. Heterosexual women are merely less inclined to embrace true liberty because they do not need to. We are disposed to be accompanied, taken care of, looked after, protected—and we expect nothing less from the male gender. For these benefits we relinquish some liberty to a standard—a gender role—a guideline upon which society is based and a segregation upon which sexism may flourish. With these factors surrounding and automatically defining us, it is plausible that with time, a percentage of the population will disagree with the segregationist standard. This group will defy their gender roles, unafraid to be considered more alike than not, more equal than separate, more human than a gender role. Therefore, how may we, as the establishment, abhor their existence when it was the establishment itself from where they came?

(Lights up on stage. Emily looks anxious. Silhouetted on a flat behind her, are the shadows of three professors, two men and one woman, sitting, reviewing a draft of EMILY'S thesis.)

DR. WHITTON

We would like to make some comments regarding your rather...ambitious thesis. Simply put, Miss Irving, we find that your project has some major problems.

DR. WARREN

Emily, in both your case studies and your interviews of homosexual women, the responses are very similar, not to mention one-dimensional.

DR. CHAVEZ

Have you had a great difficulty interviewing lesbians for your project?

DR. WARREN

We just find it odd that there's really not much said here about them.

EMILY

I document what they tell me.

DR. WHITTON

Well, perhaps their insubstantial responses have something to do with your interviewing style.

DR. CHAVEZ

It could be that the lesbians you've interviewed weren't exactly comfortable with answering personal questions about their sexual histories to a heterosexual such as yourself.

EMILY

With all due respect, I don't feel that should be an issue. Sexuality is circumstantial. That's the whole point of my thesis.

DR. WHITTON

Yes, well, one doesn't really get that from the interviews themselves...as one should.

DR. WARREN

From what we've read, it's clear that the women you've interviewed were more than just reserved. At times, they seem defensive.

DR. WHITTON

Certainly, if I were a lesbian and a heterosexual woman asked me intimate details about my sex life, I would be uncomfortable, to say the least.

DR. CHAVEZ

Your heterosexuality *does* affect the results of your interviews. I'm sorry to say that, but it does. I know it may seem unfair. We realize that there is nothing you can do to change your sexual orientation to make your subjects feel more at ease, but perhaps you could change your approach. It could be just that simple.

EMILY

Would you rather I change my interview questions? I just don't feel right about censoring myself like that.

DR. CHAVEZ

Emily, we believe in your work.

DR. WHITTON

We're giving you the benefit of the doubt here on what you've done so far. We're trying to help you, not discourage you. If you think we're being severe, imagine what others might do. Your thesis is in trouble. Emily, you are a very powerful writer. I can see that runs in your family. Your mother's work has served the intellectual community very well. Perhaps you may want to take a hint from her, since she is such a ready resource. She is a great and respected feminist.

EMILY

(with veiled sarcasm)
I'll keep that in mind, Professor Whitton.

Scene Two

(The silhouettes disappear and EMILY remains on the chair. Lights rise, revealing a cozy living room setting. There is a poster pasted on the back wall that reads, "Elect Hardy—Democrat." RICK enters from the bathroom, dressed for work.)

RICK

Sweetie, to tell you the truth, I don't know why you're so torn up about all this. If you're going to be dealing with this kind of thing, you have to be able to take harsh criticism. So they were a little rough on you... so what?

EMILY

All three of them had the same opinion, Rick. All three.

RICK

Look, not one of them even has the guts to say what you're saying. And I find it ironic that they restricted you just because you're straight. They aren't gay either.

EMILY

Well, actually...Chavez and Whitton are both gay.

RICK

Are you serious?

EMILY

I appreciate what you're doing, but let's face it, they're right. I don't know what it's like to be gay. Christ, I don't even know what it's like to be a minority.

RICK

That's not true. You know what it's like to be a woman.

EMILY

Rick. Save it for the campaign. (*pause*) I know what it's like to be the daughter of the great Margaret Irving. It can't get any cushier than that.

(*A knock at the door. RICK goes over to open it and JESSICA enters.*)

JESSICA

So, how'd it go?

EMILY

Do you know they actually advised me to ask my mother for help?

JESSICA

Oh...not so good, huh.

RICK

(aloofly)
Hello, Jessica.

JESSICA

(aloofly)
Hello, Richard.

RICK

Well, I've gotta go. I have to be at the campaign office at ten.
(to JESSICA) Maybe you'll have an easier time cheering her up. *(exits)*

JESSICA

I still don't forgive you for agreeing to marry him.

EMILY

Jess, not now.

JESSICA

All right, all right. But don't say I didn't warn you. *(pause)* Can I say just one more thing?

EMILY

Can I stop you?

JESSICA

My father was a politician. Em, he drove my mother nuts. Never marry a politician—ever. The poor woman had to divorce him three times just to get her point across.

EMILY

Rick's not a politician. Not really.

JESSICA

Oh, no. He's worse. He's a political strategist.

EMILY

And what is that supposed to mean?

JESSICA

Emily, come on. Marriage is the quintessential political game. He said, she said. I can just see it now. He'll turn your love into a terrific strategy.

EMILY

Give me a break, will you? You are the last person on earth that I would take relationship advice from. Shall I mention the string of short-term relationships that you've had in the last two years?

JESSICA

I told you, I was going through a phase.

EMILY

Can we not talk about this right now?

JESSICA

Sure, fine, whatever you say.

EMILY

I knew there was going to be a problem with my thesis. I just didn't want to admit it. I've been losing sight of my work. I know it's true.

JESSICA

Well, can it be that bad? What's your problem anyway?

EMILY

I'm straight! Somehow my heterosexual demeanor creates tension between the interviewees and myself. Like it's some repelling force that makes gay women apprehensive.

JESSICA

Well, that kinda makes sense.

EMILY

It shouldn't make a difference. If I were an African-American doing a thesis on European society do you think I would be considered wrong just because I'm not white?

JESSICA

Well, no, but...

EMILY

Some things are just not fair.

JESSICA

Sex makes a difference. It changes everything.

EMILY

It's not my fault that I'm straight and white. Tell me something, do I have any less validity because I'm straight? Should I just give up my Masters? What?

JESSICA

Listen, could you honestly tell me that it wouldn't matter to you if a big dyke grilled you about your relationship with Rick?

EMILY

It shouldn't.

JESSICA

But it would, wouldn't it?

EMILY

It shouldn't.

JESSICA

But it would! That's why your interviews suck. You put them on the spot. I agree with you that this difference shouldn't make a difference. But it does. You can't ignore sex.

EMILY

I find that so irritating.

JESSICA

Well, what do you expect gays to do, Em...change to fit your project? (*pause*) Emily?

EMILY

You know, things would be a hell of a lot easier if I were gay...

JESSICA

Yeah, right. I've said that to myself from time to time.

EMILY

(*long pause*)
You know...what if...just what if...

JESSICA

What if what?

EMILY

What if I said I was gay?

JESSICA

(*laughs*)

Ha! Yeah, right. (*pause*) Wait, you're not actually thinking about... (*pause*) No. No way! What are you nuts??

EMILY

Well, think about it! I could actually do fieldwork successfully. I could cut my hair...tone down the "obviously straight" look.

JESSICA

That is the worst idea I've ever heard come out your mouth yet. Why not go all the way and shave your head?

EMILY

Why? Why is it a bad idea?

JESSICA

Why? Why? Wha...I can't believe you're even considering this. This is a joke, right?

EMILY

No one would know, except the gay community.

JESSICA

I would know. And what about your fiancé?

EMILY

You wouldn't tell. And Rick would understand. He's a liberal Democrat.

JESSICA

People will find out. Believe me, Chicago ain't that small. And Rick would have a heart attack. It doesn't matter if he's a liberal or a Democrat, he's still a man. On second thought...maybe he wouldn't be that upset.

EMILY

People won't find out, Jess. This is for a good cause! Dr. Chavez herself said that she believed in my thesis. All I need is a little fieldwork. It's the perfect idea!

JESSICA

It's the worst idea! Emily, you're straight! Wha-what are you going to do about the sex?

EMILY

I'm not going to experiment with my sexuality. I'm not going that far. Anyway, sex is not everything that a lesbian is. It's the social exclusion I'm after. The oppression. (*smiles widely*)

JESSICA

Oh, God, Em, please ask your mother for help.

Scene Three

(*EMILY and JESSICA arrive at MAMA LOVE'S, a dimly lit swing bar known for its gay clientele. Swing music is playing. There is a bar DL. They enter UR. JESSICA looks tense and clings to EMILY. SAM is tending bar. There are various people sitting and conversing at tables.*)

JESSICA

(*behind EMILY, clinging to her elbow, crouching as if hiding*)
I don't know why I let you talk me into this.

EMILY

Relax, will you? What do you think is going to happen? We're just here for some drinks.

JESSICA

You think they know?

EMILY

Know what?

JESSICA

That we're straight. I mean, you think they could tell? What if they eighty-six us out of here for looking too *(whispering)* heterosexual? What if we get beat up?

EMILY

By the lesbian fashion Gestapo? Jessica, come on.

JESSICA

All right, whatever. Just, if anyone asks me to dance, I'm with you, okay?

EMILY

You need a drink.

(They sit at the bar.)

SAM

Can I get you two anything?

EMILY

Vodka martini.

SAM

(begins to make the drink)

What's wrong with your friend?

EMILY

She has a posture problem; slight scoliosis...runs in the family.

SAM

You two are sisters?

JESSICA

We're together!

EMILY

No, we're just friends. She's a little jumpy. Hyperthyroid.

                    SAM

Not very lucky is she? *(to JESSICA)* Can I get you anything?

                    JESSICA

Scotch. Make it a double.

(SAM finishes EMILY'S drink and pours
JESSICA'S. She drinks it all at once. A
WOMAN comes up behind JESSICA and
taps her shoulder. A popular upbeat
swing tune starts playing.)

                    WOMAN

Care to dance?

                    JESSICA

I'm with her.

                    WOMAN

(looks at the two)

Yeah, right.

(The woman grabs JESSICA by the hand and
leads her to the dance floor, exit off-stage DL
JESSICA looks for help, but EMILY urges her on.)

                    SAM

You two are new around here, I take it.

                    EMILY

No, no. Not at all.

                    SAM

I've never seen you here before. I'm Sam. Sam Bergin. *(Offers her hand.*

They shake.) Pleasure to meet you.

                              EMILY

Emily Irving.

                               SAM

Is that girl really just a friend?

                              EMILY

Jessica? Oh, definitely.

*(Lights go blue on SAM and EMILY. Lights
go up opposite stage: the dance floor. The
WOMAN and JESSICA have re-entered CR
and are swinging together throughout the
scene. JESSICA still looks a little stiff.)*

                             WOMAN

So, where you from?

                             JESSICA

Uh, Minneapolis.

                             WOMAN

Really? I'm from St. Paul! How about that. Sister cities.

                             JESSICA

Heh. Yeah.

                             WOMAN

Charleston?

*(They do the Charleston. Lights go blue
on the two dancers. Lights rise again on SAM*

and EMILY.)

EMILY

So, if you're from Philadelphia, why do you sound like you're from Boston?

SAM

You have good ears. I'm from Quincy. Moved out when I was sixteen. I've been all over, though. New York, Jersey, Pittsburgh, Florida. You?

EMILY

Well, I went to Disney World when I was eight, but...

SAM

No, I mean, where you from? Around here?

EMILY

I'm from New York. Brooklyn Heights, actually.

SAM

Nice area. So, what are you doing in Chicago?

EMILY

I'm, um, going to school, actually.

SAM

Oh really? In what?

EMILY

(sarcastically)
Finishing.

*(Lights go blue on them. Lights rise again on
our dancers. JESSICA has loosened up a bit.)*

WOMAN

You're not used to this, are you?

JESSICA

Is there something wrong with the way I dance?

WOMAN

No, I mean, you're not used to dancing with a woman. You're straight, right?

JESSICA

(pause)

I don't have a problem with dancing with you. It's just new to me.

WOMAN

Relax a little.

JESSICA

You don't mind that I'm straight?

WOMAN

Do you mind that I'm not?

JESSICA

(slightly unsure)

No.

WOMAN

Relax. Let yourself have fun. Believe me, I'm no threat. No offense, but you aren't my type. I just don't sleep with straight women....Though I do keep an open mind.

(Lights blue on them. Lights up on SAM

and EMILY.)

SAM

How come I've never seen you here before?

EMILY

(reserved)

I hardly go out. I'm a bit of a homebody.

SAM

I don't mean to be nosey or anything. It's refreshing to see new people in here. I was beginning to think that I knew every lesbian in Chicago.

EMILY

(awkwardly)

Me too. *(pause)* I guess I'm more of a day person, you know. Plus, I had this long-term relationship...girlfriend...all we did was stay home most of the time.

SAM

Oh.

EMILY

Yeah, we're not together anymore. It happens.

SAM

I'm sorry to hear about that.

EMILY

(trying)

It's okay. You know...women.

(Lights blue on them. Lights up on JESSICA and the WOMAN.)

JESSICA

This might be a stupid question but…

WOMAN

What?

JESSICA

You think I could lead? I mean, if that's okay. I've never done it before.

WOMAN

Are you kidding? Hell, ya!

(The music gets louder. The dance moves get considerably more complex; there are several flips and twists and turns. JESSICA is enjoying herself. At the end of the tune, she dips her partner.)

WOMAN

Unbelievable, Minnesota.

JESSICA

Well, uh, I'd better get back to my friend at the bar. Thanks for the dance.

WOMAN

Not that fast! The least I can do is buy you a drink for the dance lesson.

(Both exit R. Lights rise on EMILY and SAM. Both are laughing.)

SAM

That's gotta be the worst joke I've ever heard.

EMILY

It made you laugh, didn't it? Well then.

SAM

You said your name is Emily?

EMILY

That's right.

SAM

What a pretty name.

EMILY

I always thought it sounded ordinary.

SAM

It sounds friendly. I've never known anyone named Emily before. You're my first.

(The WOMAN and JESSICA enter SL.)

EMILY

Thanks. I guess I'm a pioneer of sorts.

WOMAN

*(sits down on EMILY'S left, patting an
empty seat next to her.)*

Hey, Sam! Gimme a gin and tonic, will ya?

*(JESSICA strategically sits on EMILY'S
right, acting oblivious to the gesture.)*

That woman is the best swinger I've ever met. Hey, Minnesota! This is Sam.

(JESSICA smiles and waves.)

EMILY

(offers her hand to the woman. They shake.)

I'm Emily.

WOMAN

St. Paul, nice to meet you.

SAM

She's one of those smart types. What'd you say you were?—in college?

EMILY

I'm actually getting my Masters.

SAM

(to Jessica)

You know, I'd have never guessed you be such a dancer.

JESSICA

Why not?

SAM

Well, I mean, you looked so stiff before. I thought you were going to become a permanent fixture here.

JESSICA

(sarcastically)

That's funny. You should write that one down.

WOMAN

Hey, Sam!

(The WOMAN beckons SAM over.
SAM finishes up the WOMAN'S drink
and starts talking with her inaudibly.)

EMILY

This place isn't so bad, is it?

JESSICA

I'll bet you two hundred bucks you won't pull this off.

EMILY

Thanks for the vote of confidence.

JESSICA

We look so out of place here.

EMILY

I don't think so.

JESSICA

Quit kidding yourself.

EMILY

This is going to be a good experience for me. I need this.

JESSICA

Yeah, but do you want this? *(pause)* See? You can't even answer.

EMILY

Yes. I want this.

JESSICA

It's too late. You hesitated.

(Lights fade.)

NITA YAMASHITA

A STAR IS BORN

The lights go up and a lone man stands on stage, wearing a girl's limp 1950s poodle skirt, not quite new and a little rumpled through the pleats, his hair in pigtails, saddle shoes on his feet. Even before he opens his mouth, the audience is applauding, and from the first words he speaks—"My name is Tule Lake Iwakoshi, and I'm eleven. Well, at least, I like to be 11"—to the last, there is a collective leaning forward, the way the most eager and enthusiastic audiences express their rapt attention.

Two hours later, the audience applauds for the last time and the lights go down, and Tule Lake leaves off stage left, pulling off her skirt in the wings, becoming a man once again. According to the show's press release and program, Tule Lake is the invention of C.S. Tatami, a Yale-trained and heretofore unheard-of actor turned this year's theater sensation. What only a dozen or so people know, however, is that C.S. Tatami is himself the invention of Coffin Winerip, a 32-year-old book editor and untrained actor, the man actually responsible for the phenomenally successful one-man cabaret show, "Camp," which has been selling out for the past six months at New York's Public Theater.

"Camp," last season's off-Broadway surprise hit, is the brilliant, acerbic, bitingly funny, and devastating story of twenty-six-year-old Tule Lake Iwakoshi, a Japanese-American woman living in Santa Monica with her aging parents. Tule Lake grew up in the eponymous internment camp, and the show—which includes eleven original songs and four soft-shoe dances—is told partly in flashback, as Tule relives life before and in the camps where over 120,000 Japanese-Americans spent the World War II years. At the center of Tule's story is her brother, California, a camp rebel and objector whose murder Tule witnesses as a child. It is a small, tragic story, but in Winerip's hands, it becomes a wicked little comedy, one which handles its complex and knotty issues—war, civil rights, madness, and memory—with humor and style and savoir faire along with empathy and anger and intelligence. Much of what is unique about "Camp" is, however, unreproducable in print: Winerip, who also wrote and directed the show, is a mesmerizing, highly physical actor, and the reactions "Camp" invokes come as much from his performance as the writing. Offstage, Winerip, who is tall and trim and has a face that would, twenty years ago, be described as interesting but now is considered arresting—all fine features and sharp bones—is graceful and dignified, but on-stage, as the terminally pre-pubescent Tule, his limbs contort and fold over and under one another until he achieves a sort of balletic spasticity. Similarly, his face becomes enormously, evocatively elastic—his expressions punctuate and pontificate at once. Winerip is a muscular, intense performer—along with an ebullient extravagance, he has the gift of both self-control and subtlety, and some of the finest moments in the show are when Tule, her voice becoming small, seems to herself forget that she's speaking to an audience and turns her monologue quietly inwards. Tule "fancies herself a lady," as she says, and one of the show's most touching and amusing scenes is of Tule, newly released from the camps, shopping in a fancy department store while its patrons—and we—snicker at her stylized airs, her self-conscious attempts at grace. In Tule's sturdy, ugly shoes and drooping cotton sweater, Winerip manages to convey both her gawkiness as well as her fierce, unshakable pride—the only thing that saves her from becoming a staring zombie like her once-aggressive father. It is an astonishing performance, and Winerip's passion—for the character, for the language, for the stage—is clearly evident in each song, speech, and foot-stomping tantrum Tule throws.

This on-stage rage and barely contained venom is part of what makes Winerip's off-stage life and persona that much more surprising, and during the week I spent with him—the days at the offices of Alfred A. Knopf, and the nights at the theater—I found myself marveling again and again at the ease and apparent seamlessness with which he moves through and among his bifurcated worlds and selves. Winerip is renowned and well-respected in the literary community for his keen editorial eye and erudition, and for the attention and care he lavishes upon his authors, and when I spoke with one of them, a mutual friend, about Winerip's secret history, he was disbelieving. "I've seen 'Camp' three times," the author said, "and I'm telling you that there's no way that that's Coffee. I'll bet you five grand that it's not him." I had Winerip call him to confirm his secret identity, but our friend was still incredulous. "But how?" he asked, astonished. "Why?" It is an inevitable question, of course, but one which Winerip himself is unable—or unwilling—to answer to anyone's satisfaction.

But maybe Winerip's talents as a character actor are not so unaccountable; he has, after all, been reinventing himself his entire life.

———

The son of two academics—his Jewish Hungarian father was a linguist, and his Japanese American mother a microbiologist—Winerip was born Coffin Susumu Goldberg in Santa Cruz, where his parents taught at the university. Winerip doesn't remember much about his father ("I'm pretty sure that he was kind and that I loved him, but children usually think that about this parents who die when they're young"), but he does remember his father's illness, his long struggle with cancer that began when Winerip was seven. A painful and difficult year and a half later, Willem Goldberg died of bone cancer. He was forty-three years old. "When I think of my father," says Winerip, "all I can remember are the instruments of his sickness. He died at home, and we had everything—the gurney and the IV bags and that strange sterile smell and nurses walking in and out throughout the day." Winerip, who says he and his mother had a "fractious" relationship, grew further apart from her after his father's death, and in 1979, when Winerip was almost eleven, his mother remarried, to a colleague from her lab. When he was thirteen, Winerip ran away from home. While he for the most part refuses to talk about this part of childhood, his explanation for leaving home—"Let's just say that my stepfather was rather more fond of me than I was of him"—leaves, I think, little room for misinterpretation. Winerip has not communicated with his mother in almost twenty years, and when I ask him about her, his face becomes blank and impenetrable—a perfect stage mask. "Oh my stars," he groans, and although his tone is light, his mouth becomes tight and guarded. "Speaking of mothers, did you see Lucretia Crenshaw in Macbeth recently? My god, what a performance." One of Winerip's trademarks as a performer is his remarkable voice, which translates as well off-stage as on—soft, comforting, and slightly smoky, it manages to be both crisp and slightly furry-edged through the consonants; he chooses his words carefully, but one senses an actor's energy and confidence in his cadence, in those creamy, deracinated vowels. He also has a way of wriggling out of questions he doesn't want to answer, by either smoothly changing the subject, or deflecting it with a self-deprecating joke. This happened to me so often the first couple of times I met with him that it wasn't until I looked at my notes after our interviews that I realized he hadn't answered half the questions I'd asked. If you push him toward answering, though, he will simply fall silent and, after a period too long to be misconstrued, reply gently that he doesn't want to discuss the subject raised. If Winerip is stimulating, even jolting, on-stage, he is lulling off-stage, and there is something hypnotic about the slowness and spareness of his gestures, the way he leans back in his chair so that his audience must lean forward to hear his voice dip and swell in volume.

After he ran away, he spent two years on the road. Winerip is vague and scattery about this time, and communicates with more throat-clearing and eye-wandering than words, but at one point, he pulls a small creased picture from his desk drawer and puts it in my hand. It is a surprisingly intimate gesture, and the photo—which shows a gangly, bony, fierce-faced boy wearing a stained jean jacket and dirty jeans staring into the camera bitterly—is simultaneously touching and shocking both for its image (the boy is leaning against a grafitti-covered wall, and a stretch of filthy asphalt runs alongside him) and for the lack of relation it bears to the man before me, with his fastidiously crisp clothes and level shoes. I study the photo and Winerip studies me. "I was fourteen here," he says, finally, and his voice is gentle. "This was in—let's see—in Chicago, I think. When I left home, I decided I was going to hitchhike to Boston. My father had lived there in graduate school, when he first came to the States, and the way he described it—students everywhere, cheap food—it was his idea of America, of youth, and I wanted it to be mine, too." He pauses. "It wasn't all as awful as you'd think, but the worst thing—I was a very clean kid—was the dirtiness, the inability to shower." He laughs. "Other than that, though"—he raises his hands, palms up, a shrug—"I had some interesting experiences. I could write a play." He laughs again, but something in his voice says he never will.

By the time Winerip made it to Boston, he was fifteen and "tired. I was always tired. But I liked Boston right away. I used to hang around Harvard Square, look at all the kids—I liked watching all the rich kids—they always looked so self-assured, so well taken care of. I admired their confidence." He made his living from a patchwork of part-time jobs—raking people's lawns, frying hamburgers at McDonald's, pumping gas in South Boston—and lived at a YMCA, where he paid twenty-five dollars a week for a room with a bed and a sink and one meal a day. But, as Winerip notes, his luck was soon to change. He had inherited from his parents a love of school, of learning, and he remembers being elated when he tested and was subsequently accepted into the eleventh grade at Boston's prestigious Latin School, one of the oldest and finest examples of subsidized magnet schools in the nation. He excelled at Latin, and although much of his time between the school day and his jobs was spent catching up on the two years he'd missed—especially in math and science—he did well enough in English for his teacher, Marie Auzanne, to show some of his essays to a friend of hers who was a literature professor at Harvard. Says Auzanne, "It was incredible, tough stuff, especially for a child—most kids' writing at that time is either pure fantasy or completely self-referential. Coffin's was an adult's in its anger, its perception, its compassion." Although Winerip never—and never has—wrote about the two years he lightly calls "the missing years," Auzanne said that even then his writing "always flirted with sadness, with despair even. It was a strange thing to read in a child's writing, a strange thing to read about from a child. I wanted to encourage him— I thought he'd make an excellent journalist."

When I ask Winerip about this, though, he shakes his head fiercely. "I shall be forever grateful to my teachers at Latin, especially Marie Auzanne," he says, and his voice slows. "But I think they probably thought I was some wild child, a prodigy, an uneducated waif. I was poor, but..." he sighs, resigned. "I don't think I should be given too much credit where it simply isn't due. I grew up with cultural capital, after all. My mother and father were professors. I always felt like a fraud because my life wasn't, perhaps, as difficult as they [the teachers] thought, as they think. I knew how to be comfortable around academics, around schools, I knew what teachers wanted to hear. I was a privileged kid who had learned how to play someone else. I always knew that I would go to college, and that it would be a good one. Latin didn't teach me that, although it did make it possible." Nevertheless, Winerip loved his tutorials at the university, and he and his mentor, Auzanne's friend—whose name was Jacob Winerip—soon became close. Jacob Winerip, who held an endowed chair at Harvard for the latter half of his career, was known as a sharp, discriminating, and highly original scholar and thinker and was, says his friend, historian G. Graham Craven, "chronically melancholy." A lifelong bachelor, Winerip was the only child of a very rich lawyer in New York; he sailed through Yale and Cambridge and spent his entire academic life at Harvard. In 1979, he won the Pulitzer Prize for *The Humorous Bulb*, his groundbreaking re-consideration of Chaucer. "He loved Coffee," says Professor Winerip's longtime friend and colleague, Dr. Robert LeCroix. "I think Jacob even fell *in love* with him a little bit; he had a rather Victorian sense of romance, you see. I remember telling me how he was tutoring a high school student at a friend's request, and how smart he was, and how lonely." It was true—Coffin Winerip was lonely, and struggling too—he qualified for free lunches at school, and had dinner at the Y at night, but by December of that first year in Boston, he remembers feeling "broken, exhausted, and no less tired. I remember always thinking that something had to give. When I recall that time, I can only see winter, those early Boston sunsets, and the sky navy and sad." Winerip stops suddenly and looks embarrassed, then continues. "When I was in high school, I loved Dickens. Adolescents, particularly melodramatic ones—as I was—like to imagine their lives as grim and grey as possible, if only for its promise of a happy ending. I remember floating through my days as if in a fairy tale."

But fortunately for Winerip, his story also had an ending that was Dickensian in both its pathos and its completeness, its neatness—that Christmas Eve, Winerip was working a double shift at McDonald's. When he saw his teacher walk in, he ducked, ashamed, and Jacob, recognizing him, gawked, dismayed. Remembers Winerip, "I think he really was shocked. He asked me what I was doing. It was in a bad section of Boston, and he volunteered in a soup kitchen nearby. And I didn't want to tell him, but in the end I did, and it was just as I'd quietly hoped for all that year—when I finished my shift, he was waiting outside, and asked me where I was living. And when I told him—this I remember, because he was a gentle man, and a gentleman—he was angry for me, and he told me, 'Come on. You're never going back there again.' He was, I think, childlike, idealistic in some ways, definitely old-fashioned, and he didn't think children should have to work on Christmas Eve, even if"—Winerip smiles—"they weren't Christian." That night, Winerip packed his belongings at the Y and went home with Jacob Winerip. The next day was Christmas, and the day after that, Jacob Winerip made some inquiries through the Department of Children Services (who had, apparently, no idea that Coffin was underage and living alone in a YMCA) and in the new year, adopted Coffee, who chose immediately to take his adoptive father's name. His journey, at least that part of it, was over. He would stay at Jacob Winerip's house for another year and a half before he left for Yale. "It was," says Winerip, and his smile grows soft and dreamy, "the happiest day of my life."

———

And at first glance, it appears that Winerip's life since then has kept pace with that earlier promise of happiness—he sped through Yale, where he received B.A. and M.A. in English Literature with honors in four years. Upon graduation, he won a Marshall Scholarship, and spent three years at Balliol College, Oxford, where he took a first-class degree in Classics. He toyed with the idea of becoming a professor, but upon his father's discouragement ("He told me it was no life for a young man," Winerip grins), he turned to the disgruntled academic's standby profession—publishing. So in 1992, when Winerip was twenty-three, he began his career as an assistant at Alfred A. Knopf; he has been there ever since, and if he stands to become famous as an actor, he already is as an editor. In an industry that is famously backbiting and pessimistic, Winerip is well-liked and admired among both his colleagues and his writers. Indeed, many of Knopf's recent critical and commercial successes—Robert Hart Young's *Gravitas*, Julia Plon's *The Book of Melancholy*, and Kristof Perralt's *The Marriage of Blood*—were acquired and edited by Winerip. He has, at a relatively young age, amassed a stable of loyal authors and, even in publishing's tumultuous times, all but assured himself a job.

Winerip is known among his peers for his impeccable taste and gentle and old-fashioned manners, and for his intense privacy. "He's very mysterious," says Random House editor Abigail Graves. "I've known Coffee since we were assistants, and while I consider him a friend, I'm still not sure if he considers me one—he's a very good listener and polite and witty, and you never really know what he's thinking. When people are being pretentious, or ridiculous, he'll just quirk the corner of his mouth into this delicious, ironic little smile and I'll just start snorting with laughter."

"I think Coffee is the paragon of control," says Lars Tomasson, Knopf's crusty and sharp-witted president and editor in chief. "It's very rare. He's brilliant, of course, but he also has a real sense of the subtle, which is more than I can say for most people."

When I pass this assessment on to Winerip, he breaks into a wide, spontaneous smile, as much for the compliment as for its obvious ironies. We're sitting in his office at Knopf, which is airy and light-filled and arranged as a collection of still lives, punctuated with neat, towering stacks of books and rubber-banded manuscripts. A white-flowering kumquat tree in a yellow-glazed terracotta pot sits on the window ledge, and a series of glossily polished rodent skulls, their bonework as fine and delicate as filigree, march along the edge of a bookshelf. On the desk, orangey persimmons lie in a milky gray ceramic dish. Winerip collects Japanese woodblock prints, and a tiny, color-flooded Hokusai II in an ebony-stained cherry frame hangs over his computer. It is the first piece he ever bought. Propped on a stack of books near a cork bulletin board crowded with notes, jacket covers, drawings, postcards, and invitations is an appealingly silvery photograph of a handsome young man with short dark hair and jaunty glasses. His back is turned to the camera and he is looking over his shoulder and smiling a wide, confident smile. The name of the man in the photo is Joshua Franklin, and if Winerip's adoptive father redefined his life once, Franklin would define it anew.

According to his friend Dr. Mayer Leerbohrn, Joshua Franklin was "an unapologetic character; he was flamboyantly aggressive and aggressively flamboyant at a time—college—when it wasn't too cool to be too enthusiastic about anything." The youngest child of two prominent New York attorneys (his father, Ivan Franklin, is a senior partner at Lutyens, Fraser and Stone, and his mother, Lola Lautenberg Franklin, serves on the board of directors at the Guggenheim Museum), Franklin was a leader, a popular, sunny, indulged kid who, in Leerbohrn's words, was "defiantly unbratty." Rich, attractive, fiercely bright, generous, gregarious, and supremely self-assured, Franklin quickly accumulated a large following at Yale. Winerip met Franklin their first day of school—they lived on the same floor—and gave up immediately. "I was attracted at once, as much to Josh himself as to the idea of him," says Winerip. "He was beautiful and witty, and moreover, he represented everything—ease, grace, style—that I didn't, and couldn't, have. Lots of people fell in love with him for the same reason—he seemed to be so comfortable with the very idea of himself." But Franklin, who picked his confidants carefully, pursued Winerip, and the two became friends and soon, and for the next twelve years, lovers. "I was stunned," says Winerip now, still faintly surprised. "He picked his friends, never the other way around, and I could never understand why he picked me." Franklin's old roommate, Nevada Technologies founder and CEO Darren Meryns, notes that "Josh was the kind of popular kid who's so secure that they never have to stoop to meanness, or pettiness. Moreover, he was genuinely interested in people, which meant that his circle of friends and admirers was always a pretty eclectic group. The fun of being part of that group was knowing Josh, of course, but it was also meeting people you might never talk to otherwise. I was very nerdy in high school, and if I hadn't met Josh, I'm sure I would have spent most of college hunched over a computer, playing Dungeons and Dragons. He was fast-witted and incredibly generous and had very good taste in people. He used to pride himself on it."

Meryns remembers Winerip as "dazzlingly intelligent and very private. When he trusted you, though, he was very funny, and for as elegant as Josh could be, when he was next to Coffee, with his restraint and dry humor—he seemed somehow wild, naïve, a little bit unpolished. It was an appealing combination, and Josh just loved him." The artist Alicia Olliphant, another of the couple's college friends, says Josh was "an old-fashioned dandy with an old-fashioned sense of what it meant to be gay, to be gentlemanly, to be generous. Some of it was affectation, of course—he loved anything extreme—but I think a lot of it—his good manners, for example—came naturally to him. Kids around that age like to make themselves into personalities, like to make themselves deliberately different, but one never sensed any effort from Josh—it was just who he was, and people were drawn to him because of it."

But of all of Franklin's talents, one—his ability to spot talent in others—stood out from the rest, and indeed, became something of a trademark. Says Meryns, "One of Josh's greatest gifts was his ability to draw people out of themselves—he was constantly coming up with ideas for his friends, projects that would best exploit their talents—'You should write a book!' 'You should go to cooking school!' 'You should start a technology company!'—so it's a great credit to him that so many of us did exactly what he told us to do and excelled in our Josh-chosen fields." Indeed, it was Franklin who first edged a "very dubious" Winerip onto the stage. Franklin's interests were wide-ranging and intense—he loved art (in particular, 19th-century South Asian sculpture, for which he'd cultivated a shrewd and educated eye), music (he played the bassoon and the double-bass), tennis (he was vice-captain of the Yale team), and school, but above all, he loved theater. While in high school at Groton, Franklin was a theater buff, and although he was never cast as the star in any of the school's productions, he remained fascinated with acting, and with the stage. "Josh favored older, grassroots forms of theater," says Winerip. "He liked penny dreadfuls, dance-hall routines, minstrel, cabaret, old situational comedies that relied on an actor's and a writer's resourcefulness rather than their refinement."

Their second year of college, Franklin, who had started a theater troupe called The Greasepaint Elis ("He was involved in about a million extra-curricular activities," says Meryns), convinced his friends to help him mount a production that he and Winerip had written. "Shmuel's Wig" was a musical about a young Jewish man in 1920s New York convinced he should've been born a woman (Franklin was fascinated with gender-bending themes). Winerip, who had become known for his ability as a lyricist and composer, wrote the songs and music, and Franklin took care of the book. Remembers Meryns, "It was the height of Josh's genius—you had a computer geek, a model (Olliphant), a classics scholar (Winerip), a physicist (Leerbohrn), and about a dozen others, none of us with theatrical training—all putting on wigs and long black coats and singing songs with these terrifically funny and preposterous titles, like 'Oy vey! My son is gay!' and 'The Plotz Waltz.'" The Tony Award-winning stage designer Twigg Chang, then too a member of Franklin's circle, built the sets and hand-painted the shtetl backdrops, and Andre Hilts, now an artistic director of the Alvin Ailey Dance Company, choreographed the piece. Franklin secured one of the smaller auditoriums on campus for three consecutive weekends and began mailing out flyers to his friends, classmates, and, his friends were horrified to discover, all of their professors. Franklin wanted Winerip to star, but Winerip, pleading stage fright, offered to be the lights technician instead; Franklin assumed the role of Shmuel by default. But the night the show was to open, Franklin claimed to have lost his voice, and the company voted Winerip, his informal understudy, on stage in his place. A "furious and terrified" Winerip took the stage, and sang and danced to a packed house. At the end, the cast received a standing ovation: applauding and yelling loudest of all was Franklin, who had somehow, Winerip notes wryly, regained his voice in the hour or so his boyfriend was on stage. A star was born, albeit reluctantly. Winerip completed his run of the show, and the two of them—Franklin directing and Winerip performing—went on to produce six more shows, usually vaguely (or determinedly) ethnic cabaret pieces. Together, they became rather famous for creating a sort of underground revival theater culture at the university, and to emphasize this, Franklin began showcasing his pieces in the basement of his residential college. His friends and classmates recall that Winerip would only perform in heavy makeup, a preference of which Franklin took full advantage. As the costumes and roles became increasingly ridiculous—a Jewish vampire, Queen Elizabeth in full white pancake makeup, a simian-faced six-year-old girl—Winerip relaxed into his roles. For his part, Winerip insists that acting was never a career possibility he "even remotely entertained" (and indeed, as a precursor to his future endeavors, he was usually left uncredited in the program notes), but his friends and classmates assumed he was headed towards eventual stage stardom anyway. Franklin, by all accounts, loved watching his boyfriend perform, and urged him to pursue it professionally, although even he knew that the chances of that were slim. For his part, he continued to act in his own productions; what he lacked in theatrical talent—Meryns remembers him as being "a bit thin-voiced"—he made up in sheer exuberance and enthusiasm. "Josh used to refer to Coffee as 'Cher'," says Leerbohrn. "The implication being, of course, that he was Sonny, and talentless, which of course wasn't true. But if you saw him alongside Coffee, it was clear who could've made the stage their career, and who couldn't. Josh could be electric on stage, but not like Coffee." Still, Franklin's friends assumed that he would at least attend Yale Drama School after graduating, and go on to a career as a director or producer.

But Franklin's father had other plans for him—imposing and tough, Ivan Franklin wanted his son to follow him into law, and so while Winerip studied at Oxford, Franklin slogged through law school at Harvard; he joined his father's firm upon graduating. "Everything came very easily to Josh," says Olliphant. "Friends, money, power, grades—he was inventive and spirited, but he had a hard time saying 'no' to his parents. He detested law school, and he never studied, but he ended up doing all right." Franklin loathed corporate law, and begged his father—to whom he still turned for the latter's financial largesse—to let him quit. "He did the least amount of work possible," smiles Winerip. "He was always trying to get himself fired without embarrassing his father too terribly. The obvious solutions—showing up to work absolutely snokered, or behaving lewdly and inappropriately in front of an important client—were things he simply wouldn't allow himself to consider, largely because he knew there would be wider-ranging consequences than just his own unemployment. He was responsible that way, and he did love his parents, as much as he feared them." Winerip had by then moved to New York and started his own career, and "to drown Josh's sorrows," the couple (who lived in a far-west Greenwich Village townhouse bought for Franklin by his parents) filled their nights with theater performances. "Josh would see anything," says Meryns, who occasionally tagged along. "Broadway, off-Broadway, Shakespeare in the Parking Lot…I remember once going to some solo performance art piece that was held in some filthy public restroom on White Street."

Franklin was a generous patron of the arts, and, after a period, an investor in a handful of New York productions. When one of them—Andrew Eronei's surprise hit "Life"—moved to Broadway, he was able to reap a small fortune of his own, and so, in 1994, after two years at Lutyens, he quit the firm. He decided he would write a play of his own, and for ten months (to his delight and his parents' chagrin) he shut himself in his study, five days a week, seven hours a day. ("Josh had patience in spades when it came to theater," sighs Meryns.) One bright spring day, Franklin and Winerip (who hadn't read Franklin's script) cooked a fantastic spread of food and invited some of their friends over to read the work that had consumed Franklin's life for the better part of the year. Their plates heavy with chanterelle-stuffed trout and olive oil-sauteed fiddleheads, the group gathered in the living room and sat down with the 200-page manuscript. They read straight through for almost three hours, with Franklin sitting off to the side, watching and listening. At the play's end, there was a small silence before the readers fell upon Franklin, congratulating him. "But he knew better," says Meryns, sadly. "It was awful, and I knew it, and I know he did too." "Fireworks in Brooklyn" was to be Franklin's masterpiece, the fruit of not just a year of work, but also of a brief, bright lifetime of passion. *The New York Times* theater critic St. Clair Michaels was one of the couple's friends and participated in the reading. "My heart broke for him," he says. "There was nothing I could say at its end that would sound sincere, so I left." Winerip looks pained as he remembers that night. "Of course, it was Josh's first full-length play, and well, yes, it needed work, shall we say. But he was a young man, and it was a young man's play." He pauses and sighs. "I don't think it was devastating simply because he realized he didn't have….natural talent as a playwright. It's not because he wanted to be, or expected to be, the next Andrew Eronei. But everyone wants their art to be appreciated, well-loved. I don't think Josh was any different. It's tremendous work to write anything, and certainly Josh was so talented in so many ways, I always felt he shouldn't've been as disappointed as he was, but…but I guess his devastation spoke of some deeper ambition of which none of us were really aware." Winerip pauses and closes his eyes, briefly. "It actually came as somewhat of a shock to me."

Franklin never talked about this failed play again, but Meryns echoes most of his friends' sentiments when he notes that the experience was "crushing. It's quite one thing to feel you've failed, and to feel you've failed in front of your friends, and another, more diminishing feeling to feel you're failed at an art you love which, to all appearances, doesn't seem to love you back." Indeed, Franklin went underground for a while, minimizing his once-frenetic socializing and doing pro-bono work for different legal nonprofit groups while contemplating his next move. "It seems like an extreme reaction to me now," says Leerbohrn. "Josh was so talented, so seemingly indefatigable and unshakable, that I'm afraid that we all took this mini-breakdown of his to our hearts more than we should have. None of us had ever seen Josh fail at anything, and his vulnerability was deeply unsettling."

"It was a reading of a play for Christ's sakes," says Michaels. "It really shouldn't have made a difference. It wasn't as if he had poured hundreds of thousands of dollars into this; it wasn't as if he had sacrificed his family or decades of his life for this one play. It wasn't even as if he had been publicly humiliated. But none of that made a difference in the end, because Josh felt clearly and keenly that he had failed, and in the end, that was what everyone else felt, too. It was, I think, the first time he was forced to truly realize his own inadequacy, and I'd venture to say that *that*, rather than the quality of his play per se, was what made the whole experience so miserable for him." He looks off into space for a while. "But in the end, it doesn't make a difference. We should have tried to cheer him up instead of being embarrassed for him, and the fact that none of us did—" he pauses, hands up in the air—"well, it was shitty."

One day, several months after the reading of "Fireworks in Brooklyn," Winerip was having dinner with an author when he overheard the patron next to him talking about a new cabaret series he was spearheading at P.S. 122. The man mentioned that he was contemplating accepting submissions from the general public, his companion agreed that it might be an interesting idea, and the conversation shifted routes. Winerip, though, was intrigued, and finished his dinner as quickly and politely possible, stuffed the author into a cab, and lingered outside the restaurant, waiting. When the eavesdropee came out, Winerip followed him, and, in what he now laughingly says was "a huge and excruciatingly embarrassing digression from a well-established pattern of introversion and basic timidity," introduced himself and admitted he had been listening. The man, who turned out to be P.S. 122 artistic director Lancelot Grazzi, was, fortunately for Winerip, amused, and gave him his card. "He told me that this had almost convinced him that open submissions were a bad idea," smiles Winerip, "but said to send him a script and call him at the end of the month." Winerip rushed home to tell Franklin his news, but despite his goading, Franklin remained resolutely disinterested. "He was so dispirited," Winerip recalls now, his voice soft. "By this point, I don't think it was just 'Fireworks in Brooklyn.'

In fact, I know it wasn't—it was something else entirely, but to this day I wouldn't be able to tell you what it was. But it was around that time that Josh began to—to lose his focus, perhaps, to lose his instinct for zeal itself. He lost interest and I don't think he ever regained it." That night, Winerip went into Franklin's study and sat down to write. He wrote through the weekend, and when he emerged, Sunday afternoon, he had his first script in hand. "The Sparring Susannes" was a loosely-knit collection of songs and dances between two lavishly made-up, cut-tongued, brassy middle-aged women of a certain age and class, based on the author Jacqueline Susanne, of whom Franklin was a fan. In "The Sparring Susannes," Jacqui and Lin (who would both be played by men), hack writers who believe their work is great literature, decide they're going to crash a Pulitzer Prize ceremony to which they've not been invited. Like "Camp," "The Sparring Susannes" sends up class and artistic snobbery with great vim and wicked wit, and although Winerip deliberated for some time about the show's dark irony—two trashy women with great ambition trying to write the great American novel!—he gave it to Franklin anyway. "It was my present to him, of sorts," says Winerip now with a thin smile. "I wrote it for him, because—because—he inspired it, in his way." He flinches, as if at the unpleasantness of his own honesty.

Franklin was not a sulker, and was able to shake himself out of his depression and, for the first time in months, allow himself to become enthusiastic about the theater again. He would do the piece, he said, on one condition: Winerip would have to play the other Susanne. Winerip, who'd prepared himself for this caveat, finally agreed, and after some argument and hesitation, decided to send off "The Sparring Susannes" to Grazzi. Two days later, he received a call from Grazzi.

"Why'd you send me this?" asked Grazzi. "I already have a copy."

"What?" Winerip asked.

"Yeah," said Grazzi. "Three weeks ago. I think it's fucking great. I hope you guys are ready. You guys are going to kick off the festival, twelve weeks from now. Didn't your partner tell you?"

———

Thus began Winerip's off-Broadway stage career. "The Sparring Susannes," which opened in November 1996, was an instant hit for P.S. 122, and something of an underground sensation as well—people saw it multiple times, told their friends about it, and formed long lines to wait for tickets for the Thursday, Friday, and Saturday night performances. Part of the intrigue was, of course, attributable to the actors' cloaked identities; Winerip insisted that no one know who the performers were off-stage, and although he considered it a privacy issue, the secrecy—not to mention the playbill's brief biographies: *Jacqui and Lin live in New York City*—fueled the show's cult status and generated some imaginative and witty speculation, including one "Page Six" blind item that identified the two actors as supermodels moonlighting on-stage. Both Grazzi and, later, Franklin, wanted to reveal the two actors' identities, but Winerip, in what he now concedes was an act of "supreme divaness" threatened to leave the show if any action was taken. Both Winerip and Franklin finished their seven-month run at P.S. 122 without revealing their true names.

But despite the good-natured mystery surrounding the show, its main attraction was its tooth-sharp writing, and its performers' outlandish sense of abandon. I saw "The Sparring Susannes" three times, and each time, something was tweaked, smartly and subtly changed. Both actors were very fine, but one—Jacqui—had the sort of frenetic irreverence that only the best of actors possess. Watching "Camp," I knew I was watching the same actor again, however different the role; despite Tule's extroversion, she is a more nuanced character than Jacqui—a coil of pure, brilliant, screeching id—was ever allowed to be. For his part, Winerip has fond memories of "The Sparring Susannes." "I was utterly comfortable on-stage, precisely because it was so extreme," he says. "I had a wonderful costume to hide behind"—the actors' makeup was coated so thick that it would crack and seam whenever they moved their faces—"and it was the show's and the character's utter lack of propriety that made me feel so secure—it was a chance, however contrived, to step away from myself." Besides the heavy pancake makeup, he and Franklin wore tattered flapper dresses that dropped jet beads that bounced across the floor as they danced, and cracked leather strappy sandals with teetery Roman heels. Walking—much less dancing—in the shoes was difficult, and they used to practice running around their house on those wobbly heels. Even though they eventually became nimble and sure-footed, not a week went by when one of them—tripping off-stage, or hurrying through a costume change—didn't fall and twist an ankle. "It was a wonderful time," Winerip remembers. "We were putting reality—and responsibility—on hold."

"'The Sparring Susannes' could've gone on forever, taken a life and identity of its own," Grazzi says wistfully. "Maybe it would've." Aside from singing, dancing, and a certain amount of fast-riffing improvisation, the show demanded some acrobatic ability, and its conclusion called for the two actors to do flying leaps into the wings after their curtain calls. One night, as the show was just entering its sixth month, the two jumped off-stage as always, but as Franklin landed, Winerip heard a "sharp, sickening crack—like wood clattering against pavement." Franklin fell to the ground, clutching his ankle. Winerip took him, costume and all, to the hospital. "He was unflaggingly pleasant through it," says Winerip now, with a sad smile. "And I was grateful to him for necessitating the end of our careers on stage." The couple's lives reverted to its normal rhythms —Franklin, swinging along cheerfully on his crutches, took a job as legal counsel for Actors' Equity. But after six weeks, Franklin's ankle still had not healed properly. He had been "sick more often than usual that year; he had a lot of nosebleeds, low-grade fevers," Winerip remembers. "And he was tired—fatigued. We used to say it was just old age." He gives a sharp cough of laughter and then falls silent. Upon waking one night to his partner's shallow, rapid breaths and sticky with his blood—Franklin was in the throes of a massive nosebleed—Winerip once again took him to the hospital, where Franklin was admitted for a battery of tests. The diagnosis was acute mylogenous leukemia, a particularly insidious and deadly form of cancer. Franklin would need a bone-marrow transplant if he was to hope for a recovery. His immediate family members—his father, mother, three sisters and brother—were tested, along with his extended family. There was no match. Franklin was given less than a year to live.

Thus began a long, anguishing period for the couple. Franklin, upon digesting the prognosis, decided to forgo a punishing treatment of Interferon in order to die at home. "I'm afraid I was probably an absolute wreck," Winerip says. "I respected Josh's decision, admired it even, and yet I hated him for it as well. It was the one time his parents"—who maintained a cordial but chilly relationship with their son's lover—"and I really agreed on something." Josh had been treated at Memorial Sloan-Kettering, but the Franklins took him for second and third opinions at The Mayo Clinic in St. Paul and MD Anderson in Houston, two of the nation's finest oncological hospitals. Franklin, however, "just wasn't interested," says Winerip. "It was very strange to me, awesome even. I had always thought of Josh as someone who traveled through life with a sort of impenetrable blitheness, and seemingly overnight he had become—well, certainly not resigned, or a pessimist, but someone who seemed to realize that this—life—what we consider the most important fight of all, was a battle not worth wasting his energy on. It seems hopelessly contradictory to even make a statement like that, but along the way, I think—I like to think—he learned something that made the decision less anguishing for him than it was for everyone who loved him. Josh was a smart man, and I think he knew that he couldn't hope to win against such an awful, inconquerable illness. He liked to say that the main point in life was fun, enjoyment, and anything that would have deprived him of that—Interferon, for example—would have been a personal admission of defeat. I always forgot how intuitive he was, and what a pragmatist he was, but watching him that year, I was reminded every day." Winerip pauses. "Near the end of his life, Josh told me that he had always loved the theater, and I knew that. 'Fighting against cancer,' he said, 'is more theater than I can stand. We already know the ending.'"

The two decided to travel while Franklin was still able, and Winerip took a leave of absence from work. "Josh had gone everywhere once before," smiles Winerip, "and he took me back to his favorite places—Cambodia and Patagonia, Italy and Morocco. It was irresponsible, but I hope it goes without saying that I never regretted it. I was always afraid he would get sick in some remote village, but we were lucky the entire time." Four months after his diagnosis, Franklin's health began to deteriorate, and the two returned to New York. The couple usually spent Thanksgiving with Winerip's father in Cambridge, who that year traveled to New York instead. The entire Franklin family came over as well, and they had a sober dinner. No one ate much. "Most of the time at the table was spent watching Josh, who'd fallen asleep in the middle of the meal," says Winerip. "He was always sleepy from the various medications he was on, and had lost an astonishing amount of weight—twenty-odd pounds—in the space of four or five weeks; every time any of us looked at him…" his voice trails off. After dinner, Winerip and his father were washing the dishes when his father told him, gently, that he too had cancer—advanced-stage pancreatic cancer. Winerip burst into tears, something he hadn't done "in the past decade or so. I told myself I wouldn't let Josh see me cry, but this was too much, my heart was too full. The two people I loved in the world were leaving me." Winerip's father comforted him. He was old, he said, almost eighty, and had lived a long life, and a fulfilling life. "But he didn't tell me to stop crying, or that I would be all right without him," Winerip remembers. "I was grateful to him for that. I was also livid with him for protecting me, for not letting me know, and at my own stupid, total incompetence." The next night, Winerip went to the airport with his father. The two held hands at the gate. "I don't know what to do," Winerip told him. He asked his father if he would like to move to New York, or if he wanted him to move back to Cambridge with him. No, no, his father said. We'll talk next week. Winerip returned home to Franklin, his head heavy. He called Franklin's parents, who came to sit with their son at night, and asked them if they would stay at the house, and then followed his father to Cambridge. "He tried to get me to go home, but he was in pain," says Winerip. Three days into his visit, he lay down next to his father for a nap. Jacob Winerip died—of a heart attack—in his sleep. "I couldn't speak," says Winerip now. He says nothing else, but I am reminded of a moment near the end of "Camp," directly after Tule's father's suicide, where it becomes increasingly, uncomfortably apparent that she is slipping into a madness of her own. "Oh, Pa," says Tule, "You never gave me a chance to make you proud of me. You left before I had the chance to tell you anything at all."

———

December turned into January and January into February. Franklin grew weaker and disoriented. He moved in and out of consciousness, and sometimes, at night, he would cry in short, jagged bursts. He was so emaciated that Winerip fit a cirrus cloud of shredded cottonballs around his hipbones to keep them from digging into the mattress, which Franklin said was "too hard." "It was the worst thing I had ever seen," says Meryns quietly. "I cried after every visit. It seemed the most gross injustice in the world." His illness left Franklin susceptible to everything from pneumonia to anemia, and his family snapped on latex gloves before taking his hand, which was always cold and lavender-tinted. The Franklins had long since arranged for a full-time nurse, but Winerip—who'd returned to work part-time—spent his nights curled up in a chair near Franklin's bed, holding his hand. Except for a few close friends, he told no one at work what was happening at home. He edited his books, but didn't tell his authors. "He looked awful," says St. Clair Michaels. "Gaunt, gray—my heart ached for Josh and Coffee both. Josh was a beautiful man, a dynamic man, and seeing him—supine, semi-conscious, his eyes cloudy and his skin hard and beetley from the drugs—was the most wrenching thing." Evenings, Franklin's parents would come over and they and Winerip would sit in his Josh's room, holding their son's arm, his hand—staring blankly, mutely at one another, unable to offer comfort, until they fell asleep. "It seemed my life had come full circle in a very short time," says Franklin with a quick twist of his mouth. "Willem Goldberg, my first father— and I was still reeling from Jacob's death. I cried so much those few months—my eyes and nose were perpetually swollen—that someone once stopped me in the street and asked me if I knew what all that cocaine was doing to my body." He gives an unhappy bark of laughter. By early March, Franklin, who had been slipping into comas and then awakening, frantic, confused, was unconscious more often than not. On March 7, he had a massive seizure. When he next opened his eyes, he couldn't speak or, it appeared, see. His family took turns sitting next to his bed and talking to him, so he wouldn't die alone.

Winerip was "launching" his books for the upcoming publishing season (a sales-oriented meeting when editors present the new titles to be sold into accounts by the in-house sales representatives) when his assistant slipped into the conference room and nodded at him, looking grim. Franklin's father was on the phone. He told Winerip that he thought he should come home, now. Winerip fled. When he reached his house, Ivan Franklin was waiting for him at the door so he wouldn't have to fumble with his keys. Winerip remembers that his eyes were "a startling red; a kind of electric red I had never seen before and haven't seen since." Winerip had never seen Franklin's father cry, not the entire time his son was ill, and seeing this, he knew what was going to happen. He took Lola Franklin's place next to her son's bed; he held his partner's hand and listened as his breaths grew shorter and softer and more seldom until finally, two hours later, on April 3, 1997, almost ten months after his diagnosis, Joshua Franklin died. He had never fully regained consciousness since his seizure. He had missed his twenty-ninth birthday by four days.

Winerip spoke at Franklin's memorial. He found himself unable to cry, to blink. He and the Franklins stood at the door of the synagogue and shook hands with the mourners. After the last person had left, Franklin's brother and sisters and mother walked out to the waiting car. Ivan Franklin took Winerip's hand. "He loved you," he told

Winerip gently, "and I thank you for being in his life, although I think he could have been happy with anyone. He chose you, though. And that was all right. But I want to make something clear. It's nothing personal, not really. But I never want to see you again."

Winerip has made sure he never has.

———

"Hello," says Winerip, smiling and taking my coat. It was a cold afternoon, dry and crisp, and the early-evening sky shimmers with the promise of snow. Today is Saturday, and I've come to see him at his office, where he spends his weekends, dutifully catching up on the week's work he's had to neglect in favor of the show. In a few hours he will take the bus downtown to the Public, and begin putting on his makeup for the nine o'clock show. He likes the office on the weekends, particularly Saturday, its emptiness and even its coldness, and takes advantage of its wide, high hallways to practice his scales—up, down; Tule Lake's voice is a hoarse shout of outrage and resentment, but Winerip's is astonishingly pretty, a round, winey tenor—as he answers emails and combs through one of the many stacks of paper on his desk. When I ask, he admits, shyly, that yes, he's writing a new piece, but that no, he doesn't want to talk about it, not really. "It's about death," he says, cheerfully. "But that's about all I can say. I don't want to sound pretentious."

Winerip is tremendously concerned with sounding pretentious. When he steps away from his office to the lavatory, I peer at the manuscript on his desk. "Pretentious," he has written in the margin in his even scrawl. "More subtlety, less…" The sentence cuts off. After Franklin died, Winerip spun into "a horrible place," says his friend Abigail Graves. "He was inconsolable—I mean, he didn't cry or carry on, but that was the worst part. It was as if he had retreated so far that no one would ever be able to touch him." His friends tried to convince him to enter therapy, to talk to them, to write. Winerip dismissed all of these ideas, but the last with a particular vehemence. "He said that those in grief produced the most sentimental writing," remembers Alicia Olliphant. "'Never!'" he told me. "'I never will!'" But he was, quietly, at night, although not any writing that he considered legitimate. "I'd had an idea," says Winerip. "I decided that I couldn't write about Josh, or Jacob, but I thought—maybe I could write something from further back in my memory. Just to distract me, to pretend I was another person living another sort of life." Winerip doesn't know whether any of his mother's family spent the war years in the camp—"It wasn't something I ever remember anyone talking about"—but considers it highly probable. "I'm not sure what made me think of it," says Winerip. "It was always something that had interested me, even when I was a kid, but I'm not sure what sparked my fascination at the time. It was more the idea of the character—Tule Lake came to me before the actual outline of her story—that appealed to me first. I'd find myself singing aloud, just scraps of songs, little half-tunes, really, and in the end, I formed Tule around those fragments." The first song he wrote—"Kalifornia, USA," about Tule's brother's death by the butt of a camp guard's gun—is one of the last in the show, and one of its most arresting. He wrote the music and lyrics to most of the show's other songs—"My Father's List," "I Am," "Camp/Nothing Ever Changes" and "Beauty Queen"—in a matter of days after "Kalifornia." Winerip, who wrote "The Sparring Susannes" in a similar manner—songs first, then story—points to this as proof of his own inadequacies as a playwright, something that Steven Bruce Kurtzman, "Camp"'s producer, dismisses. "That's just Coffee being modest," he says. "Playwrights compose in all sorts of ways—characters first, sets first, even lighting first—and Coffee's one of the most naturally talented writers I know, not to mention one of the most confident and versatile. He brings to the stage a strong sense of insecurity and vulnerability, both of which give him a lot of wriggle room—in both the creation of Tule as well as his own interpretation, he's allowed himself a wide margin for experimentation." And it's true—just like "The Sparring Susannes," it's unlikely that you'll ever see the same version of "Camp" twice. The first time I saw the show, Winerip delivered a throwaway line—"My brother—my brother was a Buddhahead even when he wasn't giving head"—as a goofily comic line after a tense and terse dramatic prelude, and the audience responded with relieved laughter. Another time, he delivered the words slowly, carefully, quietly, before looking out beyond the audience, who squirmed in their seats, waiting for his next words.

When Winerip returns to his office (with mugs of Earl Grey tea for us both), I ask him what he thinks makes a good actor.

"Hmm," he says, looking up at the ceiling. "It always changes. I think a while ago, when I was starting this show, I would have said…abandon, perhaps, a sort of reckless fearlessness. But now I think—now I think I'd say a sense of self-control, a sense of containment. Reserve, dignity. It's easy, I think, to convey madness on stage, but very difficult to make it truly sympathetic, to make it seem nuanced and textured and complex. It's been the hardest thing with 'Camp,' and I struggle with it constantly—am I making the character look flat? Cheap? Comedy should always be paired with tragedy, with sadness. I always tell my authors that it's easy to make people cry—mawkish writing will inevitably accomplish that—but much harder to make them laugh. I think in theater, the trick is being able to make someone stop laughing as quickly as you make them start." He sips his tea and looks up at the ceiling for so long that I have to keep myself from looking up too. "I'm not a professional actor," he says suddenly. "What people mistake for technique—and I'm flattered they think I have one—is really just uncertainty." He gives one of his sudden, surprising laughs before falling silent again.

"I think that's just modesty," I half-tease.

He tucks an end of his mouth into a faint, knowing smile, as if caught. "People approach 'Camp' differently," he says. "I like to read the fan—and hate—mail, if only because it reminds me what an acid test any piece of art is—people bring their own ideas and interpretations to a book before they even begin reading it, and the same goes for a piece of theater. If you go to see 'Camp' thinking it's a piece about race and one of the gravest Constitutional crimes ever committed, you'll respond differently than if you go thinking it's somehow a metaphor for gay and lesbian oppression. [Which, incidentally, is how both *Out* and *The Advocate* interpreted the show.] You begin to think Derrida wasn't so wrong after all."

"Now," he continues, "you, or your readers at least, will think that this show is about me, that it's about the—the human compulsion to hide, or recreate, or avoid, whatever personal or circumstantial problems arise in a lifetime. And if I tell you it's not—at least not consciously—well, there's nothing I can say that'll refute it to anyone's satisfaction." He pauses for a breath. "That's the problem discussing one's creation, as far as I can tell—the creator always, inevitably, comes off sounding pityingly defensive and unaware."

I ask him what he thinks "Camp" is about. And now he's off and running; the words pour out in a rush.

"I think people have given me—give writers in general—much more credit than I'm really due. I'm afraid I'm fairly literal—this is a play about the Japanese American internment. It's also a piece about family, about how one family does—and doesn't—cope with their circumstances, and how a person, an immigrant, learns to trust a country, only to have that country betray their trust. The drag element is, I'm afraid, a pretty obvious and simplistic message—that we, as Americans, learn to become someone else, to erase what we thought we were in favor of creating for ourselves something else, an alternate identity—and that some of us accomplish this more successfully than others. Also, I envisioned Tule as a girl, and I couldn't change it, even if I'd wanted to." He stops abruptly and flushes, stares at his hands. "It's the same reason I don't tell anyone what I do at nights," he allows. "It's not that I'm a particularly private person, as people think—anyone who's truly private would never submit to an interview—but rather that the opportunity to try on new identities without fear of criticism is, to me, an irresistible one. The fact that I'm allowed to hide behind so many layers—Tule herself, and then C.S. Tatami—is comforting to me. It allows an avenue for escape." Winerip stops and blushes again, deeply. "Good grief," he says in that distinctive cloud of a voice, "I sound like an idiot. Let's stop here. I've got a show to do." He gives me a crooked smile and half-rises from his chair, as if he's greeting someone walking through his door. It's grown dark in the office, but Winerip hasn't turned on the overhead light, and his shadow looms black and furry against the windowpane. Since Franklin's death, Winerip has, to his friends' knowledge, begun no new relationships. He still lives in the townhouse he once shared with his partner. "I will never love again," Tule Lake says at one point, and I wonder what his friends and colleagues will make of that line once Winerip is forever associated with his sassy, furious alter ego.

"This sounds terrible and cruel, and maybe it is," says St. Clair Michaels, "but in an odd way, Josh's death may prove liberating to Coffee yet. I know he doesn't think so—and I certainly don't mean anything malicious by it, because Josh was one of the kindest men I knew—but he's [Winerip] so talented, I wonder if we might not see him write a play, or something, in the next couple of years." I don't repeat this ironic bit of speculation to Winerip, but now, as his office grows darker and colder and the sky outside the window changes from purple to indigo, I wonder if Winerip may not have thought it (and know it) himself, and if behind his shy half-smile lies a more complicated explanation, a mystery he answers for himself on stage every night.

————

I go see Winerip at the Public for the last time; he has four weeks off, and then the show moves to The Mayflower Theater on Broadway for a six-month run. The first four months are, remarkably, already sold out, and Winerip's theatrical life is determined for the next couple of years—he will open the show next year in London (an event that Winerip, in his self-deprecating way, has dismissed as "doomed to failure") and has signed on as a lead to a new, as yet unspecified project at The Roundabout Theater. It is choices like these that have convinced those around him that he is moving toward a commitment he avowedly is reluctant to make: a full-time devotion to the stage. Tonight, perhaps as a goodbye to off-Broadway, Winerip gives a particularly raucous, impassioned performance, and when he dances off-stage at the end of the show, he is dripping sweat and breathing hard. Francesco Roy, the stage manager at the Public for the last seven years, stands in the wings applauding. "They'll never forget this," he tells Winerip warmly. "This'll go down in history."

Winerip returns the compliment with a gleeful grin, and his eyes refocus and beam, too. "Oh," he pants, "I don't do this for my place in history."

Roy is smiling, and together, they look like they're sharing some private joke, some extraordinarily joyous secret. "Why then?" he asks. The exchange is as inevitable and lively as on-stage banter, and Winerip is in his element.

"Well," says Winerip, and I lean forward, eager for his answer, but his eyes have already regained that flat, faraway look that actors get as they ready themselves for their entrance, the lights, the dull sweep of the audience's faces before them, "I guess it's because I get to escape." He laughs, and his voice, already slipping back into Tule's, grows louder. "It's purely selfish, darling! Fantasy!" But by now he has turned away from Roy and me, and he is gone, gone, running back out from behind the wings, his arms spread out and open like a star, gone to the roar of a stamping audience and into the spotlight which, from our angle, is a harsh white globe of unforgiving light.

TAKE OUT: QUEER WRITING FROM ASIAN PACIFIC AMERICA

CHAY YEW

WHITE

An Asian man in his sixties.

The actor should take a quick beat between sentences.

MAN

Tight
i slip in
nervously
silently
head over shoulder
into a non-descript building
corner of summit and pine
rigid
i slide
a wrinkled Andrew Jackson
across the scratched veneer counter
a man
cuban
guatemalan
lithuanian
something
with a half mutter
half wave
he buzzes me in

snugly
i wrap
a bleached white towel
around my flabby waist
snugly
i sit
in a sea of familiar faces
lost in clouds of cumulus nicotine

lost in bare arms of a couch
our deaf eyes
eyes concentrating
eyes focusing
eyes lost
on the larger-than-life images
naked flesh on flesh
porno ablaze
upon a giant technicolor screen

glistening
grinding
groping
the glow of naked bodies
it falls on our intent faces
as if a reprieve
my bespectacled eyes
they veer to
my silent companions
these silent men
men whom i have seen
men whom i have tasted
but
after all these years
these silent men
they don't know who I am
after all these years
they don't know what I do
these silent men
they never say a word to me
to them
i'm just another face
another middle-aged man
another chink
in a crowd of towels
in a crowd of possibilities

here

in this makeshift elysium
i live
the other half of my life
i live a life free
of three-piece suits
i live a life free
of disappointing children
of disappointed wife

here
amidst translucent steam
amidst sticky sweat
like these men
on the same endless mission
i venture for adventure
forever searching
forever living
for brief moments
my life
measured in moments
and a moment is all i get
surely all these moments
these pieces
add up to something

i close my eyes
adjust
tuck
get up
find my room
at the end of the hall
naked bulb
plastic ash tray
i lie
on cloroxed sheets
a creaky small cot
crack open the door
a welcome mat

and wait
for the usual parade
of gliding swans

they don't come in
these swans
instead
they glare
they scowl at me
these swans
these young
beautiful
sculpted
white swans
their faces twisted
impassive
with disgust
disinterest
their eyes
piercingly inspect
my flaccid body
deflated by age
inactivity
their eyes
carefully scrutinize
the silver of my hair
the yellow of my skin

avoiding their punishing glares
i seek shelter
in cool shadows of my narrow room
adjusting
adjusting
adjusting

after hours
lying in hopeless wait
i take a sniff

a brown bottle
punch drunk
drunk confident
i walk out
into another room
this one
larger
pitch black
where all that divides us
sounds of sighs
sounds of silence
i surrender
to jungle darkness
i let my towel
parachute
onto the cold
hard
linoleum
my body
squeezing
between
thick walls
of sweaty
pressing bodies

and once again
i feel
the drowning
the familiar wave of
hot
touches
hot
breaths
suddenly
his mouth
wetness
his
flickering

warmth
he
gagging
i
i
then
another
he
his fingers
prying
fingering
i know what he wants
he wants to
jerking
i want to
rubbing
i know i should
grabbing
be
be
but what if he doesn't
want to
kissing
stroking
what if he walks away
disinterested
and i
invisible
again
he gently slaps
it
against me
it
it
i know i should
hard
but i want it
want him

poking
i know i should
he spits
i know i should
his breath
my neck
i know i should
his hand
my head
forward
i know i should
his hand
my waist
poised
i know i
he
he
i
i

ah

i let him
in
ah
it feels good
his love
wet
naked
hard
it
it
it
penetrates
then
grinding
pounding
slamming

ruthless
rough
ecstasy

all of a sudden
scars of difference
vanish
age
beauty
race
erase
in darkness
we are one
our touch
our desire
unifies us
our hand
on hand
on stomach
on hand
on mouth
on lip
on neck
on hand
on thigh
on crotch
on pelvis
on chest
on hand
on cheek
on groin
on
on
on

we
be
come

one

one

one

i'm
home

End of Play

TAKE OUT: QUEER WRITING FROM ASIAN PACIFIC AMERICA

ABOUT THE CONTRIBUTORS

JONEIL ADRIANO was born in the Philippines and raised in California. He is a writer and community activist who now lives in Brooklyn with his partner, Jimmy McNulty. Adriano holds a bachelor's degree in Women's and Gender Studies from Columbia. "Constellations" is from his novel-in-progress, *Closer*.

NOEL ALUMIT received his Bachelor of Fine Arts in drama from the University of Southern California. His play *Mr. and Mrs. LaQuesta Go Dancing* was produced in San Francisco by Teatro Ng Tanan and his one-man show *The Rice Room: Scenes from a Bar* has been performed throughout Southern California. He is a recipient of the Emerging Voices fellowship from PEN Center USA West and a Community Access Scholarship to UCLA's Writers Program.

LISA ASAGI lives in San Francisco.

DAN BACALZO is a performance artist, poet, scholar, and activist. His first solo show, *I'm Sorry, But I Don't Speak the Language*, is also published in *Imported: A Reading Seminar*, edited by Rainer Ganahl (Semiotext(e), 1998). He's performed the show at various events and venues in the U.S., including HERE Performance Space, University of Massachusetts-Amherst, New York International Fringe Festival, Arizona State University, Wellesley College, and the Zeitgeist Theatre in New Orleans. His second solo show, *Sort of Where I'm Coming From*, was performed at The Fringe: Toronto's Theater Festival and Rhode Island School of Design. He is a Ph.D. student in the Department of Performance Studies at New York University, where he received his M.A. in January of 1996. In addition, he works with Panata, a coalition of Filipino, Filipino-American, and solidarity artists, and Peeling the Banana, a pan-Asian performance ensemble based in New York City.

REGIE CABICO is co-editor of *Poetry Nation* (Vehicule Press, 1998, Montreal). He is the recipient of the 1997 New York Foundation for the Arts Poetry Fellowship. His work has appeared in over 30 anthologies, including *The World Is Us: Gay & Lesbian Poets of the 21st Century* (St. Martin's, 2000) and *The Outlaw Bible of American Poetry* (Thunders Mouth, 1999). He was the winner of the 1993 New York Poetry Slam, a Road Poet on Lollapalooza 1994 and the opening act of MTV's "Free Your Mind" Spoken Word Tour. Regie is a cyberjay on gopoetry.com. As a performer, his solo show *onomatopoeia & a ¼ life crisis* was performed at The 1999 Seattle Fringe Festival, Queer at Here Theater (New

York), Dixon Place (NYC) and Joe's Pub at The Public Theater. He is the literary cura-tor at St. Mark's Friday Night Series, Realness & Rhythms at Different Light Bookstore and Writers on The Ledge at Dixon Place.

GAYE CHAN is an artist and a professor of photography at the University of Hawaii. She was born in Hong Kong and immigrated to Hawaii in 1969. The primary focus of Chan's work is the slippery area between the yearning for individual agency and the recognition of being mere flotsam in the tides of history. Chan's studio production is primarily in mixed-media, utilizing materials as diverse as naked ladies playing cards, termite drop-pings, and embroidery to explore subject matters ranging from capitalist colonialism, desire, and parenthood. She has had exhibitions at Art in General (New York City), Articule (Montreal), LACE (Los Angeles), Houston Center for Photography, San Francisco Camerawork, The Contemporary Museum in Honolulu, and the Honolulu Academy of Art.

ALEXANDER CHEE's work has appeared in *Big, Interview, The James White Review, LIT, Barrow Street* and the anthologies *Men on Men 2000, Loss Within Loss, His 3*, and *Boys Like Us.* He writes for *Out, Martha Stewart Living*, and *Garden Design* and teaches literary nonfiction writing at The New School University. He is the recipient of a 1999 Michener/Copernicus fellowship. He lives in Brooklyn.

JUSTIN CHIN is a writer and performance artist. He is the author of *Mongrel: Essays, Diatribes & Pranks* (St. Martin's Press), and *Bite Hard* (manic d press).

BAO LONG CHU's poems have appeared in *The Asian Pacific American Journal* and *The Viet Nam Forum.* He is currently Program Director for Writers in the Schools, a non-profit organ-ization that places writers and poets in schools and community settings in and around Houston.

KEN CHU has exhibited internationally in community-based arts organizations, alternative art spaces, and major art institutions. His work has been included in the "Brenda and Other Stories: HIV, AIDS, and You," "42nd Street Art Project," "Asia/America: Identities in Contemporary Asian American Art," "The Decade Show, Frameworks of Identity in the 1980s," and "Cultural Currents." He coordinated "Dismantling Invisibility: Asian & Pacific Islander Artists Respond to the AIDS Crisis," and "Public Mirror: Artists Against Racial Prejudice." He was a panelist on "Out in the 90's: Contemporary Perspectives on Gay & Lesbian Art," the first forum on gay and lesbian issues in the arts sponsored by The Whitney Museum of American Art. In 1990, he co-founded Godzilla: Asian American Art Network, a group of New York-based Asian and Pacific Islander visual artists and arts professionals who established a forum that fosters information exchange, mutual support, documentation, and networking through regular meetings, a newsletter, and exhibitions.

MINAL HAJRATWALA is a writer and performance poet whose work has appeared in numerous journals and in four anthologies, including *Contours of the Heart: South Asians Map North America* (Asian American Writers' Workshop). In November 1999, she premiered her one-woman show *AVATARS: Gods for a New Millennium* at the Asian Art Museum of San Francisco. Her poem 'Bodies of Water' was nominated for the Pushcart Prize after being selected by writer Meena Alexander to appear in the *Asian Pacific American Journal*. She has performed at numerous venues in San Francisco, New York, and Toronto and went on tour with the Asian American Writers' Workshop in Southern California. She is a 1999-2000 Sundance Institute writing fellow and has received writing and performance residencies. A graduate of Stanford University, she is the editor of "Perspective," the Sunday ideas and viewpoints section of the *San Jose Mercury News*.

PHILIP HUANG was born in Taiwan and now resides in Berkeley, California. He is twenty-five years old. His poems have appeared in *maganda*, a Pilipino literary journal, and his first short story, "The Widow Season" appeared in the anthology *Queer PAPI Porn*. He is thankful for the hours in the night to write, and he thanks Tim Arevelo for his unending and patient support and for his infectious love of writing. Most of all, he is thankful for being queer, for being one of the chosen ones.

T.C. HUO, author of *A Thousand Wings*, was born in Laos and currently lives in Northern California.

PAOLO JAVIER was born and raised in the Philippines. He moved to the States in 1986, and has since lived in New York, Cairo, and Vancouver. His works of poetry and prose have appeared in various American, Canadian, and international journals. In 1998, he co-founded and directed WONAX Theatre Society, a Vancouver-based company devoted to the production of one-act plays. He has taught at New York University, and recently conducted poetry workshops at the Asian American Writers' Workshop and St. Marks Poetry Project. He is currently at work on a manuscript of poems and a sequence of short films. He lives in Queens, New York.

RICH KIAMCO has been seen in Las Vegas on the Howard Stern Show and across the country performing with comedienne Judy Tenuta as her love slave/sidekick, aka 'Miss Saigon'. *POWERSHOWGIRL: unaccessorized* is Rich's first solo effort as a performer, playwright and songwriter. His one-man autobiographic romp fuses funk, hip hop, rock and blues with laughter, tears, hope, and vision. He resides in New York City where he is currently developing the next phase of the show including new music for the CD soundtrack.

R. SKY KOGACHI is an architect and graphic designer, as well as a graduate student of Industrial Design at the Art Center College of Design. He is a member of the Snazzy

Writers' Workshop, a collective of queer API writers, and the current Art Director for *dISorient,* an Asian Pacific American literary and visual arts journalzine.

JOHN KUNICHIKA received his B.F.A. in graphic design from Carnegie Mellon University in beautiful Pittsburgh, Pennsylvania. He now lives and works in New York City and dreams of the day when this book will be completed and one of the editors meets her long-overdue end.

LARISSA LAI was born in La Jolla, California. She currently lives in Vancouver, British Columbia, where she works as a community activist, writer, editor and critic. Author of *When Fox Is a Thousand,* her poetry and fiction have also appeared in *Bamboo Ridge, West Coast Line, The Asian-American Journal, CV2, Matrix, Room of One's Own, Estuaire, Many-Mouthed Birds,* and *Pearls of Passion.* She is a regular contributor to *Kinesis* and has had articles and essays published in *Fuse, Video Guide, Harbour, Rungh, Yellow Peril: Reconsidered,* and *Matriart.* In 1995 she was the recipient of an Astraea Foundation Emerging Writers Award.

DANIEL LEE is a queer (not gay) New York City-based poet-writer, photographer, artist, cultural critic, and event producer. Originally born in Kuching, Malaysia of Chinese descent, his poems have previously been seen in *Masque: A Journal of Queer Expression* and *ShoutOut!* magazines and in the forthcoming anthology *From the Mountaintop.* His sex column, "On the Down Low," can be found at dragunmagazine.com. He also recently received his Bachelor of the Arts in Writing, Asian Pacific American Studies, Chinese Studies, and Queer Theory at the Gallatin School of Individualized Study at New York University. He pays homage to all of his muses: Could-Have-Been-Beloveds and Ungrateful Betrayers, his friends (Rainbow Coalition, the Crew/Regulars), especially his best friend Manoella Gonzalez, the poet Scott Hightower, the lost mentor Wayne Buidens, his influences (Audre Lorde, Sylvia Plath, Sandra Cisneros, and other women poets), the Buddha, and his family.

DONALD LEE is still working on his bio in New York City.

JONATHAN H.X. LEE is a fifth-year senior at the University of California-Riverside majoring in Religious Studies, Sociology, and Ethnic Studies. He is Chinese, Japanese, and Cambodian.

CHING CHING LING lives in New York City.

R. ZAMORA LINMARK, a Fulbright Scholar, is the author of *Rolling The R's*, which he is currently adapting for the stage. He divides his time between Honolulu, San Francisco, and Manila.

TIMOTHY LIU is the author of three books of poems: *Vox Angelica* (Alice James, 1992), *Burnt Offerings* (Copper Canyon, 1995), and *Say Goodnight* (Copper Canyon, 1998). He is also the editor of *Word of Mouth: An Anthology of Gay American Poetry* (Talisman, 2000).

E.G. LOUIE lives in New York City.

ALEC MAPA is an award-winning actor, writer, and performance artist. His one-man show, *I Remember Mapa*, has played to sold-out houses in Los Angeles, New York, San Francisco, San Antonio, Seattle, Toronto, and Montreal. *I Remember Mapa* won the 1997 *L.A. Weekly* Award for Best Solo performance, and has been published by Grove Atlantic in the anthology *O Solo Homo: New Queer Performances*. Alec's new solo show, *Pointless*, had its world premiere at East-West Players in December 1999, and has been nominated for a 1999 GLAAD Media Award for Best in L.A. Theatre. Alec just completed filming the pilot for *Kiss Me Guido*, a 2001 mid-season replacement comedy for CBS.

DAN TAULAPAPA MCMULLIN is a Samoan writer from Los Angeles, living in Samoa and San Francisco. His screenplay "Bikini Boy" is under option with Kunewa Productions and in development with Sundance Film, and was produced onstage at Theatre Mu and Soho Rep. As a performance artist and storyteller he has performed at New Zealand International Arts Festival, Pacific Festival of the Arts in Samoa, Highways in Santa Monica, La Pena in Berkeley, the Walker Art Center in Minneapolis and on TVNZ in Aotearoa-New Zealand. His stories and essays have been published by *Bamboo Ridge*, *Cleis Press*, *Evergreen Chronicles*, *Wasafiri UK*, *Colors*, and *Resistance in Paradise*. He attended Cal Arts and was nominated for a L.A. area Emmy Award for cable photojournalism. He is currently the NEA Millennium Artist-in-Residence in American Samoa for the year 2000.

MAIANA MINAHAL was born in Manila, raised in Los Angeles, and now lives in San Francisco, where she teaches creative writing. She performs regularly in the Bay Area. Currently, she is working on her first play.

EIKI MORI, born in Kanazawa, Japan, is a photographer now based in New York City. His work has recently been featured in publications such as *Queer Japan* and *Dragün* and previously in *Fabulous* (Japan), *G & L Magazine*, *Men's Uno*, *Tomorrow* (Taiwan), and *Tofu Magazine* (Hong Kong).

MEI NG is the author of *Eating Chinese Food Naked*. She was born and raised in Queens, New York and escaped to Columbia College where she received a B.A. in Women's Studies. She has worked as a temp secretary, house painter, and waitress. She currently lives in Brooklyn.

ANDY QUAN was born in Canada with origins in the villages of Canton. His paternal grandfather arrived in Vancouver to work as a houseboy, his maternal great-great-grand-father came to Hawaii to plant rice. Currently working as International Policy Officer for the Australian Federation of AIDS Organizations, he is the co-editor of *Swallowing Clouds: an Anthology of Chinese Canadian Poetry* (Arsenal Pulp Press 1999). A singer and songwriter with self-produced tapes and a CD, he has also appeared in Canadian video-maker Richard Fung's *Dirty Laundry*, which examined issues of sexuality for Canada's first Chinese immigrants. Andy's short fiction and poetry have appeared in anthologies and literary journals in Canada, the USA and the UK, including the *Asian Pacific American Journal*, *Canadian Literature*, and the gay men's anthologies *Contra/Diction*, *Best Gay Erotica 1999* and *2000*, and *Gay Fiction at the Millennium*.

NINA REVOYR was born in Japan and grew up in Tokyo, Wisconsin, and Los Angeles. Her first novel, *The Necessary Hunger*, was published by Simon & Schuster in 1997 (paperback, St. Martin's Press, 1998). Nina has just completed her second novel, *Angeles Mesa*, for which she has already received awards from the Saltonstall Foundation and the Astraea Foundation. She lives and works in Los Angeles.

SVATI SHAH is a writer and a graduate student in medical anthropology at Columbia University. Her dissertation will focus on sex work and the politics of development in northwest India. She is a member of the South Asian Lesbian and Gay Association and an organizer in New York's progressive South Asian community. She lives in New York City.

RICCO VILLANUEVA SIASOCO was born in Iowa in 1972 and received a B.S. in Broadcasting and Film from Boston University. His work has appeared in *The Boston Phoenix*, *Flyway Literary Review*, *A. Magazine: Inside Asian America*, and the anthology *Generation Q* (Alyson, 1996), among others. He is the recipient of a C.Y. Lee Writers' Award from the Institute of Asian American Studies and a LEF Fellowship from The Writers' Room of Boston. Ricco was recently featured in PEN New England's Discovery Evening, where he was introduced by novelist Patricia Powell. His essay on the Fil-Am community in Boston was published in *Fil-Am* (PubliCo, 1999). Rico is an Internet news producer for *The Boston Globe's* boston.com and a graduate student in the Bennington College Writing Seminars.

MOHAN SIKKA is a writer and performing artist who has been in the New York and Philadelphia creative communities for the last five years. His pieces combine elements of theater, storytelling, and movement, with an emphasis on eclectic performance influences. His work has been presented at Dixon Place through The Movement Research Exchange at Judson Church, in the New Dance Alliance's Performance Mix by Philadelphia's Painted Bride Art Center, and at Toronto's *Desh-Pardesh* Festival of contemporary South Asian Culture. Additionally, his performances have been seen by audiences in Minneapolis, San Francisco, and in colleges around the northeast. He is also a New Forms Regional Grant Program awardee, which is funded by the Pennsylvania Council on the Arts, the National Endowment for the Arts, the Rockefeller Foundation and the Andy Warhol Foundation. The script of his *Curse of the Goddess* was published in the 10th Anniversary Issue of *Trikone* magazine; *The Unwritten Essay* was published by the *Toronto South Asian Review*. Interested in arts activism, Mohan helped organize the first showcase of Asian performing artists in Philadelphia, and is involved with DIASPORADICS—the first South Asian Arts & Activism Festival in the U.S. Mohan was recently an Open Society Community Fellow at The Audre Lorde Project in Brooklyn, New York.

NATASHA SINGH's fiction and poetry have appeared in anthologies and journals in both Canada and the the U.S. She teaches Creative Writing at Rutgers University and resides in New York, where she is at work on her first novel.

SHARON SOOKRAM lives in NYC and is currently working on *Between The Ears: A Guyanese Anthology* and *Sangfroid: A Guyanese Gay and Lesbian Anthology*.

ANDREW SPIELDENNER is a Vietnamese writer living in New York City. His poetry and essays have appeared in small journals, including the Vietnamese journal *Doi Dien*, and the books *Names We Call Home: Autobiography on Racial Identity* (Routledge, 1996) and *Queer PAPI Porn* (Cleis Press, 1998).

OSCAR E. SUN is a demagogic doppelganger living in Manhattan.

SEG SUN was born in Bangkok and has lived in Los Angeles for more than 20 years. He attended Los Angeles City College, where he discovered his love for creative writing. He has also taken part in local theater and church choirs around Los Angeles and is currently attending Loyola Marymount Universit, where he studies English.

CRAIG TAKEUCHI is a fourth-generation Japanese Canadian and a UBC Creative Writing student (Masters program). He has had his articles and reviews published in local magazines. His first short story was published in the anthology *Contra/Diction: New Queer Male Fiction*. His non-fiction piece, "Men and Their Shadows," has just been accepted for the anthology *Gay Men and their Journey to Manhood*.

HO TAM was born in Hong Kong and lives in Toronto, Canada. He works in a variety of mediums, including painting, photography, video, and printed matter.

JOEL BARRAQUIEL TAN is the editor of *Queer Philipino Asian and Pacific Islander Porn (PAPI)* (Cleis Press, 1998). Joel lives in Oakland, California and is completing his first novel.

JIMM TRAN was born in Vietnam, but now makes Toronto, Canada his home. He graduated from Ryerson University with a Bachelor of Applied Arts in Still Photography. He has had both solo and group exhibitions including the well-received "Self Identities" exhibition. Jimm was the previous editor-in-chief for Gay Asian Toronto's *CelebrAsian* magazine and is now the publisher of *Dragün* magazine. Jimm is an ardent traveler and has recently spent time on the back of a camel in Tunisia.

MATT UIAGALEILEI was born and raised in Honolulu. His work has appeared in the *Virgina Literary Review* and *The Hawaii Review*. He lives in California.

ERIC C. WAT is a mercenary instructor in Asian American studies, teaching wherever California state budget allows. He recently quit his other job as a waiter because he found out that was not what Mao meant when he said, "Serve the People."

VIN G. WOLFE is an elementary school teacher who currently resides in Brooklyn. She was born and raised in the Philippines and immigrated to the United States in 1988 by way of San Francisco where she lived for the past 10 years.

KATHRYN XIAN, who is a fourth generation Korean-American, currently resides in Honolulu. She studied music composition in New York under the tutelage of Joan Tower before returning to Hawaii. She thereafter founded an independent film company specifically intended to produce films that "piss people off...the 'right' people, of course." She has been working with a screenplay adaptation of her play "The Problem With Being" to do just that. Kathryn thanks Lois-Ann Yamanaka for her valuable critique and guidance with respect to "The Problem With Being" and the world of literature.

NITA YAMASHITA was born in Tokyo and raised in New York and northern California. She now lives in New York, where she works as a freelance journalist. She is writing her first book, *Authorized Portraits of Famous Asian Americans*, where "A Star Is Born" appears.

CHAY YEW's plays include "Porcelain," "A Language of Their Own," "Red," "A Beautiful Country," "Wonderland" and "As If He Hears." His performance text includes "*Home: Places Between Asian and America.*" His work has been produced throughout the world, including productions at the New York Shakespeare Festival's Public Theatre, Royal Court Theatre (London), Mark Taper Forum, Manhattan Theatre Club, Long Wharf Theatre, La Jolla Playhouse, Intiman Theatre, Portland Center Stage, Cornerstone Theatre, East West Players, Dallas Theatre Center, Studio Theatre, The Group Theatre, and TheatreWorks (Singapore), among others. For his plays, Chay has received the London Fringe Award, George and Elisabeth Marton Playwriting Award, GLAAD Media Award, Drama-Logue Award, APGF's Community Visibility Award, and the Robert Chesley Award. He is also the recipient of grants from the McKnight Foundation, Andrew W.

Mellon Foundation, TCG/Pew Charitable Trusts and the National Endowment for the Arts. His plays are published by Grove Press. Chay's plays are also anthologized in HarperCollins' *Staging Gay Lives* and the Asian American drama collection *But Still, Like Air, I Rise* by Temple University Press. A member of the New Dramatists and the Dramatists Guild, Chay Yew is the Director of the Asian Theatre Workshop at Mark Taper Forum and the Resident Director at East West Players in Los Angeles.

AFTERWORD

At a recent Q & A, I was asked by a (white) Rutgers student how it felt to be Asian and queer, the ole double-minority status whammy. I replied, "There are others!" to which he replied, "Really?!" I did go on to say that if books of poetry were to be shelved in only one section of a Barnes & Noble or a Borders, I would choose "Poetry" over "Asian Studies" or "Queer Studies," because the literary genre I work in would take precedence over the various cultural identities that I might also occupy. However, what writers wouldn't feel honored to find their book for sale on all three shelves? But the question remains unanswered: How does it feel? Conflicted. "What is it they expect from me? / What fantasy do I fulfill?" asks Dan Bacalzo in his poem "I'm Sorry, But I Don't Speak the Language." He then adds, "My body / is not the type you normally find in main-stream gay magazine ads." One might also question what kinds of texts are to be found in mainstream literary magazines. "If I work really hard, / if I went to the gym every day, / maybe I could have a body like that." After all, Bacalzo reasons, "It felt good to have men look at me. / To have my body completely objectified."

Many versions of the queer Asian body are embodied in the texts anthologized here. Indeed, many traditions are drawn from: "In zazen, roshi says, Breathe—/ Prajna paramita draws in our scattered thoughts // During sex I vocalize my breath // like the Tibetan singing bowl" says Minal Hajratwala in her poem "The In & the Out" which concludes with an outpouring of erotic syllables, "breathe me vulnerable trumpets / orchids / the cave in the heart / the vulnerable vulva / the radial ulna / the radical ulcer / the optimum hunger." And here is Daniel Lee's poem "Request" in its entirety, an instance of a haiku-like succinctness married to camp: "Fuck me / I'm bored." There is also much rage buried in outrageousness: "Not holding back/ white fetishizer! // Not holding back / Asian colonizer! // You can't /Suzy my Wong / Flower my / Drum Song" (from Daniel Lee's "When Letting Go/Fucking"). With a blues-like refrain, Lee rants, "You'll keep comin' back/ to swim / in the pool of my / homo sex drool // You'll keep comin' back /to tongue tango / between the halves / of my ass-mango." To reappropriate easy stereotypes and nullify the oppressor's linguistic darts and arrows is at the heart of this anthology's loaded title: *Take Out: Queer Writing from Asian Pacific America*. Just who's gonna take who out remains to be seen.

What to exactly do with our linguistic and cultural heritage is at the crux for Justin Chin, who takes on parents "too sensible for such comic book /chicanery" ("I Buy Sea Monkeys") as well as a group of school kids in a Chinese restaurant whom he saw "kick / the shrine sitting beside the fridge: / the pot of joss sticks, the tea cups / tumbled over, and the oranges scattered / across the floor, the fat laughing buddha / fell face-down, as if doubled over in hysterics" ("Faith"). In a world where one's ancestry is literally toppled over while one's future promises nothing more than AIDS-related deaths piling up like countless brine-shrimp corpses, what can one do but laugh at/into the American void? In getting back to how it feels to be queer and Asian, I wonder if any kind of Kinsey-scale equivalent exists for ethnicity in order to complicate matters further. Consider R. Zamora Linmark's description of Edgar in his fiction "Saved by Bertolucci": "Edgar, who normally expresses himself in the Hawaiian-Pidgin English vernacular, is speaking in a very-exaggerated tourist-from-the-mainland English. An English that is part-Valley Girl Talk and part-farmspeak." Edgar ends up bedding down James who is "strictly one hundred percent joy luck queen," no doubt through Edgar's "half-truths about being one third Filipino, one-third Spanish, and one-third Chinese," or at least his friend Vince reasons. But Edgar chalks it all up to watching Bertolucci's *The Last Emperor* while he and James act out the parts of the empress Wan Jung and the emperor Pu Yi, respectively.

Other characters are less flamboyant about their sexuality. In "A Deep Blush," T.C. Huo tells the story of "a Cal student tormented by his own untested homosexuality." A casual compliment ("You're good looking") by a white male sends our Asian-male narrator down an obsessive path where he only feels safe alluding to his newfound love-object as a "she" in his conversations, at least until therapy where "the unresponsiveness of the psychiatrist made me sense the banality of what I said, my senseless, crazed, imbecile rambling." Dan Taulapapa McMullin is even more cryptic in his triangulated pieces, which utilize radical forms. All ethnic markers are stripped away from "The Doll" as well as overt gender markers in "'O Kaulaiku." This blurring of boundaries in itself packs its own erotic/linguistic charge. As writers, do we get to choose our identities, or do they choose us? I like how maiana minahal's "poem of thanks to all the poets in poetry for the people for three nights / one hundred thirty poems" was simply inspired by Bei Dao's "A Bouquet." Or how Sharon Sookram's Indian female protagonist never thought she'd fall in love with a woman, let alone "a 39 year-old Jewish woman living on the Upper East Side" ("Searching for Love in New Paltz"). Or how an author like Mei Ng simply chooses to tell a haunting story ("Bees") about Mona and Raymond, a heterosexual couple who hardly seem to be "Asian," unless we take into consideration the "Red Hot Szechuan" that they end up ordering. It is my hope that readers will enjoy partaking of this eclectic feast.

Timothy Liu

ALSO PUBLISHED BY THE ASIAN AMERICAN WRITERS' WORKSHOP

TOKENS? THE NYC ASIAN AMERICAN EXPERIENCE ON STAGE EDITED BY ALVIN ENG

THE NUYORASIAN ANTHOLOGY: ASIAN AMERICAN WRITING ABOUT NEW YORK CITY EDITED BY BINO REALUYO

WATERMARK: VIETNAMESE AMERICAN POETRY & PROSE EDITED BY BARBARA TRAN, MONIQUE T.D. TRUONG AND LUU KHOI

BLACK LIGHTNING: POETRY IN PROGRESS BY EILEEN TABIOS

CONTOURS OF THE HEART: SOUTH ASIANS MAP NORTH AMERICA WINNER OF THE 1997 AMERICAN BOOK AWARD EDITED BY SUNAINA MAIRA AND RAJINI SRIKANTH

FLIPPIN': FILIPINOS ON AMERICA EDITED BY LUIS FRANCIA AND ERIC GAMALINDA

QUIET FIRE: A HISTORICAL ANTHOLOGY OF ASIAN AMERICAN POETRY, 1892-1970 EDITED BY JULIANA CHANG

FOR MORE INFORMATION ABOUT THE ACTIVITIES AND PROGRAMS OF THE ASIAN AMERICAN WRITERS' WORKSHOP, PLEASE CONTACT US AT:
16 WEST 32ND STREET, SUITE 10 A
NEW YORK, NY 10001-3808
TEL 212-494-0061
FAX 212-494-0062
EMAIL DESK@AAWW.ORG OR WWW.AAWW.ORG

TO PURHCASE ANY OF THESE BOOKS, PLEASE CONTACT TEMPLE UNIVERSITY PRESS
1601 N. BROAD STREET, USB 305
PHILADELPHIA, PA 19122
TEL 1-800-447-1656
FAX 215-204-1128
WWW.TEMPLE.EDU/TEMPRESS